Building an International Financial Services Firm

Building an International Financial Services Firm

How to Design and Execute Cross-Border Strategies

Markus Venzin

OXFORD
UNIVERSITY PRESS

OXFORD

UNIVERSITY PRESS

Great Clarendon Street, Oxford ox2 6DP

Oxford University Press is a department of the University of Oxford.
It furthers the University's objective of excellence in research, scholarship,
and education by publishing worldwide in

Oxford New York

Auckland Cape Town Dar es Salaam Hong Kong Karachi
Kuala Lumpur Madrid Melbourne Mexico City Nairobi
New Delhi Shanghai Taipei Toronto

With offices in

Argentina Austria Brazil Chile Czech Republic France Greece
Guatemala Hungary Italy Japan Poland Portugal Singapore
South Korea Switzerland Thailand Turkey Ukraine Vietnam

Oxford is a registered trade mark of Oxford University Press
in the UK and in certain other countries

Published in the United States
by Oxford University Press Inc., New York

British Library Cataloguing in Publication Data

Data available

Library of Congress Cataloging in Publication Data

Data available

Typeset by SPI Publisher Services, Pondicherry, India
Printed in Great Britain
on acid-free paper by
the MPG Books Group in the UK

ISBN 978–0–19–953520–0

1 3 5 7 9 10 8 6 4 2

To Chiara

Preface: The Paradox of Service Growth

Successfully building an international financial services firm is highly dependent on specific market contexts as well as the resource and capability endowments of the internationalizing company. Suggestions such as 'expand internationally or die', 'penetrate local markets as quickly as you can' or 'avoid strategic alliances' may seem alluring but are in most cases misleading. This is not surprising. 'One size fits all' strategic advice is seldom adequate or appropriate. A surprising finding in this book is that executives face a paradox while building an international financial services firm: 'more is less'. Cases such as those of Citigroup, UBS, or ABN AMRO teach that more assets and revenues can mean less profits and lower share prices, but the dominant logic for many top firms still seems to be to grow as fast and as big as they can. 'If you manage to grow your business, you are successful' becomes their credo. As a consequence, the balance sheets of financial services firms grow steadily. Royal Bank of Scotland leads the list of the world's largest companies in terms of total assets with over USD 3.7 trillion in 2007. At the time of publishing, more than 30 financial services firms will likely have reported that their total assets exceeded USD 1 trillion. But if size is not a guarantee for better performance, why do we currently see a trend towards the creation of larger and more diversified financial services firms? Do larger financial services firms create higher returns for shareholders even if these firms deliver disappointing profitability ratios? Do financial services firms face a growth paradox?

Data presented in this book suggest that the answer to these questions is 'yes' for many firms. The *Compact Oxford English Dictionary* defines a paradox as '(1) a seemingly absurd or self-contradictory statement or proposition that may in fact be true; (2) a person or thing that combines contradictory features or qualities'. The strategic imperative for many bank executives to expand across borders bears several such seemingly contradictory elements. This observation brings us back to the financial services growth paradox: 'more is less'. Many financial services firms have grown too big, too fast, and need to downsize their operations to increase profitability. In our view, the financial services growth paradox has emerged with conflicting views on five main assumptions.

Assumption 1: The portfolio logic for investments can be applied to financial services

Many executives in the financial services industry (implicitly) apply the investment rules proposed by the Boston Consulting Group (BCG) growth share matrix: 'Invest in attractive (i.e. fast-growing) markets to obtain high market shares'. As soon as investment opportunities in the home market dry up, firms start to look for growing markets abroad. This logic views a company as a portfolio of geographical businesses with a variety of risks and opportunities. A central assumption underlying the BCG matrix is that growth (of markets or share) must be prioritized to experience curve effects since relative market share is a good proxy indicator for the relative profit performance as well as cash needs. The positive impact of market share on firm profitability has been empirically demonstrated in the PIMS studies[1]— because all competitors in a given business will tend to enjoy similar price levels for their products, lower costs than competition will therefore result in superior performance.

However, several deficiencies of portfolio matrixes can be identified: the model's use of only two dimensions (growth and share) to assess competitive position, the focus on balancing cash flows rather than other interdependencies, the emphasis on cost leadership rather than differentiation as a source of competitive advantage, and the poor correlation between market share and profitability. Nevertheless, it seems that executives and shareholders alike continue to apply some aspects of the logic underlying the BCG matrix; few managers openly declare satisfaction with managing low-growth 'dog' businesses—even if they are highly profitable. It is rather doubtful that an unreflected application of the portfolio logic is adequate to build and run an international financial services firm.

In particular, the importance of size and market share needs to be better understood and revised. In principle, integrated international firms gain competitive advantages from the exploitation of differences in national resource endowments (comparative advantage), the flexibility and bargaining strength of a multinational network, and economies of scale, scope, and learning.[2] There is, however, a poor correlation between size and profitability: 'Big may be better, but big is not enough'.[3] There is little doubt about the potential existence of efficiency effects of consolidation and as a result, managers often justify their desire for scale by its assumed effect on average costs. However, the literature on bank scale economies[4] converges towards the opinion that the average cost curve shows a relatively flat U-shape at best. Medium-sized banks within the wide range of assets between USD 100 million and USD 10 billion tend to be the most cost efficient.

Empirical literature does not produce unambiguous results, but it is probably safe to say that technological progress, such as scale-dependent access

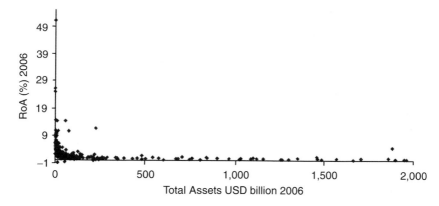

Figure 1. Effect of size on RoA of financial services firms (Data based on 254 firms of Reuters Portfolio top 500 financial services firms)

to specific products (like syndicated loans or access to loans from central banks as seen recently during the subprime crisis), has pushed the flex point of the curve higher. However, it is questionable whether cost motives can fully explain the economic rationale of mega-mergers where both companies involved exceed the level of USD 50 billion in assets. Another motive against scale as the main reason for international expansion is the increased availability of highly specialized and cost-efficient outsourcing services. Small banks have the possibility of substituting scale by outsourcing contracts with large-scale ICT providers or forging alliances for back-office integration purposes or common product development.

Although economies of scale and scope may explain national consolidation, they do not fully explain the internationalization moves of leading financial services companies. As demonstrated by Figure 1, there is no obvious correlation between asset size and return on assets (RoA). Most academic literature therefore suggests that cross-border consolidation has, at best, neutral effects on performance, and we can indeed observe that small national players often have a lower cost/income ratio than their large multinational competitors.

Very large financial services firms are not typically able to generate exceptionally high RoA. In particular, only a handful of firms with total assets of USD 200 billion generate RoA higher than 1.7 percent. It appears that small but focused and differentiated financial services firms are often able to outperform their giant competitors. In defence of the biggest financial institutions of the world, we can say that returns become increasingly stable on a fairly high level. A similar relationship (i.e. returns are stable on a high level and there is no significant correlation between return on equity (RoE) and total assets) can be observed when comparing size and RoE as depicted in Figure 2.

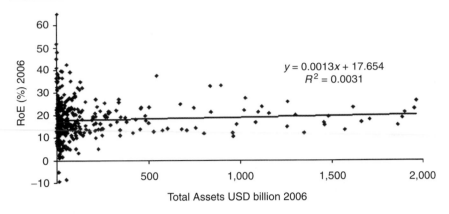

Figure 2. Effect of size on RoE of financial services firms (Data based on 354 firms of Reuters Portfolio top 500 financial services firms)

Another indication that scale/scope economies are of marginal relevance in international expansion, at least in retail banking, is evident in the battle for ABN AMRO. The Royal Bank of Scotland (RBS), Banco Santander and Fortis bid for ABN AMRO, only to ultimately divide the bank—with the Italian operations slated for Santander (and after one week sold to the Italian MPS), the Benelux operations slated for Fortis, and the rest designated for RBS. There was very little integration between the geographically dispersed units of ABN AMRO, and as a result, economies of scale and scope seemed to play a limited role in international operations.

Even though there is no general law linking size or degree of international expansion to the performance of a firm, many executives in the financial services industry act as if size is the most important business goal.

Assumption 2: Shareholders and analysts expect high growth rates

Another assumption that seduces financial services firms to accelerate growth is that stakeholders expect and value high growth rates. It might be true that shareholders and business analysts push for international expansion because this creates fantasies about future returns and high share price growth rates, but the recent moves of hedge funds to break up existing financial services giants show that growth does not create sustainable shareholder value per se. The break-up into parts of ABN AMRO provides a good example. Another recent example is the attempt by Luqman Arnold, a past CEO and shareholder of UBS, to sell several parts of the Swiss bank and split its investment banking

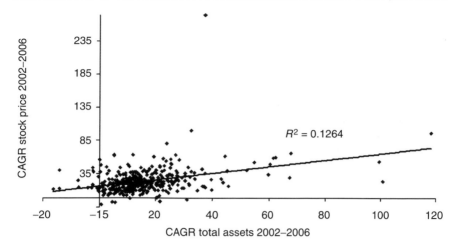

Figure 3. Effect of size on the share price of financial services firms (Data based on 391 firms of Reuters Portfolio top 500 financial services firms)

operations from its wealth management division. High growth rates might impress the markets in the short run and sometimes lead to increased total shareholder returns (i.e. increase in share price as seen in Figure 3 and dividends as seen in Figure 4). However, in the long run, it is not revenue and asset growth that matter but rather net operating profits after tax relative to equity or assets. Astonishingly, most press releases by financial services firms

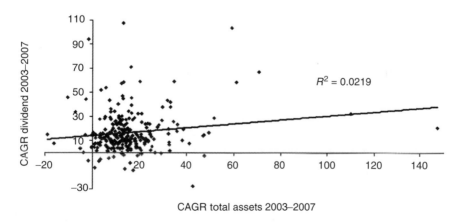

Figure 4. Effect of size on dividends of financial services firms (Data based on 266 firms of Reuters Portfolio top 500 financial services firms)

do not indicate relative performance indicators such as RoA or RoE but rather absolute profit and revenues.

Cash is king and as long as total shareholder returns are decent, business fundamentals may well be below average. Most large financial services firms are able to produce high enough absolute free cash flows to pay high dividends and impress financial markets with growth fantasies to attract new investors that bolster the share price. Due to their large balance sheets, these firms get AAA-ratings from credit rating agencies, which give the firms access to cheap refinancing and profitable businesses with large corporate accounts and institutional investors. Everything is fine until investors realize that unfocused growth can diminish the competitiveness of a firm, which leads to lower profits relative to their investments, which in turn allows the firm to pay only minimal dividends. And finally, the share price tumbles as well. Shareholders often evaluate their investments only superficially and assume that growing assets, revenues, and absolute profits indicate that all is well and do not look at business fundamentals in more detail. In the long run, financial institutions can only afford to pay high dividends and see an increase in their share price if their business results are above average.

For various reasons, practitioners have other views on this issue. Motives such as the quest for independence, empire building, growth stories for investors, redundant M&A capabilities, attractive new markets, and inefficient target banks seem to drive internationalization. Most banking executives claim to be able to create value for shareholders (and themselves) with cross-border moves—but only a few of them actually manage to deliver positive results, as shown in Figures 3 and 4.

Assumption 3: Top managers always act in the best interests of the shareholders

Top managers do not always act in the best interests of the shareholders. Strategic decisions are sometimes driven by personal interests. Because the interests of the owners (principals) and the managers (agents) of a financial services firm do not completely overlap, there will inherently be principal–agent conflicts. Agents always know more about their tasks than principals. The information asymmetries between principals and agents make it extremely difficult to align interests completely through incentive systems. Financial services firms therefore continue to grow even if shareholders prefer 'more with less'.

Top management of banks and insurance companies frequently justify their big deals with the desire to stay independent. Size protects from hostile takeover bids. But why should shareholders care about independence? If another owner is able to create more value for the firm, it is, from an economic point of view, beneficial for shareholders of the target firm to sell their stakes to another party—even if the shareholder is a government agency. However, not all companies have the capabilities to go abroad and grow. Firms with difficulties developing competitive advantage in their home market cannot hope to escape competition by entering foreign markets. Even economically less-developed markets are no Eldorado for financial institutions. Courage to establish a physical presence in those markets is not enough to ensure success. Internationalization strategies need to be based on solid sources of competitive advantages paired with strategic and organizational capabilities to transfer those advantages to foreign markets. It is natural that less competitive firms are takeover targets by firms with superior resources and capabilities. Consequently, to grow just for the sake of staying independent is a doubtful strategy.

Another frequently found argument for accelerated international exposure by top managers is that international expansion is the only way to keep their best people busy and excited. Although it is generally desirable to have highly motivated managers who act in the best interests of the owners of the firm, this is a weak motive for growth. Top executives of financial services firms at times invest in international markets because this creates exciting M&A projects and eventually increases their salaries and job security, but many unsuccessful international expansion cases of financial services firms have shown that the very opposite can, and does, happen.

Assumption 4: CAGE differences will diminish

Financial services firms sometimes assume that cultural, administrative, geographical, and economic (CAGE) differences will be reduced in the future. This evolution is expected to give internationally operating firms a competitive edge over their purely local competitors. However, most financial services segments are currently far from being integrated on a global or even regional scale. CAGE differences matter and complicate cross-border expansion substantially. Regulatory frameworks in particular are still dominated by national standards. Some large corporate customers are becoming increasingly global, but many others (e.g. retail and small corporate customers) are still local—and this is not likely to change in the near future. The competition for these super-large corporate clients is fierce and serving them often creates lower margins compared to smaller national customers. Frequently, these large potential clients prefer to work with smaller local financial services firms to get better conditions, or they decide to internalize selected financial services processes. Local financial services champions are therefore not likely to vanish from the financial services landscape.

Assumption 5: Arbitrage and aggregation possibilities will increase

Based on the assumption that CAGE differences will diminish, large multi-national financial services firms believe in increased possibilities for profit from arbitrage and cross-border aggregation. Offshoring in financial services compared to the manufacturing or consumer goods industry is still in its infancy. Financial services value chains are relatively easy to disaggregate. Most processes are highly digitalized and geographical distance should not be a big concern. As a result, offshoring of high value-added processes is not frequent in retail banking but a growing phenomenon in other financial services segments. To successfully compete in investment banking, for example, many banks decide to establish competence centres in London and New York. Geneva is an attractive location to establish a competence centre for wealth management and private banking. The emergence of these hubs boosts international integration and coordination between subsidiaries to profit from arbitrage of local resources and capabilities.

If CAGE differences are lower, financial services firms have more possibilities to implement aggregation strategies which aim to achieve cross-border synergies, primarily through international standardization. Due to high administrative differences, it is difficult to identify best practices, and standardizing processes is even more challenging. If, for example, a wealth management firm wants to assess the profitability of its global clients, it must compare local customer data at a central point. To transfer sensitive customer data outside the home country is not permitted in many countries. Benefits from arbitrage and aggregation depend on the magnitude of CAGE differences as well as on the costs and benefits of integrating those activities. Less may be more if peripheral business activities (such as the development of software, the operation of call centres, or the processing of administrative data) can be effectively outsourced. For many other processes, aggregation and arbitrage should not be organized by pure market transactions, which would justify the further geographical expansion of financial services firms. Aggregation and arbitrage opportunities therefore represent a valid basis for internationalization of financial services firms but hardly explain the desire for global presence and size.

Opening the black box of managerial decision-making and execution

The inherent conflicting views decision-makers have on these five assumptions indicate that many management teams in financial services firms are facing a growth paradox and must rethink their growth models. The objective of this book is to help management with this task by opening the black box of management excellence when building an international financial services firm. The answers to the questions raised in this book are not as clear cut as supervisory boards, CEOs, and Divisional or Strategy Heads might have hoped. There is no general correlation between the size of the firm and its economic performance, nor is there a universal causal relationship between the degree of international expansion and the profitability of the firm. Instead, it is the quality of strategic decision-making and strategy execution that makes the difference for shareholder value creation. This book identifies and addresses a set of critical questions: Do we have to grow? If yes, should we grow by product diversification or by international expansion? If we opt for international expansion, when is the right time to start that process? If the right time is now, which markets should we target? How should we enter these markets: through acquisitions, organic growth, or strategic alliances? In addition to the mode of entry decision, what should be the speed of foreign market penetration? Should we adapt our competitive positioning to the local market conditions? If yes, how? What impact does increased international presence have on our existing functional strategies? How should we design our organizational architecture to reap profits from an international presence?

Many executives have recognized that intransigent international financial services growth does not lead to higher performance and does not satisfy key stakeholders in the long run. The growth paradox of services lies in the observation that with increasing size, the competitiveness of the firm can be endangered rather than enhanced. In other words, to build an international financial services firm does not necessarily mean to grow as fast and as large as possible but rather to design and execute credible corporate and business-level strategies based on a sound analysis of core competences and market structures.

Acknowledgements

I owe a debt of gratitude to many friends, colleagues from academia, interview partners from the financial services field and reviewers from Oxford University Press. Particularly, I thank Robert Grant, David T. Llewellyn, and Steven Phelan for their comments on the initial book proposal; Vittorio Coda, Torsten Pade Hellerhoff, Jens Kleine, Monica Masucci, and Gabriella Lojacono for their observations on the final draft of the book; Giovanni Boccolini (Intesa Sanpaolo), Giampaolo Ferradini (Deutsche Bank), Felix Fremerey (DZ Bank), Joachim Fröhlich (Wüstenrot Bank), Robert Grosse (Standard Bank), Tobias Meckert (Allianz), Roberto Nicastro (Unicredit), Phil Kershaw (HBOS), Vita Rizzuto (Unicredit), Domenico Sfalanga (Intesa Sanpaolo), Martin Wohlmuth (Erste Bank), the members of the German Club of Finance, and many other executives for sharing their insights with me; my Bocconi and Steinbeis students for valuable discussions in class and many interesting research reports; and my research assistants Klaus Pietzka and Federica Massa Saluzzo for their support in data collection and interpretation. I am especially grateful for the time and effort my colleague and friend from Bocconi University Robert Grant put into this book project. A special 'thank you' goes to Vittorio Coda, who has strongly influenced the way I think about strategy and banking. He carefully read the final manuscript and contributed substantially to its quality. Finally, I thank David Musson and Matthew Derbyshire from Oxford University Press for their support throughout the project.

Acknowledgements

Contents

List of Figures   xxi
List of Tables   xxiii
List of Abbreviations   xxv

Introduction to the Book   1

Part I. Multinationality and Competitiveness

1. The Characteristics of Financial Services   23
2. Profit Impact of Internationalization   60

Part II. Strategic Decision-Making

3. Who Should Decide? Developing Strategy-Making Capabilities   73
4. Why Go Abroad? The Rationale of Cross-Border Moves   98
5. Where to Compete? The Logic Behind Market Selection   120
6. When to Enter? The Timing and Speed of Market Entry   141
7. How to Enter? The Choice of the Market Entry Mode   158
8. How to Compete? The Development of Business and
   Functional-Level Strategies   184

Part III. Strategy Execution

9. How to Organize? International Organizational Architectures   227
10. How to Accelerate Learning? Facilitating Cross-Border
    Knowledge Transfer   257
11. How to Boost Innovation Across Borders? International
    Corporate Entrepreneurship   292
    Epilogue: Sustainable International Development after the
    Subprime Crisis   314

Notes   317
Bibliography   329
Index   349

List of Figures

1. Effect of size on RoA of financial services firms   ix

2. Effect of size on RoE of financial services firms   x

3. Effect of size on the share price of financial services firms   xi

4. Effect of size on dividends of financial services firms   xi

0.1. Structure of the book   16

1.1. Organizational chart UniCredit Group (June 2007)   33

2.1. Profit impact of internationalization of selected banks   67

3.1. Formal strategic planning   85

3.2. The strategy process framework   87

3.3. Brand configuration of Erste Bank   93

4.1. Growth and value creation of the world's most valuable 225 financial services firms   100

4.2. Erste Bank—evaluating growth options   110

4.3. The cross-border strategy and organization matrix   114

4.4. Measuring the cross-border integration level of financial services segments   117

4.5. Impact of total assets on cost–income ratios   118

5.1. Assessment of market attractiveness, Allianz SE   122

5.2. Clustering geographical target markets   133

6.1. Predicting market development through analogy   148

7.1. A generic M&A process model   175

7.2. Post-merger integration level and speed   176

8.1. The impact of scale on absolute profits   187

8.2. Multi-channel distribution of Allianz in selected countries 2006   197

8.3. Towards unique strategic positions in China: multi-channel distribution of two foreign JVs in 2006   199

8.4. HBOS: product market share in UK market in 2007   207

8.5. HBOS: profit split in 2007   207

8.6. Business challenges through the evolution of the firm   219

9.1. Creating parenting advantage   229

9.2. Organizational structure of UniCredit Group in 2008   240

9.3. Organizational structure of Erste Bank before the reorganization
     in 2007   246

9.4. Organizational structure of Erste Bank in 2008   247

9.5. Erste Bank Holding structure in 2008   249

10.1. Knowledge audit   284

10.2. Knowledge development processes   285

10.3. Changing the knowledge management culture   288

11.1. An integrative process framework for corporate entrepreneurship   300

11.2. Product innovation in the certificates market   303

11.3. Extended innovation process framework in multinational firms   305

List of Tables

0.1. The biggest 30 companies of Forbes's World's 2,000 largest public companies in 2006   3

0.2. The world's largest financial services firms by assets in 2007   11

0.3. SIC codes included in the study of the financial services sector   19

1.1. The world's most valuable financial services firms in 2008   30

1.2. Strategic implications of product experience on internationalization process   49

1.3. Strategic implications of transportation costs on internationalization process   50

1.4. Strategic implications of (re-)production costs on internationalization process   52

1.5. Strategic implications of product adaptation costs on internationalization process   53

3.1. Strategy—from commodity to a unique product   81

7.1. The battle for ABN AMRO—sequence of events   172

8.1. Licensed provinces in China in 2006   200

8.2. Overview of main market conditions and characteristics of HBOS's business-level strategy in 2007   212

9.1. Corporate interventions   237

9.2. Local responsiveness versus global efficiency   254

9.3. Aligning corporate interventions to the local context   255

10.1. Developing a culture for cross-border knowledge sharing   266

11.1. Alignment of interests in entrepreneurial processes—an example   308

List of Abbreviations

AAA	adaptation–aggregation–arbitrage
ADSL	asymmetric digital subscriber line
AG	aktiengesellschaft
APE	annual premium equivalent
ASX	Australian Securities Exchange
ATM	asynchronous transfer mode
ATM	automated teller machine
AUD	Australian dollar
AUM	assets under management
BC	before Christ
bn	billion
BRIC	Brazil, Russia, India, China
BRICS	Brazil, Russian Federation, India, China, and South Africa
CA	competitive advantage
CAGE	cultural–administrative–geographic–economic
CAGR	compound annual growth rate
CEE	Central and Eastern Europe
CEO	Chief Executive Officer
CFO	Chief Financial Officer
CI	competitive intelligence
CIBM	corporate investment banking and markets
COO	Chief Operating Officer
CRM	customer relationship management
CRO	Chief Risk Officer
CV	curriculum vitae
DKK	Danish krone
DNA	deoxyribonucleic acid
DOI	degree of internationalization

ENA	Europe and North America
ESOP	employee stock ownership program
EU	European Union
EUR	Euro (€)
FDI	foreign direct investment
GCIB	group corporate and investment banking
GCM	group capital markets
GBP	pound sterling (£)
GDP	gross domestic product
GWP	gross written premiums
H1	first half of current year
HQ	headquarters
HR	human resources
I-R	integration–responsiveness
I&D	innovation & development
IB	international business
ICT	information and communication technology
IO	industrial organization
IP	Internet protocol
IPO	initial public offering
ISDN	integrated services digital network
IT	information technology
ITL	Italian lira
JV	joint venture
Kbps	kilobit per second
KM	knowledge management
L/H	life/health
LAN	local area network
LSE	London Stock Exchange
Ltd	limited
M–P	multinationality–performance
M&A	mergers and acquisitions
m	million
MBA	Master of Business Administration
Mbps	megabit per second
MNC	multinational company

MP3	mpeg-1 audio layer 3
MSOP	management stock option plan
O-L-I	ownership-location-internalization
P/C	property/casualty
P2P	peer-to-peer
PC	personal computer
PEST	political, economic, social-cultural, and technological
PIN	personal identification number
Plc	public limited company (Co)
PMI	post-merger integration
PR	public relations
R&D	research and development
RMB	renminbi (currency of mainland China)
ROA	return on assets
ROE	return on equity
ROI	return on investment
SBU	strategic business unit
SA	sociedad anónima
SE	societas europaea
SIC	standard industrial classification code
SME	small and medium-sized enterprises
SONET	synchronous optical networking
SpA	società per azioni
SRM	supplier relationship management system
SWOT	strengths-weaknesses-opportunities-threats analysis
TC	transaction cost
TCP	transmission control protocol
TQM	total quality management
UMTS	universal mobile telecommunications system
USA	United States of America
USD	United States dollar ($)
WAN	wide area network

Introduction to the book

A new era of global banking and insurance is gradually emerging. Financial services firms with the highest international exposure such as HSBC, Citigroup, AIG, and UBS started to serve international markets many decades ago. Like other service industries, internationalization in the financial services sector has lagged behind the manufacturing and technology sectors, but the international picture is changing quickly. Pioneers of international financial services have continued their global expansion. In Europe, the race for cross-border mergers has involved Banco Santander acquiring Abbey National and UniCredit taking over HVB. China's growing prominence as a financial services market is evident in the high stock market values of domestic banks and the increased overseas presence of its leading banks, above all the Industrial and Commercial Bank of China (ICBC). Meanwhile, Western companies scramble to acquire equity stakes in domestic Chinese banks. The global subprime crisis and the ensuing credit crunch have reinforced the trend for Asian financial services firms to purchase equity stakes in leading Western institutions.

One of the most prominent examples of internationally active financial institutions is Citigroup. With a history of almost 200 years, Citigroup is present in some 100 countries with around 300,000 employees in the various units of the interactive subsidiary network. As over 98 per cent of its employees are local, Citigroup must cope with cultural diversity and serve more than 200 million client accounts with a full range of financial services products. Many other financial services firms have started to catch up quickly. Through numerous merger and acquisition activities, other global financial services powerhouses have emerged. JP Morgan Chase, Bank of America, AIG, UniCredit, Allianz, UBS, and Banco Santander are just a few. US banks have undoubtedly been the leaders in forming large financial groups, but some European and Asian banks have started to aggressively expand into global markets as well. The acquisition of a 20 per cent stake of the largest African financial intermediary Standard Bank by ICBC for USD 5.6 billion in cash is a recent proof of 'inverse' internationalization—institutions from developing countries growing across national borders. As declared by ICBC, the target countries in such moves are mostly other developing countries. The world's most valuable bank (in terms of market capitalization) is no longer Citigroup but rather the Chinese ICBC. Clearly, a new dimension of international competition has started in financial services.

Five Reasons to Study the Financial Services Industry

But internationalization of banking and insurance is not a new phenomenon. A century and a half ago, Standard Chartered Bank (then two separate banks) established international operations across Africa, Asia, and the Middle East. Bank of America, HSBC, and Citibank pioneered global banking, starting from the early 1900s. Although internationalization of financial services is not an entirely new phenomenon, it merits study for several reasons: (*a*) the top players are extremely large, (*b*) many of them aggressively increase their international presence, (*c*) the motivations for creating global financial services empires are rather diverse and often ambiguous, (*d*) the impact of this increased exposure to international markets on profitability is unclear, and (*e*) many different approaches to internationalization can be observed among the leading financial services firms. The following paragraphs address these issues in greater detail.

Financial Services Firms Dominate the List of the World's Biggest Firms

The sheer size of the biggest global financial services firms has increased substantially in the past decade (see Table 0.1). Their impact on home— as well as host—economies has changed significantly. Some large banks in relatively small home economies, such as UBS and Credit Suisse in Switzerland or Fortis in the Netherlands, have become too big to die. Bankruptcy of such institutions would seriously harm the home economy.

Forbes.com ranks the world's 2,000 largest firms according to their 'bigness', measured by four different scales: sales, profits, assets, and market value. In 2006 of the Forbes's top 10, 7 are financial services firms. Of the top 30, 63 per cent are banks, insurance firms, or diversified financials. Even within the top 100, 50 financial services firms can be found. When ranking the companies by profits, financial services firms represent among the first 30 firms 33 per cent next to companies operating in the oil and gas operations with the same percentage. Most strikingly, if the companies are ranked by assets, the top 30 companies are all from the financial services industry.

Although the global subprime crisis and credit crunch has substantially damaged financial services firms along most 'bigness' dimensions used by Forbes, it is still likely that they will continue to dominate the top 100

Table 0.1. The biggest 30 companies of Forbes's World's 2,000 largest public companies in 2006[a]

Rank	Company	Country	Industry	Sales ($bn)	Profits ($bn)	Assets ($bn)	Market value ($bn)
1	Citigroup	United States	Banking	146.56	21.54	1,884.32	247.42
2	Bank of America	United States	Banking	116.57	21.13	1,459.74	226.61
3	HSBC Holdings	United Kingdom	Banking	121.51	16.63	1,860.76	202.29
4	General Electric	United States	Conglomerates	163.39	20.83	697.24	358.98
5	JP Morgan Chase	United States	Banking	99.30	14.44	1,351.52	170.97
6	America n Intl Group	United States	Insurance	113.19	14.01	979.41	174.47
7	Exxon Mobil	United States	Oil and gas operations	335.09	39.50	223.95	410.65
8	Royal Dutch Shell	Netherlands	Oil and gas operations	318.85	25.44	232.31	208.25
9	UBS	Switzerland	Diversified financials	105.59	9.78	1,776.89	116.84
10	ING Group	Netherlands	Insurance	153.44	9.65	1,615.05	93.99
11	BP	United Kingdom	Oil and gas operations	265.91	22.29	217.60	198.14
12	Toyota Motor	Japan	Consumer durables	179.02	11.68	243.60	217.69
13	Royal Bank of Scotland	United Kingdom	Banking	77.41	12.51	1,705.35	124.13
14	BNP Paribas	France	Banking	89.16	9.64	1,898.19	97.03
15	Allianz	Germany	Insurance	125.33	8.81	1,380.88	87.22
16	Berksh e Hathaway	United States	Diversified financials	98.54	11.02	248.44	163.79
17	Wal-Mart Stores	United States	Retailing	348.65	11.29	151.19	201.36
18	Barclays	United Kingdom	Banking	67.71	8.95	1,949.17	94.79
19	Chevron	United States	Oil and gas operations	195.34	17.14	132.63	149.37
19	Total	France	Oil and gas operations	175.05	15.53	138.82	152.62
21	HBOS	United Kingdom	Banking	84.28	7.59	1,156.61	79.83
22	Conoco Phillips	United States	Oil and gas operations	167.58	15.55	164.78	107.39
23	AXA Group	France	Insurance	98.85	6.38	666.47	87.64
24	Sociéte Générale Group	France	Banking	84.47	6.55	1,259.32	77.62
25	Goldman Sachs Group	United States	Diversified financials	69.35	9.54	838.20	83.31
25	Morgan Stanley	United States	Diversified financials	76.55	7.47	1,120.65	79.76
27	Banco Santander	Spain	Banking	62.34	7.37	945.86	115.75
27	Deutsche Bank	Germany	Diversified financials	95.50	7.45	1,485.58	65.15
29	AT&T	United States	Telecommunications services	63.06	7.36	270.63	229.78
30	Electricité de France	France	Utilities	77.75	7.39	233.40	133.37

[a] www.forbes.com.

list in the long run. The depreciation that most banks and insurance firms had to make after the subprime bubble burst is in many cases enormous but compared to total assets of several trillion US dollars still moderate. The highest effect is on profits and market capitalization. Citigroup, for example, lost more than half of its share price within little more than half a year (July 2007 to February 2008) but is still one of the biggest firms in the world.

Many Financial Services Firms Aggressively Increase Their Degree of Internationalization

The degree of internationalization has changed as well, making the banks and insurance companies more dependent on their foreign markets. Size has apparently become an important weapon to win against competition and satisfy demanding shareholders, but home-country consolidation is no longer an option for most banks. Even in retail banking, which was one of the few major industries of the world that was dominated by domestic players, there is at least a strong trend towards regional integration.

In Europe, in particular, the industry structure is being transformed by a wave of cross-border mergers. BSCH (Banco Santander Central Hispano) acquired Abbey National and UniCredit incorporated Hypovereinsbank (and with it Bank Austria Creditanstalt). ABN AMRO acquired Banca Antonveneta in Italy and has been taken over by a consortium led by Royal Bank of Scotland. The Spanish BBVA's bid for the Italian BNL is yet another sign that even in traditionally local businesses such as retail banking, consolidation has entered into a new phase. We can also observe regional integration driven by banks with small home markets (e.g. Nordea in Scandinavia or ING in the Benelux region). Europe is an ideal setting for studying international integration because of its attempts to reduce regulatory barriers to cross-border banking within the single market programme. In addition, the race for a good strategic position in emerging banking markets, such as Eastern European countries, Africa, Latin America, India, or China, has also intensified. A similar situation can be reported for the insurance business with inner-European consolidation such as the acquisition of the British BAT Industries PLC by the Zurich Group in 1997, or cross-triad acquisitions like the takeover of Citizens Financial Group, Inc., by RBS in 1988. A result of this worldwide consolidation process is the emergence of strong financial services firms outside the United States.

Motivations for Creating Global Financial Services Empires Are Rather Diverse and Often Ambiguous

Financial services internationalization is, however, not only driven by market-seeking motives and the desire to grow the revenue and asset base.

Increasingly, banking activities are internationalized by locating them in countries with specific factor endowments that make the provision of banking services less costly and in many instances also of higher quality (i.e. faster and more reliable). Designing offshoring strategies is not only easier for large multinational banking institutions but also accessible to small institutions through outsourcing contracts with large multinational partners in the home market such as Accenture and IBM—another good reason to study internationalization of financial services firms. In many cases, internationalization of financial services does not seem to be motivated by the desire of the management team to enhance the competitiveness of the firm to increase its overall profitability and deliver higher total shareholder returns (i.e. dividends plus share price increase). The desire to stay independent, to follow competitors, to please investor analysts, or to keep key managers excited is sometimes a doubtful motive for international expansion plans. Hence, the reasons for the existence of such ambiguous goals need to be further explored.

The Impact of Internationalization on Firm Profitability is Unclear

Unclear motivations for internationalization strategies are partly responsible for the fact that investors have run hot and cold on cross-border acquisitions. While there is some evidence that national mergers (specifically in the United States) yield savings of 40 per cent or more for an acquired entity, the cross-border merger wave in Europe during the 1970s and 1980s has, in almost all cases, failed to deliver the expected results. Two main reasons for the dilatoriness exist: international consolidation is more complex to plan and execute because financial services firms need to follow strict national regulations to which they are subject, and customer behaviour in relation to savings, investment, and transactions is nationally differentiated by culture and tradition.

For these two reasons, internationalization in banking and insurance firms is strategically and operationally more complex and interesting than internationalization in computer software, semiconductors, or soft drinks, and even compared to other service types such as business consulting, hotel services, legal services, restaurant services, and the like. International presence can create economic value by reaping economies of scale, scope, location advantages, and global learning. Unlocking such sources of returns to an international presence requires close managerial attention to trade-offs in deciding when to go international, which markets to enter, how to enter a particular market, how to compete locally, and how to organize the enlarged firm.

*Internationalization Processes of Financial Services Firms
Show Distinct Patterns*

The specific characteristics of financial services firms make a difference in how companies address these issues—another good reason to study this particular industry rather than making general statements about global strategies of all types of firms. The characteristics of services typically alter the costs and benefits of international expansion, and, as a consequence, the direction, path, and mode of foreign market entry. The challenge for financial services firms was and still is to find opportunities to apply superior and transferable (IT) systems, brands, products, marketing, and general management skills to potential new markets. As banks and insurance firms increasingly seek profitable growth through geographical diversification, we can observe that individual banks apply distinct strategies and organizational designs leading to significant performance differences. There is no 'one size fits all' approach to banking internationalization, and the 'herding' approach that many banks applied in strategy making in the past is no longer sufficient.

Is the Financial Services World Flat?

These are five good reasons to study the internationalization of financial services firms. A first glimpse at the financial services industry reveals that various segments differ in their degree of cross-border integration. To get a better understanding of the international dynamics of the financial services industry, its various sub-segments have to be distinguished. The magnitude of globalization forces has increased and a few companies like MasterCard, Visa, and PayPal are becoming truly global retail banking businesses. However, they all offer payments systems. Similarly, the ATM networks support customers globally—again, payments. It is hard to see what can be called 'global banking'. For instance, the funds for the large auto makers are spread across dozens of countries, and banks pull that all together to present a consolidated view so that their treasury management shuffles it around to optimize the usage of funds for the auto maker. That is a global activity. Global representation can be merely placing a small office in different countries. But most financial services firms are not truly global. For example, HSBC runs over 90 'local' retail banks in over 90 countries, yet these locations are self-sustaining units rather than parts of a larger, connected group.

Defining International Financial Services

Financial services may be defined as the provision of instruments and mechanisms to hold and manage savings, obtain funding, transfer funds between locations and forms, manage risks, and get advice on financial concerns.[1] Financial services include basically all organizations which have at their core the provision, packaging, and pricing of products and services in one or more of the business segments indicated below:

- investment (including deposit taking, asset management, securities brokerage)
- financing (including credit extension, securities underwriting, leveraged investing)
- protection (including insurance underwriting, derivatives hedging)
- transactions (including payments, cash management, securities exchanges, clearance, custody and safekeeping, asset servicing)

A financial services market exists when a firm has found a sustainable (i.e. profitable in the long run) way to satisfy one or more of the above-listed customer needs through selling financial products and services. Product as well as customer properties are frequently used to distinguish between different financial services markets. In their annual reports and conference presentations, executives habitually discriminate between products (banking vs. asset management vs. insurance), geographical segments (local areas vs. nations vs. regions vs. development stage vs. ICT infrastructure availability), client segments (corporate vs. private vs. institutional clients), and distribution channels (branch network vs. agents vs. online vs. telephone). All of these categories, of course, can be sub-segmented and combined. For example, in one of its strategy meetings, AIG management teams may speak about the online car insurance market for Hispanic immigrants in the United States.

If financial services have foreign currency and/or cross-country dimensions, those transactions can be labelled as international banking. Purely national banks therefore frequently engage in international banking, but do not have the characteristics of multinational banks. They can conduct international banking operations via trading activities with other financial services firms that are active internationally. For example, a client of the purely locally operating Thurgauer Kantonalbank in Switzerland wants to buy an asset management product that includes foreign assets. When the same client is using his debit card via the Cirrus network in Shanghai, the Thurgauer Kantonalbank has to engage in international banking when settling the transaction for its bank client. This example shows that all banks engage in some form of international banking, but should not be classified as multinational firms. Banks are multinationals only when they own and control banking activities in two or more countries.[2] The same applies for insurance companies, stock markets, hedge funds, or other financial services firms. But how internationally integrated are these segments?

We All Know the World is Not Flat

The contemporary debate over globalization is not conclusive on how to measure the concept of globalization or cross-border integration. There is broad consensus that globalization, whether economic, political, cultural, or environmental, is defined by increasing levels of interdependence over vast distances, yet little academic literature exists on how to measure those levels of interdependence, especially at the firm level. Many academics as well as practitioners are nevertheless inclined to agree on the assertion that globalization is accelerating and irreversible. Some even join Thomas Friedman in suggesting that the world is flat. Does geography really not matter any more? It is true that an individual or firm can compete from anywhere in the world. In the world of financial services, the business landscape is certainly fragmented: physical presence in financial centres such as London or New York still matters for investment banking and international strategy differs from national strategy in many aspects. If the world were flat, that is, without any cultural, technological, institutional, and geographical barriers, studying international business strategy would be useless. One could just take theories and concepts developed in the field of strategic management and apply them to the one big national market—'the world'. Fortunately for the field of international management, the world is fragmented, and the flattening forces described by Friedman are not likely to level the planet any time soon.

In most of its business segments, financial services is still a people business and requires local contacts and face-to-face meetings, which reduces the impact of digital communication channels and opportunities for global or regional service standardization. Product portability even within apparently would-be homogeneous financial services markets such as the Eurozone is very limited. A study[3] carried out by the US Federal Reserve in 2003 on the European banking market concluded that while numerous forces push towards globalization, many banking services could remain local. The report argues that successful banking requires local knowledge, and banking markets therefore do not necessarily need to become significantly more integrated as the globalization of other economic sectors continues. Although this study is based on survey data from 1996, and many things have happened since that time in the financial services markets, it is nevertheless an indicator of the level of integration of this sector.

It is probably true that multinational corporate clients increasingly search for multinational financial services partners that are able to serve them anywhere in the world. But clients such as the German retailing giant Metro Group often purposely search for regional or national partners to use their bargaining power to obtain better conditions that are eventually passed on to their suppliers. In many cases, retail customers find it difficult to switch from one banking branch in the United States to another banking branch of the same institution in a different country. Cross-border mobility is still relatively limited. How many US citizens own a passport that would allow them to travel abroad? Although statistics vary, an educated guess might be that around 20 per cent of the total population over 18 years of age owns a passport. How many of those would require cross-border financial services beyond credit cards or foreign currency exchange? How many of those would appreciate access to their home-country bank in the country to which they travel?

The level of value chain disaggregation and offshoring is another indicator for cross-border integration. Offshoring in financial services has historically been focused on low value-added activities and forced to fight with legal constraints and cultural barriers. Only recently have large financial services firms such as Citigroup, JP Morgan Chase, or HSBC offshored more sophisticated processes such as equity research. Suppliers of such higher value-added services are firms such as OfficeTiger (located in India and recently acquired by RR Donnelley), and Irevna, another Indian company that specialized in offshore investment research. This shows that even in knowledge-intensive services industries, it is possible to identify value chain activities that can be standardized and offshored. However, this is a recent trend. Lower value-added equity research processes that can be offshored are library functions, structured company and industry reports, and to some extent even the blending and packaging of various data on a given subject, for example an analysis of earnings estimates for a biotech company and, based on that research, the development of a valuation model. The higher value-added activities of investment banking, such as raising money by issuing and selling securities in the primary market, assisting public and private corporations in raising funds in the capital markets, or providing strategic advisory services for mergers and acquisitions, however, are still located in the richer countries.

Similarly, insurance companies have tapped into offshore resources using a variety of different models. AXA and Allianz have set up captive operations. In 2003, Allianz set up an offshore software development operation in Trivandrum, Southern India. Others, such as the world's biggest insurance company AIG, decided to directly contract an Indian supplier. Still others decide to use the offshore arms of Western services firms (such as Accenture) or a more complex 'build-operate-transfer' approach to offshoring: AVIVA first created captive offshoring operations, operated them, and then decided to spin off those operations.

These short illustrations indicate that the world is still round and not flat. But the message of Thomas Friedman is nevertheless relevant for financial services firms: international business will become increasingly important, even in formerly purely national businesses such as tax consulting, with the help of an Indian adviser or when making a hotel reservation via a call centre in Romania. Value-creating services will be located in various places around the world, customers can be served in many nations that have been formerly closed to foreign institutions, and competences and resources developed in one country can be used to create a sustainable competitive advantage in another country.

However, the costs of complexity of cross-border expansion and integration of activities are not to be disregarded. Even though information technology, another flattening force, has made it possible to connect people all around the world, coordination and control costs can sometimes increase disproportionally during international expansion. The slogan coined by Alan Rugman: 'Think regional, act local—and forget global'[4] appropriately describes the current situation of most international financial services segments. Rugman demonstrates that in the service sector, which accounts for more than 70 per cent of the workforce in North America, Western Europe, and Japan, few of the Fortune 500 companies have more than 20 per cent of their revenues from outside of their own 'triad' of the EU, North America, and Japan. Rugman's study suggests that for most service companies it is easier and more beneficial to cross country boundaries within the home triad than to enter another triad. If this is true, there seem to be higher liabilities of foreignness between triads than between inner-triad countries. Efforts to increase the integration of markets inside the triads will most likely increase those differences. Only a few attempts have been made to date to integrate financial services markets across the oceans on a larger scale.

The Industry Topography Changes Quickly

The world is not only fragmented, but the surface topography also changes quickly. Managers frequently need new maps to navigate in the financial services landscape. The market environment for global financial services experienced two decades of exponential growth with information technology and new regulatory frameworks changing the nature of business several times. Disintermediation, increased competition, product innovation, and process innovation were the natural consequences. However, Table 0.2 shows that the list of the largest (by total assets) 30 financial services firms has been relatively stable over the last 5 years: only 5 new entries can be registered. But within this top group, rankings as well as asset size changed quite substantially. In 2002, the Royal Bank of Scotland was at position 10 with just a fraction of the size it has now: RBS takes the first place in 2007 with assets of USD 3.78 trillion, which is larger than the GDP of Germany in the same year. More than half of the assets were added in 2007.

Conventional assumptions about the logic of the business had to be reviewed. Just 10 years ago several industry experts called for the end of the physical retail distribution of financial services products in favour of alternative channels such as online distribution, ATM machines, or the telephone.

Table 0.2. The world's largest financial services firms by assets in 2007[a]

Position 2007 (2002)	Company Name	Total Assets USD Million 2007	Total Assets USD Million 2006	Total Assets USD Million 2002
1 (12)	Royal Bank of Scotland Group plc	3,818,833.75	1,705,513.26	663,275.16
2 (10)	BNP Paribas	2,671,207.75	1,899,311.66	745,405.22
3 (7)	HSBC Holding plc	2,354,256.00	1,860,758.00	758,605.00
4 (3)	UBS AG	2,263,975.89	1,963,226.84	854,211.33
5 (18)	Crédit Agricole SA	2,209,637.50	1,662,204.79	530,697.95
6 (1)	Citigroup Inc.	2,187,631.00	1,884,318.00	1,097,590.00
7 (9)	ING Groep N. V.	2,048,238.13	1,617,072.59	751,755.11
8 (14)	Barclays PLC	2,022,618.75	1,056,850.38	618,885.06
9 (4)	Mitsubishi UFJ Financial Group Inc.	1,858,219.75	1,569,777.04	838,432.87
10 (5)	Deutsche Bank AG	1,757,537.50	1,485,105.82	795,813.96
11 (13)	Bank of America Corporation	1,715,746.00	1,459,737.00	660,951.00
12 (20)	Société Générale SA	1,689,570.25	1,261,740.62	526,158.27
13 (6)	Allianz SE	1,043,011.13	1,403,810.91	894,205.00
14 (47)	UniCredit SPA	1,594,503.75	1,085,425.65	223,887.72
15 (6)	JP Morgan Chase & Co	1,562,147.00	1,351,520.00	758,800.00
16 (15)	ABN AMRO Holding N.V.*	1,540,362.00	1,301,594.25	583,482.52
17 (−)	Mizuho Financial Group Inc.	1,470,797.63	1,255,614.86	—
10 (1)	Banco Santander, S.A.	1,424,640.00	1,099,500.20	40,222.07
19 (21)	Fortis N.V.	1,359,517.75	1,022,257.53	509,759.79
20 (15)	HBOS plc	1,354,509.53	1,158,260.10	571,559.66
21 (11)	Credit Suisse Group	1,352,319.38	1,028,881.79	691,152.09
22 (22)	AXA	1,135,385.50	959,454.08	466,621.89
23 (17)	Goldman Sachs Group, Inc.	1,119,796.00	838,201.00	355,574.00
24 (17)	American International Group, Inc.	1,060,505.00	979,410.00	561,229.00
25 (19)	Morgan Stanley	1,045,409.00	1,121,192.00	529,499.00
26 (−)	Industrial and Commercial Bank of China*	1,035,904.13	1,035,904.13	—
27 (23)	Merrill Lynch & Co., Inc.	1,020,050.00	841,299.00	451,375.00
28 (24)	Commerzbank AG	902,038.00	802,107.21	442,985.32
29 (27)	Dexia S.A.	944,631.25	747,336.98	368,257.90
30 (−)	Sumitomo Mitsui Financial Group, Inc.	944,233.50	898,078.70	—

* ICBC refers to 2006, ABN AMRO still traded at Amsterdam Stock Exchange

[a] Annual reports; based on Reuters Portfolio top 500 financial services firms (retrieved on 18 March 2008).

But physical branches in many countries have even increased in recent years, mostly in emerging markets. In 2006, around 70 per cent of Citigroup's new branch openings occurred in emerging economies. Sometimes the reduction in the number of branches goes hand-in-hand with the increase in the average size of the branches, as seen in the case of the English banking market. Video did not kill the radio star and the Internet did not erase all physical newspapers from the market nor will it soon replace physical branch networks. Today, most industry players have recognized that there are several viable strategic options to cope with the digital challenge.

Another change in the financial services landscape was the rise of some universal banks. A decade ago, many industry experts widely declared them as being the dominant form of strategic organization. Difficulties in making those constructs work has disenchanted the all-finance advocates: Allianz has its problems with Dresdner Bank, and the Swiss insurance company Winterthur, which had been bought by Credit Suisse, was sold in 2007 to AXA, to name just a few. Of course, there are examples of universal banks such as ING or Fortis that prove that benefits from cross-selling or the sharing of firm resources can be realized, but this business model is just one among many available.

The Flexibility–Commitment Trade-Off

As a response to an industry environment characterized by high uncertainty and dynamic change, some financial services firms prefer to create options and open up new choices rather than shut them down and commit to one basic strategy. Those firms invest in diversity, value strategies as if they were options, use internal market mechanisms to stress-test those strategies, and use venture-capital performance metrics to select winning strategies. Other financial services firms seek higher rents by making tough strategic choices in terms of product, geographical, and customer positioning as early as possible to create sustainable competitive advantages in the chosen segment.

There are many solutions to the flexibility–commitment trade-off.[5] If the future was fully known, it would be appropriate to remove all potential choices and commit to one specific business scenario. But then strategic thinking would not be needed any more. Running spreadsheet analysis would be sufficient to detect and plan for optimal resource allocation. Eliminating too many *ex post* choices is not likely to lead to increased competitiveness when substantially new information regarding customer preferences or other relevant market factors is expected to arrive in the future.

On many occasions, however, reducing flexibility pays off. To avoid negative effects of being in limbo in the post-merger integration processes, an often-cited rule of thumb in such situations is that the main strategic decisions must be communicated within the first 10 days. Managers learn to live with the new situation instead of discussing ways to sabotage the merger. When UniCredit bought the German HVB, many analysts and industry experts thought that the main objective of UniCredit was to buy the Central and Eastern European (CEE) operations of HVB affiliate, Bank Austria. The German operations of HVB, as rumour had it, would be spun off soon and sold in the near future. UniCredit's rapid integration of the two IT platforms and the creation of competence centres for specific functions in Munich and Milan halted this idle chat.

On the other hand, increased flexibility is preferable to full commitment in uncertain market environments. It was a surprise to many industry players when RBS announced it would invest up to USD 5 billion in the Chinese market in 2005, and the stock market reacted negatively to that kind of commitment. However, after RBS announced a more modest investment of USD 1.65 billion in the Bank of China, RBS shares on the London Stock Exchange gained by more than 3 per cent during the morning trade. RBS Chief Executive Fred Goodwin classified this investment as 'low-risk' with many positive returns for the bank, namely, a foothold in a very attractive financial services market with access to over 11,300 bank branches of Bank of China and a strategic alliance through a seat on the board of the most internationally exposed of the Chinese banks. The main global competitors of RBS made similar deals at the same time. Bank of America reached an agreement in June 2005 to buy a 9 per cent stake in China Construction Bank for USD 3 billion; HSBC paid USD 1.75 billion in 2004 for a 19.9 per cent stake in the Bank of Communications, China's fifth-largest lender. When drawing up a strategy for the Chinese market, financial services firms need to carefully balance the need for commitment and flexibility by carefully identifying and discussing the forces that drive industry change.

To successfully compete in international markets it is therefore a critical requirement to create and manage a portfolio of strategic options and run small-scale experiments. At the same time, financial services firms are called on to show clear commitment to a selected set of markets and options when the time is ripe. To balance this trade-off, financial services firms have to develop capabilities in deliberate strategy making and determine strategy execution on a cross-border scale. And this is where this book comes in.

The Structure of the Book

Researchers and managers alike seek a better understanding of the internationalization process of financial services firms. This book provides an overview of how expansionary strategies of financial services firms are impacted by globalization and discusses performance drivers during internationalization processes. This book explores and challenges conventional assumptions from the international management literature on topics such as the limits of international expansion, the importance of cultural and institutional distance, the nature of economies of scale and scope, the existence of first mover advantages, the logic behind the global value chain configuration, the speed and timing of market entry, and the organizational architecture. Distinct from many books that have been written in this area, this book does not focus on causes and performance consequences of cross-border consolidation of financial institutions. Instead, this book puts the reader in the driver's seat of a financial services firm on its journey towards international markets and examines the actual strategies of the firms involved in cross-border consolidation. The reader will be forced to actively think through the most fundamental strategic decisions involved in internationalization moves:

- Do we have to grow?
- If so, should we grow by product diversification or by international expansion?
- If we opt for international expansion, when is the right time to start that process?
- If the right time is now, which markets should we target?
- How should we enter these markets: through acquisitions, organic growth, or strategic alliances?
- In addition to the mode of entry decision, what should be the speed of foreign market penetration?
- Should we adapt our competitive positioning to the local market conditions? If so, how?
- What impact does an increased international presence have on our existing functional strategies?
- How should we design our organizational architecture to reap profits from an international presence?

International management theory has extensively explored most, if not all, of these questions, but often delivered conflicting results. Whenever academics have attempted to link specific competitive factors to an aggregate performance indicator such as ROE or ROA across industry, space, and time, the results have most often not been very convincing. How does the degree of product diversification influence the profitability of the firm? How does the degree of geographical diversification impact the performance of the firm? Do early movers have an advantage or is it better to be a second mover? The answer is: 'It depends.' Regarding first mover advantage, conventional wisdom says that the early bird might sometimes get the worm, but the second mouse gets the cheese. After decades of research into geographical and product diversification, the humbling conclusion is that investigators need to contextualize research and kick the habit of searching for universally valid correlations.

Recent studies of multinationality–performance relationships (M–P) in services, for example, clearly show that it is extremely risky to generalize from a few empirical studies or theoretical considerations. It is symptomatic that Hitt, Bierman, Uhlenbruck, and Shimizu[6] found a positive linear relationship in their study of US professional service firms, while in a study of German service firms Capar and Kotabe[7] concluded that the curve depicting the M–P relationship is U-shaped, at the same time as Contractor, Kundu, and Hsu,[8] using a much broader services data set, found that an S-shaped curve best represents the M–P relationship. Although over four decades of research in this area have led to different results, scholars have only recently started to address the issue of often conflicting findings.[9] Micro-level studies designed to focus on the underlying reasons for the nature of the M–P relationship,[10] rather than on the shape of the curve depicting the M–P relationship, need to be conducted.

This book seeks to provide rich insights rather than overgeneralizing findings from limited macro-studies on large databases comprising different industries. Retail banking differs from investment banking, corporate banking, or private banking and any statement about the effectiveness of internationalization strategies gains validity by recognizing those differences. Other obvious moderators of the M–P relationship are home- and host-country characteristics, entry timing, speed, mode, local competitive strategies, and organizational models. In short, to understand internationalization strategies, one needs to get a deeper look into the lowlands of managerial decision-making and implementation.

This book is structured into three parts (see Figure 0.1). The first part lays down the foundations of the theory of the multinational firm and its application to financial services. The main segments of banking and insurance, their history in international markets, and the impact increased international exposure has on firm performance will be explored. Existing literature on the incentives of internationalization, the status quo of degrees of internationalization, and their performance consequences will be discussed. Literature on multinational banking[11] has focused its attention on these issues and this book will limit itself to reporting the main findings of these efforts and showing that managers are not victims of some general economic law that predicts when to internationalize and how such a move will influence the overall performance of the bank or insurance company. Instead, unlike policymakers, managers have to consider their specific context when deciding on the occurrence, timing, and direction of internationalization. It is the quality of their strategic decisions and the level of strategic execution that will determine, to a large extent, the profit impact of international expansion. The first part therefore concludes with the deeper insight that there is no linear correlation between the degree of international presence and profitability in financial services industries. There are successful financial institutions that

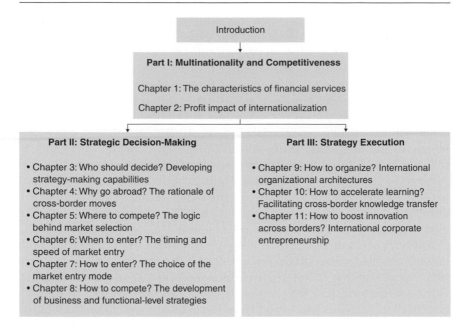

Figure 0.1. Structure of the book

have low as well as high exposure to international markets. The opposite applies as well. For that reason, it is paramount to understand the factors that drive performance in internationalization processes. Firms are not victims of a multinationality–performance curve but can define their destiny and influence this relationship through sound decision-making (discussed in Part II: Strategic Decisions) and strategy execution (discussed in Part III: Strategy Execution).

The objective of the second part of this book is to investigate the way financial services firms make decisions. The goal is to understand the nature of the main strategic decisions involved in internationalization processes such as the trade-off between product and geographical diversification, market selection, timing and speed of market entry, entry mode, local competitive formula, and the resulting functional strategies. Corporate growth into new geographical markets is one of the essential forms of strategic variation among business organizations. It is unlikely that Nordea's decision to create a Scandinavian bank or Credit Suisse's declaration to heavily invest in the Chinese market were made without deliberate decision-making processes involving top management, the board, and other key stakeholders such as business analysts, governmental representatives, or key clients. Financial services firms have to make explicit strategic choices about their internationalization process because the nature of their business involves major, discrete expansionary moves rather than incremental, evolutionary developments. Experimental entry modes through small acquisitions or organic growth are not often the most attractive strategic alternatives. There might still be space for experiments, but learning before doing clearly has predominance over learning by doing. Why are the top banks in the Eastern European countries not Citigroup, HSBC, or Bank of America but UniCredit, Raiffesen, and Erste Bank? Sandy Weil's response as former CEO of Citigroup was that they would wait until the 'dust had settled'. Numerous small acquisitions would be overly risky and energy consuming for the financial services colossus. Unlike a Sicilian producer of ceramics who may send his cousin to sell their products to the affluent Russian market, it is hard to imagine that RBS would apply for a banking licence in China 'just to find out what the market is like'. Royal Bank of Scotland's bid together with Fortis and Santander for ABN AMRO is not the outcome of a 'try, see if it works, and learn from your experience' management attitude. Rather, it was the result of deliberate strategic decisions that had a strong impact on the performance of the financial services firms involved. Part II: Strategic Decisions looks at the main deliberate decisions that take place during international expansion processes of financial services firms.

Part III: Strategy Execution investigates probably the most delicate facet of internationalization strategy—its execution. Implementing cross-border strategies is complicated by differences in culture and institutional frameworks. On paper, synergies from mergers are easily achieved but empirical evidence shows that, on average, mergers and acquisitions have, at best, neutral effects on performance. Planning and the negotiation of good terms are critical for the success of a cross-border acquisition, but it is execution that separates the wheat from the chaff. Three value creation stages in cross-border acquisitions can be distinguished: first, a target company is bought at a reasonable price (or created from scratch); second, the stand-alone performance of this entity is improved (or developed); finally, cross-border synergies are achieved. The third part of this book concentrates on the third value creation stage: the construction of a value-enhancing network of financial services units.

Most financial services firms have fairly professional M&A teams that are able to reduce the cost–income ratio of target firms substantially within the first year of integration but struggle to deliver sustained value by integrating the decentralized units and reaping profits from international presence. Key aspects that ride on the third value creation stage are described in the third part of this book: the relationship between the headquarters and the subsidiaries, the design of the multinational organizational architecture, cross-border knowledge transfer, international corporate entrepreneurship, and cultural integration.

About the Research

This book is organized around a set of strategic management issues that currently absorb much of the management attention in financial services industries. To identify those issues, two case studies with retail banks were conducted: Erste Group and UniCredit Group. In both cases, direct access to top management allowed for a rich description of their internationalization processes. Erste Group and UniCredit Group, whose main business is in the retail sector, were chosen because of the assumption that retail business is more complex to internationalize and stands at an earlier stage of internationalization than investment or private banking. Since both cases represent, so far, a clear success story of international expansion, another research project aimed at exploring the impact of international exposure on the overall profitability of a wider sample of banks. This study compared five-year performance data to the respective degree of internationalization (DOI) measured as an average of foreign assets to total assets, foreign gross income to total gross income, and foreign employment to total employment. The major finding of this study was that the performance curves found in the limited sample of five retail banks did not confirm predictions of the theory that an S-curve relationship (or any other correlation) exists between performance and degree of international presence.

Further research was conducted to identify the factors that modify the profit impact of internationalization, first with the initial sample of retail banks (Erste Bank, Bank Austria, HSBC, BBVA, and Banca Intesa). The main conclusion from this exploratory analysis was that retail banks are not victims of an exogenous, multinationality–performance relationship (M–P). Rather, they can actually positively influence the profit impact of internationalization strategies through a series of sound strategic decisions related to branch network configuration, product portfolio, branding strategy, and organizational architecture (specifically the headquarters–subsidiary relationship), and by actively building social networks in selected markets.[12]

Since the sample for this research was restricted to retail banking and only five firms, other financial services firms were included to serve the scope of this book. The decision to amplify the industry scope of the analysis was not an easy one. Financial services include retail and wholesale commercial banking, life and non-life insurance and reinsurance, investment banking and the securities industry, asset management including mutual funds and private banking, hedge funds, pension funds and private equity firms, and infrastructure services such as clearance and settlement, exchanges, custody, debt ratings, payments networks, and many more. Table 0.3 illustrates the full scope of the financial services industry as defined by the Reuters database.

The patterns of international expansion differ across those sub-segments and by including all of them, the explanatory power of the analysis could

Table 0.3. SIC codes included in the study of the financial services sector

6011	Federal reserve banks
6019	Central reserve depository institutions, not elsewhere classified
6021	National commercial banks
6022	State commercial banks
6029	Commercial banks, not elsewhere classified
6035	Savings institutions, federally chartered
6036	Savings institutions, not federally chartered
6061	Credit unions, federally chartered
6062	Credit unions, not federally chartered
6081	Branches and agencies of foreign banks
6082	Foreign trade and international banking institutions
6091	Non-deposit trust facilities
6099	Functions related to depository banking, not elsewhere classified
6111	Federal and federally sponsored credit agencies
6141	Personal credit institutions
6153	Short-term business credit institutions, except agricultural
6159	Miscellaneous business credit institutions
6162	Mortgage bankers and loan correspondents
6163	Loan brokers
6211	Security brokers, dealers, and flotation companies
6221	Commodity contracts brokers and dealers
6231	Security and commodity exchanges
6282	Investment advice
6289	Services allied with the exchange of securities or commodities, not elsewhere classified
6311	Life insurance
6321	Accident and health insurance
6324	Hospital and medical service plans
6331	Fire, marine, and casualty insurance
6351	Surety insurance
6361	Title insurance
6371	Pension, health, and welfare funds
6399	Insurance carriers, not elsewhere classified
6411	Insurance agents, brokers, and service
6512	Operators of non-residential buildings
6513	Operators of apartment buildings
6514	Operators of dwellings other than apartment buildings
6515	Operators of residential mobile home sites
6517	Lessors of railroad property
6519	Lessors of real property, not elsewhere classified
6531	Real estate agents and managers
6541	Title abstract offices
6552	Land subdividers and developers, except cemeteries
6553	Cemetery subdividers and developers
6712	Offices of bank holding companies
6719	Offices of holding companies, not elsewhere classified
6722	Management investment offices, open-end
6726	Unit investment trusts, face-amount certificate offices, and closed-end management investment offices
6732	Educational, religious, and charitable trusts
6733	Trusts, except educational, religious, and charitable
6792	Oil royalty traders
6794	Patent owners and lessors
6799	Investors, not elsewhere classified

be diluted. Nevertheless, there are some strong arguments for extending the segment range. As Berger et al.[13] note: 'for cross-border consolidation, it is particularly important to evaluate the scope and product mix efficiencies of universal-type institutions—that is, the effects of combinations among commercial banks, securities, and insurance companies—because the institutions engaging in cross-border consolidation are often of this type.'

Consequently, the analysis for this book was extended to the largest financial services firms. To further illustrate the success and failure of international expansion, smaller financial services institutions were also included. Data were first collected through publicly available sources such as Reuters, Bloomberg, Bancscope, Thomson, Forbes.com, and The Banker. Company websites were a valuable resource with investor relations material in addition to annual reports. Next, the companies were contacted and numerous interviews with top managers were conducted. Data collection was not always easy though. The databases used ensure a good degree of reliability for the blue-chips of the financial markets. Data are updated regularly and detailed information is available, often, however, incomplete or referring to different time periods. Some data on minor and more 'exotic' financial services firms, especially when located in emerging markets, had to be double checked; that is, matching information provided by the databases with that available on single web pages and annual reports. Frequent errors regarding reported currency or referred time period could be detected. Financial data available on the database were occasionally not consistent with those reported in the companies' balance sheets. To minimize data variances and to give a reliable picture of the financial services industry, most figures and tables presented in this book rely on multiple sources as indicated above.

Triangulation of data was achieved through iterated inquiries with interviewees, comparison with secondary data, and discussions with industry experts from consulting and investment banking. Insights from other industries were often used to complement and contrast data from the financial services industry.

Part I

Multinationality and Competitiveness

To have an embedded position in a large number of countries around the world, it is a great asset to act as a local financial institution while simultaneously utilizing the strength of the multinational network. To advance their understanding of the relationship between multinationality and competitiveness, financial services firms can study cross-border experiences made in other industries such as consumer goods. Unilever, for example, decided to invest early in a large global production and distribution network, especially in emerging economies, whereas its competitor Procter & Gamble decided to concentrate initially on its home market and then carefully expand into developed markets. For Unilever, the initial trigger for internationalization was to secure important input markets whereas market-seeking motives were probably more important for P&G. The deeply rooted multinationality of Unilever, which was reflected in the two headquarters in London and Rotterdam, is a strategic asset in many markets. Its high degree of decentralization and the resulting capability to adapt to local tastes, however, was penalizing its efficiency and resulted in several decades of attempts to centralize and divisionalize the organizational structure. Likewise, we can find companies in the financial services industry that have a similar approach to Unilever with strong decentralization and more than 1,000 different legal entities and other companies that have a more centralized approach with around 100 legal entities. A main point of the two chapters in Part 1 is therefore that there is no single recipe for the creation of competitive advantage in a cross-border setting but a broad variety of approaches.

Multinational financial services firms exist because they are able to successfully transfer their superior resources and capabilities to other markets. For those firms, international presence has the potential to increase their performance substantially. The CEO of HBOS, Andy Hornby, described the success recipe of his company as follows: 'Last year [2006], our international businesses grew profits 34%...our success comes from targeting markets that we know well...Australia, Ireland and Europe and North America...with skills that we have developed successfully in the UK.'[1] Similarly, Citigroup boosted its international presence when it started to develop dedicated products that could be standardized to some extent and valued by global corporate clients. To increase product homogeneity across markets, Citigroup changed its organizational structure from a purely geography-based organization with autonomous local banks to a matrix structure, at least in corporate banking, with the formation of a 'global relationship bank' serving OECD countries where geography is no longer the primary concern. Given the nature of emerging market countries, Citigroup decided to stick with geography as its main segmentation criterion but assigned the global relationship bank with the coordination task for product development.

A detailed look at the international strategies of the main financial services firms reveals that a large spectrum of approaches exists—and not all of them lead to higher profitability. Understanding the nature of the financial services markets is therefore a prerequisite to understanding the internationalization process of financial services firms such as Citigroup. International business aspects in financial services firms like the Allianz Group, UBS, JP Morgan Chase, Citigroup, or HSBC not only differ fundamentally from firms operating in other industries but also within their own industry boundaries. Organic growth, for example, for a retail bank in international markets is slow and capital-intensive, whereas insurance companies with different forms of distribution networks may find it easier to grow through internal development. In 2005, the Allianz Group in CEE had a total amount of written gross premiums of EUR 2.048 million coming from greenfield investments and only EUR 654 million from acquisitions. This makes Allianz the no. 1 foreign insurer with 13 per cent total market share in this region. Conversely, Hang Seng Bank's entry into mainland China is at a much slower pace with planned branch openings of around 10 per year.

To understand such differences, Chapter 1 describes the historical evolution of financial services and the main characteristics of its sub-segments. In particular, the impact of differences of service characteristics as opposed to physical goods on internationalization strategy is outlined. Next, Chapter 2 demonstrates that there is no universal law that links the profitability of a firm and its degree of internationalization. Performance outcomes are highly dependent on a complex set of factors related to the development, choice, and execution of strategy.

1

The characteristics of financial services

The strategic challenges of internationalization vary greatly between different financial services sectors. A retail bank such as the Italian UniCredit, as opposed to an investment bank such as Merrill Lynch or an online bank like ING Direct, will pursue distinct strategies. Different countries and regions do pose very different internationalization issues: for a European firm it is more hazardous and challenging to expand into China than to neighbouring countries within the same trade bloc. Similarly, serving different customer groups in foreign countries will pose distinct opportunities: large corporate customers tend to have less naturally differentiated needs than small corporate customers or retail clients.

Hence, internationalization strategies need to be carefully tailored to specific circumstances. The next paragraphs briefly describe how the financial services industry emerged and how the first financial institutions started to engage in international transactions. The main objective is to increase our understanding of the factors that have led to the rise (and fall) of the first internationally active financial services firms.

The Evolution of International Financial Services Firms

Financial services started to exist from the very moment wealth was accumulated and had to be protected, traded, or bartered and the risk associated had to be transferred or distributed. As early as the eighteenth century BC, in Egypt and Mesopotamia, gold was deposited in temples —the safest places at that time—and priests started to give out loans. The concept of banking was born.[1] With the emergence of trade activities along big rivers in the Chinese or Babylonian empire, not only were loans given to merchants to fund their shipments, but with these loans, the borrower would most often agree to pay an additional amount to the lender in exchange for the lender's guarantee to cancel the loan should the shipment be stolen. The concept of universal banking was born.

Before moving to more sophisticated financial services activities, coinage had to be invented. Previously, barter was the only way to exchange a product with a given price one needed less for a product one needed more. The obvious limitations of bartering were the double coincident of exchange needs, problems linked to indivisibilities of products (such as a cow), or the imprecise calculation of value, which eventually led to the invention of money. To be an effective payment method, money needs to have several properties. It must be widely used, in heavy demand, highly divisible, difficult to imitate, easily portable, and extremely durable. During times of war in the nineteenth century, cigarettes had most of those attributes, although they were not very durable, and could therefore substitute money to a certain extent.[2] With the invention of money, banking activities became more sophisticated and widespread.

With the expansion of the Ancient Greek Empire, health and life insurance emerged as 'benevolent societies' offered services to their members such as the care of families and payment of funeral expenses upon death. At the same time, the first international banking activities surfaced. Besides private persons, priests and civic entities would offer loans, deposits, currency exchange, and validation of coinage in local markets. Cross-border moneylenders in one port would write a credit note for the client who could redeem the note in another city. Interestingly, many of the early bankers in Greek city-states were foreign residents.[3] Soon, pure cash transactions were complemented by credit receipts and financial transactions were made based on accounts kept for each client. In the Ancient Roman Empire, the evolution of banking continued. As banks started to charge interest for loans, the governments amplified the regulatory framework for financial institutions.

In the Middle Ages, trade fairs played a crucial role in the development of banking. Similar to the Greek model, bills of exchange were issued that could be cashed in at any office of the issuing banker. This financial services innovation made international money transfer easier and safer. International trade, which had started to prosper by 1200 during the Templars' crusades, facilitated the fast diffusion of international payment based on securities rather than coins: merchants as well as pilgrims could use a Templar house in their home country to deposit their valuables. In return, the Templars would then give them an encrypted letter with a detailed description of their deposits. With these securities, the voyager could claim and withdraw funds from their accounts at other Templars' houses in foreign countries. This example shows that such a simple international banking activity was based on a need for safety and availability of deposits across borders by banking clients. Although the Templars did not mainly open foreign 'branches' to serve those needs, this activity nevertheless increased their power base.

The Medici Bank

In the fifteenth century, the Medici Bank emerged as the largest and most respected international bank in Europe. Soon after its foundation in 1397, the Medici Bank[4] opened foreign branches in Geneva and then later in London, Avignon, Lyon, and Bruges which quickly increased its international lending business. The Medici Bank also diversified into manufacturing of woollen cloth. As today, market entry modes were not uniform; the branch in Bruges was fully owned but in Avignon a limited liability partnership was established. The operations in Lyon were not founded as a separate branch but as a mere representative office. Those foreign branches were also responsible for the decline of the prestigious bank. The offices in London, Lyon, and Bruges suffered heavy losses due to instances of corruption or/and incompetence of local bank managers in addition to forced lending to secular leaders who ruled over trade relationships with Italian bank customers. The London branch was liquidated in 1478 and posted a loss of over 50,000 gold florins, an enormous amount of money, considering the capitalization of the entire bank only 50 years earlier was reported to be around 25,000 gold florins. The failure in Bruges added another estimated 20,000 gold florins to the list of casualties.

The subsequent period was coined by retrenchment and attempts to collect outstanding loans, which soon led to a series of bankruptcies of local businesses. The devaluation of gold against silver also played against the Medici Bank since deposits were held in gold and interest was also paid in gold. Historians have not reached a consensus as to whether the fall of the powerful Italian bank was solely due to bad management or whether generally unfavourable economic conditions were to blame. Both factors likely played a role. However, the French invasion in 1494, together with the approaching insolvency, led to the dissolving of the bank with all its branches, making Banca Monte dei Paschi di Siena SPA (founded in 1472) the oldest surviving bank in the world.

Both demand for banking services by foreign trading partners and supply of capital by a flourishing home-country economy led to the rise of the Medici Bank. The experiences of the Medici Bank offer an early pointer to the challenges of implementing internationalization strategies in financial services: to identify the right market entry mode; to develop the right governance models that allow the control of foreign operations; the importance of shared corporate values and codes of conduct; and the central rôle of risk management systems.

The Fugger Bank

With the vanishing power of the Medici as a financial institution and the rise of the Habsburgers in the late fifteenth century, the Fugger dynasty surfaced as the most influential financial institution in Europe. Similar to the Medici, the Fuggers accumulated a sizeable amount of wealth by trading with wool, silk, and other fabrics. They also invested in mining sites in Hungary and sold the extracted precious metal in Germany, mostly for coinage. The profits from that business were then used to lend money to influential secular and clerical leaders. Since interest rates in the sixteenth century rarely dropped below 10 per cent per annum and in some cases could even exceed 40 per cent, it was a profitable business although the risks were high when dealing with powerful statesmen. After roughly two centuries of flourishing activities the Fuggers went bankrupt when Philip II of Spain defaulted on loans in 1563. The Fugger family abandoned the banking business in favour of the comforts of a more settled aristocratic life.

In the meantime, more sophisticated payment instruments had been created. As in Ancient Greece, 'bills of exchange' were used to support trading between the most important European trading centres such as Barcelona, Genoa, Venice, Amsterdam, Hamburg, and Nuremberg. With this payment method, large amounts of money could be transferred without the involvement of coins. It was, however, a rather complex contract between private parties and moneylender(s). In the seventeenth century, the cheque was invented, basically a bill of exchange between banks, payable by one of the banks to whoever holds and presents the cheque.

The Rise of Commercial Financial Services

After the decline of the Medici and the retreat of the Fugger family from the banking business, other families, such as the Rothschilds, stepped in to serve kings and popes. However, by the early seventeenth century, banking began to develop traits that heralded the times of modern banking by offering commercial services for a broader range of customers. The moneylenders were gradually transformed into private banks. Barclays was one of those. The bank started its activities in 1690 with John Freame and Thomas Gould acting as goldsmith bankers on Lombard Street in the City of London. Banking offices were usually located near centres of trade such as large ports. The goldsmiths played a pivotal role, initially offering services of safe-keeping of money, later initiating lending activities and finally ceasing their original profession to focus on banking. Access to information was already a necessary business condition in the early years of financial services, and it was the coffee houses of London that advanced the craft of banking and insurance. In these coffee houses, such as the one opened in the late 1680s by Mr. Edward Lloyd, specialized shipping information by merchants, ship owners, and ships' captains could be accessed. These places soon became meeting points for parties wishing to insure ships with their cargoes and those willing to underwrite such contracts. Large-scale catastrophes such as the Great

Fire of London in 1666 added other risk categories to the list of insurance products.

The introduction of paper currency facilitated the financial services business. Around the year 650, it was the emperor of China who first began to issue paper 'value tokens' for general use. But this financial services innovation came to Europe only in the seventeenth century when Sweden started issuing paper money.[5] At the same time, the first multinational firms were created that were supposed to promote trade with the East Indies. The East India Company was founded in 1600 as the first joint stock company. Only two years later, the Dutch East India Company became the first to issue public stock.

The first National Banks emerged in Sweden and England, gradually taking up many of the responsibilities now associated with a central bank. The financial system became more vulnerable and dependent on the confidence of the public in the currency that was issued by the monetary authorities as transactions were increasingly based on paper money. The main objectives of the central banks were to keep the financial system stable and act as a source of refinancing in crisis situations. For this purpose, the central banks needed a large reserve of gold. In addition, central banks acted as clearing banks for government departments, organized the sale of government bonds, and offered depository services.

Although central banks and governments started to tighten regulatory obligations, financial systems started to become vulnerable. The first substantial shock to the financial system occurred with the crash of the South Sea Company shares in 1720. The British were at the apex of their global power and, as a consequence, people had substantial amounts of money to devote to investments. However, opportunities to invest in stocks were few and therefore the South Sea Company was an attractive investment opportunity, especially since the share price seemed to increase steadily even though the firm was badly managed and without solid economic success. Investors continued to fuel money into the company, which kept the share price high, but the bubble burst when the founders pulled out of the firm when they realized that the value of their shares did not accurately reflect the value of the firm. As a consequence, the share prices of the South Sea Company tumbled and with it, so did shares of other companies. The devastating effects of that crash could only be absorbed by the intervention of the British government and the generally favourable conditions of the British economy.

New York was also beginning to gain importance as a financial hub. In 1790, the US investment market was born as the US government raised USD 80 million in publicly traded bonds. Two years later, three government bonds and two stocks were traded. Soon, insurance stocks were added to the list and the market for securities began to grow. After the historic six-year bull market beginning in 1923, the stock market crash in 1929 was the start of the Great Depression. Nevertheless, the advancement of the financial systems continued and their global integration progressed.

International Financial Services Today

The foundation of Barclays Bank International, established in 1925 as Barclays Bank (Dominion, Colonial, and Overseas) and its constituent banks (Anglo-Egyptian, Colonial Bank, National Bank of South Africa), was one of the first attempts to create a truly multinational bank,[6] together with Citibank which had branches in 35 countries with a focus on offering loans to local customers.[7] As with most of the Colonial Banks, Barclays suffered from the general trend to decolonize the British Commonwealth zone with some members introducing different currencies and creating barriers to the free trade zone. Those foreign banks were mostly retail banks with a mission to provide local banking services and facilitate trade with the mother country.

Only in the 1960s did truly multinational banks emerge as US industrial firms started to expand geographically and needed the support of their home bank in foreign countries. Citibank, Chase Manhattan, or JP Morgan followed their corporate clients abroad and provided the services corporate clients needed to successfully establish their new operations. In less than two decades, those major US banks had developed significant international presence through branches and offices. Those banks also started to serve host country corporate and wealthy individual clients. In the 1980s, the introduction of electronic banking helped to form a network from the formerly detached and autonomous local foreign subsidiaries. Newly available ICT not only changed the communication lines within and between financial services institutions but also allowed for the offering of new products and services such as futures and options or trading on international equity markets.

The following decades saw a phase of rapid growth of international banking presence, and with it, the emergence of global capital markets and the growth of foreign exchange markets. US banks used their superior competences in the creation and provision of more sophisticated corporate banking products in combination with well-known brand names to enter developed Western European financial services markets. US banks differentiated themselves from local banks by aggressively advertising their franchise, proactively selling their services, offering access to international banking services, and substituting traditional overdraft lending with mid-term loans. Most local European banks did not have dedicated corporate banking experts and were therefore slow in responding to the new entrants from the United States. The corporate culture in most European banks was coined by the attitude of a 'seller market'. Clients that somehow found their way into a bank branch had to be scrutinized before they were served. The opposite was true for the insurance business where salesmen visited the customers at home or at work and were paid on a highly variable basis.

As early as 1974, Citibank established global account managers that coordinated the delivery of banking services to large corporate accounts. Those key accounts were able to optimize trade-offs in global marketing decisions based on a strategic controlling system that distinguished profitability measures by customers and regions.[8] At that time, Citibank's corporate structure was a matrix with corporate businesses and products on the top (i.e. 'commercial banking', 'fiduciary', and its core business 'merchant banking') and customer markets on the side (i.e. 'personal' (high net worth individuals and consumer households) and 'customer markets' (multinational, national corporate, governments, financial institutions)). As the organizational structure evolved with changes in strategy, Citibank used geography as the main segmentation criteria for most of its businesses. After a substantial restructuring in 1994, corporate banking was turned into a multi-dimensional form that would support the creation of cross-border knowledge spillovers. Today, the bank is divided into three main business groups: Global Consumer, Markets & Banking, and Global Wealth Management—in addition to one stand-alone business, Citi Alternative. This organizational structure formally continued with the devaluation of geography as a segmentation criterion and the creation of cross-border product and customer synergies.

In 2007, the level of internationalization of many sectors continues to increase. Foreign car makers, for example, sold more cars in the United States than local producers for the first time. The American consumers nominated the Honda Civic as the car of the year and Toyota took the position from General Motors as the most prolific car producer in the world. At the same time, Citigroup lost its top position as the most valuable financial services group (as measured by market capitalization) to the Chinese ICBC as shown in Table 1.1.

This brief review of selected events through the history of international banking is aimed at providing an early pointer of the motives and approaches financial services firms used to enter foreign markets. The mobility of goods and people generated the need for cross-border financial services products. In the early days of international financial services firms, the customer base was composed of a few internationally mobile merchants and pilgrims as well as a handful of powerful local statesmen and religious leaders. As international mobility increased, the need for cross-border banking and insurance rose. The first international financial institutions were born that followed their corporate clients to foreign markets and then tried to enter additional business segments in host markets.

These sections have also pointed out that not all financial services firms show similar internationalization patterns. Differences in the product/market portfolios and strategic objectives generate a considerable ample spectrum

Table 1.1. The world's most valuable financial services firms in 2008 [based on Reuters Portfolio top 500 financial services firms (retrieved on 29 February 2008); performance data and asset size refer to the last fiscal year (2007 or 2006)]

Rank	Company Name	Country of Domicile	Market Capitalization USD million	Total Assets USD million	ROA	ROE
1	Industrial and Commercial Bank of China	CHN	237,822.09	1,035,904.13	0.17	13.64
2	Berkshire Hathaway Inc.	USA	216,651.56	248,437.00	5.05	11.02
3	Bank of China Limited	CHN	198,102.70	743,961.00	0.94	13.47
4	HSBC Holding plc	GBR	178,027.08	1,712,627.00	1.08	16.1
5	Bank of America Corporation	USA	176,534.17	1,715,746.00	0.94	10.77
6	JP Morgan Chase & Co.	USA	136,884.81	1,562,147.00	1.05	12.86
7	Citigroup Inc.	USA	123,441.84	2,187,631.00	0.19	3.08
8	American International Group, Inc.	USA	118,196.70	1,060,505.00	0.73	6.28
9	China Life Insurance Company Limited	HKG	114,244.78	105,548.81	3.03	18.14
10	Banco Santander, S.A.	ESP	113,270.83	1,352,446.63	0.98	16.1
11	ABN AMRO Holding N.V.	NLD	106,499.96	1,462,295.38	0.45	21.62
12	UniCredit SpA	ITA	99,258.98	1,219,662.25	0.75	14.64
13	Wells Fargo & Company	USA	96,374.30	575,442.00	1.52	17.23
14	Mitsubishi UFJ Financial Group Inc.	JPN	92,374.45	1,788,606.75	0.31	3.07
15	Intesa Sanpaolo S.p.A.	ITA	86,347.94	852,254.06	0.86	11.02
16	Bank of Communication Co Ltd	CHN	81,088.93	236,774.92	0.81	14.86
17	BNP Paribas	FRA	81,053.95	2,510,265.00	0.53	15.14
18	Allianz SE	DEU	78,601.60	1,560,311.75	0.81	14.49
19	Banco Bilbao Vizcaya Argentaria SA	ESP	76,870.84	623,651.94	1.28	21.25
20	Royal Bank of Scotland Group plc	GBR	76,630.86	3,780,547.50	0.57	10.87
21	Ping An Insurance (Grp) Co of China Ltd	CHN	73,538.33	61,858.31	1.68	17.27
22	ING Groep N.V.	NLD	71,811.24	1,944,431.88	0.74	24.3
23	AXA	FRA	69,117.45	1,077,843.25	0.88	10.34
24	Goldman Sachs Group, Inc.	USA	67,157.76	1,119,796.00	1.18	31.52
25	China Merchants Bank Co., Ltd	CHN	66,104.27	130,497.66	0.85	17.52
26	Royal Bank of Canada	CAN	65,213.36	612,973.25	0.99	24.86
27	Banco Bradesco SA	BRA	63,257.66	199,803.47	2.64	29.13
28	UBS AG	CHE	63,052.87	2,303,894.44	0.48	26.5
29	Barclays PLC	GBR	61,756.13	1,960,519.63	0.54	23.2
30	Wachovia Corporation	USA	60,688.35	782,896.00	0.85	8.75

of cross-border strategies. To understand how financial institutions develop effective internationalization strategies it is therefore essential to get a clear view on the nature of the various market segments they may engage in. Interviews with financial services executives have shown that many of them understand a fairly narrow part of the industry very well but know little about related segments. Retail bankers admitted knowing little about investment banking. Likewise, many product specialists recognized that they knew little about their distribution channels. But to successfully guide financial services companies into foreign markets, broader knowledge about all segments is required, at least at the apex of the organization.

Segment Differences Matter

As previously mentioned, there are many criteria that can be used to segment relevant financial services markets. Most firms use a combination of three criteria: (*a*) geography (e.g. Europe, Asia), (*b*) service type (e.g. investment banking, retail banking, wealth management), (*c*) target clients (e.g. institutional vs. corporate vs. retail customers). Market definitions are imaginary lines to structure reality and distinguish a specific market activity from another. There is no single objective way to segment the market. On the contrary, market segmentation is a creative act and the logic that is applied may vary according to the strategic issue at hand. When looking at ICT issues, geographical differences might not be as relevant as product differences. When discussing corporate social responsibility, geographical differences matter more than product differences or customer groups.

Depending on the strategic question at hand, different ways of segmenting the market can be applied and examined because answers to the same strategic questions may be quite different for different segments. The use of online banking in the mortgage market differs significantly from online banking in the private banking market for high net worth individuals. The company's market segmentation and selection also influences the capabilities and resources necessary for successful activity in this market. Citigroup understood as early as in the 1970s that corporate clients have different needs than private clients and developed a dedicated corporate banking unit with specific competences and resources. This approach to segmenting the market and the development of a specific offer for that segment gave Citigroup a competitive advantage over local European banks and facilitated its entry into those markets.

The ability to tailor products to particular market segments and establish brand names is important in markets where there are opportunities for differentiation and price discrimination. Most financial services products are experience goods (customers can only identify the value of the product after experiencing it), and brands as a way to signal excellence are of crucial importance. On the other hand, there are financial services products such as mortgage loans that can be easily evaluated prior to experiencing the product. Only a few parameters like interest rate, payback period, and service fees need to be evaluated and an objective comparison of different offers can be made. In this case, branding does not play a pivotal role in customer decisions. As a consequence, online banks such as ING Direct are able to penetrate markets where the brand is not well known with their online offering. Similar arguments apply for consumer credit firms.

The way a company segments the market not only influences its strategy but also its organizational structure. Splitting the company into various divisions makes it possible for top management to decentralize decision-making authority, improving the speed and quality of strategic decisions. A clear segmentation and organizational structure also increases the chances of successfully implementing strategic initiatives; responsibilities are clearly assigned and managers that know the respective markets are also in charge of developing and executing segment strategies. Market segmentation largely determines whether a new department or division will be taken into the organization chart. High-quality decentralized decisions are more likely to be found in companies where the departments reflect the natural boundaries of the market. Only then can realistic departmental targets be formulated in such a way that departmental heads can influence whether the targets are met.

Market Definition and Its Impact on Organizational Architecture

The annual reports of the top global financial services firms do not show a uniform way to organize global operations and report financial results. For the big financial services conglomerates, it is hard to get an organizational chart from public sources. Confidentiality might be one reason for that, but another one is that the complexity of the structures is hard to clearly represent without omitting important details. In August 2007, the senior management committee of Citigroup included 126 executives. It could be simplified to three major business groups and conceal the organizational complexity within those three groups. In its first business group, the Global Consumer Group, there are nine different 'most important business activities':[9]

- United States Cards
- United States Retail Distribution
- United States Consumer Lending
- Commercial Business Group
- International Cards

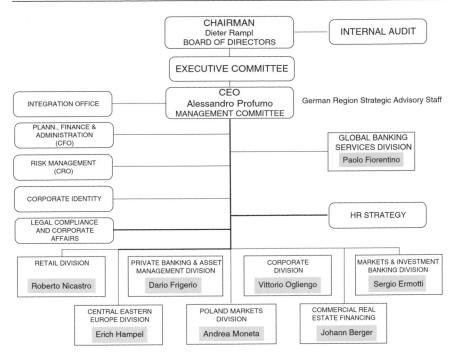

Figure 1.1. Organizational chart UniCredit Group (June 2007) (www.unicredit.com)

- International Consumer Finance
- International Retail Banking
- Citi Microfinance
- Women & Co.

This list already gives a better idea of the way Citigroup perceives the global consumer market. In most businesses (i.e. retail, consumer lending, and cards), the geographical distinction between the US market and the rest of the world is still vital. As mentioned before, just for corporate banking the step towards increased product coordination has been made and the importance of geography as a segmentation criterion has been reduced with the introduction of a global commercial business group. The existence of the units Citi Microfinance and Women & Co. shows that Citigroup has sub-segmented its client base and aims at developing appropriate products and distribution mechanisms for those target markets.

The organizational chart of UniCredit Group (Figure 1.1) shows that no single segmentation criterion is dominating. The direct reports to the CEO, Alessandro Profumo, are composed of one functional area (Global Banking Services division), two geographical areas (Central Eastern Europe division and

Poland Markets division), two divisions defined by customer groups (Retail division and Corporate division), and three product divisions (Private Banking & Asset Management division, Markets & Investment Banking division, and Commercial Real Estate Financing). This structure reflects the trade-off between local adaptation of products and services through area divisions and the need to create cross-border synergies where markets are similar. This trade-off has been resolved differently compared to Citigroup. At UniCredit, the home market, although still very important in terms of revenue and profit contribution, is not visible on the organizational chart and is formally treated as the German market. Similar to what Citigroup does in its corporate banking division, UniCredit separates the mature markets from the developing markets with one exception: Poland has only been distinguished as a separate division since 2006, which shows the dynamics of market segmentation and, in turn, the influence of political motives on the way the multinational financial services firm is organized. Prior to being a division on its own, Poland was part of the 'New Europe' division. With the new organization, the Poland Markets division does not report to the regional headquarters in Austria but directly to the Milan office. Besides political reasons, the size of the market and the fact that Poland is more advanced in its transition towards developed markets may be the justification for this move.

HSBC, a broad-based universal bank, or in its own words the 'world's local bank', offers personal financial services, commercial banking, corporate investment banking and markets (CIBM), as well as private banking products. Its core competence is consumer finance which is clearly visible in the way HSBC is organized. As of March 2007,[10] the direct reports to the CEO, Michael Geoghegan, are:

- Chief Executive Corporate Investment Banking and Markets
- Chief Executive HSBC Finance Corporation
- Chief Executive HSBC USA Inc.
- Chief Executive France
- Chief Executive Latin America
- Chief Executive Insurance
- Chief Executive HSBC Bank plc (United Kingdom)
- Chairman Hong Kong & Asia Pacific

HSBC is also organizing its operations around three product areas (i.e. insurance, finance, and investment banking/markets), as well as five geographical areas. The way HSBC segments its markets reflects its international history and its perspective on market differences. The way HSBC has solved the trade-off between the benefits and costs of cross-border integration and local adaptation differs from the solution UniCredit Group has implemented.

Many recipes exist and it is hard to predict which one will deliver superior results.

Why Include Insurance Businesses in the Study?

The examples mentioned in the previous section illustrated the difficulties of understanding and segmenting financial services markets. The decision to include insurance businesses in this study further complicates matters. It is nevertheless worthwhile to look at the broader financial services industry for two reasons. First, the industry boundaries between banking and insurance are increasingly blurring. As a result, we can see gradually more diversified financial services firms that have to approach internationalization in a holistic way by considering the linkages between insurance and banking. Second, the inherent product characteristics of banking and insurance are similar. Internationalization patterns of retail banking and retail insurance are more similar than the ones observed between retail insurance and reinsurance, for example.

The financial services industry is experiencing a return to the structure it had in its early days: originally, many banking institutions offered a complete range of services and it was the market turmoil of the 1930s which led to increased regulation of those markets and a separation of some of these activities.[11] Regulatory changes recently allowed full financial services firms such as Citigroup, Allianz, or Fortis to emerge. However, most diversified financial services firms run their insurance business as a separate unit, justified by differences in products, distribution channels, legal frameworks, and (sales) culture. The borders between these two sectors are blurring, so excluding insurers like Allianz with Dresdner Bank, Fortis and its bid for ABN AMRO, AIG with its large asset management and financial services units, AXA, ING, and many more would make the study incomplete. As banking and insurance firms face competition from alternative distribution channels as well as non-financial services firms, they look for opportunities to diversify. In addition to geographical diversification, it seems natural for most banks to enter the insurance businesses and vice versa. Although the businesses are quite different, they are increasingly interrelated, and this book therefore benefits from the inclusion of more financial services industries.

However, for most of the world's largest diversified financial services firms, it is still possible to identify a core area in terms of revenues and assets. Allianz Group, for example, is still predominantly an insurer although it bought Dresdner Bank and thereby added asset management and banking revenues of around EUR 10 billion to its total revenues of EUR 110 billion in 2006. For AXA, EUR 20 billion out of EUR 111 billion in revenues came from non-insurance areas in 2006. Accordingly, even after its merger with Travelers

Group, Citigroup has a relatively small insurance business compared to the size of the rest of its operations.

There are nevertheless some financial services firms that were 'born hybrid', like the Dutch ING Groep N.V. created in 1991 from the merger of Nationale-Nederlanden and NMB Postbank Groep. The company grew through acquisitions. The first major acquisition occurred in 1995 when Dutch ING acquired Barings Bank, Britain's oldest merchant bank (founded in 1762) and Queen Elizabeth's personal bank. Barings limped out of bankruptcy and directly into the arms of Internationale Nederlanden Groep N.V. (ING), making ING a well-known name worldwide almost overnight. Other acquisitions followed. In 1997, ING acquired the Belgian bank Brussels Lambert, US insurer Equitable of Iowa, and US investment bank Furman Selz. Two years later, ING acquired BHF-Bank, a German merchant bank. To strengthen its presence in the United States, it acquired ReliaStar and Aetna Financial, which made ING the largest insurer in South America and the second-largest insurer in the Asia/Pacific region. After this series of acquisitions, ING is now a truly diversified financial services group with 22 per cent of profits from each of its American and European insurance segments, 10 per cent from its Asian insurance segment, 25 per cent from wholesale banking, 15 per cent from retail banking, and 6 per cent from direct retail banker ING Direct.[12] These are just a few examples to show why it was important to include non-banking businesses in this study.

New Competitors Emerge

As the competitive landscape of financial services evolves, we can observe new competitive players entering attractive segments. Among these new entrants are industrial corporations like GE or Siemens, retailers like Metro, Wal-Mart, or Marks & Spencer, and car manufacturers like BMW, Volkswagen, or Ford. Banks and insurance companies have lost their well-protected oligopoly for financial services to the benefit of competitors from a variety of industries. In addition, exchanges or other financial transaction platforms increasingly enter traditional banking markets.

To defend the territory, financial services firms will have to prepare a convincing response to this threat. The competences on which new entrants often base their competitive advantage are technology based and include expert systems, customer relationship management (CRM), and distribution technologies. Financial services companies must invest in these areas to defend successfully. The threats for financial services companies exist in areas where they are unable to match service levels or product variety. Threats also exist in areas where financial services companies have insufficient information to target customers effectively.

Peer-to-peer finance is another phenomenon contributing to the erosion of the oligopoly of banks in lending. The basic business idea of companies like

Zopa or Prosper is rather simple—institutional scrutiny of finance demands is replaced by supervision within a network of peers. The mission of Prosper, America's first peer-to-peer lending marketplace, is to '... make consumer lending more financially and socially rewarding for everyone'.[13] Borrowers and lenders meet in the marketplace, the 'eBay' of consumer lending, and Prosper facilitates that process, earning a service fee for the facilitation. A good idea attracts new competitors, and the British competitor Zopa entered the American market in 2006 with its offerings.

Even the highly profitable exchanges are signalling a willingness to move towards the banking businesses. As banks increase their off-exchange business and set up exchange look-alikes of their own, the exchanges promptly threaten with backward integration. The global consolidation process of the exchanges continues, which will most likely lead to the creation of four to six dominating marketplaces. The London Stock Exchange is gaining importance with the increased weight of the Eurozone and an advantageous time zone position. While the New York Stock Exchange drives the cross-Atlantic consolidation process, the LSE is searching for a regional solution with its acquisition of Borsa Italiana. Increased scale gives the exchanges the power to respond aggressively to the disintermediation attempts of banks and alternative trading markets backed by banks. The response of the duopoly, the New York Stock Exchange and the NASDAQ, has been to buy new entrants. The next step will be that the exchanges bypass their brokers and trade directly with institutional clients. This is more likely to happen first in Europe since US regulations oblige exchanges to form trading relationships only with registered brokers.

The insurance business is being challenged as well. Robert Grosse predicts the end of insurance companies.[14] He mentions several reasons. With the abolition of ownership restrictions in the United States under the Financial Services Modernization Act of 1999, insurance businesses can be possessed by banks or other financial services firms. The generally low entry barriers that protect the insurance business are another threat to the industry. Most insurance products can be easily copied and offered by banks. The Internet as a powerful distribution channel is also eroding the market shares of incumbent insurers.

The longer-term implications will be an increase in the number of entrants into financial services markets by out-of-sector companies with strong brands, better ways of segmenting customers, and well-built service cultures. But not all of those new entrants will succeed in staying ahead of the competition. General Electric, for example, announced that it will sell off parts of its commercial and consumer finance business and focus on its fast growing areas of aerospace, energy, and disposals. However, the result of falling industry boundaries is a further pressure on basic financial product margins. The sectors most susceptible to new entrants are motor insurance, accident and health insurance, household insurance, mortgages, life insurance and pensions, leasing, and credit cards. Technology will help new entrants match existing financial services company strategies through the implementation of customer relationship management systems and developments in distribution. Existing financial services companies with a strong brand and solid financial performance will be the least susceptible to losing customers to new entrants.

However, this trend is not unilateral. Banks have also started to diversify into other non-banking businesses (besides insurance). China's fifth-biggest commercial bank, Bank of Communications, recently announced that it would diversify into the securities and trust business through organic growth as well as mergers and acquisitions. UniCredit went beyond the boundaries of financial services and created a digital marketplace called i-Faber that offers web-based procurement services to improve the efficiency of sourcing processes. With 65 per cent ownership of this venture, UniCredit is the main driver of the business.

To capture these phenomena, this study includes a wide range of financial services providers and does not just focus on banks or insurance firms. The inclusion of a wider range of financial services firms certainly complicates the analysis of internationalization processes. There are nevertheless some product properties that tie the vast variety of financial services segments together.

Product Properties of Financial Services

There are many classification schemes for services in general. Most services require physical assets and/or intermediate goods. A first distinction is therefore to separate foreign tradable, location-bound, and combination services.[15] Although banking and insurance both have the reputation of being a people business, it is not always strictly necessary for the client to meet face-to-face with the financial services consultant. New distribution channels such as the Internet or telephone (mobile or fixed) make physical proximity obsolete. When trust is not an issue for the client (i.e. when borrowing money), financial services can easily be exported within the limits of the legal frameworks in place.

Other schemes classify services according to their relative involvement of goods and the degree of commitment in a foreign country,[16] their degree of tangibility, the degree of face-to-face contact with the client,[17] and the possibility of separating production and consumption. To think through these complementary classification schemes supports the contextualization of internationalization issues. Financial services cannot be pressed as a homogeneous bloc into these classification schemes. Serving high net worth individuals requires more face-to-face interaction, less standardized products but lower resource commitment than starting operations in a foreign country as a full-fledged retail bank.

The Impact of Service Properties on International Strategy

Product differences have a substantial impact on the main strategic decisions made when expanding abroad. Consider the following example. The dynamic Australian investment bank, Macquarie Bank, managed to raise its net profit after tax by 885 per cent in the last 10 years (1996–2006) at an average of 25 per cent ROE in the same period. A main driver of that success was attributed to its international expansion. Distinct to its full-service product offerings in Australia, its home market, the bank's international strategy is to expand selectively, seeking to enter markets where its particular skills and expertise deliver real advantage to clients. To exploit those advantages and complement them with local market strengths, Macquarie Group often makes use of strategic alliances as a market entry form, specifically in their Real Estate, Investment Banking, and Capital Markets businesses. In Japan, for example, Macquarie's Investment Banking Group made an alliance with Shinsei Bank Ltd by creating the Macquarie Shinsei Advisory Co. Ltd. This joint venture delivers advisory services in relation to the acquisition and management of infrastructure assets including telecommunications, media, and transportation in Japan. Macquarie Group is no longer an Australian organization growing internationally but has instead become a global institution with the majority of its overall income in 2006 generated by just 3,200 foreign employees out of 9,400 total employees. In contrast, retail banking internationalization works differently compared to the global expansion of an investment bank like Macquarie. For retail banks, to reach a minimal market share level is important. The objective of most retail banks is to offer the entire product spectrum to international markets in the long run; strategic alliances are less frequent and the autonomy of regional markets tends to be higher.

Hence, differences in product properties alter strategic decisions. Creating value from international presence forces managers to make decisions and solve trade-offs in at least three areas: (*a*) adaptation versus standardization, (*b*) market entry speed, and (*c*) risk versus control. The following sections discuss how these trade-offs are addressed and how product differences influence them.

The adaptation versus standardization trade-off is probably the most difficult to solve in most businesses. To what extent do financial services need to be adapted to local market requirements? Too much local product adaptation would increase product variety and compromise scale and scope effects. Banks often perceive the creation of a new product as not very costly compared to the revenues generated by those products. Many thousands of different certificates are issued every year and only a few of them are sold in more than one national market. Fancy names are developed for them: airbag, double-up, reflex, x-pert, wave, etc. The costs to develop those products are hard to calculate: market research, product design, formal approval by local authorities, IT system costs, product introduction costs such as marketing and the education of the local sales force, to name just a few. To reduce these costs, financial services firms are reducing the complexity of their international product portfolio at the expense of local adaptation.

By answering the question of how much adaptation of products is required and considering the costs of local product differentiation, managers also need to be concerned with the timing of adaptation. Product adaptation, if needed, might be planned and executed before the product is offered in a foreign market or, alternatively, after consumer tests reveal what adaptation is needed after entering the market. Key differences among companies in addressing these questions are most likely dependent on how consumer feedback can be gathered and implemented, as well as the costs of product adaptation and variation. After the introduction of the A-Class series, Mercedes found out that the new model did not pass the Elk manoeuvrability test, and it was costly to repair image damage as well as redesign and re-launch the car. If only a few customers buy the latest certificate on biogas companies, it is quick and relatively easy for banks to modify product features and re-launch a new version of the product. Extensive market research before product design makes sense in the car industry but would not be appropriate for most banking segments as the lack of prior market research opportunities limits the usefulness of extensive market research. Or in other words, how managers address the adaptation–standardization trade-off depends on the specific characteristics of goods sold.

A second trade-off concerns how quickly a financial services firm should penetrate international markets. Should a firm penetrate a particular market rapidly or slowly? Should a firm enter several markets rapidly or carefully expand from one market to another? The essential trade-off managers face is either speeding up internal market penetration at higher costs and risks or slowing it down and ceding (at least in the short run) market share to competitors who move faster. Key differences among companies in addressing these questions partly depend on how fast consumer feedback can be gathered and changes can be implemented. The marginal costs of re-production of additional services, the transportation costs of goods, as well as the costs of product adaptation and variation have a strong impact on the speed of market penetration. As a result, a web-based bank will be able to penetrate the market faster than a traditional retail bank. Simultaneous market entry in many different countries is also easier to plan and execute.

The third trade-off is associated with risk exposure. Reaping returns to international presence requires risk awareness and active management of control, especially for financial services firms as the fall of the Medici Bank or the Barings Bank disaster can attest. The risk of international presence comes from several sources including language and cultural barriers, as well as legal factors, which differ between countries. A firm faces liabilities of foreignness, in essence, the disadvantages a firm faces due to lack of local market knowledge. In addition, risk exposure depends, inter alia, on country-specific resource commitment in assets that cannot be easily divested or re-deployed to other markets. There is no easy solution to control for the risks of international presence. For example, to prevent hold-up and deceit by foreign trading partners, a firm might seek control through FDI. This, however, often requires substantial resource commitment to increase asset exposure risks. The essential challenge is thus controlling foreign liability risks without driving up asset exposure risks. Key differences among companies in addressing this third trade-off again depend to a large extent on the characteristics of products sold in international markets. A private banking branch is not as resource-intensive as a retail business and not as risky as investment banking activity.

The comparison of IKEA and eBay illustrates how product differences impact internationalization strategies. IKEA, the Swedish furniture retailer, has offered highly standardized, low-cost furniture, in huge suburban stores since its inception in 1940. IKEA started a conservative policy to internation-alization entering first Norway (1963) and Denmark (1969), later expanding to Switzerland (1973) and Germany (1974)—all countries culturally similar to the home market in Sweden. Until 1991, IKEA maintained its careful international expansion strategy while leaving products largely unchanged and standardized. It was only in response to difficulties in the United States (1985–1991) that major local product adaptations were made to reflect local tastes. Across all countries IKEA entered slowly, either through wholly owned subsidiaries or through franchising, while seeking reliable linkages to local suppliers to keep risks related to foreign liability and asset exposure low.

Founded in 1995 in the United States, eBay entered language-related mar-kets in the UK and Australia during 1999 and simultaneously the culturally distant German market. Later market presence was established simultaneously during 2000 in Canada, Japan, and France. eBay established presence in the UK, Canada, France, and Italy through hiring local management teams and a combination of grass roots and online marketing programmes. Acquisitions of companies already established in local online auction activities were used in Germany and Korea. The acquisition of IBazar augmented eBay's presence in France and Italy and established business in Spain, Portugal, the Netherlands, Belgium, Brazil, and Sweden. Alliance strategies were used in Australia and Japan. Throughout its short existence, eBay has constantly adapted auction categories offered to the local markets.

eBay and IKEA are two success stories of international expansion but with substantially different approaches. These examples suggest to generalize the proposition that an internationalization process of a company offering physical products differs substantially from that of digital information goods providers like ING Direct or Egg, the online provider of borrowing, saving, and insurance services. If a producer of physical goods aspires to do business in foreign countries, the internationalization process is most often incremental and slow paced due to a lack of market knowledge. Market penetration follows a path of increasing commitment, from no regular export activities by agents to establishing own subsidiaries and production facilities. For companies like Egg, the nature of strategic decisions during an internationalization process changes substantially. Decisions on location of sites, logistics, product adaptation, and the level of output have little long-term impact on the company and are easy to reverse. As a consequence, single market entry choices and expansion across markets show fundamentally different patterns. The number and impact of strategic decisions during an internationalization process decreases with an increasing level of digitalization of the products and services of a firm. The challenge for managers is therefore to assess to what extent their product is digital and adapt their internationalization strategies accordingly.

The level of digitalization is just one out of many product characteristics to be considered when planning and executing an internationalization strategy. Most financial services products are experience goods as they are characterized by the fact that quality and price are difficult to observe before consumption. When getting a simple loan or a mortgage, the most important service parameters can be evaluated before contacting a bank. A mortgage can therefore be classified as a search good. Some financial services products are neither search products nor experience goods, but rather credence goods, that is, many clients are not able to evaluate the performance of the bank even after the experience was made. If a customer invests in a leveraged certificate and gets an annual return of 4.8 per cent, is that good or bad? Market conditions, the construction of the product, the service fees, and other parameters would have to be compared to other products and service providers—an effort that customers make intuitively, but most often not based on objective parameters. In such situations, brands are extremely important. To offer search goods, providers do not necessarily need a strong brand or a large branch network with competent consultants. Getting a EUR 5,000 loan is as simple as buying a new laptop at the computer hardware discounter Vobis. Consulting activities are hardly necessary. Creating a pension plan is more complex and requires more sophisticated consulting services and the customer has to have an elevated level of trust in the consultant and the service provider in general.

Services that are more location-bound and difficult to trade require a relatively higher degree of commitment to local markets since they involve greater face-to-face interaction with clients and include more of the 'soft' and 'capital-intensive' features. On the other hand, services that are easily traded, are not location-bound, and include more of the 'hard' and 'knowledge-intensive' features will face lower costs throughout the internationalization process. Retail banking services, for example, can be classified under the category of 'soft' services, as a significant number of banking operations are produced and consumed at the same time. They do have some 'hard' service features, such as back-end information technology (IT) systems and product offerings that can be centralized at one location far from the point of sale or consumption. One example of standardized retail banking services has been successfully implemented by ING Bank online. ING offers standard deposits to its customers in different nations in an uncomplicated manner through the Internet, consequently avoiding customization expenses, branch networks, and client consulting costs.

Retail banking services can also be categorized as knowledge-intensive, where knowledge stored in individuals and units is the key resource, and where capital investments are much lower than for other services. On the macro-level, the retail banking sector is heavily guarded by government controls, which has implications for customer loyalty. A recent banking regulation passed by the German government, for example, allows the government to monitor any personal or savings account in German retail banks. This has led to a flight of bank accounts to Austria, which negatively affects the income of German retail banks. In terms of the relative importance of incentives to internationalize, retail banks have witnessed a gradual shift from extrinsic factors (such as 'follow your client') to sector-intrinsic factors (such as 'herding'), and finally to bank-intrinsic factors (such as capitalization, performance) from 1970 to 2000.[18] Foreign expansion in the case of retail banks has also been attributed to trigger events, such as the Basel Accord of 1992, the Second Banking Directive of 1993 in the United States, and the recent accession of 10 Central and Eastern European (CEE) countries into the European Union (EU).

Hence, to better understand and interpret the nature of financial services, and their internationalization strategy, it is necessary to understand the very nature of the services. Financial services can be classified according to their inseparability, heterogeneity, intangibility, and perishability. Those categories will be explained in the following sections.

Inseparability of Production and Consumption

Inseparability of services means that services are often produced and consumed at the same time, as and when required by the customer. As such, buyer–seller interaction is quite high, and induces an element of local responsiveness or adaptation on the part of the service provider. This often makes the establishment of local facilities an essential element of international expansion. Therefore, costs increase during initial internationalization due to the capital investments required for establishing a physical presence in each of the foreign markets.[19] On the other hand, having production and consumption activities together at the same location and time reduces, to some extent, the opportunistic behaviour of employees operating at a distance, thereby helping to offset the otherwise high agency costs in the initial internationalization process.[20] Once a firm moves past initial internationalization, the inseparability characteristic allows the firm to better exploit its proprietary, firm-specific assets,[21] and generate greater market power[22] by raising the barriers to entry for competitors and making it more difficult to compete. The difficulties of potential competitors are compounded if the service in question is intangible and heterogeneous, as well as inseparable.

The inseparability aspect of retail banking involves banks' decisions regarding the size, location, design, and function of their sales outlets—decisions that have a strong impact on the costs and benefits of international expansion. Inseparability can be applied only in a relative sense. Services require simultaneous production and consumption of their output,[23] but this does not rule out the separation of production and consumption in the input functions. Researchers have distinguished between core services and supplementary services.[24] Even soft services, such as wholesale retailing (i.e. Wal-Mart and Target) and retail banking, can have centralized logistics and IT systems. These act as supplementary services, enabling the execution of the core service that involves direct contact with the customer. The production and consumption activities of supplementary services are kept separate. By avoiding duplication of a portion of the value chain activity, such service firms can save on costs and reap economies of scale benefits.[25]

As a consequence, when designing the interface with clients, retail banks invest substantial effort into optimizing their branch networks. IT integration and the central delivery of back-office services have a high priority for multinational retail banks. When the Austrian Erste Bank entered the Slovakian market, for example, it reduced the number of sales points from 441 to 349 during the post-merger integration process to optimize market coverage and reduce costs. To increase customer loyalty, some banks have looked for innovative ways to attract the interest of clients. An Abbey bank branch, located on the King's Road in London, for example, features a coffee shop inside the branch itself. Other banks decide to keep customers physically out of the branches by offering Internet banking or intelligent ATM machines, which saves time and costs. Still others try to spot the few crucial 'moments' in the lives of clients (e.g. opening of first bank account, first mortgage, pension planning) at which time the bank aims to intensify contact, while reducing client face-time during other periods. Deutsche Bank is experimenting with interactive digital product showcases in spacious, well-designed branches with long opening hours. At these branches, numerous consultants are available without an appointment. Clearly, although the production of the service requires interaction with the client in most cases, the design of the inter-action can have very different costs and benefits for both the bank and its clients.

Heterogeneity of Service Offerings

Services are usually tailored to the needs of individual consumers. They are created and delivered differently to cater to individual tastes and preferences. Product adaptation increases the costs of international expansion. During the initial internationalization phase, financial services firms face learning costs when they attempt to acquire knowledge about cultural differences and the specificities of the foreign market conditions. Institutional contexts vary significantly across countries, especially in financial services, and under-standing quickly changing regulatory requirements and gaining institutional legitimacy is a key concern for internationalizing firms. In China, for example, it is extremely difficult to pursue consistent local market strategies since the regulators are frequently introducing new norms. Cross-border standardiza-tion of services is therefore difficult and as a result foreign banks often choose to apply for banking licences that allow them to offer a limited product portfolio. Many banks start operations with relatively simple products to serve their home-market corporate clients in foreign countries or target a limited group of wealthy customers with private banking services.

The challenge for financial services firms is to find the right level of product heterogeneity. Erste Bank managed to reduce the average product heterogene-ity per client by changing the product portfolios for foreign operations to make them similar to the home market portfolio. Still, the overall product complexity for Erste Bank has increased substantially since its first cross-border moves. Fee-based services complementary to largely interest-based services offered by the entities acquired in the CEE by Erste Bank were introduced. These changes reduced IT administration costs and generated additional revenues, since services were historically provided free of charge in Eastern Europe. Erste Bank still maintained a high level of local product adaptation but used its marketing experience to identify those products that were in high demand. The consulting and selling process which is an integral part of banking services was rather standardized. Through a standardized performance measurement system applied to all international operations, best practices could be identified. Erste Bank invested a substantial amount of time and money to transfer knowledge and key retail banking capabilities to employees in Eastern European countries.

Intangibility of Services

Intangibility refers to the degree of 'touch and feel' that is required to experience a particular service. In most circumstances, services can neither be seen nor transported in a conventional way, as physical goods can be. This implies high transaction costs due to the inherent complexity of handling the services combined with the linguistic and cultural differences of customers. Due to service intangibility, quality assessment prior to consumption becomes difficult and enhances the importance of branding.

In the context of retail banking, intangibility refers to a number of factors, such as problems in evaluating and assessing credit risks in different markets. The intangibility of services makes the exploitation of market imperfections as well as the transfer of foreign market knowledge between different affiliates more arduous, thereby negatively affecting major potential benefits from internationalization. The intangibility of services adds to the need for various governments to strictly control and monitor service industries. This usually includes control over the degree of foreign participation in their service firms which, in many cases, prevents firms from operating efficiently.[26] Host-country restrictions are among the most common problems faced by international service firms.[27] Such restrictions on intangible services make it difficult for firms to keep up their high foreign market entry momentum. Another essential aspect of the intangibility of services is that it makes the services difficult to protect with patents. Consequently, first-mover advantages are often difficult to exploit and protect.

High levels of intangibility make signalling of service and product quality paramount. In most East European countries, local banks do not have a good image and, therefore, foreign banks often introduce their own brands. One of the most immediate benefits that Erste Bank could generate for its newly acquired operations in CEE countries was the development of a strong regional brand with local roots. The brand transformation was based on a thorough analysis of brand recognition in various local markets. Only after a case-by-case analysis of the strengths of the existing local brands was complete did the integration team decide how to modify the Erste brand. Brands with a local value, such as those in the Czech Republic, were kept in the portfolio. The team also found that the savings banks' symbol (a red 'S'), which had to be licensed from the German savings bank association, was a key element linking brands together.

Perishability of Services

Perishability means that services cannot be easily stored and consumed at a later time. If a bank branch has 100 safe deposit boxes and rents out only

34, the revenues from the unused service capacity of the other 66 are gone forever. Similarly, if a private bank has 10 consultants and only six of them are busy servicing clients, potential revenues from the time of the remaining four consultants have perished, unless those four consultants can use their time productively with other work. In this case, consumption and production of financial services is not fully overlapping. Whereas manufacturing companies face fewer difficulties when confronted with excess capacity—they just produce for stock—financial services firms face higher problems and costs when adjusting production capacity.

Therefore, the most efficient value chain configuration of banks differs substantially from that of manufacturing firms. Close contact with clients is needed mostly in the production of services and therefore requires a certain level of presence of well-trained personnel in peak hours, but excess capacity perishes easily. In the UK, the best banks manage to have three front-office employees supported by just one back-office staff member. In Germany, an average bank has a front-office to back-office ratio of one to one. Customer face-time as part of the total working time for Citigroup front-office employees is 53 per cent, which is a high figure if we look at the German average of around 20 per cent customer face-time. Programming productive capacity and aligning it with changing market circumstances are critical tasks.

The Impact of Product Differences: Exploiting Global Presence in the Digital World[28]

To illustrate the impact of product features on the internationalization strategies of financial services firms, this section looks at an extreme case: highly digitalized offerings such as the online bank ING Direct, the online payment service provided by PayPal, or the peer-to-peer finance offerings provided by Prosper or Zopa will be compared with less digital businesses such as cement or the furniture industry. This section shows how the digital nature of the business changes the basic economics of selected operations such as transportation, (re-)production, and product adaptation. These considerations have several strategic implications:

- Implication no. 1: Identify the degree of digitalization of products and activities
- Implication no. 2: Select foreign markets for entry that have high Internet penetration and advanced telecommunication infrastructure
- Implication no. 3: Enter new markets with low-cost but high-control modes
- Implication no. 4: Value customer learning as high as company learning

- Implication no. 5: Leverage learning from customers by developing a highly interactive subsidiary network
- Implication no. 6: Penetrate foreign markets rapidly—but not at all costs

From ING Direct to Zopa: What is the Impact of Increased Digital Product Features?[29]

Few academics and industry experts predicted the success of the PayPal (eBay) or ING Direct models, which became the fastest growing companies in the United States. PayPal now has over 120 million customers, close to the largest banks on earth. The highly digitalized value chain model made it possible to grow so quickly. The degree of digitalization is a relevant product feature of financial services. Some financial services firms, such as the online bank ING Direct or the peer-to-peer online auction site for loans Zopa, are highly (if not completely) digitalized. Others have a medium level of digitalization with most procedures supported by software applications but at times physical presence required. A low degree of digital support demands that both bankers and their clients increase face-time.

The degree of digitalization of products has a substantial impact on how firms manage their internationalization processes. The managerial challenge is twofold. First, the degree of digitalization of the value chain activities has to be assessed. Amazon, for example, was perceived initially as a purely digital sales channel and later discovered that its growth process was to a large extent conditioned by physical logistics processes. Second, managers must understand and assess the implications of the characteristics of digital goods during the process of international expansion. For a purely Internet bank, it is less crucial to analyse and understand customer tastes before entering foreign countries than it is for a traditional retail bank because with Internet banking, customer feedback is instant and the service design choices can be more easily reversed. This is just an example of the fact that digital service goods differ from other goods in several dimensions and can modify the (re-)production, transportation, and product adaptation costs.

EXPERIENCE GOOD CHARACTER

Digital information goods are often experience goods, which are signified by difficulties of consumers to evaluate such goods by sight, taste, or touch before consumption.[30] Who after all can assess the (dis-)pleasure of watching 'American Beauty' or 'Jurassic Park' without seeing the movies? Likewise, trading through eBay auctions is a unique experience, the value judgement of which may depend on consumer expectation regarding speed, payment security, number and quality of offers, etc. The more frequently one trades, the more predictable the quality of the auction experience becomes, but nonetheless there remains uncertainty as every new auction is a new experience.

Table 1.2. Strategic implications of product experience on internationalization process

	Digital information good	Physical good
Consumer experience	• Every experience is unique; difficult to evaluate the product before consumption; high need for consumer learning	• Product experiences are similar; standardized product quality makes experience predictable and facilitates consumer learning about products
Strategic implications for internationalization processes	• Digital information good providers seek to enter foreign markets through entry modes that allow control for branding and advertising strategies and gaining access to locked-in customer bases • Liability of foreignness matters but can be seen as a bilateral phenomenon with a focus on customer learning rather than company learning	• Physical good providers choose to enter countries first that have a low liability of foreignness • Internationalization is an incremental and slow-paced process mainly due to lack of market knowledge

Digital information goods often require sellers to induce buyers to acquire information before consumption to facilitate the first experience. Various strategies to do so involve sharing information content (e.g. free samples of software, free tunes of a new CD via radio, a web page for the latest movie, free listing of seller items on auction sites). Such marketing efforts are usually cheap because of low marginal costs and effective in circumventing the experience good problem. Alternatively, branding and advertising are more expensive possibilities, but both signal quality to customers. By implication, in the presence of information costs, consumers may find it useful to rely on a firm's reputation while firms seek to attract customers through branding and advertising. Because digital information goods are also associated with complementary learning investments by consumers, for example in brand recognition, there are substantial economies of scope in advertising and branding of digital information goods. If building brands is expensive, international brand leverage is a formidable way to reap economies of scope (Table 1.2).

TRANSPORTATION COSTS

The digital nature of online services allows for higher speed and lower costs of transportation compared to physical goods. Unlike agricultural goods, digital information goods do not perish or lose value during transport. Mistakes in delivery (e.g. timing, dislocation) of digital information goods can be easily corrected and traced unlike the transport of heavy physical goods. If the failure rate in cement delivery was as high as the failure rate of e-mail delivery, any cement producer would be forced to close down operations immediately. In addition, issues of storing, inventory management, and logistics are of little

49

concern to digital information goods providers. While transportation costs matter for digital information goods providers, they matter far less compared to physical goods providers. When transportation costs are low, the need to locate facilities in proximity to particular markets, or the need to be selective with choices of in-market locations, may be a lesser concern. While personal contact and local proximity between the producer and consumer appear to be an important aspect for many physical goods providers and services, it does not seem to play a decisive role in the provision of digital information goods. By implication, physical distance may matter less because decisions on location, storing, and distribution are less important to digital goods providers than market volume or the availability of advanced information communication technology.

Transportation costs of digital information goods are not zero, however. Instead, they depend on the type of information technology (hardware and software) as well as the telecommunication network the client and service provider use for data transfer. For some online services, a standard analogue voice telephony with a transmission capacity of 56 kbps may already satisfy the needs of most clients. To increase the speed of transfer, clients may choose to connect with ISDN technology (56–128 kbps), ADSL (1.5–8 Mbps downstream and 12–500 kbps upstream), cable modems (1.2–27 Mbps downstream and 128 kbps–10 Mbps upstream), or with extreme satellite (400 kbps downstream and 56 kbps upstream via analogue voice telephony). Further increases in transmission speed can be expected from technological advances (e.g. UMTS). Streaming videos illustrating products offered in online auctions are too slow in transmission and the quality is too low via telephone connections. By implication, the kind of online services that can be offered to particular clients depends on transmission capacity, speed, and costs that are largely determined by competition among complementary services providers like the telecom and computer industries (Table 1.3).

Table 1.3. Strategic implications of transportation costs on internationalization process

	Digital information good	Physical good
Transportation costs	• High speed and low cost of delivery (depending on IT infrastructure); low costs of storage; easy to correct mistakes in delivery	• High storage and logistics costs are major barriers to internationalization • Market knowledge is required to develop adequate logistics concept
Strategic implications for internationalization processes	• Digital information good providers select foreign markets for entry that have high Internet penetration and advanced telecommunication infrastructure	• Locate facilities in proximity to relevant markets • Explore low-risk transportation options with alliance partners

(RE-) PRODUCTION COSTS

Digital information goods are often costly to produce but cheap to re-produce. A movie costs millions of US dollars to produce, but very little to copy on video and even less when distributed through streaming technology over the Internet. Likewise, software, news, and auction sites exhibit relatively high fixed costs and low marginal costs of re-production. Digital information goods providers have to make capacity investments in hardware and software that also depend on the traffic volumes on websites, but marginal costs of serving additional users and the traffic they cause are low compared to the required up-front investments. High fixed costs and negligible marginal costs provide a vast potential for economies of scale in the production of digital information goods. Physical goods by contrast usually exhibit 'diminishing returns to scale', because unit costs tend to rise after a certain level. Thus, the cost structure of digital information goods providers may also provide a powerful incentive to penetrate markets rapidly for reasons of minimum efficient scale.

Not only are digital information goods subject to supply-side economies of scale, they often also exhibit demand-side economies of scale or network effects—the utility that a user derives from consumption of a good increases with the number of other agents consuming the good. For example, the benefit of any particular user of Zopa increases with the number of other users. Likewise, the value of software packages developed for an investment banking application increases as more people use them. Businesses such as gas, electricity, or telecommunication may also enjoy network effects; however, these effects are more prevalent in digital information goods because of their cost structure.

The combination of demand-side and supply-side economies of scale can lead to powerful market positions for digital information goods providers as higher sales reduce total production costs per unit while simultaneously making the product even more valuable to current and new users. If this is the case, there is substantial potential for first-mover advantages that may lead, in the extreme, to temporary monopolies in particular markets. Network effects, customer lock-in, and scale effects in production can act as entry barriers to lock out late-moving competitors from particular markets.

Competitive dynamics work with accelerated speed in product markets for digital information goods because imitation barriers are low. To the extent that digital information goods are easy to re-produce, they may also be easy to copy by competitors if they rest on common knowledge. Estimates of damages due to illegal copying of software are substantial. To replicate music stored in strings of bits takes little more than a piece of software (witness law suits between Napster and the music industry), while imitating a complex physical good often takes years of effort. Likewise, to imitate an auction

Table 1.4. Strategic implications of (re-)production costs on internationalization process

	Digital information good	Physical good
Economies of scale	• Marginal costs of re-production; demand-side scale economies • Flexible adaptation of output scale	• Diminishing return to scale • Few scale-sensitive resources and activities • Little or negative demand-side scale economies
Strategic implications for internationalization processes	• Digital information good providers seek to penetrate foreign markets rapidly and through entry modes that allow them to benefit from economies of scale in production and demand (network effects), as well as industrial networks • Protect copyrights	• To convert scale into economies of scale, firms need to pool purchasing power, limit local adaptation, and spread fixed costs globally • Rigid planning of output scale • Trade-off between scale and transportation costs • 'Natural' barriers to imitation

format is relatively easy compared to replicating complex machinery. As a result, a sustainable competitive advantage is unlikely to stem from particular product features or general IT skills in programming that are widely available. This, in turn, stresses the relative importance of other sources of competitive advantage such as branding, management of the client base, and network effects in markets for digital information goods (Table 1.4).

PRODUCT ADAPTATION COSTS

Because marginal costs of re-producing information goods are low, cost-based pricing schemes find their limits. For digital information goods providers, however, product versioning and adaptations can be cheaper and quickly achieved. This opens up new pricing and marketing possibilities based on perceived customer value. Possibilities include time-based versioning (movie producers sell movies at a higher price to cineastes and later at a lower price to less-interested consumers), disaggregation of previously packaged information content (separating specialized news from previously aggregated newspapers or journal articles), bundling of information according to consumer interest (information services like Reuters and Forester offer tailor-made information packages that are sold to different industry segments), and rapid product adaptation according to instant consumer feedback (adapting or adding an auction category to a website is far easier than changing the product design of specialized machinery).

Data on customers can also be exploited far more readily by digital information goods providers for product adaptation—not just for adapting their products to local customer needs but digital goods providers also have the possibility of selling such data. For example, Zopa charges borrowers a 0.5 per cent fee on top of their loan. On the other hand, lenders are required

Table 1.5. Strategic implications of product adaptation costs on internationalization process

	Digital information good	Physical good
Product adaptation costs	• Cheap and fast product adaptation and versioning • Fast market feedback	• Expensive and slow product adaptation
Strategic implications for internationalization processes	• Enter foreign markets rapidly and use the possibility of low learning costs and fast post-entry product adaptations • Outsourcing of product adaptation tasks • Learning by doing; experimentation with different product formats	• Slow pace of market penetration • Learning before doing; extensive market research before market introduction of new product features

to pay an annual fee of 0.5 per cent on the total amount they are lending, which declines monthly as payments come in. Zopa as well as its main competitor in the United States, Prosper, is able to monitor each successful transaction and gain immediate customer feedback. These can be used for real-time learning about customer preferences and product adaptation because transactions can be easily tracked at low cost through collaborative filtering technologies. Low cost of learning for product adaptation is facilitated not just by monitoring transaction quantities, but also through monitoring customers' movements on the web pages, how much time they spend there, and what fields they click on. This can produce customer data that is almost instantly available and allows for rapid change of product specifications and features. By contrast, providers of physical goods usually utilize more expensive and slower methods like surveys, interviews, and sales force reports to gather customer feedback.

Because gathering customer feedback is cheap, and product features are easy to adapt, digital service goods providers face lower costs than physical goods providers when experimenting with product designs and real-time learning for product adaptation. Often, it is easy for digital information goods providers to outsource local adaptations of their products, using a network of independent local content providers. This way, the cost–benefit decisions of local adaptation can be made in a flexible way without increasing fixed costs (Table 1.5).

The description of the characteristics of physical versus digital service goods has made evident the inherent differences between the two categories. Contextualizing internationalization theory with product characteristics modifies and extends existing explanations with regard to entry choices in single markets and internationalization paths across countries. To convert global presence into global competitive advantage, firms with digital product and/or process components may discuss several strategic implications.

Implication no. 1: Identify the degree of digitalization of products and activities

It is crucial for companies to assess to what extent their products and business activities are underpinned with digital processes and to what extent the business processes are tied to physical transactions. Decisions on market selection, market entry mode, product adaptation, exploitation of economies of scale and scope, as well as the speed of internationalization differ even within the category of Internet companies. Amazon still relies heavily on physical storage and distribution of goods and is therefore less digitalized than Zopa. Amazon therefore faces different effects of local adaptation of products and services on the company's cost structure and can realize fewer economies of scale. On the contrary, ING Direct was able to use a high degree of digitalization to its advantage. Search goods, such as a mortgage loan, that do not require a high level of trust, can be processed significantly faster, saving face-time for the customer and the company. As a result, the application for a mortgage loan usually takes seven minutes on average to fill out, is absolutely paperless due to full automation, and no bank fees are charged. ING Direct was able to offer higher interest rates for simple savings accounts to its customers, which increased its product attractiveness.

Even in the cement industry, differences in the degree of digitalization of the value chain activities and products may be observed. The Mexican cement producer CEMEX is well known for its strongly developed IT systems that connect its plants with a network of subsidiaries as well as business partners. The competitive advantage CEMEX gains from the digitalization of its business processes impacts the acquisition processes during international expansion. CEMEX has a fast and radical post-merger integration process of 8 to 12 months compared to its competitors Heidelberg Cement and Holcim, which both integrate their acquisitions with a 5–10-year horizon using a process of incremental improvement.

Traditional retail banking is more cost-intensive regarding marginal cost and requires people on site to serve the client. This does not apply for ING Direct as due to its high level of digitalization, ING Direct does not have many physical costs. Once the initial fixed costs are set, there are low marginal costs in reproduction of services, as mentioned in the previous section. This strengthens its position as a financial discounter and enables a faster market entry as well as penetration. It can also apply to faster product development and tailoring of services to the customer due to the possibility of direct or quicker customer feedback.

Implication no. 2: Select foreign markets for entry that have high Internet penetration and advanced telecommunication infrastructure

Digital service goods providers should plan their market entry strategies according to the availability of advanced information and communication technologies, considering as well the use of those technologies by consumers. The size of the potential market matters more than the cultural distance of the target countries. The presence of strong competitors often indicates that there is a market to attack and may therefore be seen as a positive signal for entry. It can be more costly for digital information goods providers to develop a market from scratch than to gain market share from existing competitors. Highly digitalized firms choose their locations according to government incentives and human resource availability rather than proximity to customers or logistical infrastructure. eBay, for example, entered the German market with headquarters in Kleinmachnow near Potsdam in the eastern part of the country. The rate at which Yahoo! has spread internationally over the past few years is astounding, with three to four countries entered annually. The first European headquarters was founded in London in September 1996, and just a month later Yahoo! entered France and Germany. Japan came next. ING Direct started its internationalization process in Canada in May 1997, entered both Australia and Spain in August and October 1999, respectively, followed by France in March 2000 as well as the United States in September of the same year. Finally, it entered Italy in 2001. This list shows that markets were chosen that are big and have a developed ICT infrastructure. Geographical proximity was not an issue.

Implication no. 3: Enter new markets with low-cost but high-control modes

Markets for digital information goods often show instantly high growth rates due to the introduction of new technologies or other favourable market conditions. It is therefore important to be present with a local organization when the market takes off. However, due to the specifics of the business, it is not necessary to develop full-blown local subsidiaries. Yahoo!, for example, has hardly used acquisitions to open a new subsidiary and has always built local headquarters from scratch, making greenfield investments that could be kept low by making start-ups with no more than 10 people per subsidiary.

Yahoo! only considers acquisitions for the purpose of boosting its online product development, as seen with the purchase of Geocities. With this acquisition in 1999, Yahoo! reached the largest possible community of people who created their own websites. Digital information goods providers can make small-scale foreign direct investments and thereby combine high control with low-cost entrance strategies. It is necessary to achieve high-control entry modes because of the crucial aspects of branding and access to a local customer base. Contractual agreements like licensing or franchising are difficult to develop due to the risk of losing control over the brand or customer base. Partnerships accelerate international market development but need to be managed carefully. The web of inter-firm networks should not lead to a dispersion of control over the brand and customer base.

ING Direct chose to enter the Canadian direct retail bank market using an organic growth mode. The risk attached to that strategy was twofold: on the one hand, ING Direct had no experience in starting direct online retail banking from scratch. Furthermore, no financial services firm had yet positioned itself as a discounter and demonstrated that a low-cost strategy with high volumes would work in the direct retail banking sector. But that is exactly what ING Direct pursued at the beginning of 1997 in the Canadian banking market which was mature, middle-sized, and overbanked. Electronic banking was just in its beginnings. But customers were sensitive to low interest rates and high service charges. ING Direct believed it could be successful by acquiring a strong customer base through a price leadership strategy and delivering high service at the same time. This resulted in a branchless banking and customer support via telephone service 24 hours per day and 7 days a week. That keeps operational costs low and can be converted into high interest rates for clients and no service fees charged. Despite the subprime crisis hitting the markets, ING Direct became the first mutual fund dealer in Canada in 2008 that offers paperless application to its clients regarding a new index-based product called 'Streetwise-Fund'. After four years of operating in Canada, ING Direct reached the break-even point in 2001 and grew until 2008 to become Canada's largest direct bank serving 1.5 million customers with around USD 23 billion in total assets. As mentioned previously, ING Direct reached break-even in the larger US market after two years of entry and it became the largest online bank in the country after just six years.[31]

Implication no. 4: Value customer learning as high as company learning

It is often more difficult for customers to get acquainted with the products and services of the digital information goods provider than it is for the company to learn about the local preferences and adapt accordingly. The liability of foreignness firms face still matters but can be seen as a bilateral phenomenon with a focus on customer learning rather than company learning. Post-entry product adaptations can be done rapidly due to quick customer feedback and the use of a mix of global content and locally adapted elements. Local adaptations can be developed with a network of independent local content providers as shown by Yahoo!. The cost–benefit decisions of local adaptation can be made in a flexible way without increasing fixed costs. Building on a central technical infrastructure, local product adaptation is done in a disciplined way. Yahoo!'s policy regarding content is straightforward: translate it into the local language. The local news is taken from trusted news agencies like ANSA, Reuters, etc. and interventions are made only in extreme cases. Other topics are simply adjusted to country characteristics. There are some dedicated producers who take the standard technical structure of a yahoo.com product, and then change its content, an example of which is Yahoo! Cinema.

In the United States, the hot period for films is August, which is different from Europe.

The control that Yahoo! headquarters has on subsidiaries is even clearer once we look at how there is no freedom of choice whatsoever for graphical aspects of the website. All texts have to be approved, and even if one country offers an extra online product, all of its pages have to be checked for colours, text, and writing style to get the go-ahead. This way, local adaptation can be achieved without losing the benefits of global integration. However, this procedure eventually slows production. In Italy, a special Formula 1 section was put on the web only after having undergone strict control from headquarters and several weeks of discussions.

ING Direct's strategy was to offer a fairly standardized set of products and helped the customers to appreciate their services. The online provider did not make strong efforts in trying to understand customers' needs but emphasized the importance of facilitating customer learning, or as the CEO of ING Direct, Arkadi Kuhlmann, once stated: 'To some extent, you need to reengineer the customers as well'.[32] Customers that were not able or willing to understand and follow the service procedures of ING Direct were 'kindly asked to move their business elsewhere'.[33] To rely too much on call centres and to ask for too many exceptions from the standard is generating too many costs.

Implication no. 5: Leverage learning from customers by developing a highly interactive subsidiary network

Once a country is picked, Yahoo! staffs with strictly local people. New employees must undergo a rigorous training programme that introduces them to the Yahoo! world and culture. Those in technical positions are sent on a 10-day course in London or the United States, while employees who will work in less specific positions will follow a 3- to 4-day training programme at headquarters. There they learn everything about the company. This rigorous training programme demonstrates the strength of headquarters' control over subsidiaries. Local subsidiaries are built up by local managers, supported in the first year by an experienced start-up manager from headquarters. To manage operational business, Yahoo! started a weekly report activity for subsidiaries that has now become routine. These are reports of all kinds; each and every employee prepares a report on the closing and coming week's activities to be given to the head of that specific subsidiary, who then summarizes them and prepares one of his own. This last report is finally sent to the country head who, after having read all of the other reports from the other country subsidiaries, makes the final country report. There are frequent conference calls with London and the United States in which all employees participate. There are also some functional meetings every three months where data and strategy analyses are made, and a regular European conference call appointment was set last year. Yet, these are only a few of the ways that Yahoo! keeps its employees up to date with what is going on inside the company. The need for all of these intra-company communications resides in the fact that Yahoo! now boasts more than 400 people working for the company in Europe alone.

To optimize the costs for its IT architecture, ING Direct tries to keep the different subsidiaries in close contact. This also facilitates a smooth process flow as information is retrieved from diverse departments at the same time. ING, the traditional banking parent of the online firm, is eager to create synergies between its different businesses across countries. The CEO of ING Direct declared its general willingness to comply with this request and increase the cross-border synergies—but not at any price. Too high a level of integration within the traditional ING business might damage the rebellious and differentiated image of the company. To be innovative, ING Direct attempted to leverage the learning among its own subsidiaries but kept a certain distance from its traditional parent company businesses.[34]

Implication no. 6: Penetrate foreign markets rapidly—but not at all costs

In their international expansion phase, most digital information goods providers entered three to four markets each year. Extending their global reach, they manage to benefit from economies of scale in production and demand (positive network externalities). Even though the credo of the late 1990s 'get big fast or it will be too expensive to build later' may not have proven completely accurate, it is still essential to cover international territory quickly, but not at all costs. One can frequently observe that small firms operate internationally early in their existence despite limited resources and capabilities. Early-mover advantages can come from network externalities (i.e. the more users are part of the eBay platform, the more valuable the eBay service is for the single user) as well as customer switching costs (e.g. when switching from eBay to Yahoo!, an individual trader would lose his trading history and associated reputation). However, experience shows that new entrants may win over local competition and lure customers away without necessarily buying them. New entrants use the technological superiority of their products and their speed in new product development. Successful digital information providers show competitive entry patterns that have the creation of a differentiation advantage through marketing, innovation, product quality, or service at their core. Differentiation through innovative products is often combined with a clearly focused strategy on niche markets.

ING Direct steadily increased its stake in the German DiBa AG throughout 1998–2003 when full ownership was reached. ING Direct penetrates these markets executing an approved low-cost leader strategy which is mainly achieved by efficient application of IT and aggressive marketing which are valued as core competencies. A complete distribution via Internet or telephone contributes to an efficient cost structure. ING Direct was able to quickly acquire customers attracted by differentiation advantages such as simple and easy products, high-paid interest rates, no minimum balances, no fees or service charges. At the same time high-quality service was provided through a call centre open 24 hours a day. In 2007, US operations included 500 call centre associates shared among 3 call centres. Eighty per cent of incoming calls were answered in 20 seconds and customers were never redirected. The processing speed is even tied to an employee bonus. Employees receive a broad and intensive training covering 5 products in 20 days. These and other measures helped ING Direct to gain a certain level of market share to be able to afford their infrastructural investments. However, the biggest chunk of its growth in most markets came from relatively controlled organic growth without risky acquisitions.[35]

2

Profit impact of internationalization

The previous chapter showed that service characteristics substantially influence the way financial services firms internationalize, highlighting the ever-growing importance of digital goods. Different financial services sub-segments require different approaches to cross-border strategies. Building on this insight, the aim of this chapter is to understand performance patterns of internationalizing firms. Should all financial services firms aim at becoming international? Is there an optimal degree of internationalization expansion that can be calculated? Previous studies have claimed that there is an S-curve relationship between profitability and the degree of internationalization. Internationalizing firms first reduce overall profitability because they need to make initial investments in foreign markets. Once they have accumulated knowledge about host markets and overcome the main liabilities of foreignness and newness, profitability will increase up to a point where the complexity of the organization increases coordination costs and reduces overall profitability again.

Although this S-curve logic is comprehensible, it has little impact on the decisions of executives in financial services firms. The main message of this chapter is that performance outcomes of cross-border moves are highly dependent on a complex set of factors related to the development, choice, and execution of strategy. Managerial excellence has a substantial impact on the performance of an internationalizing financial services firm. The readers of this chapter will get a broader view on how to measure the degree of internationalization in financial services firms: increasing a bank's multinationality does not just mean to increase foreign assets and revenues. It may also mean to increase the presence of foreign managers in key positions, more international strategic alliances, and more competence centres in foreign countries. Second, the S-curve hypothesis will be discussed and abandoned. Finally, the reader will get an early pointer on the factors that modify the multinationality–performance relationship based on a series of case illustrations.

Measuring 'Multinationality'

To understand and model the profit drivers of international exposure, the concept of 'multinationality' (or degree of internationality), which goes far beyond foreign assets or foreign sales, must first be defined. Measurement problems complicate the study of multinationality–performance (M–P) relationships. Measuring the degree of international exposure is, to some extent, discretionary. Single-item measures of multinationality only give a partial view of the picture.[1] Many academic studies are nevertheless based on single-item measures such as the ratio of foreign sales over total sales.[2] To construct an index including several multinationality dimensions certainly improves the accuracy of the measure.

However, gathering this data is not an easy venture. Ongoing domestic merger activities cause substantial data collection difficulties. BBVA, for example, emerged out of nine Spanish banks. Understanding how the degree of internationalization (DOI) changed over time would mean trying to reconstruct the internationalization history of the observed banks. Changing accounting standards also complicates the definition of a DOI: in 2006, Banca Intesa did not separately account for retail banking activities (reported figures include corporate banking) and their annual reports list retail activities for foreign clients (but managed out of Italy) as foreign sales. Furthermore, some firms move their headquarters to a different country as HSBC did in 1993, or refer to neighbouring countries as part of the 'extended home market' (as Erste Bank does with some CEE countries) or as the 'second home market'[3] (as does Banca Intesa). In addition, countries change their boundaries (the former Yugoslavia) and thus alter DOI measures.

In other words, measuring the DOI of a financial services firm is always arbitrary and subject to discussion. The construction of an index including several dimensions nevertheless gives an approximate sense of the degree of international exposure of a financial services firm. To construct such an index, several dimensions of multinationality can be used:

- Foreign sales to total sales
- Foreign assets to total assets
- Number of foreign countries with direct presence
- Number of foreign employees to total employees
- Cultural distance index of foreign subsidiaries
- Number of international strategic alliances
- Number of foreign top managers to local top managers
- Number of international competence centres to total competence centres
- Percentage of foreign ownership
- Number of foreign clients to total clients

Most of these measures, however, assess merely the level of international presence but reveal little about the level of cross-border integration. Especially in retail banking, most international subsidiaries today may share a common ICT backbone but are fairly autonomous entities in terms of strategic decision-making and resource allocation. They are often close to being completely independent banks with a foreign financial services firm as shareholder. In a truly transnational or globally integrated bank, however, the subsidiaries are incomplete economic entities and their value derives largely from relationships with others. Increasing cross-border integration implies an increased coordination control of business activities and resources.

Currently used DOI measures by international business (IB) literature capture the international exposure but do not reveal much about the evolutionary state of the network of subsidiaries. Many studies in IB literature draw on the concept of integration of international operations as a key element of international strategy[4] and some even suggest that the international integration of value-added activities is the essence of global competition.[5] Few contributions actually measure the concept of 'geographical integration' on a firm level. The Globalization Index published by A. T. Kearney[6] is an attempt to measure the level of integration of single countries. The index is composed of several items including the following:

- Trade and investment flows
- Movement of people across borders
- Volume of international telephone calls
- Internet usage
- Participation in international organizations

Not surprisingly, this list is headed by relatively small economies that started their globalization processes early: (a) Singapore, (b) Hong Kong, (c) Netherlands, (d) Switzerland, (e) Ireland, (f) Denmark, (g) United States, (h) Canada, (i) Jordan, and (j) Estonia.

Based on previous empirical studies on the firm level,[7] measures of global integration or transnational integration for financial services firms may be used on three levels of competition: products, capabilities, and resources. Global integration grows with increasing coordination and control within the organization of the following:

- Product and services standards
- Business processes (e.g. risk management, CRM, product development)
- International transfer of tangible and intangible assets (e.g. human resources, best practices, technology, brand, expertise)

An attempt to measure the degree of global integration of the financial services industries is made at the end of Chapter 4.

The S-Curve Hypothesis

Because multinationality can be defined and measured in multiple ways, it is not surprising that research linking multinationality to performance generates mixed results. What is the impact of international exposure on the profitability of Citigroup or Morgan Stanley? Did BBVA increase its profitability when it retreated from some Latin American countries? Do financial services firms with higher international presence generally have higher levels of profitability? Many decades of research on the relationship between multinationality and performance offers no clear answers. The bottom line is that no universal law is able to link the profitability of a firm to its international presence. Too many factors modify the relationship between international presence and the cost and revenue structure of financial services firms.

The size of the home market is one such factor. While Swiss firms such as UBS or Credit Suisse, the Dutch ING, or the Belgian/Dutch Fortis soon found limits in their national growth ambitions, Bank of America was able to grow within its national boundaries for a long time. The large US market makes the early internationalization process of Citigroup even more remarkable. The choice of the target market and timing of entry are further modifiers of the multinationality–performance relationship (M–P). Banca Intesa (now Intesa Sanpaolo), for example, would have had a splendid development of its M–P curve from the year 2000 onwards if the unfortunate venture into the South American markets had not been undertaken. The ability to integrate operations from various countries and create cross-border synergies is another obvious factor that can affect the economic success of international expansion. ABN AMRO hardly integrated its international operations and, as a consequence, is now facing the issue that its geographical break-up value (as estimated by the RBS-Santander-Fortis consortium) is higher than the company value offered by Barclays Bank.

From a managerial standpoint, internationalization has been driven by three main factors. First, leading companies list their desire to stay independent as the first motive for their international expansion. Second, regulatory barriers to international expansion in numerous developing countries in Eastern Europe or Asia are relaxing and many trade blocs have harmonized their institutional frameworks. The third driver of internationalization is the fast development of ICT and with it, the lower cost of coordinating and controlling a large subsidiary network and higher economies of scale by using superior financial services software. However, there appears to be considerable difference in opinion between practitioners and academics as to where the principal benefits from internationalization lie. Academics are often more sceptical and suggest that many financial services firms have not lived up to their promises of exploiting economies of scale and scope (by exploiting assets such as financial resources, reputation, and technology across multiple markets), reaping profits from entering higher growth and less saturated over-seas markets, increasing revenues from serving multinational customers, or fostering innovation and knowledge sharing from the international diffusion of local knowledge.

Some financial services firms clearly did substantially improve their perfor-mance by increasing their multinational presence. Erste Bank is one of those firms. The retail bank improved its return on equity from 1.3 per cent in 1997 to 17 per cent in 2005 by moving from foreign employment of 17 per cent to 73 per cent in the same time period. Its share price increased fivefold from 1997 to 2005. It is evident that internationalization has benefits and costs. The relationship between higher levels of global presence and profitability depends on market contexts as well as firm idiosyncratic factors. Interna-tionalization allows firms to reconfigure their global value chains to exploit country differences in resources and capabilities, and to identify and mobilize globally dispersed knowledge and activities. International presence alters and complicates decisions on offshoring, outsourcing, and the creation of centres of excellence. A critical managerial task is therefore to assess the returns from internationalization in financial services, for the financial services firm itself as well as its stakeholders such as employees, customers, and host governments.

Early studies on the topic found a positive linear relationship between inter-national expansion and the exploitation of foreign market opportunities;[8] others found a negative correlation,[9] and still others, no relationship at all. Some studies explored the effect firm size has on the M–P relationship and concluded that large firms show an inverse U-shaped relationship and small- and medium-sized enterprises (SME) showed a U-shaped form. Lu and Beamish[10] deduced from those studies that a firm might pass through an S-shaped relationship as it grows, combining an inverse U-shape correlation at an early stage of its development with a U-shape correlation. In their model, performance is measured using an accounting-based indicator (return on assets) and a market-based financial indicator (Tobin's Q = market value of assets divided by the replacement value of assets). The measure for inter-nationalization includes the number of overseas subsidiaries as well as the number of countries in which the firm has subsidiaries.

According to the Lu and Beamish model, internationalizing firms go through three phases as they increase their degree of internationality. The first phase of geographical diversification shows high costs mainly due to liabilities of newness and foreignness. Coordination costs in the early phase of internationalization do not play a significant role. The main indicators used in the empirical literature to measure the liability of foreignness are elapsed time of operations in the foreign market, international experience of the entrant firm, and lack of knowledge about foreign markets. The concept of liability of newness suggests that selection processes favour older, more reliable organizations and failure rates are expected to decrease monotonically with age.[11] Older organizations have an advantage over younger organizations because it is easier to continue existing routines than to create new ones or borrow old ones.[12] The costs associated with liability of newness facing young firms are efforts to train employees, develop internal routines, and establish credible exchange relationships.[13] The development patterns of these three costs determine the overall benefit curve. Learning about foreign markets and the development of routines and legitimacy as an established firm will not increase any more as opposed to coordination costs, which increase exponentially.

The benefits of international expansion, on the other hand, develop slowly. Due to established market entry barriers such as customer switching costs or access to distribution channels, it is hard to lure foreign customers away from their local suppliers. Net gains from internationalization grow exponentially if an initial dry spell has been overcome. Increasingly, economies of scale from growing output and experience as well as economies of scope from pooling resources and capabilities such as R&D or the brand name start to benefit from international exposure. Firms often take a loss in this early phase of geographical expansion.

Only if a firm manages to penetrate foreign markets with success and learns how to establish and run a foreign subsidiary will the costs of newness and foreignness be lowered and eventually, the benefits will exceed the costs of geographic diversification. In this second phase of the Lu and Beamish model, both costs and benefits rise exponentially. At some point, the benefits from penetrating new markets reach their peak, indicating that there are limits to globalization. In phase two, the benefits curve flattens out and eventually decreases when penetrating countries from different triads. These dynamics will turn profits eventually below zero, which marks the beginning of phase three of the Lu and Beamish model. The result of the higher complexity costs with increased levels of multinationality is that the 10 biggest financial services firms are not global but at best bi-regional[14] with ICBC, the world's most valuable universal bank, being strongly rooted in one large economy—China—and only recently moving into international markets (e.g. into Africa with the purchase of 20 per cent of Standard Bank).

Performance Patterns in Financial Services Industries[15]

Many studies have been conducted that link levels of geographical diversification to the overall performance of the firm. Few of these studies focus on financial services firms. The work by Alfred Slager[16] is probably the most complete study of the banking industry. Slager aimed to identify the patterns and efficiency of international strategy and concluded that not all banks naturally expand their degrees of international exposure. The study identifies five different internationalization strategies and concluded that many banks reduce their levels of multinationality and consequently, manage to increase performance. He concludes that internationalization has in most cases not contributed to profitability and shareholders have not gained by investing in banks with more international activities.[17] In addition, he finds that foreign profitability tends to be lower than domestic and the DOI-Performance curve is 'J-shaped', suggesting that up to a certain degree of internationalization (roughly 40 per cent foreign staff, income, and assets), costs tend to outrun benefits. His study shows that a similar pattern emerges for shareholder return: banks that either strongly or moderately increased their internationalization activities generated the lowest shareholder return as a group, while banks that retreated from international markets generated the highest. Furthermore, Slager found that foreign banking activities did not improve stability of earnings.

Generally, it is widely accepted that alternative ownership models (e.g. private vs. state owned; low vs. high concentration) show different profitability, cost efficiency, and risk patterns.[18] One would therefore expect to see a positive effect on the profitability of financial institutions when privately owned banks buy foreign state-owned banks. Nevertheless, a study on banking mergers and acquisitions in the EU shows that no improvement in cost efficiency and little improvement in profit efficiency are achieved in cross-border transactions.[19] However, the same study also concluded that most domestic bank mergers in Europe fulfilled their objective to cut costs although they failed to achieve revenue synergies. Cross-border mergers, instead, were proved to better exploit revenue synergies due to geographical diversification.

Building on the results of these studies, we have reconstructed the M–P relationship of five retail banks for a five-year development period (1999–2004). Although with a fairly small sample and therefore without statistical relevance, it is obvious that there is no clear pattern linking international exposure to performance (see Figure 2.1). The M–P relationship varies significantly depending on firm strategy, structure, and contexts in which the firm operates. As a consequence, managers in charge of international strategy need to reflect on how to design those factors. For managers, another collection of M–P data sets is not of great use. Instead, rich case data describing the trade-offs are more valuable because firms are not 'victims' of the S-curve described by Lu and Beamish but can actively influence the M–P relationship.

Each retail bank shows a rather different M–P curve. Their strategies, structures, and competitive contexts vary substantially even though the general banking environment was generally very favourable in the 1999–2004 period.

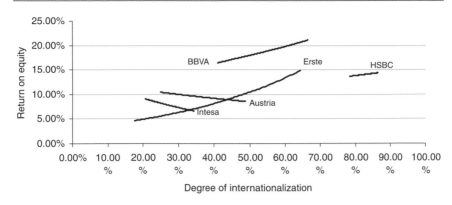

Figure 2.1. Profit impact of internationalization of selected banks

The first bank in the sample, Erste Bank, was founded over 180 years ago and aggressively internationalized only in the late 1990s. At the time of the IPO in 1997, the group had total assets of EUR 49 billion, a market capitalization of EUR 2 billion, and a customer base of 0.6 million. In 2004, the bank had total assets of EUR 139.7 billion, a market capitalization of EUR 10 billion, and a customer base of over 11 million. The company now employs more than 35,000 employees—a steep increase compared to the workforce of 9,300 in 1997. In its core business, retail banking, today Erste Bank is the leader in its extended home market and in CEE countries, and has managed to increase its share price by 350 per cent as well as its key performance indicators during its internationalization process over the last six years. Erste Bank announced its intention to grow into CEE markets in 1997 and presented a clear strategy that was communicated to the market and has never changed since. The core pillars of the bank's strategy were to focus on its retail banking business and enlarge its branch network into the emerging markets of CEE. Buying a bank in the Czech Republic with a retail network of over 1,000 branches was a brave and visionary move, as most other banks at that time moved their interest into investment banking and online retailing.

Bank Austria is Erste Bank's main competitor in the low-margin Austrian home market but occupies complementary positions in Eastern European markets. Although Bank Austria started its internationalization process about five years earlier than Erste Bank (early 1990s), it has achieved a substantially lower DOI than Erste Bank. Similar to Erste Bank, Bank Austria started its internationalization process after a phase of national consolidation. The group's CEE network comprises over 1,000 offices in 11 countries, with 20,000 employees serving 4.7 million customers. Whereas Erste Bank attempts (and actually has achieved in most countries) market share of 20 per cent,

Bank Austria's share in the individual countries ranges from 5 per cent to 10 per cent. This figure will, however, be boosted after the post-merger integration process of the Italian UniCredit Group and the German Hypo-Vereinsbank, the latter being the parent company of Bank Austria. Together with UniCredit operations in Eastern European countries, Bank Austria will have a consolidated presence in those markets.

The Hongkong and Shanghai Banking Corporation Limited (HSBC) was originally founded and headquartered in Hong Kong in 1865 to promote and finance British imperial trade. The internationalization process started in the late 1950s with the acquisition of the Middle East and Indian Mercantile Bank and was followed by a strong acquisition-based, cross-border expansion process. In 1993, HSBC Holdings was set up in London after the purchase of Midland Bank one year earlier. The objective of HSBC in the mid to late 1990s was to build the world's biggest financial services group, well underlined by its mission statement: 'The world's local bank'. With a DOI in 2004 of 86 per cent, the internationalization strategy of HSBC today is to exploit economic and credit growth in emerging markets that show increased consumer demand. Like Erste Bank but opposed to Citigroup, JP Morgan Chase, or Deutsche Bank, HSBC committed to the retail banking sector as a main strategic focus at the expense of the investment banking business.

The consolidation following the deregulation in the Spanish retail banking market created two major Spanish banks in the late 1990s: Banco Santander and BBVA. With more than 88,000 employees in 32 countries BBVA is a strong player in Spain and Latin America (especially Mexico). In the United States, the company started off successfully serving Mexican immigrants and aims at extending its presence in the US Hispanic market. BBVA applies two criteria for every expansion: it must fit the bank's strategy and generate value from the beginning—focusing on (a) markets with strong growth potential in which BBVA is not already present, (b) target banks that can reinforce the growth capacity in markets where BBVA is present and complement the current strengths and/or improve the range of products and services, and (c) potential target banks that have room for further improvement.

Finally, in the late 1990s, Banca Intesa was formed through the integration of three Italian banks: Banco Ambrosiano Veneto, Cariplo, and Banca Commerciale Italiana. In 2004, Banca Intesa had over 55,000 employees and 3,698 branches (of which 618 were abroad). With the lowest current DOI of the sample, the bank's main international focus lies in the Eastern European countries, hence competing with Erste Bank, Bank Austria, UniCredit, and local players for market share. According to their business plan 2005–2007, the future target companies are in the Ukraine, Romania, and Turkey. The internationalization strategy shows that Intesa seeks to grow its businesses in proximity to Italy and other Intesa assets.

These snapshots of internationalization strategies of five primarily retail banks are not representative of the financial services industry but indicate that the design and execution of internationalization strategies is complex and needs to be done by carefully considering the specific market and firm contexts. These five examples also show that internationalization strategies can potentially generate higher firm performance and create shareholder value by making good strategic decisions (Part II of this book) and by reaching a high level of excellence in their execution (Part III of this book).

Part II

Strategic Decision-Making

The first part of this book has described the nature of financial services firms and how they attempt to create value from cross-border moves. It was argued that there is no universal law able to link the degree of international expansion to profitability; too many factors influence this relationship between multinationality and performance. Some of those factors, such as the attractiveness of the home market or the regulatory frameworks of target markets, are hard to influence by managers. However, managers have, of course, an impact on the destiny of their firms. It is the quality of strategic decision-making and execution during internationalization processes that influences the overall profitability of the firm. In this second part of the book, the main strategic decisions that firms have to make when crossing geographical borders will be identified and discussed.

Market entry strategies[1] include decisions on the choice of a target product/market, the entry mode, or the competitive local strategy. These and other decisions are strongly interdependent and dividing them into distinct modules may create artificial sequences that managers in reality will most likely not find. Country selection and market entry modes, for example, may have to be discussed at the same time. The availability of certain entry modes may determine the attractiveness of a potential market. But before analysing the content of strategy, the second part of this book starts with a discussion on how strategy formation as a process actually works. How do financial services firms actually make strategic decisions? How are their strategy processes designed?

Most financial services firms appear to engage in fairly formal strategy-making activities. They seem to believe in the identification of 'best practices' by studying and benchmarking their peers. However, innovative strategies rarely emerge from a myopic study of the micro-activities of competitors. The safest approach to strategy formation is often a process of copying successful products and strategic moves of competitors or trusting in the strategic advice of consultants. Most firms have recognized that strategy formation is neither the production of a static plan nor a 'long, subtle, and difficult process of learning'.[2] The planning process certainly creates some sort of written document—a plan—but strategy is more than producing plans; it is about setting the preconditions for innovative ideas. Strategy is neither the execution of random experiments nor the abstract creation of new concepts and business plans.

The goals of Part II are mainly three: first, to show how strategic planning processes in financial services firms can be designed; second, to identify the multiple strategic options for the occurrence, timing, speed, mode, and direction of organizational growth available to financial services firms; and third, to illustrate some of the actual strategies that selected financial institutions employ to drive cross-border initiatives.

3

Who should decide? Developing strategy-making capabilities

Managers sometimes refer to their 'gut feelings' or intuition when making important strategic decisions. 'None of our decisions regarding internationalization were based on rocket science', declared a head of strategy of a European retail bank. Executives often have difficulty in explaining exactly why they favour one strategic alternative over another. Because intuition by definition has no traceable train of thought, and choices are often made without formal analysis, intuitive thinking often makes people, especially analysts or shareholders, nervous. Formal planning meetings reassure organizational members that the decisions are made based on sound analysis, even though the 'deep' strategic decisions have already been made elsewhere. This chapter explores how financial services firms can establish strategy-making processes that can generate successful strategies.

Strategy making in many financial services firms is dominated by the desire to control risks, steer resources into profitable areas, and make incremental adjustments to the existing business model. Innovative strategic thinking that penetrates the organization from the lower ranks of the firm is rare. The narrow regulatory framework and inflexible IT systems often contribute to a fairly centralized approach to strategic decision-making in financial services firms. Nevertheless, some financial institutions have started to encourage decentralized strategic thinking with higher degrees of autonomy. This chapter describes how financial services firms can accelerate their strategic metabolisms and fuel strategic thinking processes with energy. To improve strategy-making capabilities in the firm, top managers need to give away their monopoly on strategic decisions and stop viewing themselves as 'oracles' that are endowed with the wisdom and decision power of the Greek gods. This chapter calls for the end of the strategy factory frequently found in financial services firms in which strategies have become commodities frequently represented in well-designed Power Point slides. The final part of this chapter shows how strategy processes should be designed if they are to lead to unique strategic positions.

Accelerating the Strategic Metabolism

Metabolism is defined as 'the chemical changes in living cells by which energy is provided for vital processes and activities and new material is assimilated'.[1] Similar to human bodies, firms have a metabolism that provides energy to their employees by assimilating and processing strategic issues and converting them into visions that guide and motivate daily activities. It is this strategic metabolism that helps firms pick relevant issues and process them within the firm. Like food gets converted into calories and then energy, strategic ideas get converted into actionable plans that motivate employees. To compare strategy processes to the human metabolism certainly has its limits. Whereas the human body gets food only from outside, employees can generate strategic ideas and thereby feed the strategic metabolism. However, many parallels exist. Strategic decision-making capabilities in firms depend to a large extent on the ability to process relevant information within the firm. It is this process capability that lays the ground for sound strategic decisions. Like human beings, a firm's metabolism tends to slow as it ages and often, organizations seek processes to accelerate their lagging metabolism. They need a system to capture the innovative and quite often intuitive ideas of talented people both inside and outside their organization. Relying only on the 'gut feeling' of the CEO or an experienced investment banker, trial and error, or just simply pure luck may lead to a successful strategy one time, but it is highly unlikely that a second superior strategy will be crafted once the current one is outdated. Managers therefore need to understand the fundamental principles under-lying successful strategies and develop strategic capabilities. To rejuvenate a firm, its strategic metabolism must be high, and the firm has the chance to channel the energy into the appropriate initiatives.

But many executives doubt that the investment of management attention in strategy really leads to superior performance. The question of whether investing time and energy into strategy making will pay is as old as the strategy field itself and frequently emerges in management discussions as well as academic articles. Based on a survey among top managers of large multina-tional firms, Michael C. Mankins[2] discovered that, on average, management teams meet for 250 hours and only 15 per cent of that time is dedicated to strategy development and approval. Most of the top management time is consumed by operating performance reviews, administrative issues, or 'the crisis of the moment'. As a consequence, only 12 per cent of the surveyed executives believed that their top management meetings consistently pro-duced decisions on important strategic or organizational issues, which leads to the conclusion that those decisions are made elsewhere. Do these results indicate that firms invest—on average—little time in strategy because they do not expect huge returns from strategy or because they lack the capabilities to create effective strategies? Do firms that invest a substantial amount of time in strategy making outperform firms that instead focus on operational issues?

As with nearly all answers in management issues, the most adequate first response is probably, 'it depends'. The general dissatisfaction of executives with their strategy-making process does not indicate that strategy making is unimportant, but that most firms have strategy-making processes that fail to produce innovative and actionable strategies. Although general guidelines for good strategy-making practices exist, industry differences almost certainly matter in addition to cultural differences or business models. The ways in which media companies integrate innovative ideas into their regular and systematized strategic planning processes is entirely different from cement companies. German executives may have a different view on the value of strategic analysis than their American colleagues. A cost leader relying on heavy product standardization and scale efficiencies like Siemens in most of its divisions may decide to move decision-making power far up the hierarchy whereas more dynamic or complex markets may need a decentralized, participative, and dynamic strategy process. Even within the same company, different divisions may have distinct strategy processes in place.

In a fluctuating and competitive environment, strategy formation abilities may be a more likely source of competitive advantage than a clever strategic position. Decreased sustainability of competitive advantage due to weakened barriers against imitation and substitution has given rise to a phenomenon labelled 'hypercompetition'.[3] Firms need to destroy their competitive advantages themselves before their competitors do it; strategies can only be short-term by nature; logical strategic behaviour leads to predictable actions and should be avoided; the ability to identify and develop surprising sources of competitive advantage is the only sustainable competence in hypercompetitive markets. To survive in a hypercompetitive environment, firms need to develop superior strategic capabilities—and not just at the apex of the organization.

The organizational chart of the UniCredit Group reveals an option for businesses in emerging economies to use a decentralized approach to strategy whereas developed countries may be led by central product divisions. The recent break-up of the Poland Markets division from the Central Eastern Europe division shows that, apart from political pressures, Poland was in need of more attention and decision freedom. Similarly, local IT departments of UniCredit Group continue to lose decision power as regional ICT platforms are developed and a distinct global services division emerges. At Credit Suisse, the IT division itself is organized as a matrix with the product lines dominant over the regional IT organizations. In summary, there is no 'one size fits all' approach to strategic management and this makes the task of designing strategy processes in large multinational firms both interesting and challenging. Firms need to find their own way to increase the speed and quality of strategic thinking and review their approaches as their business changes.

There is little recorded evidence of companies being able to successfully link personal intuition from various places in the company to formal strategy processes. One of the few remarkable exceptions is the study by Robert Grant.[4] On the basis of in-depth case studies of the planning systems of eight of the world's largest oil companies, he concluded that planning continues to play a central role in the management systems of large companies through the provision of mechanisms for coordinating decentralized strategy formulation within a structure of demanding performance targets and clear corporate guidelines. Grant calls this process 'planned emergence', attempting to reconcile the 'rational design' (i.e. strategy is planned and explicit) and 'emergent process' (strategy is consistent behaviour without clear plans) schools of strategy formation.

Strategic thinking has the potential to add value to the firm but as with most good things, too much of it can certainly destroy value. Some companies may fall into the 'paralysis by analysis' trap because they think too much before they act, if they ever act, and some companies may destroy value because they act before they think, if they ever think. What may reassure strategists is that Glaister and Falshaw[5] conclude their empirical study on strategic management practices in the UK by stating that '... strategic planning is currently perceived to be of benefit and is still going strong'.[6] However, other studies undertaken on the impact of strategic planning on company performance have not always come to the same positive conclusion. So what are the characteristics of an effective strategy process?

The Myth of the 'Oracle Manager'

Strategic management is about achieving superior performance, and as a consequence, it is about the search for sources of profitability—both in market contexts and in the resource and capability endowment of the firm. Strategic decisions are distinct from operational decisions. Strategic decisions have a long-term impact on the development of the firm, commit a substantial amount of resources, and, most importantly, are hard to reverse. Similar to Fortis's decision to create the 'One Fortis' brand, ING launched its first ever global marketing campaign to launch a single brand through national media in 25 countries with 85 per cent of the investment spent on local retail markets and through the sponsorship of a Formula 1 team. This decision has all the prerequisites of being strategic in nature, like the decision of HBOS to not create an umbrella brand but use its local identities in foreign markets or of Credit Suisse to offshore 2,000 IT jobs to India or the decision of the London Stock Exchange to merge with Borsa Italiana. Questions remain, though. Why do so many strategy projects fail? Why are strategy statements often meaningless to employees? How do management teams develop collective intuition[7] about the future? How do individuals share strategic knowledge across the organization?

The essence of corporate-level management has been described as giving directions and allocating resources, much like a parent gives guidance and boundaries to a child.[8] A hierarchy of authority underpins this process. The company CEOs gain the backing of investors based on their understanding of the commercial environment. The corporation develops a strategy based on this understanding; the strategy is then accepted by the major stakeholders by virtue of the corporation's authority for the various businesses. Managers impose this strategy on their subordinates by virtue of their authority and so on down the hierarchical line. This process can be designed in various ways.

One approach to develop strategies is to concentrate decision-making authority at the apex of the organization. The top managers of such organizations act like an oracle because they are able to be closer to the reality than all the others. The oracle manager functions like the host in a mainframe computer system. The rest of the organization consists of terminals that get a share of the reality provided by the host. The three directives for the oracle managers therefore are: increase the speed, power, and reliability of information flows. Consequently, organizing means to follow the principles proposed by Frederick Taylor or Herbert Simon. These ideas of management emerged when industrial recruits came directly from agricultural work. The recruits were relatively poorly educated and unsuitable for complex tasks. Over time the growing industrial society gave rise to most theories and practices of how companies are organized and managed today. In many business schools, 'management' is still primarily the means of mastering a variety of analytical techniques resting on conventional assumptions of knowledge.

An alternative to perceiving the multinational financial services firm as an organization run by oracle managers may be to look at the firm as a network of self-organized clusters of subsidiaries composed of relationships and driven by communication. Corporate staff focuses on processing information by finding and connecting experts around the world. Such a networked organization may be compared to a client-server computer system. Every employee can potentially contribute to the knowledge base of the organization. Hence, the three rules of thumb in the networked company are connect people with people, connect people with information, and stimulate heedful, collective action. Organizational forms that support those principles centre around the idea of 'self-organized networks'.

The ancient oracles were not the first to understand the power of knowledge, but they were skilled at keeping it to themselves. As long as people thought the oracles alone had the ability to see into the future and know the secrets and needs of every individual, then their positions of power and authority were secure. If other sources of knowledge arose or if their prescient abilities waned, then an oracle's time in the limelight passed quickly. To keep powerful, the oracles had to know things others did not or could not know. They had to remain the source of all knowledge and wise counsel. Of course, oracles were not seen as line managers that had the power to give orders, but not to respect the recommendation of the oracle was tough to do.

At first glimpse, a manager's lot is not so different. Most managers have worked hard, and worked smart, to gain their unique knowledge on critical issues such as the likely moves of their competitors, the nature of customer demand, and special advantages of their products or services. Many have had long careers rising through the ranks, learning what it is like at each level so that they can make informed judgements about which policies will work throughout the organization. With every step up the organizational ladder, more and more information is channelled through the managers until they reach the office of CEO, where they, and they alone, have access to all information generated by the entire organization.

With this knowledge comes great power and, as for the oracle, there are expectations that the pronouncements coming from the executive offices are based on a unique and comprehensive knowledge base. Due to their hard work and intelligence, managers are granted the privilege of thinking strategically for their organizations. Extraordinarily prescient and effective judgements are expected to result from the concentration of knowledge into the hands of these few individuals. This is the myth of the oracle manager.

The world has played a cruel trick on those who still subscribe to this myth. The economic landscape is changing constantly and becoming incredibly diverse. The 'diminishing returns to scale' predicted by classical economic theory are giving way to increasing returns. There is a simple rule cascading the business of companies like Microsoft, Google, ING Direct, and eBay: 'the more you sell, the more you sell!' Likewise, knowledge seems to be the only resource that follows that principle: 'the more you know, the more you know.'

Whoever can create or capture the 'knowledge leadership' in an emerging market has an enormous advantage over those who follow. As with many other fast growing companies, the challenge lies in how to grow the knowledge base at the same rate as sales. For most foreign banks in emerging economies, one of the main challenges is to find and keep talented people. The saying 'if you are not living on the edge, you are taking up too much space' is becoming increasingly relevant for companies in all kinds of businesses, not just at Silicon Graphics, where this phrase originated. The conclusion is straightforward: any organization with the bulk of its people waiting for the prophetic pronouncements of management runs an enormous risk of being pushed aside by more agile competitors, especially those with a better way of creating relevant knowledge and exploiting their power and organizational methodology to do this effectively. Yet, outdated management schemes are difficult to change. It is hard to give empowerment; people have to take it. Yet, for most managers, it is hard to accept that teams can self-organize and self-control.

Many workers today have a college education, speak foreign languages, and have their own Internet blog. If the knowledge level of the workforce changes, our management theories and practices need to change as well. Phrases like 'learning organizations', 'core competences', and 'knowledge management' are in common use in companies, but this is only the beginning. Knowledgeable employees challenge conventional management practices at work. Not surprisingly, managers have to search for different sources of inspiration on how to manage, and conferences on knowledge management are attracting more than twice as many paying executives as before. Academic journals and business magazines run special issues on the search for new strategy paradigms, knowledge in organizations, knowledge transfer, cooperative strategies, information technology, and the networked organization. Not surprisingly, consulting and accounting firms are attracted to these ideas, eagerly jumping on the train of this development. Teachers and managers are up against the same challenge: rethinking the inherent parent–child assumptions of current managerial practices.

In a knowledge-based society, with knowledge-based competition, where knowledgeable workers discuss employability, managers must focus on this challenge and abandon the seductive myth of being an 'oracle manager'. Knowledge is increasingly the most essential dimension of business and concentrating it into the hands of a few individuals may be dangerous. The sole oracle manager of a company becomes its Achilles heel. Managers must be aware of this threat and work to prevent this weakening. Alessandro Profumo, CEO of UniCredit, announced his full retirement at the age of 60, an attempt to reduce his central role in the company, and allow for other knowledge centres to flourish.

There will always be critical roles for managers, but the nature of their work, the focus of their knowledge development, and the basis of their power is altering irreversibly. In short, strategic decisions should be taken not only by top managers but also by decentralized units. Managers in financial services firms need to identify (or create) their strategic autonomy and improve the quality of decision-making within the strategic guidelines provided by the headquarters.

The End of the Strategy Factory

Following William Ross Ashby's belief that 'only variety is able to destroy variety', some financial services firms have started to design and implement complex strategic management and control systems. However, as the dynamics of change have thickened the haze of uncertainty, believing in traditional strategic forecasting tools may become increasingly hazardous. Management teams are tempted to give up on sustaining conversations on a strategic level and instead of searching for foresight, they focus on the problem of how to live without it. Many firms experience situations of 'absence of strategy'[9] and are forced to look for substitutes for strategy, such as increased organizational flexibility.

However, substituting 'organizing' by 'planning' can be a very expensive and hazardous move. Deutsche Bank's decision to split its retail business into three separate units and brands in 1998 is an example. Only four years later, after failed merger talks with Dresdner Bank and speculations about selling the retail business to Allianz, Deutsche Bank reintegrated two of the newly created divisions. This shows great organizational flexibility but limited strategic vision. Corporate planning diffused during the 1960s and 1970s consisted mostly of 'scientific' decision-making techniques including cost–benefit analysis, discounted cash flow appraisal, linear programming, econometric forecasting, and macroeconomic demand management.[10] Most of those planning techniques take a reactive approach to external changes and provide limited results when coping with increased uncertainty. As uncertainty, complexity, and global exposure increase, the role of intuition in decision-making increases. Intuition has the power to increase the speed and quality of decision-making, especially in situations characterized by high uncertainty, but how does intuition grow in an executive? How does individual intuition travel? How can intuition be shared among executives?

The survival motto for strategists in an uncertain world may sound trivial—simplicity wins. The most frequently used strategy tools are the simplest ones. Relatively unsophisticated techniques, such as spreadsheet 'what if' analyses, 'key' or 'critical' success factors analysis, financial analyses of competitors, scenario techniques, SWOT analysis, and core capabilities analyses are still the preferred strategy tools. More elaborate methodologies like soft systems methodology or real options are rarely used by financial services firms in strategic planning activities. Although the market environment is growing increasingly complex, the strategic tools used to cope with that complexity are the well established and, at a first glance, simple ones. Option valuation, game theory, or models based on complexity theory do not have a substantial impact on management practice (yet?). The real option approach, for example, is not popular among management practitioners because academic discussion has so far centred around 'arcane equations and models'[11] and is

Table 3.1. Strategy—from commodity to a unique product

Value chain activity	Strategy as commodity	Strategy as unique product
Market research and planning: What products should we offer to which customers?	Intensive analysis of the stakeholders' interests and the political environment; key decision-makers as 'customers' for strategy development; production highly linked to formal planning process	Strategic ideas/topics often emerge from middle managers through an informal process; the impact on the end-customer of the firm is the central concern; level of explicit analysis often very low
Procurement: What is our level of outsourcing?	Very high; external partners deliver content and process competences; brand image of partners highly important	Very low; if outside providers are involved, they often add strategy process competences
Research and development: How do we facilitate innovation?	The strategy production process should be standardized to produce 'stable' results; innovation comes from new data that is processed	When strategy production becomes routine, new process tools are used and different people participate in the process
Marketing and sales: How do we introduce the product in the market?	Market introduction of strategy as a product starts when the product is ready; the 'buy-in' of customers is considered to be a secondary issue	Marketing and sales often start before thinking about procurement activities; strategy implementation starts with strategy formulation
Engineering: How do we actually fabricate the product?	Sequential engineering and consumption of strategy	Simultaneous engineering and consumption of strategy
Packaging and delivery: How do we make sure that the product reaches the clients?	Strategy is delivered in complex reports and PowerPoint slides; the communication process does not create memorable experiences for the employees	The delivery of strategy aims at creating a strong experience for the employees; prose texts, metaphors, simple and shared language, repetition, various media, and substantial time is dedicated to this phase
After-sales service: How do we follow up on our sales?	The follow-up of strategy initiatives is very weak; strategy projects start as 4-laned highways and end as crossroads	Mutual feedback, strategy roll-outs, performance measurement, and the communication of first success stories make the strategy process a cybernetic cycle

too complex to be pragmatically applied to management issues. But this does not mean that Ashby's law of requisite variety is wrong. Strategy processes in many firms are indeed becoming more complex. The tools that are used to structure data may be simple, but the number of managers and their level of interaction have increased.

The Strategy Production Process

Let us consider, for a moment, that strategy can be considered a product, that is, the result of an industrial process with several value chain activities involved (Table 3.1). The commodity 'strategy' is manufactured in large strategy factories with corporate staff and consultants eagerly engaged in creating

PowerPoint charts and Excel spreadsheets. To be effectively sold, the packaging of the strategy is as important as the content itself. Outstanding strategic ideas, based on a sound analysis of the environment and company itself, are hard to get. To cover up for the lack of creativity and entrepreneurial spirit, huge masses of data are processed and sometimes copied from consulting reports or even from conference presentations of competitors. The production of strategy has become a fairly standardized process in most companies. Some staff organization or external consultants analyse the company and come up with strategic alternatives and the senior management team then chooses one alternative to pursue. The result in the best case is that a firm has a no-frills strategy similar to those of its competitors, while in the worst case you get unrealistic business plans and negative economic performance.

The market for strategies is mature. Strategy as a product is close to a commodity and therefore easy to substitute. The market for strategy is oligopolistic in its nature; big consulting companies and some strategy gurus set the industry standards and sell the same products to their clients with little variation. The value chain of strategy production has been standardized and it seems that at least the formal part of strategy formulation has become routine. Therefore, most strategies are easy to predict by competitors. Efficiency of production seems to be more important than the effectiveness of the resulting plan. The huge number of pages in strategy reports indicate that economies of scale, and with it cost advantages in strategy production, are more important than creativity, innovation, and risk-taking to develop a unique strategy. To contrast this recent trend towards 'me too' strategies, firms need to think about value-creating activities in the production of strategy and identify differentiation drivers. The question must be: How can financial services firms create a sustainable competitive advantage based on the production process of the firm's strategies?

In sum, strategy should not be a commodity but a unique product which is the result of superior strategy production capabilities. Consider the Erste Bank case. In 1997, the small Austrian bank announced its intention to expand into the Central Eastern European markets and presented a clear strategy that was communicated to the market and has never changed since. The core pillars of the bank's strategy were to focus on its retail banking business and enlarge its branch network into emerging markets. Although very simple, this strategy was unique and challenging at a time when most competitors abandoned retail banking and focused on the more profitable businesses of investment banking and asset management, and numerous business analysts and strategy consultants predicted the end of physical branch networks in favour of digital distribution channels. Buying a bank in the Czech Republic with a retail network of over 1,000 branches was a brave and visionary strategic move. This position was described by a JP Morgan report in 2001 with the title 'Erste Bank: The Loneliness of the Long Distance Runner', which indicated that Erste

Bank needed a lot of staying power to reach its long-term goals. The decision to buy a Czech bank was largely based on a qualitative analysis of the current situation and managerial intuition. The strategy development was not rocket-science and the management team believed that '... as soon as the numbers show that this is the right strategy, everybody (including competitors) knows it. If we had known with certainty in 1999 that the Czech Republic would join the EU and wealth would increase as it did, we would have had at least 20 competitors from day one.'[12]

Companies that have superior process skills in the production of strategies are able to outperform their competitors in many aspects such as time to market, degree of consensus among stakeholders, and the quality of strategy (consistent, unique, value-creating, built on company strengths and market opportunities, feasible, and easy to understand). Generic strategy means generic commitment. Firms need to appreciate personal intuition and creatively integrate those 'gut feelings' into formal strategy processes. The more uncertain the environment, the more firms tend to rely on intuition of single, powerful executives. However, if the strategy factory is reduced to a single source, implementing strategy will always be troublesome. The challenge of companies navigating in fast-moving industries is therefore to link personal intuition with formal strategy planning routines in a way that facilitates the production of unique strategies.

A Beautiful Strategy

So what are the roadblocks that stop financial services firms from developing unique strategies instead of settling for a banal strategy? If for a moment, one could forget about political, resource, or other constraints, what would the 'ideal' strategy process, leading to the 'perfect' strategy, look like? Such an ideal strategy process certainly does not start as crisis management. Instead, the management team should have enough time to deal with the strategic issues at hand because an early warning system should have identified those issues as important for the future development of the company ahead of time. Strategic issues can come from anywhere in the organization and are prioritized according to their urgency and impact on profit. To discuss those strategic topics, a stable management team should develop a common understanding of critical strategy concepts.

In an ideal strategy process, frequently held strategic conversations build on each other and the results of strategy meetings are easy to communicate. Operations are not discussed in those meetings. Metaphors, stories, and visual representations support the broad understanding of the strategy. During strategy meetings, it is not important to slice the pie of existing activities and exercise power but rather enlarge the pie and use power to create new wealth for the firm. Consensus is easy to reach after a hard but fair discussion. The management team has a clear focus on decision-making but not on discussions per se. Before reaching a decision, executives have clear strategic alternatives from which to choose. The goal is to get strategic issues off the agenda without letting them sneak back on the agenda any time soon.

Team members come prepared to the strategy meetings. All strategic issues are classified as (*a*) for information, (*b*) for discussion, or (*c*) for decision. Background material on these issues is made available through a common and secure web platform. Before starting the strategy production process, it is already clear to everyone how the strategy will be chosen and what other process parameters will be in place. The management team develops a good feeling for the mix between planning (learning before doing) and experimentation (learning by doing). Already in well-known territory, the management team emphasizes the development of a plan. When uncertainty increases, and the level of risk is acceptable, small-scale experiments and learning by doing help to avoid 'paralysis by analysis' problems.

The ideal strategy process takes into account that markets have become increasingly complex, and simple standard strategy tools such as the SWOT analysis or the key success factor do not facilitate strategic thinking. If strategy becomes routine, an ideal strategy process is able to reinvent itself and managers change the methodologies and tools. The worst thing that can happen to the strategy process is that it boils down to that of an annual rolling budget round in which all numbers within the Excel spreadsheet are simply multiplied by a standard annual growth rate.

If firms manage to integrate some of these characteristics into their strategy production process, they will soon realize that strategy making emotionally involves employees and generates rich experiences. Most people have a clear memory of masterpieces in visual arts such as Leonardo's 'Mona Lisa' or the structure of the Eiffel Tower. Most people remember the moment they heard the news of the Twin Towers in New York falling. Yet, strategy in many organizations involves employees less than a postcard from Paris. Test your friends: at the pub, ask them to draw the strategy of their company on the back of a beer mat and have them describe how these lines influence their daily activities. Have you ever had the experience of reading a book for more than an hour and not remembering a single concept after closing it? Despite the quality of the book, the abstract representation of ideas makes it more difficult to connect them to your world. If this is the case, how can we expect commitment to the company's strategy if the strategic messages do not conquer a space in the minds of employees? The fact is that it is not enough for your employees to remember the strategy. In order to trigger action, they have to remember it as being beautiful.

Designing Strategy Processes

What are the design elements of a beautiful strategy? The content of strategic plans has changed over the past decades. Strategy plans are increasingly shorter, have less detail, and emphasize performance planning.[13] Instead of full-fledged strategy plans, many corporate headquarters are shifting their expectations towards a planning output that delivers strategic direction rather than micro-instructions from an oracle manager. Even though most strategic decisions are discussed in the corporate hallways, formal strategy meetings and workshops as a context for strategic decision-making are still important. Many different formats for such events exist, from large-scale top executive conventions to small management retreats. These events all follow a different logic and course of action. However, many formal strategy processes of financial services firms follow the timing as indicated in Figure 3.1.

Managing Strategy Workshops

Strategy workshops are organized frequently and often have the following setting: a top management team of 5–15 members meets for around two days to identify the most important strategic issues and address those issues within the limits of the very little time at their disposal. This is quite a challenge and many executives consider their strategy meetings to be a big waste of time. In fact, most senior management teams can hardly sustain a conversation on a 'strategic' level for more than one hour. Faced with strategic issues that are prickled with unpredictability, uncertainty, complexity, chaos, contradiction, and unsolvable tensions, managers often prefer to deal with tangible issues of operations that have an immediate effect on the bottom line.

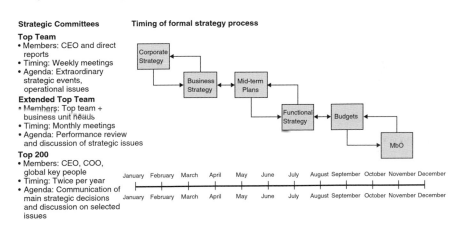

Figure 3.1. Formal strategic planning

Instead of talking about the next 5 or 10 years of evolution for the company, managers often find themselves discussing the purchase of new computers, the high social costs of employment in a particular country, or the last lost contract.

The future seems to be unmanageable, and executives frequently react with ambivalence and become uncertain in the face of strategic decisions. When discussing a strategic issue and developing more knowledge about it, the issue in question becomes increasingly paradoxical as more components and interrelations of the phenomenon are revealed. How else can so many firms have excess capital and yet not know how to profitably invest the money? Are business opportunities missing or are management teams unable to carve out a growth path? How can we explain that Unilever paid a multi-billion-dollar extraordinary dividend to its shareholders and only one year later had to raise money to make a large-scale acquisition?

Many firms seem to be good at restructuring the portfolio, downsizing headcount, re-engineering, and constantly improving their processes to become better, but have difficulties reinventing their industries and developing growth strategies. Only efforts in all areas can make a company bigger, better, and different; exploitation and exploration capabilities need to be balanced. Reasons for this lack of regenerative strategic activities and meaningless strategy workshops are numerous. Often, the notion of strategy is unclear and perceived differently by top management team members. Clarifying the main strategy concepts is essential to the functioning of strategy workshops. Another reason for difficulties in conducting strategy workshops is that the operational pressure is too high. There is not enough time for contemplation of strategy, no time for reflection and sense-making.[14] To cover for the lack of time, the strategy-formulation task is delegated to a strategy department where once again, key decision-makers are not involved in value-generating strategic conversations. Often, the environment is perceived as overly complex and unpredictable, and strategy is reduced to resource allocation decisions or in a worst case scenario, it is decided that no strategy is needed because the company's leading market position is not perceived as being in danger.

Figure 3.2 suggests a simple strategy process that supports a management team in strategic discussions. The process follows a simple but effective problem-solving process: identify the strategic challenges—analyse the actual situation—describe an ideal future setting—identify a solution to get there—and carve out an action plan. It is the responsibility of each management team to develop its own personal toolbox and strategy approach, and the process depicted in Figure 3.2 is far from being the only valid method to define a solid strategy. The common use of instruments in a firm builds a substantial first pillar of an improved understanding of strategic issues and accelerates strategy development and implementation. To get a flavour of

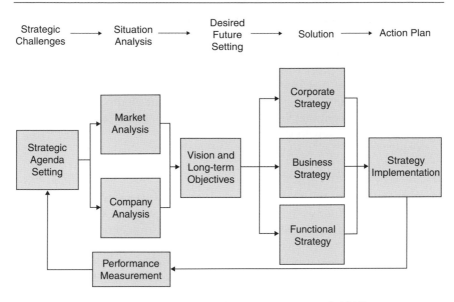

Figure 3.2. The strategy process framework (Venzin, Rasner et al. 2005)

the logic behind the process, but without pretending to deliver a detailed description of the decision scenarios, let us again consider the case of Erste Bank.

Performance Measurement

It is not imperative to start with the performance measurement box. Good strategies can start with an entrepreneurial vision, a resource analysis, or the identification of a market gap. However, 360° strategy analysis often starts with performance measurement, which is the engine of the strategy process. Managers understand and respect numbers. Even if a strategic issue is already well identified, to show with numbers why the issue is urgent (e.g. rapidly worsening performance indicators) and has a high impact on profitability (i.e. the cost structure and/or revenues) is creating the right level of attention. Looking at Erste Bank in 1997, it had an overall ROA of 0.10 per cent, a ROE of 1.3 per cent, a cost/income ratio of 73.5 per cent, net profits of EUR 46.57 million, and a share price of EUR 11.44. In addition to purely financial performance indicators, a fully balanced scorecard should include customer-centred indicators, organizational indicators, and innovation indicators. To illustrate the process at Erste Bank, financial indicators will suffice.

The performance indicators in 1997 show that the bank was significantly underperforming its European peers such as Banco Santander, Société Générale, or UniCredit on all levels. For the peer group, ROE is typically close to 20 per cent and the cost to income ratio typically below 60 per cent. Although markedly low, Erste Bank's performance indicators did not hint at a very urgent strategic issue. Erste Bank generated profit and was well capitalized. A further analysis of the various product and geographical segments indicated that it would be quite hard, if not impossible, to reach or even outperform its European peer banks without modifying the business definition. This meant that Erste Bank was a takeover target by a more efficient national, or more likely foreign, bank.

Setting the Strategic Agenda

In 1997, the strategic issue that was consequently raised by the newly appointed CEO, Andreas Treichel, was: 'How can we raise the overall profitability of the bank to remain independent?' Even though apparently broad and bold, not all stakeholders were immediately convinced that profitability targets should be aggressively raised. The Austrian banking sector has long been dominated by the strong ownership and involvement of the Austrian State. Bank directors were often politicians rather than banking experts. For them, it was frequently more important to extend the revenue base and grow larger than to increase profitability. The pursuit of producing returns that even matched the cost of capital was not considered a priority. A result of this close connection between the state and the banking system was that political rather than economic motivations were considered when making credit assignment decisions or launching new products. In the early 1960s, for example, when bank accounts and transactions started to substitute physical pay packets when paying employees, banks did not charge a service fee. Account management was offered for free. To explain to customers why they had to pay for a service that was once free is a difficult process—an experience that numerous Internet-based firms also had to undergo. In other words, 'If we could charge as much as the banks in the UK, we would probably be the most profitable bank of the world.'[15] To raise the attention for profitability issues was not easy. With a lot of patience during six months of meetings and face-to-face discussions, it was finally possible to create a broad consensus for addressing the strategic issue of independence and profitable growth.

Market Analysis

After the identification and prioritization of strategic issues, the analysis of the various market segments—their attractiveness, competitive forces, and key success factors—is the first step in gaining a deeper understanding of the issue at hand. The core market segment of Erste Bank was the retailing market in Austria with profitability close to zero. The reasons for this profitability were attributed on one hand to the overall low industry attractiveness, and on the other hand to firm-related factors. What has characterized the banking sector in Europe in the past 15 years is the large number of mergers and acquisitions that have taken place among major players. Between 1991 and 1992, the period coinciding with the liberalization of banking regulations and the establishment of the single European market, there were approximately 380 transactions, suggesting that banks chose to combine forces to cope with these changes. During 1997 and 1998 this number decreased to around 125. France and Italy had 290 and 375 transactions, respectively, showing significantly more action than the other countries from 1991 to 1998. M&A activities across Europe were constantly high, with most operations domestic rather than cross-border. The low concentration ratios in Germany, Italy, and Austria indicate that there is sufficient room for further consolidation in these countries.

To analyse the attractiveness of single geographical markets, consider the profitability pressure (composed of cost–income ratios, ROI, and ROE) and structural pressure (market share of the five biggest banks, banking density, and average total assets). Even though the structural pressure for Germany is only marginally higher than in Italy, the profitability of German banks is much lower. Therefore, the profitability gap between Italian and German banks cannot be entirely explained by structural issues, more so if one considers the German banking market as split into three competitive groups (three-pillar system): private and commercial banks, savings banks, and cooperative banking institutions. In the late 1990s, Austria was considered to be the 'lousiest' banking market in Europe—overbanked, overbranched, overstaffed, and with poor margins. The country had 103 national banks per million inhabitants in 2002, which was the highest bank density in Europe. However, the relatively high market share (43 per cent) of the five biggest banks shows that there has been some consolidation in the market. In fact, the number of banks was reduced by 20 per cent in the 1990s.

To operate profitably in such a market is a difficult venture. In 1997, Erste Bank faced fierce competition from other savings and commercial banks in Austria and had only marginal exposure to attractive geographical markets with limited growth options in the home market. To successfully compete in the home market, a bank does not just have to be best in class but must be able to somehow change industry logic. With marginal efficiency gains, it was very unlikely that an acceptable profitability level would have been reached. Analysis showed that the most important issue was to improve the collaboration between savings banks in Austria.

Company Analysis

A second (or parallel) step in the situational analysis is the analysis of the bank's resources and capabilities. Which resources and competences form the basis of a sustainable competitive advantage? How are these resources utilized by capabilities to create products and services? What are the cost and differentiation drivers? Sometimes it is easier to get orientation from the analysis of the firm rather than from the market analysis. Such resource-based approaches to strategic management work best in dynamic markets in which it is hazardous to make long-term forecasts on the best market position to be reached. Implementation efforts take too long to allow for a reactive strategy. Orientation does not come from the market position but rather from the specific resources and capabilities of the firm. Competitive advantage sometimes does not result from the capability to recognize and exploit changes in the industry structure but instead from firms' unique resources and capabilities. The management task is therefore to identify the resources and capabilities of the firm and appraise their rent-generating potential. This analysis showed Erste Bank that their core capabilities were clearly rooted in retail banking, among other issues. Although investment and private banking seemed to be appealing market segments, to develop or acquire the capabilities needed to successfully operate in those segments would take a long time and/or be very expensive.

Development of a Vision and Long-Term Objectives

Erste Bank decided to commit itself to retail business based on a sound analysis of the bank's identity and capabilities. One of its main competitors in the CEE markets, UniCredit, has a crystal clear vision statement: 'We want to be the first truly European bank.' The vision for Erste Bank is less aggressive but not less articulated: the goal is to remain independent and strengthen the presence in the extended home market while further consolidating the collaboration with savings banks in Austria. Given the changes in European financial services markets and the high consolidation pressure within the Austrian market, to embark on a growth process seemed to be the only way to remain independent. Consequently, the bank set clear strategic targets for itself:

- To optimize the profitability of core product areas
- To develop closer ties with the 64 independent member banks of the savings bank organization
- To broaden the home market to include retail banking operations in selected CEE countries and target the extended home market potential of 40 million clients
- To develop a leading multi-channel distribution network, to include offering premier online access to innovative products

Development of Corporate Strategies

The strategies are designed to allow the firm to reach its ambitious goals. On the corporate level, the main tasks are the following:

- Steer resources to attractive market segments and business ventures
- Directly contribute to the resource and capability endowment of the business units
- Initiate coordination and control of interrelationships between business units
- Evaluate profit prospects of each business unit and steer corporate resources into the most attractive strategic opportunities

The foundations for a successful corporate strategy were laid in 1993, when the business division of Erste Bank was turned into a stock corporation. The entire banking business of DIE ERSTE österreichische Spar-Casse-Bank was transferred to DIE ERSTE österreichische Spar-Casse-Bank Aktiengesellschaft, a newly created joint stock company that became the operational bank. DIE ERSTE österreichische Spar-Casse remained in existence as a holding company for the stocks of the new subsidiary company, changing its name to DIE ERSTE österreichische Spar-Casse Anteilsverwaltungssparkasse (AVS).

In 1997, Erste Bank merged with Girocredit as stipulated in a merger contract (the assimilation of Girocredit into ERSTE) and DIE ERSTE österreichische Spar-Casse-Bank AG changed its name to Erste Bank der öesterreichischen Sparkassen AG. The same year, Erste Bank acquired 83.66 per cent of Mezöbank, the tenth largest Hungarian bank in terms of total assets. Mezöbank operated the fifth largest branch network in Hungary and allowed Erste Bank to establish an excellent initial position in Central Europe as well as to have its first experiences with acquisition and post-merger integration processes.

In December 1997, Erste Bank launched the biggest IPO at that time in Austrian history with a volume of EUR 508 million. The investors liked to bet on a 'bad' company with a consistent investment story and highly credible management team. Consequently, the steep growth of the company was financed by two additional fund-raising activities on the Austrian stock market (EUR 282 million in 2000 and EUR 642 million in 2002). In fact, Erste Bank top management did not see cash availability as a constraint. They were convinced that good ideas would always be funded. The investors were awarded for their trust in the bank's venture with a substantial increase in the value of their shares. It was much easier for Erste Bank to deal with shareholders than with a private equity partner.

The cornerstone of Erste Bank's corporate strategy was to invest in its international expansion towards the opening CEE markets. The internationalization process of Erste Bank was stimulated by the desire to remain independent and the difficulties of creating profit in the home market. Of course, the geographical proximity to emerging and attractive markets facilitated the process. Another component was the analysis of the identity of Erste Bank, which clearly showed that Erste Bank had its roots and core capabilities in retail banking. As a consequence, Erste Bank dismissed the possibility of growing through product diversification and moving towards a model of the universal bank or even offering a full range of bank-assurance services. In addition, the regulatory framework in the EU seemed to move towards a harmonization of banking regulations and Eastern European countries that sooner or later would join the EU. The last major motivation for internationalizing Erste's activities was that the target banks had substantial potential in performance improvement. By implementing the business-proven Erste Bank processes— its IT systems, changing the product portfolio towards service fees, reducing headcount as well as the number of branches, optimizing capital utilization, and much more—Erste Bank could improve key performance indicators such as the cost/income ratio and ultimately, profit.

Development of Business Unit Strategies

On the business unit level, competitive strategies have to be developed for each business segment. A major pillar of the success strategy of Erste Bank was to uncompromisingly tackle low-return domestic businesses. A key element was to give the 64 independent savings banks, for which it acted as central banker, branches owned by Erste Bank in return for an increased equity stake in the main savings bank. This approach led to a reduction of Erste Bank's own branches from 270 in 1998 to 144 in 2004 and gave rise to a better exploitation of the synergy potential. In fact, the Austrian savings bank sector seemed to be more willing to consider moves towards cooperation than can be seen in other markets. Erste Bank increasingly served as the backbone for the affiliated savings banks that signed a cross-guarantee agreement in 2001. Now, Erste Bank additionally provides IT support, pools marketing budgets to promote a single brand for all savings banks, and develops new financial products for the entire network.

This increased collaboration helped to minimize the structural causes for low profitability in the Austrian operations but there were some firm-specific issues to tackle. Erste Bank attempted to improve its retailing business performance through improved customer targeting: distinguishing between Individual Clients (around 110,000 customers with an after-tax income of above EUR 2,000 per month) and Standard Clients (around 420,000 customers with an after-tax income of below EUR 2,000). The main goal was to increase the average income per client by 8 per cent in 2005 from EUR 220 for Standard Clients and EUR 1,540 for Individual Clients in 2003.

Figure 3.3. Brand configuration of Erste Bank

Development of Functional Strategies

One of the most immediate benefits that Erste Bank could generate for its newly acquired operations in Eastern European countries was the development of a strong regional brand with local roots (Figure 3.3). The brand transformation was made on a thorough empirical analysis of brand recognition in different local markets. Only after a thorough analysis of the strengths of the existing local brand did the integration teams decide to modify the brand on a case-by-case basis. Brands with local value, for example in the Czech Republic, were kept in the portfolio. Although the savings banks symbol (a red 'S') had to be licensed from the German savings banks association, it was a key element linking the various brands.

Furthermore, cross-border integration allows Erste Bank to standardize its products. Since new products are generated from the daily business of the decentralized units, Erste Bank utilizes a fairly large product portfolio. However, since customer needs in different regions are quite similar, and since customers do not request a large range of products, there is room for standardization that reduces the bank's costs substantially. The expensive part of a new product is developing IT processes around product management.

Through cross-border collaboration in areas such as marketing, IT, production, training, and of course the cross-guarantee system that came into effect in January 2002, Erste Bank has increased the performance of the decentralized units. Its customers have the choice between various distribution channels, from expert advice at its branches to its Net-banking and Net-trading platforms. In this way, customers enjoy 24-hour access to Erste Bank's vast range of services. The distribution channels are being continuously upgraded and seamlessly integrated into the overall portfolio. Erste Bank's multi-channel marketing cuts the administrative workload for branch staff, thus adding valuable capacity for need-based customer advisory and support.

Strategy Implementation

The execution of this strategy in the Czech Republic included the development of a more focused distribution with 50 Full Service Branches

(15–25 staff), 94 Limited Service Branches (5–15 staff), and 9 Self Service Branches. In the course of the reorganization, 15 per cent of branch management has been changed and branch managers were assigned direct responsibility for 20 clients. Furthermore, measures to increase cross-selling and client migration to more sophisticated financial services products as well as improved targeting based on a new Customer Relationship Management (CRM) system helped to improve retail branch performance. A new management incentive system allowed successful branch managers to profit directly from increased branch income, volume (excluding loans), and cross-selling volumes. Although the bonus payment represents only 8–9 per cent of total compensation, it increased awareness of performance goals substantially.

To underpin this awareness, Erste Bank introduced both an Employee Stock Ownership Programme (ESOP) and a Management Stock Option Plan (MSOP) in 2002. The ESOP allows all Erste employees to buy shares on an annual basis with a 20 per cent discount on the market. Under the MSOP for top management, options priced 'at the market' were granted. Moreover, options were also granted to 'key performers' regardless of their hierarchical position. Consequently, today approximately 2 per cent of the bank's capital is held by its employees. Management has announced the target of at least 5 per cent to be achieved in the coming years.

Erste Bank managed to change its company culture from a bureaucratic, old-fashioned, purely domestically oriented savings bank to a modern bank. The focus on economic results was one of the major cultural changes the bank experienced, but smaller changes in people's behaviour, such as a CEO who would cross the corridor without his jacket on, were signals that a new era had begun.

Erste Bank also developed sound capabilities in executing market entry strategies. In 1999, for example, Erste Bank entered the Czech market, where it already had a small corporate banking unit with approximately 100 employees. The bank used local knowledge to make major strategic acquisitions and later integrate minor existing operations. This substantially facilitated further penetration of the market. The decision to increase investments in the Czech market was initiated and strongly supported by CEO Andreas Treichl. Some of his closest collaborators attribute as much as 90 per cent of Erste's success in the Eastern European markets to him. He did not rush into the implementation of a decision. On the contrary, he spent four months in internal discussions persuading his colleagues until the first steps were taken abroad and a core team of key executives started to believe in his foresight and vision.

The reasons for such a move were evident: if the bank aimed at keeping its independence, it had to grow. The market in Austria was limited and internationalization towards Eastern European countries was a unique chance to gain access to a large customer base that has potential for growth over the next 20 years. The profits from international expansion, Andreas Treichl believed, would not come from increased sales due to developing a customer basis in a mid-term perspective; however, there was a clear opportunity to create value in the short term by improving and restructuring the existing business. Most banks in Eastern Europe were overcapitalized with cost/income ratios at 90 per cent and upward. However, the opportunity to internationalize was brought forth in a period when nobody liked retail banking very much in general and nobody liked Eastern European countries specifically.

Erste Bank had already learned in Hungary that it is difficult to succeed in such a venture. Many investors did not believe that Erste Bank would learn from the first experience and successfully enter other Eastern European markets. In addition, the proposed acquisition in the Czech Republic seemed much too big. It seemed that 'the tail tried to wag the dog'. Entering the Czech market demanded a great deal of Erste Bank employees. The due diligence process had already made it clear to the teams involved that they would have to travel frequently to Prague and that there would be few opportunities to leave the office by early evening. To complement the strong management team, Erste Bank found the help of an experienced banker in Jack Stack, who, as CEO of Ceska sporitelna, supported the preparation and execution of their strategy.

The first step in the acquisition of Ceska sporitelna was the due diligence process, carried out painstakingly by several teams of approximately 60 people in total. The composition of those due diligence teams reflected the key processes of the bank and therefore included controllers, IT managers, and risk managers. Each team was led by a member of Erste and a manager from Ceska sporitelna. Since the large investment could take the shape of a life-threatening venture, negotiations were rigorous and lasted for a year. At one point, the Austrian negotiators interrupted the process because their offer already represented the upper limit of their capacity.

The so-called 'ring-fencing' agreement with the local government was a central element of the acquisition contract. This innovative contract chapter aimed to collateralize credit risks through the possibility of reviewing receivable credits ex post, that is, after closing the acquisition deal. Since it was impossible to analyse the entire credit portfolio in less than a year, the ring-fencing agreement allowed Erste Bank to scan all the credits Ceska sporitelna had on its balance sheet case-by-case and decide whether to keep them or to eliminate those credits by moving them to a government agency. If the credits remained with Erste and the Austrian bank managed to readjust them, the benefits were shared with the government. An arbitral court was created to resolve cases of discordances. This type of agreement reassured not only the management team of Erste Bank but also the investors who saw that their downside risk was limited. However, it was only possible to get the government to work with a ring-fencing agreement because Erste Bank did not have numerous co-bidders in the sales process of Ceska sporitelna. Nevertheless, Erste Bank developed excellent skills in bidding for government assets, a process that is often less transparent with a winner who is not always the bidder with the most appropriate business fit and price package.

The success of the post-merger integration (PMI) process comes from three main factors: speed, milestones, and people. A dogma during the integration process was 'implement today, perfect tomorrow' (Jack Stack, CEO Ceska sporitelna). This helped reduce PMI time to 18 months. The PMI team defined clear milestones and communicated them to stakeholders outside the company. Communication to investors, in particular, created transparency as well as a high level of commitment. Every delay in implementation had an effect on the share price and the possibility of accessing additional capital. The PMI process was sustained by the best people in the company. Even if it had a negative effect on the performance of the home-country operations, it was essential to send the best managers to the newly acquired unit. This was one of the central insights Erste Bank gained from its failure in Hungary, where Erste Bank sometimes chose expatriates simply because they did not know how to use them in the Austrian operations. Another important decision was to hire Jack Stack for the Czech Republic acquisition. Jack Stack, 54, started his banking career in controlling at Chemical Bank in 1977. He soon moved into Chemical Bank's retail operations, assuming responsibility for customer alignment and strategic branch repositioning. He was prominently involved in orchestrating the merger of Chemical Bank with Manufacturers Hanover. Appointing him was a smart move to avoid choosing between an Austrian and a local manager.

The restructuring process was possible because it is much easier to lay-off people in Eastern European countries than in other European countries. This workforce flexibility had been negotiated with the government before the acquisition contract was signed. Erste Bank further slimmed down and optimized most, if not all, of its business processes. The result is that the cost–income ratio could be reduced from over 90 per cent to 55 per cent. Although the interest curve was flat and very low in the Czech Republic, it was possible to earn additional income because the bank managed to charge for services that were free or priced at a lower level in the past. Non-interest income has risen steadily to almost 40 per cent of total income.

The Result: Unique Strategic Positions

The result of the strategy process Erste Bank went through is that in the period from 1997 to 2007 the customer base grew from 0.6 to 15.9 million and increased its employees tenfold from 5,000 to 50,000. In the same period, the share price rose from EUR 12 to EUR 60. The group cost–income ratio decreased from 73.5 to 59.9. Return on equity increased from 1.3 per cent to 13.5 per cent but had its peak in 2004 at 18 per cent. A large part of the success story of Erste Bank is the result of superior strategic capabilities and the achievement of a unique strategic position.

The 'ring-fencing' agreement with the Czech government that allowed Erste Bank to renegotiate bad loans of the acquired bank, for example, was made possible because the Austrian bank was the only bidder for the local financial services firm. After observing the initial success of early movers, the competitive turf in the CEE countries has increased significantly and the 'me too' strategies in Romania or Russia are much more expensive to execute. As a consequence, the economic results of Erste Bank have slightly worsened and the management team decided to decelerate the international expansion process and consolidate its businesses abroad.

The discussion of strategy-making capabilities in this chapter has shown that the quality of strategy largely depends on the ability of the financial services firm to fuel the strategy process with energy, as demonstrated by Erste Bank. The often standardized planning meetings should be complemented by more decentralized ad hoc processes. As financial services firms grow internationally, it will be increasingly important to decentralize strategy-making capabilities. As in other industries, also the financial services sector will continue to feature examples of more centralistic leadership styles as seen with Sandy Weill of Citigroup, with Warren Buffet of Berkshire Hathaway, and with Alessandro Profumo of UniCredit Group as well as more decentralized management models as seen with Nordea, Macquarie Bank, or Erste Bank. In many financial services firms, the CEOs earn just a fraction of their best performing executives. As a result, the autonomy of those managers increased. The investment banking division of Deutsche Bank, for example, is headquartered in London and enjoys a substantial degree of decision-making freedom. The foreign operations of HBOS are supported by just six central staff members and local decisions are taken by local management teams. At Allianz, foreign operations are mostly run by German expatriates to reinforce central control. Many viable strategy process models exist. Financial services firms need to make conscious design decisions that fit best with their firm and market contexts.

4

Why go abroad? The rationale of cross-border moves

After having spent some time on the discussion of how strategy processes should be designed, this chapter now addresses a first essential strategic choice internationalizing financial services firms face: should cross-border markets be served or not? Financial services firms can potentially benefit in several ways from increased international presence. Many of them are just pure market seekers since their primary motive for cross-border moves is to find new customers for their services. Resource-seeking, efficiency-seeking, or strategic asset-seeking motives have been of secondary importance in the past but are starting to be more important as the financial services value chains become increasingly disaggregated and offshored. This chapter offers a detailed description of the major benefits and costs of international growth initiatives.[1] Several major benefits will be distinguished: economies of scale, economies of scope, X-efficiencies, access to key factors and location-related advantages, firm-specific assets, satisfying growth expectations of shareholders, accumulation of market power, and agency motives. On the other hand, three main costs categories are addressed: liabilities of foreignness, liabilities of newness, and coordination costs.

The following section confronts growth via international expansion with alternative growth options such as local market consolidation or product diversification. For many financial services firms in many countries, market consolidation as well as product diversification have reached their regulatory limits. International expansion seems to be therefore the natural choice to grow, at least for the larger financial institutions in developed economies. This section concludes by advancing the speculation that focused international growth is more successful compared to cross-border expansion offering a broad range of products.

Next, this chapter discusses the magnitude of the potential benefits and costs of international expansion. Whether a financial services firm enters into foreign markets depends on the availability of alternative growth options and on the benefits of cross-border moves in relation to their costs. The balance of benefits and costs of internationalization, in turn, depends on three factors: (*a*) the need for local adaptation; (*b*) the possibility of global integration of activities; and (*c*) the opportunities for global arbitrage. Different views on these three elements have an effect on the decision to internationalize and on the strategic positioning if cross-border activities are pursued. The chapter concludes with a short reflection on the limits of global expansion and whether all financial services firms need to be present internationally.

Value Creation in Multinational Firms

The presentation of Alessandro Profumo, CEO of UniCredit Group, at the Capital Markets Day on 5 July 2006 in Munich left no doubt regarding the capacity of the UniCredit management team to create value for its shareholders. Earnings per share rose from EUR 0.02 in 1994 to EUR 0.37 in 2006. In the same period, the market capitalization rose from EUR 2.5 billion to EUR 60 billion, with the return on equity rising from 1.4 per cent to 19 per cent. The steep rise in performance cannot be entirely attributed to UniCredit's exposure to international markets. However, in 2005, around 51 per cent of total group gross operational profit came from abroad, with the Central and Eastern European (CEE)[2] countries contributing an impressive 21 per cent overall, exceeding Austria's 11 per cent and Germany's 19 per cent. At the same time, the leading Italian bank is more exposed to risks coming from international markets. When the American mortgage crisis first rattled global markets in late 2007, the UniCredit shares suffered disproportionately compared to its national peers, losing over 6 per cent in just one trading day, due to its presence in the German market. Like UniCredit, many financial services firms have started creating most of their shareholder value in foreign markets.

How Managers Justify International Expansion Plans

At the Capital Markets Day in Munich in July 2006, Alessandro Profumo announced: 'It is our goal to create the first truly European Bank.' What are the reasons for that ambition, and does the Italian bank have the prerequisites to be successful in international markets? There are many forces that push financial services firms across national boundaries. The aim to create shareholder value is just one. Often, self-interests of managers or short-term effects on the share price have a strong influence on the decision to internationalize. Very few financial services firms will take their decision to internationalize based on a hypothetical multinationality–performance curve discussed in Chapter 2. Interviews with executives in the financial services industry and investor relations statements of internationalizing banks showed that several managerial arguments for international expansion can be identified:

- 'We have something to teach to banks in other markets.'
- 'Our home market is saturated.'
- 'Internationalizing companies are traded at a premium price.'
- 'We want to stay independent.'
- 'International exposure attracts and keeps better management talent.'
- 'Foreign markets are more attractive.'
- 'Major competitors in important markets are not domestic and have a presence in several countries.'
- 'New information and communication technology makes international operations easier to govern.'
- 'We need to follow our clients to international markets.'

These are the arguments that were the most frequently mentioned by top executives. However, stakeholders of financial services firms may have different motives for promoting cross-border expansion. There is a risk that corporate governance structures do not sufficiently align the interests of managers and shareholders, and as a result, cross-border moves are put forth that destroy shareholder value but satisfy top management's needs of empire building or salary increases.[3] As Figure 4.1 shows, growth does not always mean increased

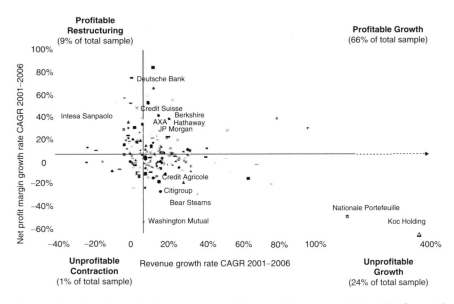

Figure 4.1. Growth and value creation of the world's most valuable 225 financial services firms [Reuters top 500 financial services firms (retrieved on 25 January 2008)]

profit margins and shareholder value creation. But 66 per cent of the largest financial services firms in terms of market capitalization have managed to grow their revenue base and at the same time their net profit margins. Only 24 per cent of the firms have reduced their margins while growing. Only 20 of the 225 firms observed have increased their net profit margins by reducing their revenues.

Figure 4.1 shows that most, but not all, financial services firms are able to grow their revenues and contemporaneously increase their overall profitability. This suggests that there are most likely also performance differences in cross-border expansion. This raises the question of how they can be explained and how the mechanisms behind success stories of international growth such as that by UniCredit in the CEE region and later in mature markets such as Germany and Austria can be explained. The following section therefore explores the main theoretical frameworks that describe the ways multinational firms can create value from their international presence.

Fundamental Sources of Value Creation

Since its inception in the late 1960s, the literature on international business has been concerned with the reasons of existence of the multinational company, its competitive advantage compared to local competitors, and their organizational architecture and governance modes. An integrated framework or theory of international management does not currently exist.

The early days of international management research were coined by studies on export behaviour such as the work by Adam Smith[4] on absolute comparative advantage, Ricardo[5] on relative comparative advantage, the Heckscher-Ohlin theory first published by Ohlin[6] on sources of comparative advantage of nations, Posner[7] on temporary comparative advantage of nations, and Linder[8] on demand similarities as catalysts for export relationships. With the seminal work of Hymer,[9] the international management field started to become more differentiated. Apart from exporting, other market entry modes such as licensing and foreign direct investment (FDI) were studied. Researchers attempted to explain why multinational firms exist, exploring topics such as

- the extension of oligopolistic competition to the international arena[10]
- the product life cycle model where firm-specific advantages yield temporary monopolies in host markets[11]
- a discussion of coordination costs between MNC (multinational corporation) units compared to external contractual relations in foreign countries, so that intermediate markets are internalized in the modern MNC[12]
- firm-specific advantages that compensate for liabilities of foreignness (i.e. the difficulties of doing business abroad)[13]

Dunning[14] combines such market power arguments, transaction cost reasoning, non-tradable firm-specific advantages, and location-specific advantages in his eclectic paradigm to explain why MNCs exist. The main message: FDI occurs when three sources of competitive advantages (O-L-I) exist:

- Ownership advantages: to overcome liability of foreignness, firms need to have possession of sources of sustainable competitive advantages over local competitors. A superior operational model of a retail insurance firm, a better pool of investment bankers, superior market segmentation capabilities, or a stronger wealth management brand are examples of such resources and capabilities that create ownership advantages.

- Locational advantages: some resources cannot be moved economically and therefore it is more convenient to locate the value-creation activity in a foreign country. Most financial services businesses are tied to local markets because they require a certain level of trust and face-to-face contact with customers. In addition, regulatory restrictions oblige financial institutions to establish a local presence to offer their services.

- Internalization advantages: to exploit sources of competitive advantage in a foreign country, hierarchies are more efficient than market structures. In other words, financial services firms prefer ownership of foreign operations if they believe that they are more efficient in organizing their activities internally than through market contracts with a local partner. This implies that in some instances market mechanisms are less efficient than administrative mechanisms because the coordination through active planning creates value.

Although eclectic, Dunning's attempt to integrate various theoretical perspectives gravitating around the international management field is probably still the most widely used frame of reference for researchers attempting to explain why MNCs exist. Studies that have identified the sources and magnitude of advantages available to firms following international strategies[15] may help to explain ownership advantages in Dunning's framework. These include economies of scale and scope, tapping into location advantages, escaping or hedging local business cycle risk, as well as sharing activities and knowledge. Similarly, studies concerned with the effective and efficient management of MNCs explain why and when hierarchies are more efficient than markets. Specifically, these studies document the complex task of managing a global firm and identifying processes that can be adapted by MNCs to manage this complexity.[16] The inquiry into the internal organization of MNCs has followed a rather discontinuous path. Starting with the path-breaking work of Stopford and Wells,[17] which applies Chandler's[18] contingency framework to the analysis of MNC structures, the initial investigation focused on the structural fit between an MNC's expansion strategy (represented in terms of product and geographic diversity) and its organizational structure. The essential prediction is that matrix structures become more likely with greater product diversity and geographic dispersion.

The following literature emphasizes the trade-off that an MNC often faces between being globally integrated and being locally responsive.[19] This second stream of research, often known as the integration–responsiveness (I–R) framework, shifted focus from the notion of structural fit onto the question of balancing two conflicting competitive pressures. The well-known formulation of the I–R framework is the transnational model of Bartlett and Ghoshal[20] who described an MNC's organizational form that is multidimensional and relies on normative social control instead of the traditional structural control. In the meantime, a third stream of work also emerged that applies economic theories of firm growth and organization to the analysis of MNC structures, pointing to the nature of a firm's knowledge-based resources as the critical factor in the design of MNC structures.[21] In this view, the organizational structure of the modern MNC is co-determined by the knowledge sources, which might be locally dispersed, and the integration needs occurring in the pursuit of global innovation.[22]

This brief review gives only a taste of the various options available to explain the incentives, approaches, and effects of internationalization of financial services firms. Although there are many theoretical arguments as to why firms should internationalize and predictions on what outcomes these moves have on firm performance, customer value added or the performance of the financial services system of a country, the empirical results on these issues do not give a very clear picture of the performance implications of international expansion. The following sections dive deeper into specific benefit and cost dimensions of international expansion.

Benefits of International Expansion

We can find several examples of banks that obtain a large part of their profitability from their foreign markets. For Erste Bank the net profit contribution of 2006 from CEE (Central and Eastern Europe) was 60.5 per cent, with the remaining 39.5 per cent coming from Austria, their home market. Whereas this figure might be an indication of the degree of internationalization rather than foreign profitability, the 2006 cost/income ratio of 62.6 per cent in Austria as opposed to an average of 56.1 per cent in the CEE countries is a stronger indication of foreign market profitability. Similarly, the CEE division of UniCredit Group (which does not include Poland) produces a cost/income ratio of 54.2 per cent and the Poland Markets division has an even lower cost/income ratio of 48.4 per cent as opposed to the average cost/income ratio of the total group of 56.5 per cent. This illustrates that even for a bank operating out of an attractive home market such as Italy, servicing foreign markets can boost operational performance, not to mention the effects that the presentation of an international growth story into growing markets has on the share price. The potential benefits described in the following sections may justify the enthusiasm for growth of financial services firms.

Economies of Scale

Economies of scale in the production of goods or services exist when an increase in the scale of the firm causes a decrease in the long-run average cost of each unit and/or an increase in revenues. Large scale gives rise to increased operational efficiency by eliminating redundant facilities and personnel, as well as improving the quality of management.[23] To reap economies of scale is easier within a single home country as compared to cross-border operations. However, numerous national as well as international examples of firms that managed to achieve economies of scale exist. When Fortis Group acquired the Belgian bank Générale in 1998, the operation was predicted to lead to at least a 10 per cent reduction in employment in the following five-year period (equal to about 2,500 jobs). When the Royal Bank of Scotland took over National Westminster Bank, its success was due to its pledge to cut costs by more than GBP 1 billion, mostly by eliminating an estimated 18,000 jobs. The acquisition of the UK's Abbey National by Spain's Banco Santander in late 2004 is an example of how modern core systems can contribute to an acquisition.[24] Banco Santander estimated it could realize EUR 300 million in annual savings by reducing technology costs.

A closer look at these and other examples of mergers and acquisitions in the financial services landscape helps to identify several categories of economies of scale:

- *Cost-based economies of scale in production.* Cost efficiency is achieved by lowering average cost per unit of output through expanding a single line of business. Digital elements of most financial services products make reproduction often very cheap. Although it is not easy to replicate financial services products across national boundaries, it is nevertheless likely that the harmonization of the global financial services institutional frameworks will allow multinational firms to profit from size, especially in investment and private banking segments but increasingly in retail insurance and banking markets. The emergence of regional product factories in many banks and insurance companies and more homogeneous regulatory frameworks across borders is an indication of the intention to reap scale economies.

- *Brand-based economies of scale.* Large size will allow brand recognition to be obtained at a lower cost. Most financial services are experience goods where the quality of the service can only be judged after the experience is made. Consequently, brands that are able to signal value play an essential part in the business models of most financial services providers. In practice, we can observe different approaches to brand-based economies of scale. RBS, HBOS, or Erste Bank believe in local brands and eliminate them only if they are not profitable. UniCredit, UBS, or Allianz attempt to establish regional or global brands.

- *Revenue-based economies of scale.* A large capital base is often the entry ticket for underwriting larger loans and securities issues. Therefore, size has a positive impact on the demand for underwriting services, but not exclusively. Some customers need or prefer bigger banking institutions.

- *Safety net-based economies of scale.* As a bank becomes very large, it is more likely to be perceived by customers, business partners, and public authorities as 'too big to fail'. This would provide a competitive advantage in terms of both a lower funding cost for a given level of capital (as seen when some big banks had to get additional funding from central banks) and risk and larger positions accepted by counterparties.

Economies of Scope

The previously described economies of scale refer to efficiencies related to supply-side factors. Economies of scope refer to demand-side effects and arise when a firm decides to broaden its range of products or services and/or its distribution. Such changes can have a positive impact on costs as well as revenues. Many of the economies of scale we have identified in the previous section can be exploited across different products and geographical markets and are therefore called economies of scope. Several categories can be distinguished:

- *Cost-based economies of scope.* Cost efficiencies are achieved by offering a broad range of products or services to a customer base. These could originate from the large fixed costs incurred in creating an information database or developing an ICT backbone that can be used to provide a large set of services. An existing retail branch network, for example, can be more efficiently used by offering a broader set of products.

- *Sales (revenue)-based economies of scope.* Some financial services firms manage the cross-selling of new products to an existing customer base. Sales-based economies of scope arise when investors or customers of financial services products have a preference for one-stop shopping, buying insurance products from the bank consultant or vice versa.

- *Risk diversification-based economies of scope.* Standard portfolio theory states that a portfolio of imperfectly correlated risks will reduce the overall volatility of profit. Greater earnings stability from asynchronous businesses or smoothing out foreign exchange volatility with multi-currency flows can reduce the overall risk of a financial services firm.[25]

X-Efficiencies and the Transfer of Superior Managerial Capabilities

X-efficiency refers to a firm not operating with maximum cost efficiency, that is, cost structure is too high given a current volume of output. This source of efficiency is often cited as the prime motivation for a domestic merger, as two banks merging can more easily coordinate the reduction of the size of an overly large branch network. Expanding the geographical scope gives the financial services firm the opportunity to exploit its resources and capabilities which then create a competitive edge in the home market. The transfer of a firm's proprietary assets and competences across borders is a central strategic goal of many internationalization moves.[26] Although it is more difficult to create X-efficiencies across borders than within a single market, it is nevertheless a major motive for many international M&A transactions.

Arbitrage through Access to Key Input Factors and Location-Related Advantages

Resource-seeking motives for international expansion have been historically less important in the financial services industry. Nevertheless, financial institutions can benefit from increased international exposure by gaining access to valuable strategic assets such as low-cost programming capacity (e.g. in India or Eastern European markets) or specific knowledge (e.g. investment banking in London or New York). The international firm's presence in several nations increases its ability to pick up on knowledge that domestic or less multinational rivals cannot access.[27] Location-related advantages may also come in the form of tax benefits.[28]

Follow Captive Customers to Attractive Foreign Markets

An often cited motive for financial services firms to go abroad is that they follow their clients. Knowledge about clients is a competitive advantage that needs to be both protected and exploited. Selected corporate banking, investment banking, and private banking operations are therefore often offered in early stages of foreign market entry and only later are broader retail services added to the foreign market portfolio. Shareholder value can potentially be created by taking advantage of opportunities in the foreign banking markets if the home market is saturated, highly regulated, small, or has an unattractive competitive structure.[29] Multinational banking grows in concert with direct foreign investment as banks try to meet the demand for banking services of multinational firms abroad. Banks go abroad to serve their domestic customers who have gone abroad, which is sometimes called the 'gravitational pull effect'.[30]

Satisfy Growth Expectations of Shareholders and Follow the Leader

Most financial services firms are under constant pressure from their shareholders and analysts to deliver new and more exciting growth stories. For universal banks that operate in an unattractive or saturated home market, international expansion is often the only investment story that can be created. Banks also tend to follow one another in their foreign commitments. They decide to enter the same markets at the same time by choosing the same mode of entry.[31]

Accumulation of Market Power

Horizontal mergers, which reduce the number of firms operating in one market, may lead to less competition and higher margins. Mergers across industries may allow higher profit due to strategies that allow the firm to package a bundle of goods. Increasing market power by raising market share helps firms to widen cost–price margins, establish preferred technical standards and protocols, and create global brand equity.[32]

Agency Motives

The argument is that higher profit driven by economies of scale or market power can be captured by management in the forms of higher salaries, perks, reduction of risk, or just a more 'quiet life'[33] due to the possibility to create slack management without any severe consequences. Managers sometimes make risk-reducing decisions that may be misaligned with the interests of the more risk-tolerant shareholders. Cross-border moves may be instrumental for top managers to preserve independence and as a means to ensure job security. Achieving size and capital clout can act as a defensive measure against takeover. Management hubris and self-aggrandizement, driven by management's utility function, which may be different from the shareholder's utility function, can drive international expansion plans. The benefits of international diversification can be generated for the shareholders, customers, and the financial services system in general or the management of a single firm. In some cases, however, the increase in the wealth of shareholders does not correspond to increased social welfare. Exploiting the benefits of a public safety net or market power will create economic inefficiencies. The 'quiet life' argument for international expansion might be appealing to managers but is certainly not serving the best interests of shareholders.

Costs of International Expansion

The efficiency obstacles particular to international mergers, such as geographical distances, cultural and linguistic differences, as well as hierarchical and regulatory structure differences, cancel out part of the gains from cross-border consolidation. Distance still matters—cultural, administrative, geographical, and economic differences[34] between home and host markets create additional costs for internationalizing firms. Managing a subsidiary in a neighbouring country that can be reached with a two-hour flight differs fundamentally from interacting with a subsidiary that is six time zones away. For a Western firm, dealing with the regulatory bodies in China or India requires substantial resources. Understanding customers' needs and managing the workforce across cultures are costly. These are just a few reasons why many practitioners and academics believe that even in the mid-term we will have a 'semi-globalized'[35] rather than a fully integrated world economy. To reduce and manage complexity is a major challenge for multinational financial services firms, as illustrated by the following cost categories.

Liabilities of Foreignness

Financial services firms doing business abroad face costs arising from the unfamiliarity of the environment due to cultural, political, and economic differences, and from the need for coordination across geographical distance.[36] The costs of geographical distance, such as transportation, travel, and coordination, seem to be relatively small for financial services firms compared to manufacturing companies. However, many executives who have been interviewed mentioned the strong impact of geographical distance on management costs. Other firm-specific costs arise from a firm's unfamiliarity with the local environment, in particular local regulations and market mechanisms. In addition, a foreign financial services firm might face costs resulting from the host-country environment, such as the lack of legitimacy of foreign firms and economic nationalism. In some countries that have been closed to foreign financial services firms for a long period of time, however, foreign banks and insurance companies can often bond on reputational advantages since local firms suffer from low efficiency and deliver mediocre services. Another category of liability of foreignness may come from the home-country environment in the form of restricted management practices or regulations.

To overcome the liability of foreignness and outpace local firms, multinational financial institutions need to provide their cross-border sub-units with firm-specific advantages in the form of superior resources and organizational and managerial capabilities. Multinational firms have to resist the natural tendency of their decentralized units to mimic local competitors. Instead, they should arouse the local industry landscape and signal to customers that foreign financial institutions can provide superior services.

Liabilities of Newness

The concept of liability of newness suggests that selection processes favour older, more reliable organizations and failure rates are expected to decrease monotonically with age.[37] Older organizations have an advantage over younger ones because it is easier to continue existing routines than to create new ones or borrow old ones.[38] The costs associated with the liability of newness that young firms face are due to efforts to train employees, develop internal routines, and establish credible exchange relationships.[39]

Coordination Costs

In an organizational model of 'perfect decentralization',[40] single units within multinational financial services firms maximize their own profitability, utility, or wealth while completely disregarding other units' decisions. In such organizations, hierarchical authority does not play a role when resources are assigned and strategic decisions are made; instead, transactions are made at arm's length in which all parties involved act in their own self-interest and are not subject to any pressure from third parties. In such a world, coordination costs, by definition, do not occur—but neither do the benefits of multinational presence described earlier. In many instances, however, integrated financial services firms exist because they are more efficient in organizing the production of services than market contracts between independent units. This implies that in some cases it is less efficient to manage the relationship with a fairly independent contractual partner than with an internal unit that is owned by the firm.

But as the number of foreign units increases and greater task interdependency between those units is created, the coordination costs can increase exponentially. Increased coordination and control implies that several administrative cost items accrue.

- Interests between the headquarters and the subsidiaries need to be aligned, monitored, and reinforced.
- Information asymmetries need to be levelled out through additional information-processing.
- Specialized capabilities need to be developed and applied where needed.
- Organizational flexibility decreases due to many interdependencies that have to be considered.
- As a result of increased interdependency and compliance, the compounding risk of failure increases.

Some of the costs associated with management complexity will be discussed in Part III of this book.

Evaluating Alternative Growth Options

Such cost/benefit considerations of international expansion have to be made in comparison to alternative strategic growth options. Before choosing internationalization as the dominant growth strategy, alternative growth options such as market penetration, product development, or (unrelated) diversification have to be carefully analysed. Figure 4.2 offers a general framework for evaluating different growth options.[41] As illustrated by the example of Erste Bank's decision to internationalize in the late 1990s, a firm can expand

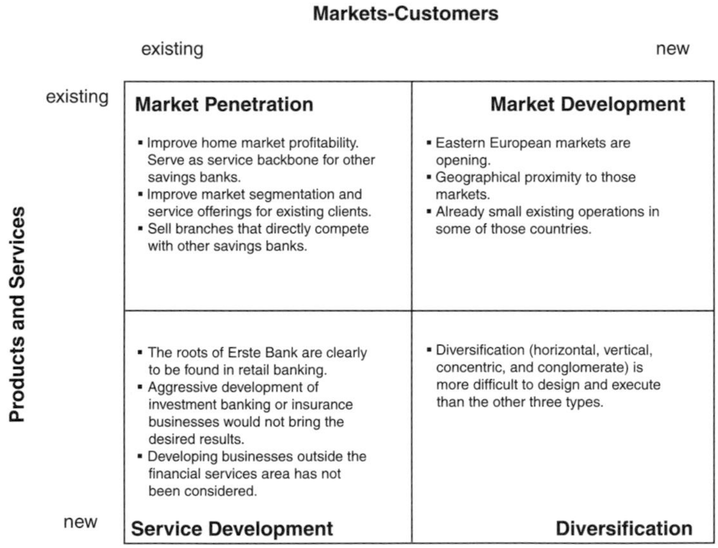

Markets-Customers

	existing	new
existing	**Market Penetration** • Improve home market profitability. Serve as service backbone for other savings banks. • Improve market segmentation and service offerings for existing clients. • Sell branches that directly compete with other savings banks.	**Market Development** • Eastern European markets are opening. • Geographical proximity to those markets. • Already small existing operations in some of those countries.
new	• The roots of Erste Bank are clearly to be found in retail banking. • Aggressive development of investment banking or insurance businesses would not bring the desired results. • Developing businesses outside the financial services area has not been considered. **Service Development**	• Diversification (horizontal, vertical, concentric, and conglomerate) is more difficult to design and execute than the other three types. **Diversification**

(Products and Services)

Figure 4.2. Erste Bank—evaluating growth options (Ansoff 1957)

by four general avenues: market penetration, service development, market development, and diversification.

The heuristics of this model bear three simple suggestions:

- A firm should only expand into new geographical and/or service markets out of a solid position in its home markets.

- The timing of such growth projects depends on the level of saturation of the home market as well as the attractiveness of potential target markets and the firm's disposal of superior capabilities and resources.

- Simultaneous service and market diversification carry a higher failure rate.

The strategic choice of Erste Bank to push its international businesses was largely stimulated by the desire to remain independent and the difficulties associated with creating profitable growth opportunities in its home market. Of course, Erste's geographical proximity to emerging and attractive CEE markets facilitated the process. Another component was the analysis of the identity of Erste Bank, which clearly showed that Erste Bank had its roots and core capabilities in retail banking. As a consequence, Erste Bank discounted the possibility of growing through product diversification and moving towards a model of the universal bank or even offering a full range of bancassurance services. In addition, the regulatory framework in the EU appeared to be moving towards a harmonization of banking regulations, and Eastern European countries sooner or later would join the EU. In addition, the target banks had substantial potential in performance improvement. By implementing the business-proven Erste Bank processes, its IT systems, changing the product portfolio towards service fees, reducing headcount as well as the number of branches, optimizing capital utilization, and much more, Erste Bank could improve key performance indicators such as the cost/income ratio and ultimately, profit.

As opposed to less-regulated businesses, not all service development and diversification initiatives are permissible. National or regional central banks monitor the scope and scale of financial holding companies to ensure that proper competition exists, and that no conflicts of interest arise within different operational units. Most of the large multinational banks have expanded into mortgage banking, investment banking, or even insurance as a way of diversifying cash flows and offering more services to their clients in addition to the traditional interest-based business.

One of the few big financial services firms with a balanced banking–insurance revenue model is Fortis. Created in 1990 by the merger between N.V. AMEV, a large Dutch insurer, and VSB, a Dutch bank, Fortis performed its first cross-border acquisition and incorporated AG Group—a large Belgian insurer—in the same year. In 2006, Fortis had a financial services portfolio with 45 per cent of total profits from merchant and private banking, 31 per cent from insurance, and the remaining 24 per cent from retail banking. With total profits (ROE) consistently exceeding 20 per cent, Fortis is also one of the most profitable diversified financial services groups worldwide. The management believes in the universal banking model, and not only because their all-embracing financial services are appreciated by their corporate clients. To follow clients in their international expansion is just one avenue to global markets. Another advantage of having both banking and insurance activities is the positive effect that product diversification has on total risk exposure. Fortis claims to be able to reduce the economic capital, an indicator Fortis uses to measure and manage risk, substantially by offering all major financial services products. Economic capital is defined as the amount of capital required to protect against economic insolvency. It reflects the real risks Fortis is actually taking by exposing itself to unexpected movements in the value of assets and liabilities. Economic capital differs from regulatory capital, which is needed to protect the group against statutory insolvency, or the capital-level rating agencies might be comfortable with or require.

Some of the universal banks changed their business model and product mix during their internationalization process. Deutsche Bank, for example, became an investment bank but is still one of the largest commercial banks in Germany. Similarly, the Swiss banks UBS and Credit Suisse are among the largest wealth management firms but maintain their retail banking identity in Switzerland. The bancassurance model has often not lived up to its promises. A recent example is Credit Suisse, which incorporated the large insurer Winterthur only to sell it again to AXA a few years later. The issue of business model suitability is closely connected with historical and cultural aspects of a country. While in countries such as Spain and France the process of integration has been evolutionary, in other countries, such as the United States or the UK, integration was much more painful. The convergence of banking and insurance can take many forms, from simple cross-sales agreements to full corporate integration. The initial fascination in the 1990s for easy-to-realize synergies in terms of economies of scope and, to a lesser extent, economies of scale gave way to a more realistic assessment of the promises of bancassurance models. Therefore, one can find many specialized financial services firms that concentrate on particular types of financial services but convergence towards universal financial services firms that are able to use their powerful brands is still a major business trend. A recent example is JP Morgan Chase: CEO Jamie Dimon suggested to his supervisory board that they should be prepared for stiffer competition from European banks as well as from Indian and Chinese banks. He sees the lack of an international retail bank within the JP Morgan Chase Group as a significant strategic shortcoming and plans for a major acquisition once the consolidation brought forth larger units that are up for sale.[42]

Since Nobel Laureate Harry Markowitz demonstrated mathematically in 1952 why putting all your eggs in one basket is an unacceptably risky strategy, many firms have experienced diversification that reduces the overall profitability of one firm. Risk reduction may well be a motive for top managers to diversify because they reduce the risk of losing their jobs, but for investors, the easiest strategy to reduce risks is via alternative investments on the capital market. However, there is no clear empirical evidence or convincing theoretical arguments able to predict the impact of diversification on the profitability of firms in general, or on financial institutions in particular. Since many allowable types of activities are truly financially related, the diversification of financial services firms is nevertheless limited in most countries. The bottom line is that for most financial services firms, international expansion appears to be the growth option promising the highest returns.

Exploiting Cross-Border Differences

The benefits and costs of international market expansion depend on the magnitude of cross-border differences and the firm's ability to use those differences to create sources of competitive advantages. Not all financial services firms necessarily have to and will expand their international presence in the short and medium term, but most, if not all, have to understand and process the impact globalization has on their businesses. In his book[43] on global strategy, *Redefining Global Strategy*, Pankaj Ghemawat strikingly demonstrates that the world is indeed semi-globalized and differences still matter. Using industry examples as diverse as soccer and soft drinks, he illustrates how cultural, administrative, geographical, and economic differences can indeed give local companies a competitive edge over large multinationals that overstress the similarities between markets. Large MNCs have the challenge of managing the well described and researched trade-off between local adaptation and global standardization (or adaptation aggregation trade-off, to use the words of Ghemawat) by redesigning their input and output market strategies according to a triple A triangle: Adaptation–Aggregation–Arbitrage. Figure 4.3 combines the matrix proposed by Bartlett and Ghoshal with the AAA model of Ghemawat. The similarities of both matrixes are evident and trigger a further distinction between integrated and undifferentiated arbitrage.

- *Undifferentiated arbitrage within an international firm*: Mainly in early phases of their internationalization, firms opportunistically export their products and services designed for the home markets. Many foreign wealth

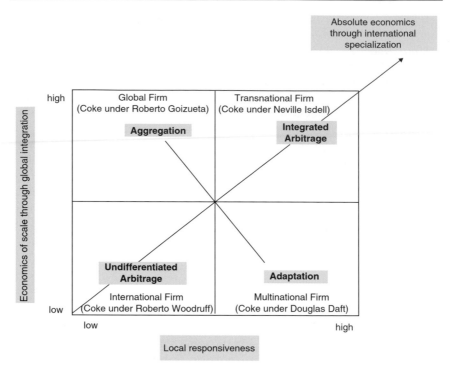

Figure 4.3. The cross-border strategy and organization matrix (based on Bartlett and Ghoshal 1991; Ghemawat 2007)

management firms, for example, used their representative offices to divert local demand to the investment products designed for their home markets. Arbitrage—the exploitation of CAGE differences—between local operations does not happen frequently, and if it does, transactions are handled by arm's length principles.

- *Aggregation within a global firm*: Firms that follow aggregation strategies aim to achieve cross-border synergies primarily through international standardization. The organizational form reflects the firms' aim to coordinate across borders by businesses, customers, or regions. Products and services are designed to serve the global customer with homogeneous needs across country boundaries. Most segments within financial services do not allow for complete standardization and centralization. Even asset managers and investment bankers have to satisfy local norms and customers' needs, and cross-border transactions and knowledge transfer are still limited. Perhaps the only global businesses to date utilizing aggregation within financial services are payment services.

- *Adaptation within a multinational firm*: The main purpose of a multinational firm is to achieve local relevance through the delegation of wide local decision-making autonomy in an organizational chart that distinguishes countries on a primary level. Many retail banks are organized following this model. The local banks are fairly autonomous. A few business processes and resources are coordinated at the centre, among them the core banking system, risk management system, and sometimes aspects of branding.

- *Integrated arbitrage within a transnational firm*: One is inclined to agree with Ghemawat when he states that the slogan 'think global, act local'[44] is (mis-)used to describe far too many different views and situations. However, the nature of the transnational firm indeed aims at combining the benefits of local adaptation with the global economies of centralization. HSBC claims to be the 'world's local bank' and TV advertising campaigns show how moving to another country for retail clients becomes much easier with the support of HSBC. Although many industry experts agree that there is currently no truly transnational financial services firm, remarkable attempts to combine local market presence with global economies of scale and scope do exist. Integrated arbitrage by the creation of competence centres that fuel the network of interdependent units with specific resources, competences, and products/services means moving into the third stage of value creation as described in Chapter 9.

To illustrate his ideas on the AAA triangle, Ghemawat uses the international evolution of the Coca-Cola Company. In the early days of its existence, the US soft drinks giant under Robert Woodruff aimed at 'colonizing' foreign countries by exporting product and utilizing FDI in fairly autonomous local bottling, attempting to replicate the US Coke approach in their contexts. In 1981, it was with Roberto Goizueta that Coke embarked on an aggressive globalization strategy with a firm belief in almost endless cross-border economies of scale. National differences mattered little and headquarters was in charge of the most critical functions such as consumer research, advertising, or product development. With Douglas Daft in the early 2000s, the pendulum of cross-border strategy swung back in favour of local adaptation and autonomy at the expense of global standardization. The consequence was massive layoffs at the headquarters level and marketing budgets moved the local entrepreneurs who did not have the necessary capabilities to perform the new charters. Soon Coca-Cola realized that it had to again centralize some of the functions, which resulted in frustrated, dethroned local kings and desperate central HR managers forced to again build up the necessary skills they had relinquished just a few years before. Since 2004, Neville Isdell's strategy has been to find a less extreme compromise between local adaptation and centralization.

As the Coke example shows, finding the right position in the cross-border strategy and organization matrix is not trivial and needs to be constantly reviewed as market environments and firm conditions change. However, not all firms that expand into foreign markets necessarily decide to integrate operations across borders. There are clear limits to international expansion, as discussed in the next section.

Limits to International Expansion and the Viability of Purely Local Firms

What is the optimal geographical scope for financial services firms? Can we expect to see a narrower spectrum of viable strategies in terms of multinational presence? Or in other words, is there a future for local and regional financial services firms? Will we finally see global financial services firms in the near future? As discussed, there are several factors that make it easier for financial services firms to compete on a cross-border scale and reap the benefits of multinationality. However, the financial services industry currently remains far from being globalized, even after adapting the full effects of deregulation and technological progress.[45] Despite the increasing cross-border financial activities within the individual industrialized countries, market shares of foreign-owned banks are generally below 10 per cent, with some exceptions to be found in the CEE countries. A study conducted by Berger et al.[46] examined the issue of how much the banking industry is, and potentially will become, globalized. They examined more than 2,000 foreign affiliates of large multinational corporations for their choice of banks for cash management services in each of the then 20 European nations. Cash management was selected as it covers a variety of core banking services including liquidity management, short-term lending, foreign exchange transactions, and assistance with hedging, and it generally requires a physical presence in the nation in which the service is provided. Cash management can be provided by local banks that operate only in the host nation, by global banks headquartered in a few financial centres but with offices in many nations around the world, and by institutions between these two extremes.[47] On the basis of two dimensions of globalization—nationality of a bank (which refers to the location of a bank's headquarters) and reach of a bank (which refers to geographic scope and size of the chosen bank)—Berger et al. investigated whether multinational companies are more likely to choose a home nation bank (headquartered in the same nation as the multinational corporation's headquarters), a host nation bank (headquartered in the nation in which the affiliate of the company operates), or a third nation bank (headquartered in neither the host nor the home nation) for cash management services. The study concluded that the nationality of the bank has an impact on the degree of the bank's reach, as its nationality is of primary importance in choosing a bank for cash management services, because banks can only expand across international borders to the extent that customers are willing to purchase services from foreign-owned banks.

In this study, only 8 out of the total sample of 255 banks were identified as global (e.g. Deutsche Bank, Citibank), each providing services to firms in at least 9 of the then 20 European nations and had USD 100 billion in consolidated assets at the end of 1995. Local banks only provided services to sample firms in the nation of their headquarters and had assets of less than USD 100 billion. The 73 regional banks operated in more nations or were larger than a local bank but smaller than a global bank. When internationalizing, less than 20 per cent of the multinational corporations selected a bank from their home nation, but nearly two-thirds chose a bank headquartered in the host nation due to the local market knowledge, culture, language, and regulatory conditions in the host countries. However, the study also concluded that the reach of the banks showed variation across host nations. Only 26.2 per cent of the firms operating in the former socialist countries used a host bank and 42.6 per cent of these firms selected a bank from their home or a third nation. Nevertheless, since most of the multinational corporations that were examined are based on host nation banks with limited reach, the study suggests that the extent of globalization may remain limited.

The degree of globalization obviously depends on the nature of the business. Retail banking and insurance are supposedly the most local businesses, followed by servicing corporate clients and wealthy private clients. Asset management, investment banking, and capital markets are regional businesses, with securities markets and payment services being the most globalized. Figure 4.4 shows an attempt to classify financial services industries

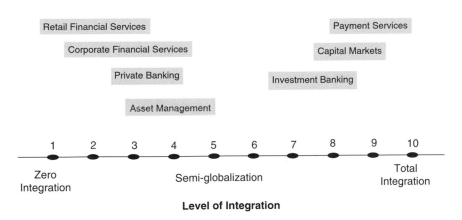

Figure 4.4. Measuring the cross-border integration level of financial services segments

117

according to their degree of integration.[48] Based on a limited number of expert interviews and therefore without empirical validity, this figure hypothesizes that most segments of the financial services industry are not semi-globalized (yet) but still bound to national borders or fairly integrated on a global basis. If we were to sub-segment the markets indicated in Figure 4.4, we would see that it is difficult to place entire segments on a level of integration. Corporate banking for large clients is much more globally integrated than for small clients. Most payment services are less integrated than payments based on credit cards.[49]

The level of integration can be measured by the degree of product/service standardization, the international transfer of tangible and intangible assets, and the creation of dedicated competence centres for key processes. David Llewellyn[50] argues that size per se does not lead to higher profitability but rather the ability to create efficient and well-focused financial institutions that secure long-term survival. While a trend towards the creation of larger and more diversified financial services firms can be recorded, this does not at all exclude opportunities for small- and medium-sized firms to compete successfully alongside giant financial services firms. Llewellyn concluded that internal efficiency, or X-efficiency, largely determines a bank's cost level and suggests that scale economies are more likely to be found in bank processes (such as credit card administration) rather than on the firm level. Figure 4.5 confirms this view. There seems to be no correlation between total assets and the cost–income ratio. What can be observed though is that with increasing

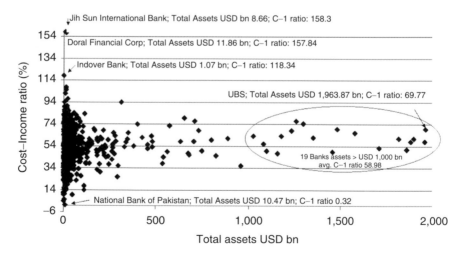

Figure 4.5. Impact of total assets on cost–income ratios (annual reports; The Banker 2007)

size, the cost–income ratio variance diminishes, probably due to positive portfolio effects.

A focus on processes rather than firms indicates that small financial services firms have strategic options to generate scale economies by deconstructing value chain activities and bundling demand for process capacity through strategic alliances and smart outsourcing strategies. Overall, Llewellyn[51] concluded that small- and medium-sized firms have a chance to survive in the long term if they have a credible business strategy based on a sound analysis of core competences and an effective sourcing strategy—with all the consequences that this might have on the organizational structure.

5

Where to compete? The logic behind market selection

The previous chapter discussed the main benefits and costs of going abroad without distinguishing what markets to choose. Many of the benefit and cost dimensions mentioned there address no single market but increased international scale in general. However, some dimensions like liabilities of foreignness and newness or the possibilities of arbitrage and the exploitation of firm-specific assets are country-specific. The goal of this chapter is therefore to advance some of the arguments presented in Chapter 4 and develop a heuristic model that supports managers when choosing their next target market.

Executives frequently view market selection as a relatively simple task: 'A bank is a "leveraged" play on the underlying economy; therefore, the key challenge is to select the better performing economies and to attract the most valuable clients in our chosen economies.'[1] This quote indicates that the profitability in overseas markets depends on the long-term attractiveness of the single country and the potential competitive advantage a foreign firm can develop in this country. In other words, financial institutions choose foreign markets based on two items:

- Their inherent attractiveness: the structure of the market that leads to a certain level of profitability as well as the potential future possibilities for any new entrant.

- Their penetrability: the potential ability of a specific firm to use its strengths to gain market share in this specific geographical segment.

A commonly found approach to market selection is a three-step process: (*a*) identify a country based on its attractiveness, (*b*) conduct in-depth research, and (*c*) decide whether to enter the market. Initial identification is often based on accidental elements such as language proficiency, cultural understanding of top management team members, the availability of an acquisition target, or the last holiday trip of the president of the board. But successful organizations undertake systematic quantitative analysis on the attractiveness and penetrability of potential world markets and distinguish three market selection processes: screening, identification, and final selection.

The first step consists of a cost-effective method of screening potential markets based on macro-level indicators to eliminate countries that do not meet the firm's long-term vision and objectives.[2] The result of the market screening phase is a short-list of the most attractive countries—between three and five. Normally, the screening process uses secondary data on market attractiveness. As a second step, the short-listed markets have to be explored in detail. An assessment of the industry attractiveness and forecasts of potential benefits and costs of market entry are the objectives. The competitive intelligence methods of this phase move towards more costly processes like the generation of first-hand onshore experiences. The market choice stage determines the country market(s) that best match the company's objectives and available resource leverages.

Market selection and market entry mode choices often coincide and are hard to separate and as such are often treated as one decision.[3] Once a country has been selected for entry, it automatically has to be compared to the existing portfolio of geographical presence. Most financial services firms use portfolio matrices as a basis for their geographical investment decisions that measure the relative strengths of own operations and the attractiveness of foreign markets. This chapter describes those two factors, the usefulness of portfolio matrices and then discusses process aspects of market selection, that is, how management teams actually collect data on foreign markets and set investment priorities.

Assessing Market Attractiveness

According to the US Department of State,[4] there are 223 sovereign countries in the world[5] as of 27 November 2007. Even if a management team deliberately reduces choice and focuses just on the largest 72 economies, which make up 97 per cent of the world's GDP and 88 per cent of the world's population,[6] the number of potentially attractive markets still remains high. Reducing choice by clustering countries into regions is hazardous as well. Despite attempts to harmonize financial services markets in Europe and throughout the globe, national markets differ substantially from each other. Just consider the structure of branch networks. In Germany, for example, 1 million inhabitants were served by 494 banking branches in 2003 whereas in the UK 234 branches sufficed. The United States with 287 branches per million inhabitants and Japan with 317 were in a similar range. Even though Germany has many more branches, it still has the highest number of employees per branch with 12, followed by the UK with 10. The asset growth rate in emerging

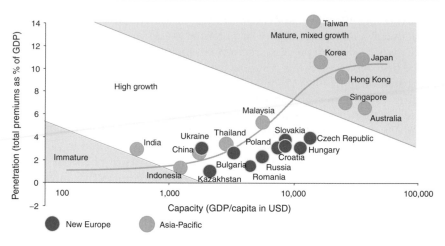

Figure 5.1. Assessment of market attractiveness, Allianz SE (Zedelius 2007: 4)

countries is more than double that of developed economies. While in some CEE markets clients with assets of EUR 10,000 get access to private banking services, in other markets (such as Switzerland) clients have to have of assets exceeding EUR 1 million to be considered wealthy. Therefore, detecting and understanding differences like these is the basis for a sound selection of target markets.

There are no clear-cut rules to assess the attractiveness of foreign markets. Many firms construct matrices around market size, market growth, profit margin of existing players, or general macro-economic elements that attempt to assess the development stage of a single country. Figure 5.1 shows an example of such a map.

Such maps build the basis for market selection and entry decisions. Interestingly, it seems that with a GDP per capita of around USD 7,000, the penetration of the market with insurance products starts to increase exponentially. Also, it appears possible to forecast market development since the countries seem to follow a systematic pattern depicted by an S-curve. Segmentation is not a science but an art, and consequently there are many ways to cluster countries to discuss attractiveness and market entry timing. Since financial services are among the most regulated markets, the institutional frameworks strongly impact the attractiveness of markets.

The Role of Institutional Frameworks and Governments

Governments have a strong impact on the international expansion plans of firms—especially in the financial services industry. In Poland for example, the government fiercely opposed UniCredit's plans to merge its Polish bank with a rival bank owned by HVB (Bank BPH) and approved the merger only after UniCredit agreed to sell 200 of the 480 branches as well as the name of the acquired bank in an international auction. The local government argued that, in creating the largest bank in Poland, the merger would cost too many jobs and banking would become less competitive. A condition of the deal was that Poland should change its banking law to allow for BPH to be split—a law which the Parliament had little time to decide. Finally, the legislation was rushed through the Parliament and the Senate at the last minute and signed by Lech Kaczynski, Poland's president, just a few hours before the expiry of the deadline in the UniCredit agreement. In return, UniCredit agreed to create a separate market division for Poland that would report directly to headquarters in Milan. This is just a short episode that shows how important regulations and the government are for financial services firms.

Governments are aware of the fact that good financial systems are an essential ingredient for sustainable economic growth and prosperity. In developing countries, the participation of foreign banks can contribute to the development of a more efficient and stable financial system. Many governments therefore facilitate the entry of foreign banks through accelerated and liberal privatization of state banks and insurance companies and access to financial services licences.

However, there are not only positive effects of foreign bank entry on the local economic system. Tighter entry requirements are sometimes negatively linked with bank efficiency and can lead to higher interest rate margins as well as overhead expenditures.[7] Consequently, some governments aim to control the process of liberalizing the entry of foreign financial services firms more strictly. The challenge for governments is to specify and evaluate the effects of the entry of foreign banks on domestic banks and the financial services system on a case-by-case basis. Extensive empirical research has studied the effects (i.e. quality and availability of banking services, efficiency of production of services, degree of innovation) of foreign bank entry and has created a consensus around the proposition that increased competition leads to higher efficiency of the banking system.[8] Relatively less work has been done on the negative effects on certain customer groups and local banks. Foreign banks, for example, tend to cherry-pick their customers and thus do not engage in significant lending activities for small firms,[9] which can hamper economic growth. Small firms are the growth engine in developing countries, and domestic banks can be exposed to increased lending risks. Bank concentration seems to have a negative and significant effect on the efficiency of the banking system in emerging countries, but in rich and developed economies with well-developed financial systems and economic freedoms, bank concentration can have positive effects for local firms, customers, and other stakeholders.[10]

The Appeal of Emerging Markets versus Economically Developed Markets

Despite the often difficult regulatory environments, doing business in emerging markets has been attractive to many financial services firms for several decades. However, reaping high returns from presence in emerging countries is challenging. Citigroup opened its first branch in Shanghai in 1902, making it the first American bank in Asia. Soon, branches in Manila, Yokohama, Singapore, Hong Kong, Calcutta, and Panama City followed. The financing of large infrastructure projects such as railway networks or the Panama Canal often drove international business, but many setbacks had to be absorbed. In China, for example, Citigroup had to close its branches twice; first in 1941 with some branches reopening four years later, only to be closed again in 1950. Similar experiences were found in Hong Kong, India, Indonesia, Spain, Malaysia, and Russia.

Nevertheless, many Continental European banks are increasingly looking at market entry strategies in emerging non-European economies. Acquisitions that were announced and completed in 2007 are numerous and include most major European players and many emerging countries—not just the BRICS (Brazil, Russian Federation, India, China, and South Africa) areas. Société Générale, for example, is among others active in the emerging markets of Croatia, Russia, Brazil, India, Slovenia, Montenegro, Georgia, and Algeria. Growth does not just come from acquisitions but also from organic development. In 2006, Société Générale opened a total of 399 new branches in the markets of Romania, Russia, Morocco, and Serbia. In addition, they launched new activities in Kazakhstan, Bulgaria, Cyprus, and Slovakia, mostly to grow their consumer credit business.

Allianz is another case of a financial services firm that invests substantially in emerging economies. In Pakistan, Allianz AG formed a joint venture with EFU General Group to found Allianz EFU in 2000 as Pakistan's first health insurer with a majority shareholding of Allianz AG. EFU General Insurance Company Ltd. is a Pakistan-based company engaged in general insurance business comprising fire and property, marine, and motor. The company operates through 57 branches in Pakistan and one branch in Jeddah, Saudi Arabia. It has four business segments: fire and property, marine, motor, and miscellaneous. Through the joint venture, Allianz EFU is market leader in the Pakistan health insurance market with a 35 per cent market share, covering both life and non-life risks. Its core business in Pakistan is to manage a full health care programme for families and employees. In Africa, Allianz is represented by its company subsidiary, AGF Afrique, which had EUR 70.5 million in turnover in 2005 and EUR 1.605 billion in asset management. Its affiliates in Africa include Benin, Burkina Faso, Togo, Central African Republic, Cameroon, Côte d'Ivoire, Madagascar, Mali, and Senegal. Allianz is represented in Africa by Allianz Insurance Limited, a locally licensed short-term insurer and a wholly owned affiliate of the Allianz Group. Further activities of Allianz AG in emerging markets are carried out in Bermuda, Brunei, Indonesia, Cyprus, Kazakhstan, and Sri Lanka.

The French AXA Group also aggressively invests in emerging countries. In 2004 the AXA Group created the 'Mediterranean' region including, among others, subsidiaries operating in Turkey, Morocco, and Lebanon. Moreover, investments were put not only into joint ventures with banking partners in the Philippines and Thailand but also into a joint venture with Bank Mandiri, Indonesia's largest bank. In 2005, AXA exited its insurance business in Uruguay while reinforcing its position in the Middle East by creating AXA Gulf (Qatar, Bahrain, Oman, Saudi Arabia, and the United Arab Emirates), operating in life, property/casualty, and asset management markets. The AXA Group is represented in emerging markets in Africa including Cameroon, Gabon, Ivory Coast, Morocco, and Senegal. In Asia, China, Hong Kong, India, Indonesia, Malaysia, Singapore, and Taiwan are targeted. Finally, AXA Asia Pacific Holdings recently acquired MLC Hong Kong and MLC Indonesia.

The CEE remains highly attractive for banks, first and foremost for market-seeking reasons, but importance is increasingly given to those markets as places for new talent and resources. The CEE economies grow on average three times faster than the eurozone and consequently banks grow three times faster than the CEE economies. In 2005, the balance-sheet total of all banks in the CEE increased by almost one-third. The total assets of the banking systems grow at a rate of over 20 per cent in countries such as Bulgaria, Ukraine, or Slovakia, but even if this pace is maintained, it will still take decades for these countries to reach assets/inhabitant figures similar to the eurozone.

This clearly indicates that there is sustainable potential for growth in the CEE, with a growing middle class and rising incomes. Innovative banking products are established in retail as well as corporate banking: credit cards, leasing contracts, mortgage loans, and investment funds. Margins of those products are often higher in developed CEE countries (such as Poland) than in Western European countries. At the end of 2005, international banks controlled about two-thirds of the banking assets in 'established' markets with a market share of around 78 per cent (excluding Russia, Turkey, and Ukraine). Banks like UniCredit or Erste Bank consider the CEE area to be a 'second home market' and contribute significantly to the further development of the banking system in these markets. In most of the CEE countries, the major banks have been privatized and growth through acquisitions is becoming increasingly difficult and expensive. The dominant position of UniCredit makes it difficult to find additional targets. Furthermore, price-to-book value have more than doubled since the first acquisitions occurred. The Hungarian bank OTP paid a price-to-book value of 4.9× for DSK Bank in 2003, whereas the price-to-book value of most large banks lies between 1.5× and 2×. The race for emerging markets long ago became a crowded competition and the price that foreign banks are willing to pay for targets in emerging markets is fast converging towards a pain barrier that will stop future aggressive moves.

These short illustrations show that the attractiveness of emerging markets depends on many factors that are linked to the market structure such as the intensity of competition, the expected changes in the legal framework, the development of demand for financial services products, or the plain availability of acquisition targets. Different product sub-segments have a different inherent attractiveness and require distinct investment decisions. Many financial services firms intensified their engagement in emerging markets, but the opposite is happening too: financial services firms from emerging countries have started to invest in international markets—a phenomenon labelled here as 'inverse internationalization'.

Inverse Internationalization

India's Tata Group won a competitive bid for the British luxury car brand Jaguar while introducing a home-made car for EUR 1,800. Its co-national Mittal bought a 20 per cent stake in the soccer club Queen's Park Rangers. ICBC bought a 20 per cent stake in South African Standard Bank. These are only a few examples of recent 'inverse' internationalization moves. Increasingly, institutions from developing countries are also growing across national borders and buying stakes in the world's most prestigious firms. Financial services firms are no exception, as shown by the recent USD 5 billion deal of China Investment Corporation (CIC) with Morgan Stanley. CIC, the Chinese state investment company, was set up in September 2007 with an initial capital of USD 200 billion from the country's enormous foreign exchange reserves. The initial investment strategy of CIC was to use around one-third of the funds to buy Huijin Investment Co., an investment vehicle of the Chinese government. Another third of the capital would be used to restructure shareholdings of some of the state-owned banks. The remaining USD 70 billion is allocated to a wide range of overseas investments.

The global credit crisis at the end of 2007 opened many sealed doors for mostly passive investors from emerging economies, as shown by the substantial capital injections into UBS and Citigroup by state funds of Singapore and Abu Dhabi. However, the CIC–Morgan Stanley transaction may be of more strategic importance. The investment in Morgan Stanley allows CIC to reveal 9.9 per cent of the American investment bank by August 2010. On the other hand, this transaction secures Morgan Stanley direct access to China's fast growing capital markets and the local governments that regulate them. Morgan Stanley is even in possession of a mainland commercial banking licence—which usually takes several years for a foreign bank to obtain—through its recent 100 per cent acquisition of the small Nan

Tung Bank. This licence allows Morgan Stanley to offer commercial banking products denominated in the local currency.

The phenomenon of inverse internationalization happens quickly and forces financial services firms from economically developed countries not only to constantly search for sources of competitive advantages to defend their home markets but also to carefully select the foreign markets they aim at. The times in which financial services firms could easily find countries with lucrative takeover targets and a free avenue to increased market share are gone. As a result, market selection and the subsequent definition of entry strategies have to be addressed in a more careful way.

Assessing Market Penetrability

Besides the inherent attractiveness of geographical markets, the market penetrability influences the entry decision of financial services firms. 'Given that the market is attractive, can we use our specific resource and capability endowment to penetrate the market?' is the main question to be addressed. Management teams try to understand at this point whether there are ownership advantages (e.g. superior process capabilities, strong brand, and specific expertise) that can outweigh the liabilities of foreignness and newness as well as the coordination costs described in the previous chapter.

Many executives consider cultural differences to be crucial in the market selection process. They acknowledge that many aspects of business success depend on cultural fit. Before entering a country, financial services firms should therefore assess whether their managers are able to deal with multiple ethnic groups with very different cultures. It is important to recognize that people from different cultures are different in a variety of ways: how they dress, look at things, interact, and in their values and general assumptions about life.

Besides cultural aspects, financial services firms need to assess their ability to transfer their ownership advantages to foreign markets. When Erste Bank entered the Central Eastern European markets, they carefully analysed in which markets they could contribute with superior resources or processes to local markets. A central issue of concern in this analysis is the value of the foreign brand. Erste Bank's brand transformation was made on a thorough empirical analysis of brand recognition in different local markets. Only after a thorough analysis of the strengths of the existing local brand did the integration teams decide to modify the brand on a case-by-case basis. Brands with local value, for example in the Czech Republic, were kept in the portfolio. Although the savings banks symbol (a red 'S') had to be licensed from the German savings banks association, it is a key element that links the various brands together.

Furthermore, cross-border integration allowed Erste Bank to standardize its products. Since new products are generated out of the daily business of the decentralized units, Erste Bank disposes of a fairly large product portfolio. However, since customer needs in different regions are quite similar, and since customers do not request a large range of products, there is room for standardization that would reduce the bank's costs substantially. The expensive part of a new product is developing IT processes around product management.

Through cross-border collaboration in areas such as marketing, IT, production, training, and of course the cross-guarantee system which came into effect in January 2002, Erste Bank has increased the performance of the decentralized units. Its customers have the choice between various distribution channels, from expert advice at its branches to its Net-banking and Net-trading platforms. In this way, customers enjoy 24-hour access to Erste Bank's vast range of services. The distribution channels are being continuously upgraded and seamlessly integrated in the overall portfolio. Erste Bank's multi-channel marketing will cut the administrative workload for branch staff, thus adding valuable capacities for needs-based customer advisory and support.

However, there is consensus inside the bank that there are natural barriers to Erste Bank's internationalization process. The home market consists of two main markets with differing structures. Apart from the mature and stable Austrian market, the bank focuses on Central Europe with its attractive growth prospects. Erste Bank's Central European Extended Home Market comprises the Czech Republic, the Slovak Republic, Hungary, Croatia, and Slovenia. Due to the overall scarcity of modern banking products, when compared to the European Union, these markets present enormous growth potential. Erste Bank focuses on candidates for accession to the European Union because the expected rise in income levels will likely generate increased demand for banking products.

The management of Erste Bank is developing those markets instead of aiming at penetrating other European countries or more exotic markets such as India or China. On the contrary, international businesses (i.e. markets outside the extended home market) are of limited strategic importance and have been subsequently downsized. The network of offices established in Mexico City, Santiago, Sydney, Singapore, and Madrid was closed after the IPO in 1997. Only the branches in New York, London, and Hong Kong were kept open and run out of Vienna with the strategic objective of running niche businesses such as participating in syndicated credit markets or aircraft financing.

Erste Bank's market choices were probably made based on just a few factors: they believed in the emergence of the CEE as an economic area and they chose markets where governments allowed for full ownership, interesting acquisition targets were available, and they already had some market knowledge. The detailed analysis related to the transfer of ownership advantages to those markets was made only after the entry happened.

The Pitfalls of Portfolio Strategies

The analysis of single dimensions of market attractiveness and penetrability helps to develop a gut feeling on which markets would be the most interesting ones. Portfolio matrices are often used to formalize market selection decisions and to set investment priorities. This section discusses the usefulness of such portfolio matrices and the pitfalls that may come with them.

The BCG Matrix

The Boston Consulting Group's (BCG) matrix and modified portfolio planning tools have for a long period of time occupied a fundamental position in corporate planning departments as well as in business school courses. With this section, we attempt to show that the BCG matrix has a number of flaws and its application is rather problematic. Firms should therefore construct their own portfolio matrices and use them as a learning tool rather than an expert system that automatically generates investment strategies.

The BCG growth share matrix is one of the best known and persistent tools in strategic management. This matrix measures market attractiveness by just one measure, that is, 'market growth', and market penetrability by another single item, that is, relative market share. Although the GE-McKinsey matrix modified the matrix by including several other dimensions to assess attractiveness and relative strength (or penetrability), the major critique of the BCG matrix applies also to younger portfolio management tools. At the height of its success between 1972 and 1982, the BCG matrix was used by around 45 per cent of the Fortune 500.[11] The JSTOR database reports that no fewer than six major journal articles were authored on the BCG matrix in 1982. However, in the first decade of the twenty-first century, the BCG matrix is certainly in the decline phase of its product life cycle, perhaps qualifying for 'dog' status in its own terminology. References to the BCG matrix have disappeared from graduate textbooks and academic journals, and are slowly being phased out of undergraduate and marketing texts except, perhaps, as historical footnotes.

There are several sound reasons for this decline, including the model's use of only two dimensions (growth and share) to assess competitive position, the focus on balancing cash flows rather than other interdependencies, the emphasis on cost leadership rather than differentiation as a source of competitive advantage, and the poor correlation between market share and profitability.[12] Despite the numerous theoretical critiques of the BCG model, empirical studies that directly examine whether the BCG matrix delivers superior profitability as a portfolio management system are surprisingly scarce.[13] In fact, Armstrong and Brodie[14] report that they could find only one empirical study prior to their own that directly tested whether firms adopting the BCG

129

matrix outperformed those that did not. Furthermore, while 66 per cent of students familiar with the BCG matrix thought it would produce better decisions under certain circumstances, the same students were unable to describe any such circumstances. This is not surprising given that such studies do not exist.

The BCG matrix explicitly recognizes that a diversified company is a portfolio of businesses, each of which should make a distinct contribution to the overall corporate performance and should be managed accordingly.[15] Portfolio planning has its roots in the late 1960s as firms started to become larger and more diversified. Corporate headquarters were created with the aim to add value to their collection of businesses by allocating funds, creating synergies, or directly influencing their activities. A central concern of corporate managers was to allocate funds in a strategic way and thereby to ensure that the company balances the cash needs of its business units. Alternative resource allocation methods such as basing investment decisions on track records or the complex prediction of discounted project cash flows did not seem to entirely satisfy corporate managers. The BCG matrix on the other hand helps to allocate limited resources based on one single graph. As such, it serves as a simplifier that links a market dimension (i.e. market growth) to a company dimension (i.e. relative market share).

A central assumption underlying the BCG matrix is that growth (of markets or share) has to be prioritized due to experience curve effects since relative market share is a good proxy indicator for the relative profit performance as well as cash needs. The positive impact of market share on firm profitability has been empirically demonstrated in the PIMS studies.[16] Because all competitors in a given business will tend to enjoy similar price levels for their products, lower costs than competition will therefore result in superior performance. The market share is expressed in relation to the biggest competitor as an indicator for market share dominance which would invert cash needs. Market growth as the second axis of the BCG matrix has a substantial effect on the cash needs of a business unit. Growing businesses require cash for fixed assets, working capital, and similar investments that ensure that the firm can keep or extend its market share position, even though market share can be acquired at lower cost during high growth phases.[17]

The positioning of all businesses according to their relative market share and their market growth results in a one-spot representation of the business portfolio. The goal of management should be to have a balanced portfolio to ensure an optimization of the cash streams and with them the overall performance of the company. Hence, the sustainable growth rate of a company is seen as a function of its portfolio of cash-generating businesses and cash-using businesses. The experience curve effect explains why high market share businesses generate more cash than they can meaningfully redeploy and therefore create opportunities for new businesses in growing markets. The BCG claim was that the four different business categories in the different squares of the matrix have indeed different tendencies to generate or consume cash and therefore need to be treated accordingly:

- 'Question Mark' businesses (high growth and low relative market share) have high cash needs and firms should therefore do whatever is necessary to increase market share or divest quickly.

- 'Star' businesses (high growth and high relative market share) are frequently roughly in balance on net cash flow and may exceptionally need more cash than what is generated by their own business. The main focus of star businesses is to protect the market share, hence to get a bigger portion of the market growth than their competitors. Star businesses will ultimately turn into cash cows, assuming that markets cannot grow for ever or become dogs if they fail to protect the market share.

- 'Cash Cow' businesses (low growth and high relative market share) are characterized by high profit and cash generation. The remaining cash after covering costs to run the business and to protect the share in a mature market should be redistributed to other businesses.

- 'Dog' businesses (low growth and low relative market share) often generate poor profits and cash needs are frequently higher than the cash that is generated. To improve the overall performance, firms should minimize the proportion of their assets that remain in this category by focusing on a specialized segment, harvesting by cutting costs, and maximizing cash flow by divestment or liquidation.

The apparent simplicity of having reduced a complex decision problem to a two-dimensional matrix was of intuitive appeal. The central assumption was based on academic research (i.e. the PIMS study) and managers located in corporate headquarters were able to show their value added for their businesses. The proliferation of portfolio planning as a resource allocation tool was accelerated by the BCG consultants and their competitors like McKinsey and Arthur D. Little who developed similar matrices together with their clients. The intense academic critiques presented in the next section did not slow down the rapid spread of the new management fashion.

The assumptions and decision rules proposed by the BCG matrix have been criticized from three main angles: measurement issues, pitfalls in the assumptions, and the feasibility of strategies.[18] When using the BCG matrix as a decision support, probably the most instant difficulty a management team faces is measurement issues. Both axes, relative market share and market growth, depend on managers' subjective interpretation of what the relevant market is. Broad versus narrow definitions of markets reflect different views on the long-term development of the business. In numerous markets, it is difficult to gather data about the total market size, its growth rate, and the share of the biggest competitor, not to mention the measurement and forecasting of product life cycles. The impact of re-launches and face-lifts on product life cycles is highly uncertain and further complicates growth rate predictions. The measurement problems may lead to different recommendations for the same situation.[19]

Critiques around the BCG assumptions address two main arguments: the impact of market share on profit and more precisely the cost position of the firm and the nature of the business life cycle and its influence on the cash needs of a business unit. Day[20] argues that the BCG approach emphasizes the relative profitability in comparison to competition while absolute profitability should be the more important consideration. Christensen et al.[21] state that a low-cost position is not necessarily based on a high market share. The assumption that all competitors have the same experience curves and therefore market share dominance can be used as a proxy for the relative profit performance has several flaws. The correlation of ROI with market share is much less than 100 per cent and varies across markets: experience does not guarantee cost advantage, neither does scale.[22] Experience curves vary across industries and across competitors and it is sometimes difficult to keep experiences proprietary. Furthermore, differences in price levels due to differentiation advantages are not considered to have a substantial impact on profit. The claim that all competitors manage to achieve similar prices for their products and services may be true for mature (commodity) markets but certainly does not hold for growing markets.

Moreover, the feasibility of the normative strategies proposed by the BCG matrix has been criticized. Business units may not be the right level of aggregation and some companies take the single investment project instead of entire geographical segments as units of analysis. If the corporate level has allocated a certain amount of money to a single business unit, the problem of allocating the money to single projects still remains.[23] Another major implementation problem is the difficulty one faces to unequivocally operationalize strategic guidelines such as 'milk for cash', 'harvest', or 'selectively invest'. Although intuitively appealing, those normative strategies need to be contextualized and refined.

In particular, the strategies for dog businesses have been criticized.[24] The BCG logic implies that firms have the ability to shift resources from one business to another. Sometimes it might be costly to liquidate or divest a dog business. Barriers to exit due to legal or political constraints may complicate the implementation of the BCG guidelines. In addition, divesting a dog business might negatively affect other businesses if strong interrelationships exist. Christensen et al. argue that one aspect of strategy is to choose the competitors carefully, and '... dying dogs and sleeping cows may well be attractive competitors'.[25] This assertion seems to be well supported by the many strategic moves of Richard Branson's Virgin Group to challenge the big players in mature industries such as the soft drinks market.

Another reason why dog businesses may be kept in the portfolio comes from the shareholders' attitude towards risk: the desire to reduce vulnerability is a possible reason for keeping, or even acquiring, a 'dog'.[26] It might make sense to keep dog businesses that provide modest returns but do not increase the exposure of the company to additional risk generated by entry into new markets. That may be the reason why Morrison and Wensley refer to the low share–low growth box as 'pets' (instead of 'dogs') which are 'nice to have' because they deliver a constant, though modest, drain of funds or small contributions.[27]

Construct Your Own Portfolio Matrix

Although the critique of the BCG matrix is well grounded in theoretical and empirical research, we believe that the portfolio methodology can and should be customized to meet the individual market circumstances of the users instead of rejecting it as a decision aid. Management teams should discuss the two dimensions of the matrix (market attractiveness vs. market penetrability) and use the newly constructed matrix as a learning vehicle in strategic planning processes instead of a deterministic expert system. Figure 5.2 shows an attempt to bring market and company factors together in one matrix and to assign generic strategies for each quadrant.

The matrix has to be constructed by taking into account the firm's specific situation and industry specificity. Hence, key decision-makers have to be

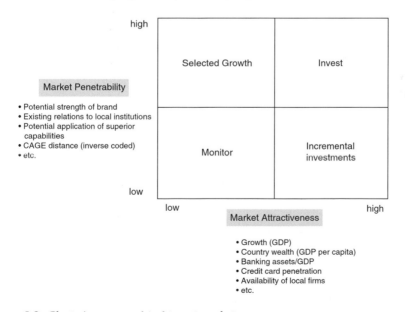

Figure 5.2. Clustering geographical target markets

133

involved when designing the matrix. A uniform model will not suffice. For an insurance company, for example, industry attractiveness may be measured by total market volume of insurance premiums, market growth, or the regulatory environment for a specific product category. Allianz SE may use 'penetration' and 'capacity' to assess market attractiveness. 'Capacity' of each country is measured by its GDP per capita in US dollars. 'Penetration' levels represent total premiums as a percentage of the countries' specific GDP. Other financial services firms may come up with different portfolio models. The result of the portfolio exercise is that countries can be clustered regarding their attractiveness as well as the firm's potential to penetrate them and that each cluster gets a different underlying investment strategy. But this analysis is only valuable if based on sound data. How to collect market data is the subject of the next section.

Competitive Intelligence

Competitive intelligence processes help firms to select appropriate markets by providing in-depth data on a narrow set of potential target markets. Internationalization strategies of financial services firms are often not characterized by success. One reason for difficulties is that markets often have not been selected carefully or/and the timing was not appropriate. BBVA and Banca Intesa Sanpaolo in Latin American markets are examples of unfortunate market selection. In 2000, the home markets of BBVA (at that time BBV) and Intesa Sanpaolo (then Banca Intesa) were saturated and highly competitive. Latin American markets promised cheap acquisition targets in rapidly developing economies, and therefore new streams of revenues due to privatization and deregulation of financial markets during the 1990s. Among the most important motives for market entry were the following:

- *Asset seeking*: The Latin American markets seemed to offer cheap options for quick growth through acquisitions. The target firms seemed to be attractive also due to familiarity with the region through already-existing representative offices and a commonality (or affinity in the case of Intesa) of language and culture. However, the integration of the acquired firms proved in many cases to be more hazardous than expected.

- *Asset exploitation*: The banks believed that they could introduce efficiencies through relevant skills and experience, obtained by going through the transition from non-competitive to highly competitive markets in their home markets (maybe less applicable for Intesa). With these experiences, BBVA and Intesa tried to follow an asset exploitation strategy because they believed they could improve the cost/income ratios of targets through improved cash flow management and other associated policies. This worked out only partly.

- *Herding*: For BBVA, the choice of Latin America can be described as an oligopolistic reaction to the location choices of its local rival, Santander.[28] To copy what others do by definition does not lead to a competitive advantage and is therefore a strategy of questionable value added.

Nevertheless, the two banks decided to build market power and develop their brands in these markets. These moves should help, in a first phase, to finance international trade, to service home country customers, and to finance local governments. Asian countries did not allow foreign companies to acquire local commercial banks and therefore seemed to be less attractive.

2000 was a successful year for BBVA (with a ROE of 21.1 per cent compared to 13.7 per cent in 2002) and Intesa (with a ROE of 13.8 per cent compared to 1.6 per cent in 2002). The Argentine economic crisis, which started in 1999 and lasted until 2002, caused an economic downturn and compelled companies to undertake better risk assessment. Banks were not able to foresee the implosion of Argentina's fixed exchange rate system; they did not take the risk of default seriously and were not expecting to bear the full costs of devaluation.[29] The Argentinian Currency Board secured low financial volatility in good times but during the crisis high real volatility was inevitable. In addition to the Argentinian economic crisis, the slowdown in US economic growth and instability generated by the elections in Brazil, which raised the country's risk level, caused a strong depreciation of Latin American currencies. Additionally, signs of economic stagnation and a decline of foreign direct investments influenced the depreciation of Latin American currencies against the Euro. In 2002, the Argentinian Peso lost 75.1 per cent against the Euro, the Venezuelan Bolivar lost 53.5 per cent, and the Brazilian Real lost 44.8 per cent. This caused a reduction of the investment flow of BBVA due to increased risk aversion. Nevertheless, BBVA is still present in South America today and showed a 35 per cent increase in operating profits in 2006 compared to 2005.

For Banca Intesa, the retreat from the South American markets was even more painful. In August 2003, Intesa sold its Uruguayan banking operations for USD 1 to the local unit of France's Credit Agricole. In December 2003, Banca Intesa sold its Brazilian unit, Banco Sudameris Brasil, to the Dutch bank ABN AMRO in order to concentrate on its Italian business and complete a total exit from Latin America.

The resulting losses for Banca Intesa were substantial. In 1999, Intesa denoted a net income drop of ITL 656 billion (–26.7 per cent) and an ITL 2,303 billion decrease in the operating margin, which resulted in a –8 per cent growth rate of operating income. This profitability drop was attributed largely to reorganization projects of acquired banking groups in Latin America.

These brief examples show that market selection needs to balance the temptation of large profits with the ability to predict when a country might encounter economic difficulties. These examples also show that, like many other strategic decisions, firms do not always select markets based on a clear rationale and analytical method but on personal beliefs, preferences, past experiences, and networks.[30] Consequently, a more systematic approach to market selection is imperative.

To improve the quality of market selection strategies, firms need to engage in a process of competitive intelligence. The more managers know about a potential market, the more likely it is that a market entry strategy will be successful. The Society of Competitive Intelligence Professionals (SCIP) describes competitive intelligence (CI) as 'a necessary, ethical business discipline for decision making based on understanding the competitive environment . . . '[31] Competitive intelligence processes support the identification, evaluation, and selection of foreign business opportunities with the objective to make those decisions with less guidance from intuition or instinct. Sound market data allow firms to compare foreign market conditions with the home market and detect key differences in the CAGE (cultural, administrative, geographical, and economic) dimensions. Needless to say, the bigger the differences are, the more important data collection is. Firms are often more reluctant to conduct international market research in foreign countries than they are on their home turf, for many reasons: managers are unfamiliar with data sources in other countries; they look at internationalization as an experiment and engage in 'learning by doing' planning approaches; they have an opportunistic approach to international markets built on unsolicited customer requests; or they believe that the world is flat and cross-border differences do not matter.

Market intelligence is a process of enhancing the competitiveness of a firm through the systematic gathering and analysis of data on the general market environment for the purposes of improving the robustness of strategic decisions. Often, the focus of research activities is on competitors and the data collection process is then called competitive intelligence. The goal is to anticipate the reactions of competitors to the market entry moves and to avoid strategies that can be nullified easily by competitors.[32] A market intelligence process can be split into five fundamental steps: planning, gathering, analysis, distribution, and the application to strategic decisions.

Planning

This first step is to identify the major strategic decisions that need to be made in the future. Data gathering has to be directed towards a specific purpose if it is to be efficient. Beyond the pure selection of markets, what are the decisions that a firm has to make when entering a foreign market that commit substantial resources, have a long-term impact on the future development of the firm, and are hard to reverse? Clearly listing the strategic issues at hand improves the market intelligence process substantially. For example, if one knows that the market selection and entry strategy greatly depend on the value of the foreign brand name, market analysis can be focused on that point. Managers (especially international sales directors) are often frustrated about their involvement in market intelligence processes because they feel that they contribute with substantial efforts to the process but rarely see an outcome. This first step of identifying the data needs is therefore crucial.

The financial services industry is not R&D intensive and intellectual property rights today cannot effectively protect innovative products or business processes. Competitive intelligence processes are therefore not necessarily product-related activities but rather supportive of other strategic questions. A Swiss bank, for example, engaged in CI to address an organizational issue: 'What is the appropriate size and role of the corporate headquarters?' The role of CI was to benchmark the organizational models of peers and other service segments to support the design of a new organizational architecture. An insurance company addressed another issue: 'Are we creating any advantage for our subsidiary in Mexico or can other firms create more value for it?' CI processes supported the identification of potential best owners and their strategies, and helped estimate the interest level of managers and shareholders of those firms as well as calculate potential synergies.

In summary, clear strategic issues should be the starting point of any competitive intelligence process. Complementary to a focused CI process are continuous efforts of market screening, that is, the periodical observation of selected relevant market data.

Gathering

After listing the major strategic issues such as the selection of target markets, sources of information have to be identified and classified (e.g. according to their level of reliability). Appropriate data collection methodologies need to be chosen (e.g. interviews, surveys, secondary data). Most of the interesting data can be found in a legal and ethical way, but many approaches are borderline cases. Is it legal and ethical to conduct phoney job interviews, pretending to look for a key position but in reality just spying on interested managers from competitors? What about quizzing customers and buyers about the sales of competitors' products, infiltrating customers' and competitors' business operations, quizzing competitors' former employees, interviewing consultants who may have worked with competitors, or buying competitors' paper garbage? Many of these activities are not ethical and some are even illegal. Spying in financial services plays a limited role since most services and processes are transparent. The market players are forced by the regulators and shareholders to disclose sensitive financial and business details. In what other industry can one find a 200-page strategy document on the web with many intimate facts on future business and corporate strategies? In specific instances, for example when internally discussing the final price of a bid for an acquisition, it is advisable to protect the M&A team from more sophisticated electronic spying methods such as wiretaps or electronic listening devices that contain a radio transmitter able to tap conversations. Such electronic devices are particularly efficient if meetings are held in external locations but they also find their way into most intimate boardrooms.

With the right equipment and access to information, even cellular phones that are turned off can be used to record meetings. By using the phone's tracking device, it is possible to activate the phone's microphone and thereby sneak into the most critical of business conversations. The only effective way to protect against such spying is to take the battery out of the phone. A phone battery suddenly using more power than usual or feeling warmer than normal can be indications that the phone is busy transmitting conversations to third parties. Another indication that something wrong is going on with a GSM cellular phone is that one can hear a continuous interference buzz when the phone gets too close to other audio equipment, even if it is turned off.

Similarly, it is easy to infiltrate answering machines, voice mail, instant messaging programs, fax, baby monitors, cordless microphones, or dictation machines. Cordless microphones, for instance, transmit clear audio signals from the distance of about a quarter of a mile. This means these should not be used for confidential meetings. Regular switching of long and difficult passwords is also advisable. Additionally, hidden MP3 players are able to record several days of conversation or fake smoke detectors can be equipped with a camera to illegally monitor action. PC monitors can be targeted as well. Specialized software programs are able to record a screenshot in a desired interval without being detected. This software can capture all activity performed on a PC, no matter who performs it. Electronic spying methods have become more and more sophisticated and easier, as well as cheaper, to receive.

Analysis

Unstructured data are of limited use for the firm. To organize data in tables, benchmark analysis, competitor profiles, segmentation analysis, or other industry analysis tools are crucial to increase the efficiency of the market intelligence process. The process of analysis turns information into intelligence. The former is factual and of little strategic value if not processed. Intelligence, on the other hand, is pieces of information that have been filtered, distilled, and analysed. Intelligence—or in other words 'knowledge'— is what managers need to make decisions.

Distribution

Ensuring that market knowledge is distributed to decision-makers is the third step in the CI process. Several formats can be used: from organizing dedicated CI presentations to creating Intranet forums and databases to sharing intelligence reports. Particularly effective in distributing information is assigning knowledge broker roles to managers for certain key competitive intelligence areas. This step is critical to the success of competitive intelligence. Many initiatives kick the bucket because data is gathered, mainly from the proper sales force, but they never receive a feedback on what has happened to their input.

Application to Strategic Decisions

Companies often develop strategies that are fairly detached from the analysis efforts. We all know that hundreds of PowerPoint slides do not make an effective strategy. Covering slides with a nicely formatted collection of bullet points does not of itself produce logical consistency. As a consequence, many strategy processes do not follow the simple logic proposed in Chapter 3: issue identification–analysis–solution–implementation–monitoring–control.

To tie analysis to strategic decision-making, first of all, firms have to make sure that decision-makers are actually minimally involved in the analysis efforts. If staff functions work completely detached from the decision-makers, the CI process will be of limited value. Firms must create appropriate strategic decision-making formats. Chapter 3 discussed how to design effective strategy processes and strategy workshops in particular. However, strategy workshops are not the only vehicles in which strategic decisions are made and formalized. On a functional level, market intelligence can be used to make the sales warm-up more realistic.

Corporate war gaming exercises are another active way of using market intelligence. Like in chess, the goal of corporate war games is to identify possible future competitive situations and deliberate strategic moves. A possible way to initiate such a process is to have a group of managers outline an intended strategy. Managers from the same company then form groups that simulate competitors or other key stakeholders. 'Competitors' are then given time to develop a counter-strategy and asked to present it to the first group, which has the task of revising the initial strategy as needed. A good chess player is able to think many moves and counter-moves ahead and consequently develops an idea about which strategy will lead to victory. Similarly, companies can develop robust strategies by stress-testing them in corporate war gaming exercises.

6

When to enter? The timing and speed of market entry

Once the target market has been selected, the right timing and speed for market expansion has to be identified. Financial services firms frequently face the trade-off between penetrating new countries quickly (speed) and entering the next country without consolidating the position in previously served countries (timing). Again, general advice is difficult to provide: as mentioned in Chapter 1, service characteristics such as the extent of digitization have a strong impact on timing and speed decisions. In other words, sometimes the early bird gets the worm, but the second mouse gets the cheese. Sometimes being first in a market pays off, but at times the superior strategy is to watch competitors make mistakes and enter later.

Most financial services firms exploit home market growth opportunities before they seriously invest in cross-border initiatives. Erste Bank, for example, only significantly invested in foreign markets when home market consolidation was difficult and unprofitable. After more than a century of contemplative development, Erste Bank successfully launched an aggressive geographical expansion strategy into CEE markets as a 'late mover' compared to its local competitor Bank Austria (now part of UniCredit Group) but as an 'early mover' compared to most other foreign banks.

An analyst statement in 1999 pointed out that the Erste Bank share was a call option on the EU enlargement. Most local CEE governments recognized early that they had to improve the efficiency of their banking system in this process and consequently started to privatize their banks with foreign investors as partners. Several CEE banking systems grow at a rate of over 20 per cent, but even if this pace can be maintained, it will take decades for these countries to reach assets/inhabitant figures similar to the Eurozone, indicating that there is sustainable potential for growth. This raises fundamental questions for international banks: should they first consolidate their CEE presence and consolidate national presence through organic growth, or quickly expand into other remote places? In other words, what should be their speed of internationalization?

At the end of 2005, international banks controlled about two-thirds of the banking assets in more advanced CEE economies with a market share of around 78 per cent (excluding Russia, Turkey, and Ukraine). Banks like UniCredit or Erste Bank consider the CEE area as a 'second home market' and contribute significantly to the development of the banking system in these markets. However, there are still a few markets that are less internationalized and consolidated. International banks in Turkey, for example, currently have a market share of only 19 per cent, and in Russia, only 9 per cent. The highest concentration of international banks is to be found in new EU member states, with Estonia leading the pack with a 99 per cent market share of foreign banks, followed by Slovakia with 98 per cent, and Croatia with 91 per cent. Will countries such as Russia or Turkey allow foreign banks to take up a dominating role? If yes, when will that most likely happen? These and other questions have to be addressed when deciding upon the timing and speed of internationalization.

Observing market development is critical when getting the timing right for successful internationalization but internal resource and capability conditions need to be considered as well. For the second-largest Italian bank, Banca Intesa, the rush towards the international markets of its peers seemed to come too early. In 2006, Intesa had not consolidated its IT platform and fully integrated the business processes of its operational banks in Italy. For Intesa, it seemed to be harder to export a successful and robust banking model to foreign markets. As a consequence, its international moves were less aggressive than its national rival UniCredit, especially since Intesa still had an attractive national merger project with Sanpaolo. Home market conditions, a dynamic view of the attractiveness and the penetrability of host markets as well as the resource and capability endowment of internationalizing firms need to be assessed when making market entry timing and speed decisions.

This chapter starts with a discussion on how financial services firms predict market development. The role of uncertainty and ambiguity and tools that attempt to reduce them are presented. Next, early and late mover advantages are discussed. We will see how firms that enter markets early try to protect their advantages through isolation mechanisms such as the creation of technological standards, the pre-emption of assets, and buyer switching costs. Late movers can take advantage of free riding, the early resolution of technological or market uncertainty, shifts in technology or customer needs, and incumbent inertia. This chapter concludes with a discussion of factors that typically lead to accelerated international expansion.

Creating Market Foresight

Forecasting techniques are relevant for all major strategic decisions during internationalization processes. To get market entry timing and speed decisions right, financial services firms' need to predict market development and develop market foresight[1] is particularly relevant. By expanding the awareness for the dynamics of emerging situations in foreign markets, companies can avoid risks and 'stress-test' strategies for market contingencies. Forecasting is, however, particularly helpful to get the timing and speed of market entry right. However, experience shows that many firms prefer alternatives to creating formal market outlooks:

- They rely on guru or oracle forecasting by believing in the opinion of just one expert;
- They glorify past successes and thereby develop a feeling of invulnerability;
- They engage in window-blind forecasting by developing foresight in a narrow area such as technology development without analysing other aspects like customer demand or regulatory changes.

The first step in creating market foresight is to recognize that strategic decisions are always made under conditions of uncertainty. Therefore, before choosing a forecasting methodology, it is advisable to understand the type of uncertainty facing a strategic decision.

Conditions of Uncertainty

Four levels of uncertainty can be distinguished:[2]

- In a 'clear-enough future', traditional strategy tools such as regression analysis may work because the past can be an adequate predictor for the future.
- On the next level of uncertainty, one may identify 'alternative futures', such as new government structures after an election. The strategy tools to apply are decision analysis, option valuation models, and game theory.
- Uncertainty level 3 consists of a 'range of futures', when trying to predict the oil price, for example. No obvious scenarios can be identified and therefore latent-demand research, technology forecasting, or scenario planning may be adequate strategy tools.
- Uncertainty level 4 is 'true ambiguity' where no basis for forecasting is possible, such as when deciding whether to enter the Russian market in 1992. In a situation of true ambiguity, the strategy tools that may

be applied are analogies, pattern recognition, or non-linear dynamic models.

After identifying the nature and extent of residual uncertainties, adequate strategy tools that best fit the amount of uncertainty should be chosen and applied. A more comprehensive strategy tool kit should therefore include scenario planning,[3] game theory,[4] system dynamics,[5] agent-based models,[6] and a real options approach.[7]

Which Strategy Models Really Work in Uncertain Environments?

Beinhocker,[8] in his article on the 'origins of strategy', suggests taking an evolutionary approach to mastering uncertainty. Strategy in an environment of true ambiguity may be seen as an 'evolutionary search' on a 'fitness landscape'[9] where the strategic goal becomes to create options and open up new choices rather than shut them down.[10] The survival motto for an uncertain world suggested by Beinhocker therefore reads as follows: invest in diversity, value strategies as if they were options, categorize the mix of strategies, stress-test your strategies, bring the market inside, and use venture–capital performance metrics.

Contrary to the indications of Beinhocker, an empirical study[11] analysing 113 public limited UK companies discovered that the most frequently used strategy tools are the simplest ones. Among the most often used strategic tools are first spreadsheet 'what if' analyses followed by analyses of 'key' or 'critical' success factors, financial analyses of competitors, SWOT analysis, and core capabilities analyses. More sophisticated methodologies like soft systems methodology were found in the last position of the ranking list.

What might be surprising is that although the environment gets increasingly complex, the strategic tools to cope with that complexity are the well established and, at first glance, simple ones. Option valuation, game theory, or models based on complexity theory do not seem to have a substantial impact on management practice (yet). The real option approach, for example, is not popular among management practitioners because academic discussion has so far revolved around 'arcane equations and models'[12] and has appeared to be too complex to be pragmatically applied to management issues. Even if the strategy tools are simple, the thinking processes taking place around the use of those tools is rather complex and, in the end, crucial for the creation of a successful strategy.

Reducing Uncertainty and Ambiguity

The second major issue that we regard as critical for the foresight process is the desire to reduce uncertainty and ambiguity. Uncertainty arises from perceived inaccuracy in estimates of future consequences conditional on present actions.[13] While predicting and forecasting the future are essential to the long-term survival of firms, predicting and forecasting are not sufficient in themselves, because the future is highly uncertain. Often, it is not possible to reduce uncertainty and ambiguity of situations, and firms need to learn how to respond to unpredictable events. However, uncertainty can often be reduced by applying the right forecasting methodology and ambiguity of situations can be reduced by a careful interpretation of the available data by the top management team. Ambiguity hints at the confusion created by the existence of several different interpretations of available data at the same time.[14] To reduce ambiguity, management teams should engage in strategic conversations.

In strategic conversations, data is interpreted and distinct meanings are then integrated into shared understanding. Winning strategies emerge from a decision process in which executives develop collective intuition, accelerate constructive conflict, maintain decision pacing, and avoid politics.[15] Deep conversations about the future of the firm play an essential role in an internationalization process. It is necessary that managers interpret data they gather about new markets. Interpreting is a process in which managers explain their opinion to their colleagues through words as well as actions.

Interpretation is facilitated by the use of metaphors, analogies, stories, or more assertive hypotheses and models. Excessive use of PowerPoint presentations often limits the capacity to truly understand the meaning of data at hand. 3M therefore decided to replace most of their PowerPoint presentations at strategy meetings with short strategic stories in Word documents.[16] It is rare that PowerPoint presentation with issues displayed in a bullet point format triggers deep thought or inspires commitment.

Throughout the interpretation process, words may help, but common experiences are central to the communication of intuition. Meaning is generated if managers look at what they have done and then try to make sense of these events. The clue may be to generate memorable strategic experiences that people remember and continue to discuss. Why did Steve Balmer of Microsoft start one of his presentations by screaming, shouting, and jumping for one minute in front of his audience? He created a memorable moment and definitely captured the attention of his spectators. The more the message is wrought with uncertainty and ambiguity, the more difficult it is to create similar interpretations among organizational members. Common experiences need to be created and new forms of communication such as visual thinking[17] should be developed to help integrate divergent interpretations.

Intuition and Market Foresight

Decisions about market entry timing and speed are, like most other strategic decisions, not made in a purely technocratic way on the drawing board of a strategy staff member. Managers often refer to their intuition when post-rationalizing important strategic decisions: 'I just had a gut feeling.' However, few top executives have the power to steer their companies based on their gut feelings alone. At some point, it may be necessary to communicate individual feelings about the company's future course of action, be it to get support from the shareholders or to facilitate implementation. In times of uncertainty and ambiguity where strategy may be reduced to a 'gut feeling', which is hard to express in words, the communication process becomes challenging. Distributing leaflets with vision statements, an occasional article in the in-house magazine, or number crunching in strategy meetings may have to be complemented with other forms of communication. Developing a shared vision entails developing redundant information about the future, or shared meaning that is stored in more than one brain or body, yet how can 'gut feelings' become shared information?

Intuition generated by past experiences influences foreign market entry timing decisions substantially. Intuition can be defined as 'the preconscious recognition of the pattern and/or possibilities inherent in a personal stream of experience'.[18] Intuition is an individual rather than a group or organizational phenomenon. It refers to a stock of knowledge that is tacit and inherently hard to express in words.[19] The attention for the role of intuition in strategic processes has centred around the question of whether intuitive decision-making leads to better organizational performance in highly turbulent environments. Some authors claim that overly formal and systematic thinking is outdated and should be replaced by a more intuitive mode of thinking; Nonaka and Takeuchi,[20] for example, suggest that Western managers need to revise their assumption that knowledge can be acquired, taught, and trained through manuals, books, or lectures, accept the less formal and systematic side of knowledge, and start focusing on highly subjective insights, intuitions, and hunches that are gained through the use of metaphors, pictures, or experiences.

Empirical studies in psychology have shown that individuals can learn complex rule structures without being able to articulate them. In such instances, managers may refer to their gut feelings or intuition, defined as '. . . a non-conscious, holistic processing mode in which judgements are made with no awareness of the rules or knowledge used for inference and can feel right despite one's inability to articulate the reason'.[21] Inherent in this definition are three main building blocks of intuition:

- The source of intuition occurs at a non-conscious level and one is therefore unable to identify what caused it (intuition is therefore distinct from judgements with clear thought structures).

- Intuition allows understanding of not only the variables involved in a complex situation but also their relationships.

- Intuition often involves a feeling of being 'right'.

Intuition is a psychological function that allows one to see the totality of a given situation and synthesize isolated data and experiences into an integrated group; intuition is subconscious, complex, quick, distinct from emotion, not affected by cognitive biases, and part of all decisions.[22] However, it is most likely that the combination of both intuition and formal thinking leads to sound strategic decisions. Research conducted by Khatri and Ng[23] or Shapiro and Spence[24] suggests that intuition should be used cautiously in combination with rational analysis in stable and moderately unstable environments, but should be used more often in highly unstable contexts. Well-structured problems that established decision rules can be applied to seem to be less frequent in fast-moving industries than ill-structured problems for which no explicit and widely accepted decision rules exist.

Selected Forecasting Methods

As discussed previously, there are many methods available to create foresight. These can be divided into two broad categories: judgemental and statistical. The former are based on expert opinions and role playing. The latter are based on quantitative data. Effective forecasting combines both methodological approaches.

The Delphi methodology, for example, is a valid alternative to 'guru forecasting' as it aims at obtaining the opinion of a larger number of experts. The Delphi Technique[25] was originally conceived as a systematic interactive forecasting methodology with a panel of independent experts without necessarily involving them in face-to-face meetings. In two or three rounds, the experts are confronted with carefully designed questionnaires detailing a key uncertainty. After each round, the facilitator of the process provides the experts with a summary of the answers of the entire panel. The experts have the possibility to revise their opinions on the basis of the answers of the other panellists. At the end of the process, a panel session where the experts discuss open issues may add additional value to the quality of the analysis.

Another option is scenario planning. The objective of scenario planning is to expand the imagination to envisage a wider range of possible futures. Scenarios challenge the prevailing mindset and identify early strategic issues that could shape the future of the firm. They also help create a risk/return profile of strategic options and assess the robustness of strategic options. The scenario technique is a disciplined method to depict several archetypes of potential future worlds. It is complementary to other foresight processes, and can even integrate other methodologies such as the Delphi Technique or cognitive mapping. Constructing scenarios allows for the exploration of joint impacts of various uncertainties. A sensitivity analysis of several variables at the same time can be performed without keeping others constant. While engaging in and interpreting scenarios, subjective interpretations will be formed and communicated and a picture of the future as well as the path that leads there can be shared. This methodology requires the intellectual courage to reveal evidence outside the actual way of thinking and the ability to hold two conflicting ideas in mind without losing the power to function.

Scenarios can be constructed in a multiple-step approach:

- Identify factors: scenarios should be created around factors that (*a*) have a strong impact on the industry, (*b*) are hard to predict, and (*c*) are hard to influence by the firm.

- Create initial scenarios: an initial scenario can be created by choosing different discrete outcomes of one or two core factors. A morphological frame can be used to combine several factors. Consistency, plausibility, and probability of scenarios must be checked.

- Choose decision scenarios: the most significant scenarios should be further developed and applied to strategic decisions.

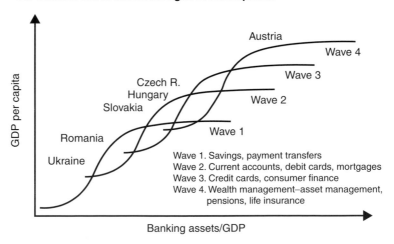

Our markets are at different stages of development

Figure 6.1. Predicting market development through analogy (Erste Bank Annual Report 2006)

When forecasting the development of demand and sophistication of geographical markets for financial services products, a historical analogy can be an effective methodology. As Figure 6.1 shows, one can assume that markets are at different stages of development and that they will follow similar historical patterns of more developed markets.

These and other forecasting exercises put management teams into the position to assess the development of geographical markets and prepare decisions on market entry timing and speed. However, even under conditions of reduced uncertainty of foreign market development, an internationalizing financial services firm still must make policy decisions on whether it is easier to profit from early mover advantages or whether it pays off to be a late entrant.

Early Mover Advantages

Innovation speed is generally positively related to firm profitability.[26] To be an early mover in internationalization means to be able to exploit local opportunity first and pre-empt scarce resources. It seems to be common sense that it pays to be first or at least early in the race for new competitive positions but in management literature there is no clear empirical evidence supporting the claim that it pays to hit the market first.[27] Most empirical studies on first mover advantage focus on product innovation, and when applied to geographical diversification, evidence of positive effects of early entry is not clear at all. Too many factors can influence the relationship between early market entry and commercial success.

First, it is not always easy to identify the first mover. Which foreign bank entered the British market first? Historians would probably say the Medici Bank was the first foreign bank. It might therefore make more sense to call it 'early' instead of 'first' mover advantages and relate it to a shorter time period. Does a financial services firm with a representative office in a foreign country for 100 years have a competitive advantage over firms that opened a full-fledged subsidiary 10 years ago? Probably not.

Second, early market entry is not sufficient for success in a foreign market. The specific capabilities of the financial services firm obviously have a strong impact on foreign market success. Assuming that financial services are distinct in nature, it is legitimate to predict that late entrants with superior resource and capability endowments can quickly make up for lost time. The disadvantage of entering later can be compensated by better service offerings, a larger branch network, or by simply buying market share.[28] Furthermore, second movers can take advantage of free riding on innovation, specifically when it is hard to protect, or technological and market uncertainty favour delayed investments.

Third, general market conditions have a substantial impact on the value of early entry. In some markets, ING Direct gains no advantage by entering early because the ICT infrastructure has not yet reached a critical standard and customers still have to be educated on how to use new service offerings. Being the first and the only player in a market is not always positive. Although a firm may enjoy the privilege of operating in a monopolistic market, the costs of developing this market may outweigh the benefits and once the market is big enough and profitability increases, new entrants will be hard to keep out.

However, reflecting about when and under what conditions early mover advantages develop and at what magnitude is essential for several reasons. First, it increases the understanding of firms on competitive structures of an industry segment. Second, it supports the decision on when (timing) and how fast (speed) to enter new geographical markets. Finally, it gives an indication on how to make effective use of early entry by identifying and protecting all available sources of first mover advantages.

Isolation Mechanisms

Early mover advantages allow pioneering firms to obtain higher levels of market share, earn positive economic profits, and survive longer than competitors. 'Isolating mechanisms'[29] generate and protect early mover advantages from imitation. Although many attempts have been made to categorize early mover advantages, the most common division of isolating mechanisms is to distinguish advantages from technological leadership, pre-emption of assets, and buyer switching costs.[30]

First, early mover advantage may derive from the pre-emption of scarce assets. Early entrants in new geographical markets may be able to pre-empt resources, such as geographical space (e.g. prime physical location), technology space (e.g. patents), or customer perceptual space. Pioneers may be able to expand and defend their position by blocking product space with a broadening product line. Allianz, for example, uses a multi-channel approach when it enters new foreign markets. The German financial services firm makes extensive use of existing retail banking networks, as shown by its agreement with ICBC and other banks in China. Although few Chinese banks will grant exclusive distribution rights for insurance products, the chances to defend the product space for early movers are nevertheless higher. Pre-emption of superior human resources is also possible, but employee mobility makes such an advantage difficult to sustain. A retail bank that enters emerging countries early may gain access to superior information and purchase assets such as sales outlets at strategic locations at relatively low market prices.

Second, first moving companies may be able to develop buyer switching costs that force new entrants to invest extra resources to attract customers. In the internationalization literature, the speed of market penetration is often described as dependent on the costs and possibilities of acquiring market knowledge.[31] However, the costs and possibilities of customer learning about the firm's products are equally important. Early entrants have the chance to influence the utility function of customers[32] because customers often favour the initial position of the pioneer.[33] Empirical evidence shows that consumers learn more about a pioneer than a late entrant.[34] Once customers have learned how to use an innovative product or service, they are hesitant to switch to another one because of the potential hassle of new learning.

In addition, and perhaps even more important, are the switching costs that relate to transaction records and trader reputation in the case of online auctions. When switching costs lead to lock-in effects, firms have to offer a huge advantage and/or compensate for switching costs to attract consumers from competitors. Buyers are often confronted with imperfect information about newly introduced goods. The experience character of service goods amplifies that effect since value judgements may only be possible ex post. Acquisition decisions are therefore influenced by brand reputation and other signalling effects because buyers may rationally choose and remain with the brand they first encounter. Buyer choice under uncertainty is consequently another potential source of competitive advantage from first mover activities.

As customers accumulate experience with the pioneer's product, they develop switching costs,[35] giving rise to demand-side economies of scale for pioneering brands. These are usually understood as positive consumption externalities in which 'the utility that a user derives from consumption of a good increases with the number of other agents consuming the good'.[36] This creates a positive feedback loop and markets are characterized by increasing returns,[37] which often leads to market structures that exhibit path dependencies and in which even inefficient products may prevail as the dominant product.[38] In this case, customers enjoy lower costs (or greater benefits) when using the standard product, which allows compatibility with the largest base of external users or complementors.[39] Firms may profit from those advantages and seek to enter a 'winner-takes-most' market first.[40]

Third, firms may gain first mover advantages by sustaining leadership in technology, which leads to reduced costs through learning or experience effects. However, those learning effects can only lead to a competitive advantage if they remain proprietary. Inter-firm diffusion of technology often leads to increasingly short periods during which firms may exploit cost advantages. Diffusion mechanisms like workforce mobility, research publications, dissection of products, or other competitive intelligence activities lead to an early erosion of technology-based first mover advantages. Patents may help to protect proprietary technology but it is often not possible to secure legal protection of new technology. On the contrary, early patenting of new technology may even make it easier for competitors to detect new technology for the scope of imitation. Therefore, technological advantages seem to be less important as a reason for an internationalizing financial services firm to enter a new market early.

Empirical Evidence of Early Mover Advantage

In banking literature, Berger and Dick[41] find that there is anecdotal and very limited empirical evidence of early mover advantages. Early mover advantages mainly result in higher market shares and derive from consumer switching costs as well as economies of scale. In their study of 10,000 bank entries into local urban markets within the United States between 1972 and 2002, Berger and Dick analysed whether there were any differences in deposit market shares among banking firms in a given market based on how early they entered. Their data show that there is indeed a robust relationship between a bank's entry timing and its market success. Assuming that all banks have equal capabilities and resources, the study suggested that early entrants would have, on average, higher market shares than late entrants. Empirical studies exploring the timing and speed of cross-border market entry of financial services industries are not known to the author.

Late Mover Advantages

When entering a new market, early entrants typically face the highest market and technological uncertainties. There are numerous examples of companies that have failed to profit from pioneering new product categories; it is very often the fast second mover[42] that is able to transform a low-volume niche product into a mass market product. Gillette did not invent safety razors, Microsoft did not develop the first DOS software, nor did Procter & Gamble develop disposable diapers.[43]

According to the timing of their entry, firms can be classified as early followers, differentiated followers, me-too followers, or late entrants. They may benefit from not being first in different dimensions and magnitudes, but in general, several late mover advantages can be distinguished:[44]

- *Free rider effects*: companies may profit from free riding on the investments made by the first movers such as R&D, buyer education, and infrastructure development.

- *Resolution of technological or market uncertainty*: especially in financial services markets where firms often have little influence on how uncertainties are resolved (e.g. regulatory frameworks), it can be beneficial to enter the market only after industry standards have been set and clear trends are visible.

- *Shifts in technology or customer needs*: late entrants can use disruptive events in the industry to replace incumbents.

- *Incumbent inertia*: late entrants are more alert to such changes and can mobilize the firm more quickly and at lower cost. Incumbents have a higher risk of immobility because they have invested in specific fixed assets or might be reluctant to cannibalize existing products. Often, incumbents also have deadlocked routines that are hard to change.

A pertinent example of a successful challenger of incumbent firms is ING-DiBa in Germany. The direct bank managed to make use of a shift in technology and customer needs to gain market share in a very short period of time. In 1965, the 'Bank für Sparanlagen und Vermögensbildung AG in Frankfurt am Main' was founded, but it was only with the strategic alliance with the Dutch ING in 1998 that the German bank started to shake the local market structure. By 2005, the bank had more than 5 million accounts, and just one year later ING-DiBa had total assets of EUR 72.8 billion. This rapid growth catapulted ING-DiBa to third place in Germany in terms of numbers of customer accounts behind Postbank (15.8 million) and Deutsche Bank (8.2 million) but before incumbents like Dresdner Bank (4.9 million) or Commerzbank (4 million) in 2005.

The CEO of Dresdner Bank, Herbert Walter, admitted in 2006 that ING-DiBa has long been underestimated.[45] However, the concept of late mover advantage takes a different shape when focusing on just the category of direct online banks; ING-DiBa is the indisputable leader in direct online banks in terms of number of customers, with more than five times that of its closest competitors, DAB Bank and Comdirect Bank.[46] Late movers had little chance to catch up with the more established direct online banks. The project of the Swiss Vontobel 'y-o-u, the evolution of Swiss Private Banking', the Finnish E-Brokers eQ Online, or the Berlin-based bank Systracom are just a few. These efforts never managed to attract even 10,000 clients despite substantial efforts in marketing and infrastructure.

Are Employees Loyal?

Early entrants may be able to pre-empt resources, such as geographical space, technological space, or customer perceptual space. Pioneers may even be able to expand and defend their position for some time by blocking product space with a broadening product line. However, not all sources of early mover advantages are easy to protect. Pre-emption of superior human resources, for example, has been frequently mentioned as an important early mover advantage but employee mobility makes such an advantage difficult to sustain. Specifically, in strong growth markets like CEE or Asian areas where employee loyalty is considerably lower than that of more developed countries, it is often possible to lure talented employees with only slightly higher salaries.

Are Customers Loyal?

Customer loyalty is at times not as high as early entrants may wish although there is empirical evidence that consumers learn more about a pioneer than about a late entrant.[47] Pioneering brands such as ING-DiBa in Germany are more likely to be retrieved from memory, considered for choice, and actually chosen.[48] As customers accumulate experience with the pioneer's product, they develop switching costs giving rise to demand-side economies of scale for pioneering brands. However, with aggressive marketing campaigns based on a few simple 'killer' products and the offer to take care of all administrative as well as financial honours of switching from incumbents, late comers frequently manage to catch up or even overtake early entrants.

Accelerated Internationalization Processes

The essential choices managers face are between speeding up internal market penetration at higher costs and risks or slowing it down and ceding—at least in the short run—market share to competitors who move faster. The ability to derive early mover advantages obviously depends on the quality of resources and capabilities that new entrants have in relation to local competitors, yet some firms manage to successfully accelerate internationalization processes. From the late 1980s, researchers have increasingly explored small firms that operated internationally early in their existence despite limited resources and capabilities in industries including high technology, software, art, and craft.[49]

International New Ventures

Some firms are able to accelerate their internationalization expansion processes despite limited international experience and resources. They frequently use hybrid governance structures (e.g. joint ventures and other forms of strategic alliances) during international expansion. Theoretical explanations offered for accelerated internationalization emphasize the increasing importance of network relations, industrial conditions, manager/

entrepreneur's capabilities and mindset, and, perhaps most importantly, technological change that facilitates cross-border communication.[50]

The international new venture literature addresses factors that contribute to the understanding of 'accelerated internationalization'. International new ventures may reflect the adaptation of the Japanese keiretsu model, where the internationally expanding small firm in mature markets follows as a dependent supplier of a large internationally expanding firm. Following the client to foreign countries has historically been one of the most important drivers for internationalization. Allianz, for example, followed Siemens to China by offering export insurance products as well as expatriate insurance policies for operations in Shanghai in the first decades of the nineteenth century. Recently, the presence of Allianz was increased exponentially by the strategic investment they made in China's largest bank, ICBC, and the bancassurance agreement they forged.

The Italian insurer Generali, on the other hand, boosted its presence in China after it forged a 50/50 joint venture with the National Petroleum Corporation (CNPC)—the 'Generali China Life Insurance Company Limited'. After Generali China Life received its group life licence in 2004, the company was able to offer a broader range of products, from life and health to pension benefits. In March 2005, it successfully executed the largest annuity plan in the world with a volume of USD 2.4 billion in collaboration with its partner CNPC. The group insurance policy provided a retirement scheme covering 390,000 CNPC retirees. This deal ranked Generali China Life second among foreign joint ventures operating in the Chinese insurance market with a market share among foreign insurance firms of 22.4 per cent in 2007, of which about 17 per cent can be assigned to the group insurance policy segment. In 2005, this deal made Generali China Life the largest foreign insurance company measured by total premium income in China's then USD 55 billion insurance market, of which foreign insurers claim a 2.7 per cent share. AIG's 12-year lead in the Chinese insurance market was interrupted by this mega case for a very short period of time. Nevertheless, in 2006, AIG was once again number one, 7 per cent ahead of Generali's 22 per cent market share of foreign joint ventures.

The Role of Networks

These two short examples give a taste of what it takes to penetrate foreign markets quickly. To a large extent, fast-paced internationalization depends on an organization's set of network relationships rather than specific company advantages. Foreign firms seek to obtain a position in an industrial value network. Such networks can be based on strong personal relationships or institutional ties. In Germany, for example, the term 'Deutschland AG' (i.e. Germany Ltd.) has been coined to indicate the cross-shareholdings of large companies and the cross-company supervisory board memberships. In Japan, such networks are called 'keiretsu' and describe a set of companies with interlocking business relationships and shareholdings. In South Korea, such business groups are called 'Chaebol'. If such industrial value networks are already developed across borders, they could support a late mover to tap into complementary resources in established industrial networks in the host country. Hence, international expansion may proceed faster, compared to firms that operate in industries where international industry networks have not yet been established. Such networks may well be instrumental for firms during rapid internationalization because networks often allow access to complementary resources to compensate for lacking own capabilities and assets.

Personal international networks may also contribute to manager/entrepreneurs' experiences and open attitudes. Individual managers with an international mindset may have international access to social networks. This, in turn, can contribute to early and accelerated internationalization. Network relations may become bridges to foreign markets.[51] If managers have acquired prior foreign market knowledge, the internationally expanding firm may not need to independently acquire knowledge, and one would expect faster internationalization and higher commitment modes.

International Niche Markets

However, even independent new ventures operating in niche markets may exhibit patterns of accelerated internationalization. If firms operate in niche markets or narrow product lines, growth objectives will be constrained by limited home demand: if international expansion provides the only growth path, internationalization may be required to achieve economies of scale[52] or to leverage differentiation advantages gained at home. Hence, the speed of market entry depends on the need to achieve economies of scale and scope.

Many financial services firms offer a vast product range in their home countries but focus on a few main products in their international markets. Firms such as UBS, Credit Suisse, or Deutsche Bank offer retail services in their home markets but focus on wealth management and/or investment banking in foreign markets. The Australian Macquarie Group, headquartered in Sydney, is another example of a financial services firm that chose to internationalize with a focused service offering. It seems that with increasing geographical distance, the bank narrows down its service range. In 2007, more than 55 per cent of bank income was generated from clients and activities outside Australia. Macquarie Group strategy is to 'expand selectively, seeking only to enter markets where our particular skills and expertise deliver real advantage to the clients. This approach allows the flexibility to enter new sectors and regions as opportunities arise and to respond to the specialist requirements of individual markets'.[53]

The Role of International Governance Mechanisms

Speed of market entry and penetration are also dependent on the modalities of governing international expansion. International expansion in financial services firms has in the past seen many mergers and acquisitions but relatively fewer strategic alliances. This tendency towards higher commitment market entry modes depends on the nature of the financial services business and the difficulties of limiting transaction costs of an alliance agreement.

If a financial services firm judges the risk of imitation by local firms to be high, it may refrain from joint ventures, since these may expose the firm to substantial expropriation risk by incumbents who act as partners. There are obviously also many reasons why mergers and acquisitions may not be the best mode of entry. If a foreign bank has to pay four times book value for targets in Eastern European markets and is forced to buy at the same time a large portion of undesired assets, mergers and acquisitions might not be the ideal option.

Scaling Capabilities

The growth of the firm is limited by the speed with which it can replicate its knowledge-based resources.[54] The design of internal knowledge management systems, however, is a neglected aspect in current theory on the internationalizing firm. If economies of scale and scope are essentially economies of knowledge re-use and the internationally expanding firm acts under constraints of rapid imitation, then bottlenecks in the internationalization process of the firm might depend not only on the speed with which it acquires market knowledge through experience-based learning, but additionally how it develops absorptive capacity[55] and the ability to replicate proprietary knowledge across international markets through the design of its internal knowledge management system.

7

How to enter? The choice of the market entry mode

While deciding on the timing and speed of market entry, financial services firms have to choose the most appropriate market entry mode among the available alternatives. Strategic objectives such as timing and speed of market entry certainly influence the choice of the market entry mode. Acquisitions allow for an immediate and quick entry but are risky. Organic growth is slower but easier to control. This chapter reviews the strategies companies in the financial services sector pursue to enter foreign markets. The modes of internationalization vary between financial services industries and companies. Even though international banks developed their presence mostly through acquisitions, and the availability of true greenfield investments is shrinking, organic growth options and strategic alliances are still inalienable elements of cross-border growth initiatives of most financial services firms to achieve the desired market presence.

In general, firms can internationalize in a number of ways, including through exports, contractual agreements, and foreign direct investment (FDI). International financial services markets have traditionally been entered using equity modes such as mergers and acquisitions or FDI. Relatively fewer joint ventures and contractual arrangements have occurred. In the past, high-control entry modes in financial services have been by far the most common,[1] but alternative entry modes are becoming increasingly common.

Citigroup, for example, acquired Bank Handlowy in Poland but chose to pursue organic growth in Russia, where they built a fairly successful retail bank with 21 branches from scratch in less than three years. Another example of successful organic growth is the Austrian Raiffeisen Bank (RZB), which started as early as 1987 to build its presence in Hungary and subsequently other CEE countries. Only recently, after foreign markets became more stable, has the RZB Group complemented its organic growth model with selected acquisitions.

The objective of this chapter is to describe available entry modes and discuss how financial institutions select among these entry modes when expanding internationally.

Entry Mode Decision Variables

For a nice American breakfast with ham and eggs, a farmer needs a chicken that is willing to be 'involved' but a pig with a lot of 'commitment'. Financial services firms have to calibrate their entry mode commitment and decide whether to go for the 'chicken strategy'—putting many eggs in several baskets—or a higher commitment mode. Reaping superior returns from international presence requires risk awareness and active management of commitment and control. The risk of international presence comes from several sources including language and cultural barriers as well as legal factors, which differ from country to country. A firm faces 'liabilities of foreignness', or in other words, disadvantages due to lack of local market knowledge. In addition, risk exposure depends on country-specific resource commitment in assets that cannot be easily divested or re-deployed to other markets. There is no easy solution to control the risks of international presence. To prevent hold-up and deceit by foreign partners, a firm might seek higher control through FDI. However, this requires substantial resource commitment, which in turn increases the risk exposure of assets. The essential challenge is therefore to control foreign liability risks without driving up asset exposure risks.

Entry Mode Decisions are Context-Sensitive

An overwhelmingly large set of factors has been identified that influence the entry mode choice of financial services firms.[2] Among those factors are the following:

- Industry characteristics
- Restrictions on foreign investments
- Country risk
- Availability of partnerships
- Cultural distance
- Market size
- Competitive advantage of foreign firm
- Political control over international operations
- Resource availability (human, financial) to execute strategy
- Strategic importance of target region
- Nationality of internationalizing firm

An extended literature review would certainly further extend this list. The transaction cost (TC) theory is probably the most frequently used theoretical lens to explore market entry mode choices. TC theory suggests that asset specificity (i.e. resources that may lose their value if applied for different purposes), behavioural uncertainties (i.e. the inability of the financial services firms to predict the behaviour of potential partners in a foreign country), and environmental uncertainties (i.e. risks associated with the host country such as the ability to enforce contracts) create market transaction costs as well as control costs. Based on an analysis of costs associated with alternative organizational structures, firms can decide to adopt either a market structure (i.e. non-equity modes) or hierarchies (i.e. equity modes).

In general, firms choose market entry modes to minimize transactional risks associated with lacking foreign market knowledge or controls for foreign country risks by limiting resource exposure until market knowledge has been acquired. TC theory suggests that firms may select entry modes that balance the advantages of integration (e.g. protect proprietary know-how and minimize market transaction costs) with the additional costs of control. A first critical contextual factor is the capital intensity of the business.

Capital-intensive service groups such as retail banking prefer a full-control entry mode (i.e. greater control and resource commitments) in countries with both economic and political stability and in which marketing assets can serve as a source of competitive advantage. This can be explained by the fact that valuable assets in these sectors are linked to brand, an existing customer base, or a physical distribution network.

On the other hand, knowledge-intensive service segments, such as investment banking or wealth management, call for a shared-control entry mode when they are driven by market-seeking motives, asset-seeking motives (like capital, labour resources, host-market knowledge, local contacts, and technology), or when they have prior experience in shared-control modes. Financial services firms often form strategic alliances with local distribution channels to market their products. There are several examples: the AXA Asia Pacific Holdings joint venture, Aviva's joint venture with AIB, or the joint venture Global Payments Asia-Pacific Limited, arranged by the parties Global Payments and HSBC in 2006, to mention just three.

From the organizational capability perspective, service firms with international experience tend to use higher-control entry modes for new markets than firms with less experience. The degree of digitalization also influences the mode of entry. Higher degrees of digitalization allow for low-commitment and high-control entry modes. ING Direct, for example, is able to enter retail banking markets in a full-control mode, exposing its assets only marginally to risks as market exit, sunk, or switching costs are very low.

Industry characteristics are among the more important factors influencing market entry decisions. A study of telecommunication carriers concluded that there is a need to enrich prevailing theory with contextual factors that characterize specific industries.[3] For example, internationalization decisions in the telecommunication sector are influenced by institutional factors such as government policy, opportunistic decision-making in the face of industry deregulation, and possibilities to obtain governments' ex ante and ex post resource commitments. Since financial services have comparable degrees of regulation, they may be subject to similar dynamics.

Another group of researchers explores the question of whether international activity of small firms differs from large MNCs. A study[4] of 187 small software firms from Norway, Ireland, and Finland found a rapid, non-incremental internationalization process to be most common among these small firms, and noted that while some firms entered close markets with low psychic distance (i.e. the perceived cultural difference between home and foreign country), others made commitments to markets that were distant. The same study concluded that commitment to foreign markets was manifested by exporting to new markets rather than deepened commitment through increased FDI in currently served international markets. A study[5] of 60 New Zealand-based small software firms found that network relations with clients and supply chain partners were associated with rapid international growth and influenced market selection and entry behaviour more than other explanatory variables suggested in internationalization theory.

This brief overview shows that there are a vast amount of interconnected and dynamic factors that influence entry mode decisions. It is therefore not feasible to find a universal law that definitively helps companies to choose the optimal entry mode choice. Instead, firms need to be able to discuss selected important decision variables, knowing that the variables are highly context-sensitive.

Balancing Market Commitment and Control

Since many factors influence market entry mode decisions, firms have to balance the commitment they make for single markets and the level of control they have over foreign operations. Market commitment can be defined as a combination of the amount of resources committed and the degree of specificity of those resources (i.e. how difficult it is to find alternative uses). Stage models of internationalization are concerned with determinants of increasing commitment of the internationalizing firm, both within a single foreign market and across several foreign markets.[6] This line of research argues that internationalization follows a path of increasing commitment from transaction market entry modes, such as spot export activities, through export by agents and licensing agreements to the more commitment-intensive establishment of sales subsidiaries, joint ventures, and overseas production units. As experiences are accumulated and knowledge develops about markets, theory suggests that firms escalate their commitments from low to high investment-intensive foreign entry modes. The greater the uncertainty and distrust surrounding international business, the more managers seek control through internalizing transactions.[7] It is therefore through the gradual acquisition, integration, and utilization of knowledge that firms are able to successively increase commitments to foreign markets. The RZB case appears to confirm the stage models of internationalization theory. The Austrian banking group mentioned in their annual report from 2006 that the company preferred to enter with low-risk entry modes and increase commitment as markets stabilized and the firm acquired more international experience.

Commitment-intensive entry modes including FDI may be explained not only through ownership advantages of the MNC and opportunities of internalization in intermediate product markets, but additionally through location advantages of the host country that serve to induce international expansion.[8] Location advantages occur with the possibility of using resource endowments that are specific to a particular location. Firms might want to tap into local knowledge sources (e.g. Indian or Eastern European software engineers; access to a network of investment bankers in London), exploit low labour costs (e.g. call centre operators in North Africa), or take advantage of physical resources (less relevant for financial services firms). If managers believe that location advantages can be beneficially combined with firm-specific capabilities like technological skills, reputation, and know-how, and the latter are difficult to trade, then firms may be required to engage in FDI.

Financial services firms sell mostly experience goods. Because the quality of experience goods can only be evaluated after their consumption, brands play a crucial role in market success. If a multinational financial services firm can more credibly convey quality assurance through branding relative to a host country licensee, internalization may also help buyers to overcome uncertainty about the good in question. Similarly, to leverage its brand internationally, McDonald's owns its restaurants in Moscow but runs restaurants in New York City by franchising. In other words, by pooling ownership, incentives to haggle, cheat, and default are reduced. More generally, the less property right and strategic protection against misappropriation of rents by host country partners is possible, the more firms will tend to international expansion by FDI via mergers, acquisitions, and greenfield investments. Consequently, entry modes chosen by the internationalizing firm can depend on the costs and benefits of alternative governance arrangements with firms seeking to minimize transaction costs.

In conclusion, the higher the perceived uncertainty and expropriation hazards that foreign entrants face, the more firms will choose foreign entry modes that allow for control. Such modes are usually associated with high resource commitments and FDI. International expansion via commitment-intensive modes of market entry seems appropriate if location advantages can be combined with non-tradable ownership advantages of the internationalizing firm. On the other hand, companies enter markets they know little about with resource-lean entry modes such as a representative office or a non-equity strategic alliance. This can allow the company to learn more about the market and increase familiarity with specific market conditions. Only when the company has reached a higher confidence level will it choose a market entry mode the company can control, such as FDI.

Organic Growth

From a transaction cost perspective using control and costs as the main decision variables, market entry modes could be divided into three main categories: exporting (direct vs. indirect), contracts (e.g. commercial agreements), and investments (e.g. greenfield, financial participation, joint venture, mergers and acquisitions). In financial services industries, organic growth models in foreign markets can take several legal and organizational forms, from low commitment modes like corresponding banking, representative offices, or strategic alliances to high commitment modes such as branches or full subsidiaries.

Main Organic Entry Modes

A recent study conducted by A. T. Kearney[9] reveals that future growth for most financial services firms should come from organic strategies. Firms in Europe derive 71 per cent of growth from organic strategies compared to 75 per cent in North America, and as much as 88 per cent in Asia. Acquisitions, according to the report, will still be part of the growth strategies of financial institutions but merely to cover geographic or capability gaps. Internal development or organic growth is preferable if there is no time pressure to grow and enough resources (financial, capabilities, technologies, market knowledge) to seek new opportunities. A strong corporate culture that might cause problems in alliances or acquisitions is another good reason to opt for organic growth rather than M&A. In addition, organic growth often keeps cash flows uniform and predictable. Another reason why some financial institutions are refocusing on organic growth models is that many firms have reached a critical mass and no longer fear that they are an easy takeover target themselves. Firms still struggle to integrate previously acquired companies and therefore are not eager to venture into new M&A operations. The main avenue to organic growth is customer intimacy: to be able to segment customer groups, get a deeper insight into their needs, and translate this customer understanding into effective business models and efficient operational processes. To grow organically, financial institutions need to create switching costs and satisfy existing customers while acquiring new clients. Several forms of organic growth into new markets can be identified:

- *Corresponding banking/insurance*: Many financial services firms start their international activities by following their corporate clients to foreign markets. Local financial services partners are identified and a cooperation model is developed without local presence of the foreign firm. Corresponding financial services models are a low-risk and less costly way to safeguard captive clients in foreign markets. The main risk may come from reputational problems a low-performing local partner may create.

- *Representative office*: This is the most basic banking/insurance establishment that does not perform independent financial services activities. In many countries, such as China, it is mandatory to have a representative office for several years before being able to apply for a banking or insurance licence. The main objective of representative offices is to gather market intelligence, lobby with the local government, and attract business for the parent firm abroad.

- *Branch office*: With a branch, a financial services firm engages in regular operational activities, backed by the capital of the parent company. With the branch as a legal extension of the parent firm, this market entry mode exposes the financial services firm to substantial risk: it is possible to sue the parent indirectly through one of its branches. On the other hand, with a branch, a financial services firm signals to foreign clients that it is willing to guarantee all its global assets for the local activities.

- *Subsidiary*: A subsidiary represents a legally independent unit and therefore secures its activities with its own capital. The subsidiary operates under host country law and is controlled by a large majority stake of the parent firm. In contrast to a branch, a subsidiary is allowed to open branches in foreign countries.

In many markets it is, however, difficult to grow just by realizing internal growth options: mature markets have only modest growth rates and to lure customers away from competitors is difficult. In many emerging markets, successful market entry requires a certain level of speed which is difficult to achieve with organic growth. In other fast growing markets such as China, governmental restrictions limit the opening of branches by foreign financial services firms. The case of Generali in China illustrates how organic growth often needs to be supported by a strong alliance with a local partner.

Generali Goes to China

Operating since 1831, Assicurazioni Generali S.p.A has accumulated experience in the insurance business for more than 170 years. The company engages with its 66,000 employees in over 40 countries through 315 affiliates world-wide. In 2006, the group's total premiums accounted for EUR 64.5 billion and the consolidated net profit reached EUR 2.404 billion, representing a 25.3 per cent rise compared to 2005. The entrance into the Chinese insurance market was undertaken in 1996 when Generali opened representative offices in Bei-jing and one year later in Shanghai. To increase its long-term commitment to the Chinese market, Generali invested in a strategic alliance with China National Petroleum Corporation (CNPC). Together they founded the 50/50 joint venture Generali China Life Insurance Company Limited. The approval of the China Insurance Regulatory Commission was given on 15 January 2002 after licensing Generali for the individual life segment.

CNPC is a large state-owned energy corporation located in China. It engages in businesses such as upstream and downstream operations in the area of oil and gas, petroleum material, and equipment manufacturing and supply. In 2006, the company reported a total profit of RMB 185.76 billion, correspond-ing to EUR 17.442 billion. Both parties can contribute complementary assets in the joint venture. Generali contributed specific know-how in the insurance business alongside technological and financial skills and CNPC contributes local market resources and a service network.

Generali Life entered the group-life business by receiving a licence in 2004 and since then offering a broad range of products from life and health to pension benefits. In March 2005, it successfully executed the largest annu-ity plan in the world with a volume of USD 2.4 billion in collaboration with its partner CNPC. The contracted group policy 'provides a retirement scheme paying out a lifetime immediate annuity'[10] covering 390,000 CNPC retirees. This deal was possible with the sophisticated expertise and support of the Generali Employee Benefits Network (GEB). Moreover, the product was customized to the needs of CNPC by ensuring that those employees who contributed more to the success of CNPC received a better lifetime benefit. This deal pushed Generali's image and generated a huge volume to further develop the infrastructure in the Chinese market.

Measured by GWP, Generali China Life ranked second place among the foreign joint ventures operating in the Chinese insurance market with a market share of 22 per cent in 2007, of which approximately 17 per cent can be assigned to the group policy closed with CNPC. In the year 2005, this deal made Generali China Life the largest foreign insurance company measured by total premium income in China's then USD 55 billion insur-ance market, of which foreign insurers at that time claimed a 2.7 per cent share.[11] Within this segment AIG's 12-year lead in the Chinese insurance market was interrupted by Generali China Life closing this mega case. Nevertheless, in 2006, AIG was again the market leader, 7 per cent ahead of Generali's 22 per cent market share of that claimed by foreign joint ventures.

Generali Complements JV Business with Organic Growth

In 2004, Generali China set up its Beijing branch and then two additional branches in Shanghai and Guangdong. The latter is in charge of further development of the South Chinese market and has a mission as a coordination centre, providing guidance and support to local business management and service centres. To increase market reach, the life insurer set up sub-branches or service centres in six other cities: Foshan, Foshan Shunde, Guangzhou Tianhe, Beijing Dacheng, Shenzhen, and Foshan Xiqiao.[12]

In June 2006, the CIRC gave permission to the insurer to set up a new branch in Jiangsu (Generali China Jiangsu Branch) located in Wuxi, an old industrial city in the Jiangsu province, famous for its wealth, with a great economic potential. In February 2006, Generali China relocated its head office from Guangzhou to Beijing to improve efficiency of communication and coordination with its local partner CNPC and also with the CIRC. By 2007, Generali China had accomplished three capital increases due to its steady growth and rapid development in the Chinese insurance market.[13] Generali started its property and casualty (P/C) segment in 2007 after receiving the non-life licence from the CIRC.

Organic growth is slow and costly, especially in the Chinese insurance market, but a necessary element to create an independent identity and value proposition in the market. The Chinese insurance business accounts for only 0.89 per cent of Generali's worldwide total premium income. To justify the managerial attention of the Chinese market, the operations of Generali have to be quickly lifted up to a suitable level and live up to their promises.

Generali's Competitive Strategy

Another important lever to grow sustainably is a sound competitive strategy in chosen business segments. Apart from the captive business with its JV partner, there are several essential elements of Generali's strategic position: (a) a decentralized multi-brand and multi-channel distribution approach which includes bank sales and 4,500 single brand agents and (b) the Generali employee benefits network.

The strategic plan 2006–2008 foresees an extension of up to 10,000 agents by the end of 2008 in order to gain critical mass. The JV's current businesses include life, health, and accident insurances as well as property and casualty. The products are offered to individuals as well as groups, corporate as well as private clients. Future plans include an enhancement of its position among the top foreign joint ventures, for instance through continuing geographical expansion and further leveraging its multi-channel distribution and bancassurance platform (e.g. more bancassurance agreements with major domestic banks).[14]

The second important facet of Generali's strategy is the Generali employee benefits network founded in 1966 with the goal to focus on the needs of multinational corporate customers. The organization itself consists of 50 international employee benefits experts and around 80 local network partner specialists that carry the expertise for complex international employee benefits plans. The basis that builds the network is composed of 100 local insurers in 74 countries that contribute daily global risk analysis and technical underwriting support, such as Generali China Life. GEB offers three products tailored to the needs of large and multinational firms:

- *Multinational pooling* combines the multinational company's employee benefits insurance contracts established in various countries into one unique account (or pool) for the purposes of experience rating.[15] The cooperating company has only one interface for the entire employee benefits plan and can tightly control costs and, by this, realize economies of scale.

- *Reinsurance to captive companies* aims at the reinsurance of inter-company risk plans. GEB finances the employee benefit risk, which can be offered starting from a contract with at least 3,000 lives to be insured.

- *Expatriate solutions* provide the customer with a benefit plan for international employees of the firm.

The services and products offered are the output of a three-level organization. The foundation is the actual network of local Generali representatives, which provide the first contact to clients. The second level monitors and controls local activity and coordinates the relations between network and international clients. Furthermore, regional coordinating offices observe and communicate changes in local legislation and the resulting impact on products like group insurance programmes. The countries served are organized in the following divisions: The Americas, Western Europe and Middle East and Africa, UK and Ireland, Central and Eastern Europe, Asia-Pacific. Regional managers report to the head office, which has the function of coordinating and directing as well as serving as the interface for financial reporting.[16]

Mergers and Acquisitions

A speedier way to grow compared to organic modes is mergers and acquisitions. Although it is admittedly difficult to measure their success, there is a strong case against mergers—many fail. On average, acquiring firms' performance does not improve and is often negatively affected by the operation. Acquisitions are the largest capital expenditures most firms ever make, yet they are often the worst planned and executed business activities. Acquisitions are frequently paid at a premium, which often has a strongly negative effect on shareholder value of the acquirer. It is not unusual to see an acquisition premium of 25–50 per cent compared to its stand-alone value. Creating benefits of this magnitude to offset the acquisition premium is a massive hurdle for the acquiring firm. Another critical issue is often a mismatch in managerial salaries. US top executives sometimes earn 10 times more than their European peers, which might explain why European top executives sometimes have personal interests in acquiring overseas. Competitors often launch aggressive attacks to take advantage of the M&A chaos. UniCredit used the post-merger integration uncertainty of its local rival Intesa when it merged with Sanpaolo by launching a forceful marketing campaign to lure away customers. Andreas Treichel, CEO of Erste Bank, once remarked that

the fact that the two financial institutions will as a result of the activities connected with their merger be busy for several months or even years with their own internal affairs, means an enormous market opportunity for the other banks, as they will be able to persuade clients who are unsatisfied with this situation to try their services. . . . Apart from this, there will be many chances to acquire top people from central Europe for other positions, as there is certain to be some overstaffing.[17]

As a result, not all mergers and acquisitions generate wealth. Early literature within the field of industrial organization (IO) economics[18] suggested that economies of scale, scope, and market power can be realized through related acquisitions, which will in turn lead to superior performance of the acquiring firm.[19] However, the results of this research have been somewhat ambiguous, with the result that many additional structural and organizational variables have been suggested as possible determinants of acquisition success. These include market share, relative size, pre-acquisition experience, timing relative to the business cycle, and business relatedness.[20]

Nevertheless, in many cases, acquisitions are the best strategic alternative to grow, and if well planned and executed, can create shareholder value. Mergers and acquisitions appear to make the most sense if cultural aspects have not caused major problems in the past and the target company fits strategically and culturally to the organization, generating obvious synergies. An intensive due-diligence process with access to auditing material must be undertaken prior to the purchase to understand the risks. On average, the success rate of M&A also seems to increase if the buyer is not significantly larger than the seller in terms of turnover.

In summary, there are many success recipes for M&A found in the pertinent literature; however, none of these recipes can be considered a one-size-fits-all solution. The next section looks at a specific M&A case: ABN AMRO. This case illustrates how missing cross-border and cross-product synergies as well as low overall profitability can threaten the independence of large financial services firms. The case highlights the role of shareholder activism and the power that hedge funds can exert with minimal shareholdings. Despite the desire of top management to remain independent, or at least not be broken up, the case shows that even financial services giants are takeover targets if they do not generate enough value. The ABN AMRO case shows that neither poison pills (such as the sale of LaSalle) nor strong trade unions or the support of the local government could stop the consortium composed of RBS, Santander, and Fortis. Although not a typical M&A case, the battle for ABN AMRO represents a new breed of market transactions that threaten the quiet life of top executives at large financial services firms like UBS, Citigroup, or Dresdner Bank that struggle to keep up with the high performance expectations of their shareholders. The case shows that even with a very small ownership share, an activist fund was able to force the sale of ABN AMRO to a consortium of three banks that aimed to split up the target.

The Battle for ABN AMRO

ABN AMRO is a Dutch bank founded in 1991 from the merger between Algemene Bank Nederland (ABN Bank) and Amsterdam-Rotterdam Bank (AMRO Bank). Continuous growth led to ABN AMRO becoming number 15 in the world. In 2000, a new organizational structure was implemented to better fit with the dimensions and activities of the bank: 150 branches were closed and 2,500 jobs had to go, cutting staff at the Dutch operations by 10 per cent. Despite this reorganization ABN AMRO's losses proceeded consecutively for seven years. In 2006, after insistent calls for expected returns of stakeholders, the option of takeover was taken into consideration. ABN AMRO became an interesting takeover target, and its strategic goals were reduced to finding a counter-party who would offer to buy the Dutch bank at an appealing price while granting coherence in strategic management.

ABN AMRO continued to deliver a low performance and it seemed that the company would not be able to manage a turnaround on its own. The board of directors saw the independence of ABN AMRO endangered after The Children's Investment Fund (TCI) suggested a break-up or sale of the bank. TCI was known for its aggressive shareholder activism. With a total ownership of just 1 per cent in ABN AMRO, the investment fund managed to mobilize enough shareholders to put pressure on the board of directors. TCI demanded fundamental changes in the ownership structure of the bank to increase returns for shareholders claiming seven years of poor performance. The situation was critical for the board, forcing them to look for a white knight to save them. Barclays agreed to play this part and quickly made a EUR 63 billion offer to acquire ABN AMRO.

However, ABN AMRO was appealing to other players at the time. Based on a break-up hypothesis, a consortium composed of the Royal Bank of Scotland, Fortis, and Santander managed to make a counter-offer in less than two weeks. The battle started and with it, the commencement of one of the most turbulent and expensive takeovers in the history of financial services. On 5 October 2007, after six months of bid adjustments and court sentences, investors representing 85 per cent of the Dutch bank's shares accepted the consortium's offer of EUR 70 billion.

The Banker[21] positions Barclays PLC in 12th place in terms of tier one capital strengths and in first position in the UK for total assets. In March 2007, Barclays decided to make a bid to take over ABN AMRO. It soon became the only and privileged interlocutor because of its declaration of being aligned with ABN AMRO's strategic vision. Barclays declared that they planned to keep ABN AMRO uniformity while delivering ABN AMRO's global product lines (BarCap, BGI, and Barclaycard) via a combined global distribution base. Barclays' price premium was based on its desire to develop operational synergies and generate additional margins by covering additional geographical regions. In particular, Barclays' retail business was most focused on the UK; ABN AMRO had franchises in the Netherlands, Italy, the United States, and Brazil. The new entity would have presented a widespread geographical presence, becoming the second largest bank in the world. The deal aimed to create a global investment bank that would have been a leader in risk management and financing, the world's largest institutional asset manager and the eighth largest wealth manager, with a leading European onshore franchise and attractive positions in growth markets.

The consortium of the Royal Bank of Scotland, Fortis, and Santander had different strategic objectives and approach. In April 2007, the Royal Bank of Scotland, Fortis, and Santander submitted a joint letter to the Chairmen of the Supervisory and Managing boards of ABN AMRO to express the consortium's interest in making a proposal for the acquisition of ABN AMRO. At first, the main interest of the consortium lay in the acquisition of the US subsidiary, LaSalle, but it suddenly switched towards ABN AMRO when the offer for the US affiliate was declined in favour of Bank of America. On 29 May 2007, the consortium made an offer to take over ABN AMRO.

Each component of the consortium had clear objectives in mind when they formed the coalition: Fortis aimed to acquire ABN AMRO's Dutch business, its fund management, and private banking operations; the Royal Bank of

Scotland aspired to take the US retail banking operation, ABN AMRO's whole-sale banking business and all other operations, including those in India and the Far East; Santander of Spain wished to buy ABN AMRO's operations in Brazil and Banca Antonveneta in Italy (Table 7.1).

A Process Model for Managing Mergers and Acquisitions

As the example of ABN AMRO shows, it can be quite hazardous to plan and execute a merger or an acquisition. Figure 7.1 describes a generic process to manage M&As that can be used to structure such operations. In the course of this process, financial services firms have to overcome several critical points. A recent study conducted by A. T. Kearney[22] reveals that the most important factors with the power to influence the success rate of M&As are found at the beginning and at the end of the process: to have a sound strategy from day one, to be able to break down cultural barriers, and to master the integration process.

One of the most critical steps in the above described process is the post-merger integration. Value creation through post-merger integration processes is not a completely predictable, planned activity but rather an evolutionary and emergent process.[23] Integration management must incorporate the trade-off between speed and the quality of the integration in terms of utilizing the potential of the local operation without alienating key personnel. Reaching the desired end state quickly in terms of post-merger integration organiza-tional rearrangement is desirable to be able to enjoy the benefits of merging sooner, and to avoid dissipating value through indecision and aimlessness, which is especially pressing if high premiums have been paid. Fast inte-gration is also better to minimize the uncertainty of target employees and reduce 'post-merger drift' in terms of efforts and pain, and to demonstrate the value of the combination to both sides. In contrast, slow integration has the benefit of avoiding sudden disruption to the purchased entity and creating ill-conceived changes, both of which can result in capability dilution and a de-motivated workforce.[24] In addition, by delaying commitment and implementation of a specific organizational arrangement, slower integration offers more flexibility for potential changes precipitated by environmental shifts.

Acquisition success is a function of the two parallel processes of task integra-tion and human integration. Task integration is defined as the identification and realization of operational synergies, and human integration is defined as the creation of positive attitudes towards the integration among employees on both sides. Overall acquisition success is thus contingent on the effec-tive management of both sub-processes. A high degree of integration of the target into the acquirer allows for benefits of economies of scale and scope of functions, tighter control and uniform incentives, and facilitates human

How to enter? The choice of the market entry mode

Table 7.1. The battle for ABN AMRO—sequence of events

ABN AMRO announces further restructuring (30 October 2006)	ABN AMRO announced the intention of closing some commercial client operations in various countries as a response to concerns about its low performance. The bank decided to divest EUR 10 billion in risk-weighted assets allocated to commercial clients to be re-invested elsewhere. The company also intended to cut 4,500 head-office jobs, and mulled additional divestments to fasten measures to improve profits.
Barclays makes bid for ABN AMRO (18 March 2007)	Barclays made a tentative takeover bid to ABN AMRO. The British bank was supposed to assist in the prevention of the break-up of ABN AMRO. On the side of convenience of the deal, Barclays had a smaller geographical overlap with ABN AMRO than other suitors and this appeared as something negative on the side of cost savings but positive on both geographical extension and the quality of the relationship between Barclays and its Dutch target.
Barclays in exclusive talks with ABN AMRO (18 March 2007)	Barclays was understood to be in exclusive talks with ABN AMRO over a possible merger. These early stage discussions nevertheless unveiled widespread interest from other potential suitors such as ING, the Royal Bank of Scotland, Fortis, and Banco Santander.
Barclays' concessions bring ABN deal closer (20 March 2007)	Barclays and ABN AMRO settled the basis for the establishment of the new entity. The features would be: • UK PLC with a primary listing on the London Stock Exchange and secondary listing on Euro next Amsterdam • UK unitary board • First Chairman nominated by ABN AMRO and the first Chief Executive Officer nominated by Barclays • Head office in Amsterdam • Dutch Central Bank (DNB) acting as lead regulator for the new entity
RBS plans break-up bid for ABN AMRO (13 April 2007)	The Royal Bank of Scotland set up a consortium constituted by Santander and Fortis to enter the battle with a potential break-up bid.
Barclays and ABN in 48-hour deadline (15 April 2007)	Barclays and ABN AMRO gave themselves 48 hours to agree on a merger. The consortium was pressuring ABN AMRO and Barclays, claiming it could offer a better deal in terms of bid price and portion of cash. In these crucial hours, ABN AMRO and Barclays were discussing further details on how the combined institution should be regulated.
ABN agrees to EUR 67 billion takeover by Barclays (22 April 2007)	ABN AMRO agreed to be taken over by UK rival Barclays. This choice would bring EUR 3.5 billion in annual savings, according to ABN AMRO analysts' estimates. In addition, 10% of the workforce would be cut and half of it moved offshore. This agreement nevertheless allows ABN AMRO to hear details of a rival bid from the Royal Bank of Scotland, Santander of Spain, and Fortis.
Shareholders to contest ABN sale of LaSalle (24 April 2007)	VEB, the Dutch Investors Association, threatened a legal challenge, claiming that the rushed sale of LaSalle could provide too big an obstacle for the consortium. As a consequence, ABN AMRO started contacting other potential suitors attracted by the acquisition of the US subsidiary.
RBS wades into battle for ABN with EUR 72 billion offer (25 April 2007)	The Royal Bank of Scotland-led consortium declared it would pay EUR 72.2 billion for the Dutch bank if it abandoned its USD 21 billion sale of LaSalle to Bank of America. After this offer, ABN AMRO decided to disclose its books to the three banks and agreed to allow due diligence on the same terms as it had granted Barclays.

Table 7.1. (*Continued*)

BofA threatens legal action against ABN (29 April 2007)	Bank of America threatened to take legal action against ABN AMRO if there is any attempt to delay the sale of LaSalle. Under the terms of the contract between ABN AMRO and BofA, potential rivals could buy LaSalle if they make a higher bid but ABN AMRO would not be able to accept a conditional offer without triggering a lawsuit from BofA.
Judge blocks ABN's sale of LaSalle (3 May 2007)	An unexpected strike occurred when Amsterdam Commercial Court blocked ABN AMRO's plans to sell LaSalle to BofA for USD 21 billion.
ABN rejects RBS offer for LaSalle (7 May 2007)	ABN AMRO rejected a USD 24.5 billion offer for LaSalle from the consortium. As a consequence, BofA sued the Dutch bank, seeking an injunction that would block the unit's sale to any other party.
ABN AMRO's Chief Financial Officer resigns (10 May 2007)	Hugh Scott-Barrett, ABN AMRO's CFO, announces his resignation.
RBS consortium outlines EUR 71.1 billion offer for ABN AMRO (29 May 2007)	The Royal Bank of Scotland and its partners disclose their offer for ABN AMRO: EUR 71.1 billion, 79% cash. The offer creates chaos and raises claims among players: ABN AMRO still firmly supports Barclays' bid while the VEB suggests putting the two rival bids before shareholders.
Unions demand talks on ABN AMRO's future (4 June 2007)	The situation gets edgy around the bloody battle for ABN AMRO and unions from more than a dozen countries demanding detailed talks with rival banks bidding for ABN AMRO in order to achieve a rapid and satisfying solution.
ABN AMRO legal decision (13 July 2007)	The Dutch Supreme Court allowed ABN AMRO's sale of LaSalle to Bank of America to go ahead as planned. This choice was taken without the shareholder vote. This, however, does not diminish the interest that the consortium is paying towards the ABN AMRO deal. The next step expected was the declaration of a revised offer of the consortium.
RBS-led consortium revises bid for ABN (16 July 2007)	The Royal Bank of Scotland-led consortium makes its revised offer. Total price stays stable but a lifting in the cash element to 93% to EUR 71.1 billion (USD 98 billion) total value was presented. The offer appeared to be highly profitable for ABN AMRO because with the exclusion of LaSalle from the new deal, RBS's projected cost savings dropped from EUR 2 billion to EUR 1.2 billion and revenue savings halved from EUR 0.85 billion to EUR 0.48 billion.
ABN presses Barclays to raise bid (22 July 2007)	The chief executive of ABN AMRO called on Barclays to raise its offer. It is the first time that Barclays has received a reminder of this type. The aim, according to the CEO of ABN AMRO, was to emphasize the reliance of ABN management on the preference accorded to Barclays.
Barclays back in the game for ABN (23 July 2007)	Following ABN AMRO's recommendations, Barclays submitted its new EUR 71.1 billion offer. To do so, the bank had to seek support of two additional investors: China Development Bank and Temasek. According to the BBC, 'if the talks succeeded, China would hold a 7 per cent stake in the merged bank, while Singapore would own a 3 per cent stake'.
ABN opts for neutral stance on bids (29 July 2007)	ABN AMRO now took a neutral position by not recommending any offer either from Barclays or from the consortium. Barclays' offer is formally conditional on a recommendation from ABN AMRO but it reserved the right to 'extend the date to 30 July for satisfaction of the pre-condition in case of improvement in its share price or waive the pre-condition in the event that it doesn't increase'.

(*cont.*)

Table 7.1. (*Continued*)

Fortis close to EUR 13 billion rights issue agreement (6 August 2007)	Fortis gained support from its shareholders to buy a stake in ABN AMRO. Though the shareholders' vote was highly supportive, concerns were expressed about the investors' desire to absorb such a large share issue.
Investors in Barclays back bid for ABN (14 September 2007)	Barclays' shareholders approve their bank's offer. The battle is still open even if the consortium's offer is EUR 5.50 per share higher than Barclays'. Citing John Varles, Barclays' CEO, the drive of this offer is not to prevail over the consortium through a highly profitable deal but through a better strategic fit: 'ABN allows us to do what we are already doing, but more quickly.'
RBS and Santander seek funds for bid (20 September 2007)	The Royal Bank of Scotland and Santander start issuing preference shares and convertible bonds to pay the bid for ABN AMRO. In this phase, ABN AMRO kept a neutral position though it is commonly felt that the preference is now shifting towards the consortium's side.
RBS raises EUR 6 billion for ABN bid (26 September 2007)	In accordance with the designed plan, the Royal Bank of Scotland raises more than EUR 6 billion through an issue of preference shares. The end is close.
Barclays concedes defeat in battle for ABN AMRO (5 October 2007)	A dramatic fall in Barclays' share price determined the end of the six-month battle between the white knight and the consortium. A EUR 200 million break fee would be paid to Barclays as the pending deal terminated.
Victory formally declared in ABN tussle (9 October 2007)	A formal declaration of victory was made by the consortium after shareholders representing 86% of ABN AMRO's shares accepted the group's EUR 70 billion offer. Next steps include the completion of the rights issue by Fortis and, in the longer term, the reorganization of ABN AMRO's retail and wholesale activities.
RBS consortium to take control of ABN (10 October 2007)	Mark Fisher is named chief executive of ABN AMRO, replacing Rijkman Groenink.
Banca Antonveneta goes to MPS (8 November 2007)	The world's oldest bank, Monte dei Paschi di Siena, announced the acquisition of Banca Antonveneta. Surprisingly, MPS enters the scenario of mergers and acquisitions in the banking sector by buying Banca Antonveneta for a price of EUR 9 billion (Antonveneta was valued at EUR 6.6 billion at the time of the ABN AMRO offer). Santander accepted the offer as an unexpected gift that raised core capital to about 6.2% of risk-weighted assets.

Based on lead articles of the *Financial Times*.

integration due to the increased potential of contacts and interactions. On the other hand, a low degree of integration (i.e. a high degree of autonomy) enables the preservation of capabilities that could otherwise be diluted if the routines underlying those capabilities were disrupted.[25] Moreover, a low degree of integration offers more flexibility in rearranging the resources if necessary as environmental circumstances change. Thus there is an explicit trade-off between high and low levels of integration.

The integration of physical assets, organization processes, and people of two organizations that have decided to merge plays a critical role.[26] The combination of the assets and processes, or in other words 'task integration', by which the resources and activities of the firms are assimilated, is essential

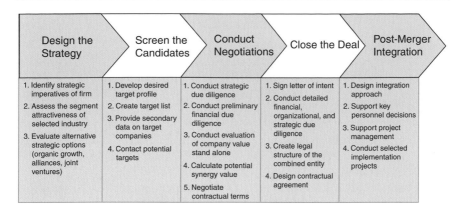

Figure 7.1. A generic M&A process model

to conducting business operations and thereby creating financial gains from a deal.[27] Likewise, the blending of the employees from both sides to generate interaction and productive cooperation, human integration to achieve organizational culture convergence and shared identity, motivation, and goals are necessary enablers to allow the commencement of business operations, especially because specialized employees can be critical components of the competences purchased.

Mergers and acquisitions are attractive because they allow a firm to grow rapidly, but problems during integration processes can push firms to prefer organic growth options. Defining the right level and speed for integration is crucial to get the post-merger integration process running. Figure 7.2 distinguishes four approaches to post-merger integration.

- *Preservation*: After the acquisition, little integration is made without any time pressure. When financial services firms such as Nordea decide to acquire healthy businesses that show few interdependencies with the existing organization, preservation as an integration mode can make sense. The newly acquired unit is seen as a strategic option for future growth plans. Sooner or later, the question whether the acquiring firm is the 'best owner' for the local operation will come, as seen with the ABN AMRO case.

- *Quick wins*: Fast changes in selected areas can make sense if a financial services firm acquires a small unit in a foreign country and decides to support the local unit in its fast but autonomous growth plan to quickly achieve a critical mass. This mode deliberately sacrifices operational efficiency for accelerated local growth. This mode also makes sense if the nature of the business does not allow for substantial cross-border synergies

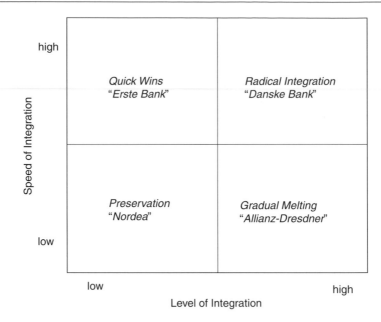

Figure 7.2. Post-merger integration level and speed

and requires local entrepreneurship. Erste Bank's post-merger integration approach follows this strategy in most of its acquisitions.

- *Radical integration*: To achieve cross-border synergies, this mode aggressively integrates the two companies. This mode makes sense if a sufficiently large acquisition target is in bad shape and a quick (i.e. 6–12 months) integration process can help the local firm improve its performance. Radical integration often assimilates the acquisition target by imposing the acquiring firm's processes on the local firm. Danske Bank can be placed into this quadrant for most of its acquisitions.

- *Gradual melting*: When acquiring a relatively successful, large local operation, it takes more time to create adequate symbiosis between the two firms. With increased possibilities to disaggregate financial value chain activities, the design of the integration blueprint deserves a thorough study, which can take time. Even though it might make sense to declare a post-merger integration phase as concluded after one and a half years, the fine-tuning of human and task integration can take several more years to reach desired levels. The acquisition of the German HVB by UniCredit may serve as an example of this integration category.

Post-merger integration processes are tainted with pitfalls and often fail or take more time than expected. Organic growth models or strategic alliances can be valid alternatives in many situations.

Strategic Alliances

Strategic alliances balance risk and control and are therefore a compromise between an acquisition and organic growth. They represent a compromise between short-term, pure market transactions and long-term, pure organizational solutions like mergers and acquisitions. A strategic alliance between two firms is created when they agree on a durable sharing or pooling of resources for undertaking activities of strategic importance to one or more of the partners. The term 'strategic' is justified if a significant proportion of the overall resources of the partners is committed for a longer period of time and there is a sufficiently high degree of interdependence between the partners. Strategic alliances are further defined by their central importance to the strategic objectives of the partners. Strategic alliances in the financial services industry can take many forms and serve several objectives. Let us briefly consider two examples.

The joint venture Macquarie Shinsei Advisory Co., Ltd (MSAC) between the Australian Macquarie Group and Shinsei Bank was formed in April 2006 based on the public-to-private sector shift in Japan. The Macquarie Bank Group currently employs a network of about 11,000 people in 25 countries. Its core businesses are financial services such as infrastructure investment, advisory, and funds management. In 2005, the Macquarie Bank Group had USD 38 billion in total assets. Shinsei Bank is based in Japan with currently 2,248 employees. It offers a full range of financial products and services in the areas of institutional banking, consumer and commercial finance, and retail banking. The joint venture's main objective was to serve the Japanese market and exploit opportunities in the enormous amount of public and private infrastructure.

Another example is the AXA Group, currently expanding extensively into emerging markets in the Asia Pacific area. Consistent with its strategy to be among the top five in the Asia Pacific area by January 2003, AXA Asia Pacific Holdings signed a bancassurance joint venture with Bank Mandiri. AXA Asia Pacific owns 51 per cent and Bank Mandiri owns 49 per cent of the joint venture. In September 2002, Bank Mandiri had total assets of USD 28 billion and a market share of deposits of 23 per cent. With its then 17,572 employees, Bank Mandiri was the largest Indonesian bank. Together with AXA Asia Pacific, which had 4,500 employees at the time, the joint venture provides financial protection and wealth management products to Bank Mandiri's 6.7 million customers. Aspirations of the joint venture included 3 per cent penetration of Bank Mandiri's customer base and USD 350 million of AUM (assets under management) within five years. Synergies were seen in the common use of Bank Mandiri's distribution system and AXA's product capabilities. Furthermore, the joint venture sought economies of scale from local, regional, and global operations of both companies. In addition, AXA is active in the Philippines through the joint venture with the Metro

Bank named AXA Philippines, in Thailand through the joint venture with Krungthei Bank, and in China through the joint venture with Minmetals.

Strategic alliances are not limited by industrial barriers. Nordea signed an agreement with the Finnish department store chain operator Stockmann in 2007 to finance and service their credit cards. Many retailers, such as Carrefour, Tesco, or Marks & Spencer, have also started to partner with banks and insurance companies to offer a vast array of products. Initially, simple services such as savings accounts, consumer financing, and credit and debit cards were offered, but increasingly, the product range has been enlarged and now includes home mortgages, investment funds, and a broad range of insurance products (from life, car, health to even household pet insurance policies).

As these short examples indicate, motives to form strategic alliances in the financial services industry are frequently distribution agreements to facilitate international expansion. Several other strategic motives for the formation of alliances exist:[28]

- Risk sharing
- Product rationalization and economies of scale
- Technology transfer
- Shaping competition
- Conforming to host government policy
- Strengthening vertical linkages with suppliers and distribution channels

This list is by no means complete; several other motives for the building of a strategic alliance exist. An essential trait of strategic alliances is that the participating firms agree on mutually defined goals. It is not necessary that all partners have the same view on the goals but it is vital that they explicitly agree on a common set of goals and how to contribute to achieving those goals.

However, strategic alliances also have several negative aspects that need to be considered: the costs of negotiating and controlling strategic alliances are often too high. The possibility of choosing the wrong partner is also high and can have severe consequences on the participating companies. Two risk types can be distinguished:[29]

- *Relational risks*: Alliances are built and governed by managers with individual interests and behavioural patterns. The interests of the alliance are most of the time less relevant than the proper interests, which may lead to opportunistic behaviour.

- *Performance risks*: Even if the alliance partners are committed to common goals, they sometimes fail to fulfil the expectations due to firm or market-based factors.

It is therefore not surprising that around 50 per cent of strategic alliances fail.[30]

The Case for Cross-Border Alliances

Strategic alliances are nevertheless increasingly used by financial services firms to expand abroad. A strategic alliance can be labelled as successful if both partners are able to achieve their strategic goals and consequently recover the financial costs of capital. A study[31] on 49 cross-border alliances concluded that two-thirds of the alliances analysed had difficulties surviving the first two years due to managerial or financial problems. Nevertheless, 51 per cent of the sample alliances were successful for both partners and only 33 per cent resulted in failure for both. This success rate is comparable with that of cross-border acquisitions. The authors of the study offered several observations:

- Strategic alliances appear to be more effective when entering new geographical areas and non-core businesses.
- Alliances between strong and weak companies are less likely to survive.
- Strategic alliances need to evolve beyond their initial mission and objectives and maintain a certain degree of autonomy from their parent companies.
- Clear management control is more important than financial ownership and successful strategic alliances are therefore more likely to have an even split of financial ownership.
- A large portion of strategic alliances end with one partner assuming complete ownership.

The London-based Credit Suisse First Boston may serve as an example to illustrate these insights. Founded as a 50–50 joint venture in 1978 by Credit Suisse, it gave the Swiss bank access to a non-core business area: the creation of US-based corporate bonds and other innovative financial products. The joint venture served the interests of First Boston because it provided that bank with access to European customers. Both banks were probably equally strong at the point of the formation of the joint venture until the late 1980s when First Boston ran into trouble with its engagement in the collapsing junk bond market. Credit Suisse first acquired 44 per cent of First Boston in 1988 and later acquired a controlling stake in 1990. The original name of the joint venture was 'Financière Crédit Suisse-First Boston', quickly rebranded into Credit Suisse First Boston, to finally phase out the First Boston name completely in 2006.

To bring in the proper brand name into joint ventures can be risky if control over the joint venture is lost or if it is impossible to sell the stake without the brand name. If Siemens were to sell its stake in the household appliance JV Bosch-Siemens, it would only achieve a satisfying price if it left its brand name with the JV and consequently lost control over its end-consumer branding strategy. With Credit Suisse First Boston the opposite happened: the 'First Boston' brand increasingly lost appeal in the market and Credit Suisse decided to follow an umbrella brand strategy of its local competitor UBS, which eliminated the previously acquired brands Dillon Read, Paine Webber, and SG Warburg. Similar moves can be observed by Citigroup, which abstains from using the Salomon Brothers name, or the UniCredit Group, which carefully pushes its umbrella brand in the CEE areas.

Governing Strategic Alliances

As previously indicated, strategic alliances are a relatively low-commitment market entry mode that allows an internationalizing firm to develop local market knowledge and gradually increase its presence in a foreign market. The downside of alliances is that lower degrees of control come with lower commitment. The shape of the governance mechanisms is central to the functioning of strategic alliances. Organizational structures and managerial processes need to be defined to reduce organizational costs, enhance the competitive position of alliance partners, and ensure better knowledge acquisition.[32] The governance mechanisms of an alliance are of course context-sensitive and therefore case-specific. Based on previous experiences, several indications can nevertheless be given:[33]

- *Simplicity*: Not all aspects of a strategic alliance can be controlled and codified in a contract. To recognize this aspect of collaboration and to define simple and flexible structures is central to the functioning of strategic alliances. Contracts cannot substitute a minimum level of trust between the partners.
- *Clear conflict resolution mechanisms*: Conflicts are a natural part of management and will probably occur in any alliance. Mechanisms that avoid arbitrary escalation of such conflicts need to be developed before the conflicts occur.
- *Command structures*: Even in a seemingly frictionless relationship based on mutual trust and esteem, task and human integration must be coordinated.
- *Incentive systems*: They indicate how performance is measured and link performance to rewards.
- *Standard operating procedures*: Firms need to develop routines to be efficient. The same applies for strategic alliances. Standard operating

procedures reduce behavioural and task uncertainty and accelerate operational as well as strategic decision-making.

- *Transfer pricing*: A crucial point for strategic alliances is the measurement and pricing of the contributions of each partner when market prices cannot be found or applied. This is particularly delicate if the alliance evolves and collaboration specifications change.

- *Early recognition of warning signals*: Effective governing mechanisms must be able to perceive soft signs of dissatisfaction early enough to make timely interventions more successful.

- *Relational quality*: Alliance partners need to invest in relational quality and thereby facilitate mutual trust. Relational quality depends on (*a*) the reputation of alliance partners, (*b*) the quality of the initial negotiation process, (*c*) the direct experience with the behaviour of the partners, and (*d*) the partners' behaviour outside the context of the strategic alliance.[34]

Market Entry Mode Choice

Given this broad spectrum of market entry modes, how do financial services firms choose? In general, four main approaches to market entry mode choice can be distinguished:[35]

- *The sales/opportunistic approach*: A firm largely implicitly chooses to follow an opportunistic approach. Market entry modes are selected without any clear strategy. This approach is chosen because the firm aims at maximizing short-term sales and therefore does not apply systematic selection criteria and as a consequence does not adapt its products and services to local needs. Little effort is made to control overseas distribution.

- *The naïve approach*: Some firms decide to apply the same or a similar market entry mode that has been used in the past. This approach follows pragmatic rules that have worked in the past with other countries.

- *The strategic approach*: The market entry strategy is based on an analysis of the market. The entry mode is chosen considering the most important factors that influence the success of alternative modes.

- *The imitation approach*: Second movers may decide to copy successful entry recipes. This approach is used frequently with financial services and is often labelled as 'herding'.

Assuming that the readers of this book are inclined to follow a strategic approach to market entry mode choice, the following sections offer some additional reflection on the topic. As discussed earlier, the choice of the market entry mode depends on several factors such as a financial institution's motivation, the product market being entered, the cultural distance, and the location advantages. A firm's motivation for its presence abroad usually has a strong influence on the choice of the organizational forms it adopts, at least when host country regulations do not constrain choice. The higher the financial services firms' motivation, the higher the level of commitment.

The organizational form that foreign financial services firms adopt in foreign markets reflects the product market they are entering. When banks wish to operate in the wholesale and corporate markets, they typically choose to open a branch or a representative office. On the contrary, banks wishing to operate in a retail market in a foreign country tend to operate via local subsidiaries, which trade on the basis of their own capital and reputation.[36] Larger firms are likely to prefer higher levels of equity ownership and commitment.[37] Larger banks, which enjoy more financial and managerial resources, have a higher propensity to grow in foreign markets by both internal and external growth and to set up foreign units requiring a higher level of commitment. In fact, constraints and the lack of complementary assets afflicting small-sized firms leave small-sized firms with fewer means of reducing uncertainty and induce them to favour entry modes requiring less commitment. Therefore, smaller banks would orient their internationalization strategies towards prudent arrangements (representatives' offices and/or affiliates), which allow both set-up costs and the risks involved in FDI to be reduced.

FDI in banking is significantly influenced by the size of the bank as well as by its multinational experience.[38] This phenomenon of 'incremental internationalization',[39] that is, a step-by-step increase in the firm's involvement in a foreign market, is empirically well documented. The propensity to augment the ownership level in foreign units tends to increase while experience in dealing with international operations is accumulated.[40] Empirical evidence confirms that earlier operations in the target country by the parent company increase the probability of choosing a wholly owned subsidiary.[41]

Cultural distance decreases the propensity of a bank to become heavily involved in the foreign country through the acquisition of local companies. The integration of an acquired company into a parent firm is complicated by the differences between the organizations involved and differences in organizational culture and management style. Many studies have found that cultural differences increase the probability that acquisitions will fail.[42] FDI by banks can be negatively influenced by the target country's political and economic risk.[43] As a result, the higher the wealth, size, and development of the market, the higher is the level of involvement of a bank and the lower the host country's political and economic risk.

This glimpse of some studies on market entry modes shows how difficult it is really to take a strategic approach to market entry mode selection. There are, in theory, many variables to consider and many studies deliver conflicting results on how these factors impact entry mode choice and ultimately, the performance of the internationalizing financial services firm. Fortunately, managers have learned to reduce complexity by applying 'simple rules' or 'collective intuition'.[44]

8

How to compete? The development of business and functional-level strategies

Once a presence in a foreign country is established, either through mergers and acquisitions, an organic growth mode, or a strategic alliance, financial services firms need to develop effective business and functional-level strategies to outpace their local competitors. There are various examples of successful business-level strategies to be found among the leading global financial services firms. This chapter explores how positional competitive advantages such as the early mover advantage as a foreign bank in the Czech Republic of Erste Bank as well as firm-based sources of competitive advantages such as the proprietary IT system of UBS can lead to superior performance.

This chapter has several objectives. It shows why profitability variance among financial services firms exists not only on an international level but also on a national scale. Size stabilizes profitability close to the industry average level, but relatively small and focused banks can show high profitability rates. Higher profitability depends on the ability of a financial services firm to understand the local market structure and develop positional advantages. This chapter also shows that another avenue to higher profitability is to deploy superior resources and capabilities in the local market. A third common way to internationalize in a profitable way is to concentrate on a narrow industry segment (or client group) and leverage superior capabilities on a global scale. This chapter introduces and illustrates these concepts with two case examples: Allianz and HBOS. These short case descriptions show how financial services firms can create unique strategic positions by developing differentiation and cost advantages as well as by focusing on well-defined target segments.

Where Does Competitive Advantage Come From?

Business-level strategies indicate the general direction of the firm in a specific market segment in terms of its cost position and/or differentiation position and define the breadth of the target segment. The choice of the business strategies is closely linked to the home-market competitive strategy, the rationale of internationalization, the choice of the entry timing and speed, as well as the entry mode. Successful internationalization strategies show a high degree of consistency among the various strategic choices. If the principal motive for internationalization is to follow large corporate clients to selected foreign markets, organic growth modes with a similar competitive strategy as in the home market are probably more appropriate than large-scale acquisitions that introduce radically different competitive strategies. If a bank enters India primarily for resource-seeking reasons it will have a different local strategy as opposed to a bank that aims at developing new markets. Similarly, competitive recipes in many emerging markets differ quite substantially from those in mature markets. What all competitive strategies have in common is that the goal of any financial services firm should be to reach a unique strategic position that is valued by the customers. At least three fundamental questions have to be asked for each new geographical segment the firm enters: What are we going to offer? Who are we going to serve? How are we going to deliver our services?[1]

Most financial services firms attempt to transfer their sources of competitive advantages that made them strong in their home markets to foreign countries. Fortis, for example, claims to grow by internationally leveraging core skills built in the Benelux (Belgium, the Netherlands, and Luxemburg) countries. Each of the major business segments of Fortis has a distinct internationalization strategy. The retail banking arm grows by rolling out the consumer finance platform within Europe. The insurance business is developed by leveraging the bancassurance model internationally (except in the United States). The growth strategy of the commercial and private banking arm is built around a pan-European product offering and a network for international multinational firms. The merchant banking activities of Fortis have a global reach with a focus on a specific industry (e.g. energy, commodities, or transportation) as well as selected products (e.g. custody, fund administration, or clearing). All business units are linked together by group-wide horizontal functions of risk, legal and compliance, human resources, ICT and operations, and facility and purchasing. Despite various global growth initiatives, Fortis still remains a regional star with 80 per cent of net profits in 2006 from the Benelux countries, with a goal to reduce the weight of Benelux to 70 per cent by 2009, which is reflected in the fact that over 50 per cent of the new senior managers are recruited for non-Benelux markets.

The Fortis illustration shows that it is a delicate task to gain competitive advantage as a foreign financial services firm, and not all business units have the same preparation and use the same strategy to internationalize. Instead, many financial institutions realize that international expansion has not been largely characterized by success and reduce their exposure to international markets. Citigroup sold its private banking business to the Italian Credem and HSBC is expected to sell half of its 800 retail branches in France to focus on the Asian high-growth markets, to mention just two examples.

The Origins of Performance Differences

Financial services firms are often accused of herding and of little differentiation. However, a closer look at the strategies shows that substantial differences in approach and business performance exist. In general, the overall profitability of a firm depends on the attractiveness of the industry and its ability to obtain positional advantages compared to rivals as well as the resource and capability endowment of the single firm. Market as well as firm-based conditions are of course highly dynamic. The steel industry was by far less attractive 10 years ago compared to today due to increased global demand and reduced international rivalry. The real estate finance business was attractive in the early 2000s but has now lost its appeal in many markets.

On the other hand, one can observe a high variance in profitability of firms competing in the same industry. An analysis[2] of the top 35 firms in terms of market capitalization within the global life insurance business (SIC code 6311) showed that profitability can vary significantly within a segment and market capitalization as an indicator of size is an unreliable predictor of profitability. ROA of the sample varied from 0.38 per cent to 4.57 per cent and total assets vary between USD 5 billion and USD 120 billion with a flat correlation between total assets and ROA.

In some markets, the profitability differences can be small. The top seven banks in France, for example, are placed within a ROA range of 0.97 per cent (HSBC France and Groupe Caisse d'Epargne) and 0.73 per cent (BNP Paribas).[3] In less consolidated banking markets, the performance differences can reach higher levels. In Italy, the lowest profitability reported by The Banker in 2007 is registered by Banca Popolare Intra with −2.71 per cent ROA and the highest profitability shows Banco Desio with 2.49 per cent ROA. A similar pattern can be observed in the German market: the lowest profitability is registered at −1.56 per cent (Allgemeine Hypothekenbank Rheinboden as of December 2005) and the highest at 2.25 per cent (Santander Consumer CC-Bank as of December 2006). The biggest 10 German banks are all to be found in the range of 0.26 per cent to 0.72 per cent ROA.

Size seems to stabilize profitability close to the industry average level, but relatively small and focused banks can also show high profitability rates. In Germany, the locally focused cooperative bank of Frankfurt (Frankfurter Volksbank) shows a profitability of 1.70 per cent ROA and the product-focused Volkswagen Bank reports a ROA of 1.68 per cent. Both of these top firms have a narrowly defined business model. The Frankfurter Volksbank concentrates on basic retail business in a limited geographical area where it successfully buys

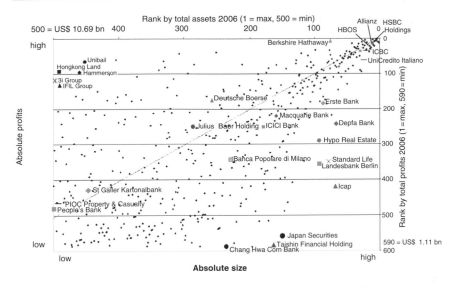

Figure 8.1. The impact of scale on absolute profits (based on www.forbes.com)

and integrates very small cooperative banks. Volkswagen Bank, on the other hand, offers a narrow range of highly standardized leasing and insurance services to semi-captive clients.

The speculation that firm size reduces profitability variance finds confirmation in Figure 8.1 which compares total asset rankings to absolute profit rankings in 2006. What one can observe is that relatively small financial services firms have a much higher profitability variance than the biggest 100 financial services firms. In addition, we can see that relatively small financial services firms manage to outperform even very large peers in terms of absolute profits because they have a narrowly focused business model and excel in what they do. Unibail-Rodamco, for example, is the leading pan-European commercial property investor and developer. In 2006, the bank reported total assets of USD 14.30 billion and USD 2.82 billion in profit, which is higher than the absolute profit of much bigger (i.e. 34–56 times by assets) peers like

- Danske Bank in Denmark: USD 2.4 billion in profit with total assets of USD 484.52 billion
- Commerzbank in Germany: USD 2.0 billion in profit with total assets of USD 801.18 billion

Even considering that Unibail-Rodamco had a splendid year in 2006 and an understandably more difficult year in 2007 with net profits decreasing by 55 per cent, the French firm still has a relatively better performance than many of its larger competitors in the financial services industry.

It is therefore not surprising that leading the pack in the German banking market in terms of profitability is not one of the biggest banks but rather a small subsidiary of a large Spanish bank—Santander Consumer CC-Bank. In 1987, the Spanish Santander Central Hispano acquired the 30-year-old German CC-Bank AG and immediately introduced the first private label visa credit card of a German bank. Other innovative services such as telephone banking, financing of dental prostheses, or vacation trips allowed the bank to reach over EUR 14 billion in credit volume. A peculiarity is that Santander Consumer CC-Bank was turned into an equal equity stake strategic alliance with the Royal Bank of Scotland in 1988. Just eight years later, the Spanish bank ended the alliance and bought all the shares back from RBS.

As these short examples show, at the root of profitability differences are market-based positional advantages as well as firm-based sources of competitive advantages.[4] These are briefly described in the following sections.

Financial services firms can develop positional advantages (see discussion of early mover advantages in Chapter 6) if they are able to map, interpret, and forecast the development of the industry structure. Changes in the forces that shape the industry such as the regulatory environment, customer needs, or information and communication technology can lead to a re-allocation of competitive advantage among incumbent firms. Some financial institutions might be able to react faster to external changes and/or the changes matching their existing resource and capability equipment. Financial services firms need to reduce the complexity of the competitive environment and distinguish lasting developments—which matter for the company—from short-term swings. Even drastic events such as the subprime crisis of late 2007 and the resulting credit crunch may only have a short-term impact for some financial services firms. However, there might be a long-term impact on firms that managed to stay out of the subprime market in the first place. Zurich Financial Services, for example, had an excellent performance in 2007 and its CEO stated proudly: 'We looked at some of these yield enhancing products. But we couldn't understand how they could make money and meet our risk criteria.'[5] Even though the Swiss company was able to avoid taking those risks and was minimally affected by the short-term global turmoil, it will still have to bear the consequences of the global credit crunch as well as changed regulations in risk management and product regulations as a consequence of the subprime crisis.

The second factor influencing the profitability of individual firms is their resource and capability endowment. The ability to differentiate their product range from others in the market, or offer it at lower prices, leads to a strong competitive position. Company resources such as patents, marketing capabilities, efficient and large-scale production processes, or excellent customer service strengthen the competitive position of firms.

Towards a Unique Strategic Position

To outperform local competition, foreign financial services firms must define and create a unique strategic position. As mentioned earlier, a rough way to define a unique strategic position is to find a new combination of answers to several fundamental questions of (*a*) who are the target customers; (*b*) what products or services should be offered at what price; and (*c*) what distinctive functional strategies should be put in place to operationally deliver the chosen products or services. Strategic positions change over time and firms attempt to play the game better (i.e. increased efficiency), or to play the game differently (i.e. increased effectiveness).

Many well-known scholars in the field of strategic management have put more emphasis on the benefits of playing the game differently. The end of incrementalism has been announced by several authors in the field of strategic management. They describe how rule breakers such as IKEA, the Body Shop, Charles Schwab, Dell Computers, Swatch, or Southwest Airlines have managed to shape their industries. Strategists and senior executives need to set preconditions that can give rise to strategy innovation rather than developing strategies themselves; planning and strategizing are even seen as two distinct activities.[6]

The financial services industry produces fewer examples of revolutionary new business models, mainly due to its highly regulated markets. Nevertheless, we have seen radically new business segments emerge such as direct banking/insurance, peer-to-peer financing, or micro-financing. Within established business segments, many examples of firms that question the dominant industry logic exist: Banco Santander, for example, challenged established players in the Spanish market with aggressive interest rates on savings accounts. UniCredit abolished the EUR 50 fee customers had to pay to close a savings account a few months before banks in Italy were legally obliged to do so. It is, however, more difficult for established companies to strategically innovate. Banca Mediolanum quickly gained a substantial market share in the Italian and Spanish retail segments with an innovative distribution concept based on well-trained financial advisers who visit retail clients at home. Many examples of revolutionary strategies can be found when analysing the way financial institutions organize their back-office processes.

One avenue to create strategic innovation is to identify gaps in the industry and turn them into mass markets. To overcome the structural and cultural inertia of success is to monitor the strategic health of the company, create a positive crisis, challenge the strategic planning process, and institutionalize a questioning attitude. Successful strategic innovators are faster at selling new strategic challenges to stakeholders outside and inside the firm. Firms that are able and willing to activate their thinking at different starting points are more likely to escape existing assumptions and stereotypes and ultimately see or discover something new.[7]

To strategically innovate and create industry breakpoints means to come up with a new offering to the market, clearly superior in terms of the value perceived by the consumer and the delivered cost of the offering, that changes the rules of the competitive game.

- *Divergent industry breakpoints*: They are usually product/market driven and lead to an increasingly innovative variety in the competitive offerings. Organizational capabilities that are needed to create divergent industry breakpoints are direct innovation (largely based on the creativity and market sensitivity of senior managers) and spontaneous innovation as bottom-up initiatives and stakeholder networking.

- *Convergent industry breakpoints*: These involve improvements in the systems and processes employed to deliver the products or services. The main capabilities that may lead to convergent industry breakpoints are systematization (turning a task into mass production), continual improvement, and process re-engineering.[8]

High-growth companies tend to focus less on competition than their less successful rivals do. To create value innovation,[9] senior managers need to identify, articulate, and challenge the strategic logic of the firm and think with the logic of a new entrant. However, this is a difficult task, as shown by the research on 'dominant logic'.[10] The concept of dominant logic refers to 'a mind set or a world view or conceptualization of the business and the administrative tools to accomplish goals and make decisions in that business'.[11] The two main sources of dominant logic are the reinforcement of a world view by market success and complex problem-solving behaviour (cognitive simplifications by drawing on conventional wisdom or past experiences as well as cognitive bias due to inadequate or missing information). To overcome phenomena of dominant logic and innovate strategically, firms need to develop the ability of the firm or its dominant coalition to learn, or perhaps 'unlearn'[12] first, to get rid of previously acquired mental models. Top managers are less likely to respond appropriately or quickly enough to situations where the dominant logic is different. These difficulties caused by distinct dominant logics represent additional hidden costs of geographical diversification.

In a fluctuating and competitive environment, strategy formation abilities are more likely to be a source of competitive advantage than clever strategic positioning.[13] Decreased sustainability of competitive advantage due to weakened barriers against imitation and substitution has given rise to a phenomenon labelled 'hypercompetition'.[14] Firms in the financial services industry need to destroy their competitive advantages themselves before their competitors do it and strategies can only be short-term by nature. Logical strategic behaviour leads to predictable actions and should be avoided. In a recent auction process for a bank in a Central Eastern European country, a competing bank reported that its rival in the past always increased the final bid by 20 per cent. It was obviously easy to win the bid against that bank. The conclusion is that predictable behaviour does not always create competitive advantage.

The ability to identify, develop, and protect surprising sources of competitive advantage is an essential competence in hypercompetitive markets. To survive in a hypercompetitive environment, firms may need to develop superior strategic capabilities (e.g. how decisions are made and implemented). Most unique strategic positions therefore last only for a limited period of time, but there are several ways to protect the sources of competitive advantage (CA):[15]

- *Make CA hard to identify*: Some of the most profitable financial services firms are not listed and have no obligation to report profitability in detail. To obscure performance is a viable way to protect sources of competitive advantage.

- *Make CA hard to understand*: If CA is based on multiple sources and the interface of several processes, it is more difficult for competitors to understand where true CA comes from.

- *Make it hard to replicate*: Even if it is possible to diagnose CA, financial services firms can make it hard to replicate CA because it is based on tacit knowledge and less mobile resources.

- *Make CA hard to imitate*: Financial services firms can create and keep first mover advantages by exploiting all interesting investment opportunities first; imitation barriers can also come from the ability to credibly threaten potential imitators with retaliation.

The following two examples, Allianz[16] and HBOS,[17] illustrate how internationalizing financial services firms attempt to build up and protect unique strategic positions in foreign markets.

Allianz in China

Activities of Allianz in China started in 1917 when it provided insurance coverage to salesmen of export firms or tradesmen living in the main coastal cities like Shanghai or to companies like Siemens that aimed to control the machine transportation risks. At the beginning of the twentieth century, the then named Allianz Stuttgarter Verein established commercial relationships with companies operating in China, just nine years before Allianz's current leading foreign competitor AIG entered China. At that time, signing and handing out German insurance policies to clients in Shanghai was easy because there was no regulating authority as there is today, the China Insurance Regulatory Commission (CIRC).

The business of Allianz in China was nevertheless marginal until the beginning of the 1980s when the German insurer developed its activities in the Chinese market through cooperation agreements with the People's Bank of China (PBC) and Chinese insurance companies like PICC (People's Insurance Company of China), China Life, PAIC (Ping An Insurance Company), and CPIC (China Pacific Insurance Co. Ltd). Allianz contributed with their technical know-how and supported mainly reinsurance businesses. The know-how transfer happened primarily in small meetings with Chinese politicians and financial specialists who wanted to know how the European bank and insurance system operates. First, the know-how transfer was confined to fairly open conversations and only later was it converted into more structured workshops and training courses of 20–30 participants. The overall objective was to build relationships as these were extremely beneficial for the approval of requested insurance licences. There was no service that Allianz received in return from its Chinese alliance partners, and the creation of relationships with Chinese partners emerged as a long and difficult process.

In 1994, Allianz subsequently set up representative offices in Shanghai, Beijing, and Guangzhou. Allianz had big plans to further expand in China but new limitations on foreign companies were passed in 1995, which complicated Allianz's operating business. For instance, foreign insurance firms were not allowed to own more than 51 per cent within a strategic alliance. Furthermore, joint venture partners were assigned by the regulatory body and could not be chosen by the foreign financial services firm. Insurance licences were approved in favour of companies with longer established economic as well as political relationships.

Strategic Alliance with Dazhong

Despite a difficult regulatory environment, Allianz increased its commitment to the Chinese market and found a valuable partner in the local company Dazhong, which had operated in the segment of property insurance since 1995 and appeared to have seemingly compatible strategic objectives. The joint venture Allianz Dazhong Life Insurance was founded, and after two years of lobbying a licence was granted to operate its business starting from January 1999. As the business evolved, it was soon obvious that Allianz was eager to expand more aggressively and could no longer align with Dazhong's 'wait-and-see' strategy. Dazhong, on the other hand, underestimated Allianz's commitment and ambitious business goals for the Chinese market. Due to

Dazhong's difficulties in its property business, the Chinese partner was not able or willing to sponsor the planned growth with the required financial resources necessary for the 49 per cent ownership of the joint venture. As a result, Allianz's business was involuntarily confined to the area of Shanghai where it was confronted with the highest concentration of competitors and the most demanding customers. The JV was therefore doomed to languish due to its inability to grow. This was reason enough for Allianz to scan the market for another partner that would be more compatible in terms of strategy, objectives, and resources.

Building Strategic Alliances

Soon Allianz identified CITIC Trust (CITIC Trust and Investment Company Ltd.) as a matching partner who bought Dazhong's shares and thus received 49 per cent of the joint venture in October 2005. The new joint venture was named Allianz China Life Insurance Co. (AZCL) to prevent confusion for the customers, since CITIC Trust was already engaged with Prudential Plc in a 50/50 joint venture in the life insurance segment (CITIC Prudential). CITIC Trust is one of China's largest business conglomerates with total assets of RMB 929.2 billion in 2006, corresponding to EUR 87.8 billion. The first three years of cooperation so far confirmed Allianz's initial assessment that CITIC would be a valuable partner in a market growing more than 30 per cent per year. CITIC, on the other hand, found in Allianz a partner with technical expertise and access to the bancassurance distribution channel in China through Allianz's equity partnership with Industrial and Commercial Bank of China (ICBC). AZCL managed to achieve gross written premiums (GWP) of EUR 120 million in 2006, which represented an increase of 310 per cent compared to the previous year. As a result, AZCL ranked 4th (from 8th place in 2005) among the 26 foreign life insurance joint ventures in China in 2006.

Within AZCL, both parties were able to merge their complementary assets, contributing extensive know-how of the insurance business with deep knowledge about local market conditions in order to drive business successfully in mainland China. As one of the three national trust and investment companies controlled by the People's Bank of China, CITIC Trust is equipped with a robust financial structure and a well-developed network of influence ('Guanxi'). Due to Allianz's international risk management expertise and CITIC Trust's local capital management and financial know-how, AZCL was able to grow its reputation as a provider of professional services and tailor-made products. It offers a broad range of insurance services to individuals as well as corporate customers.

The increased sales volume in 2006 built a stable foundation for the further development of AZCL's infrastructure. The joint venture grew its presence from two cities in 2004 to a presence of 38 sales service centres in 16 cities within 6 provinces at the beginning of 2008. The current five provinces (Sichuan since November 2006, Shenzhen since May 2006, Guangdong since January 2005, Zhejiang since April 2006, Shanghai since January 1999) list an average GDP growth of 13 per cent and the disposable incomes per urban resident promise sustainable growth potential. Further penetration was supported by the mass recruitment of single brand agents and the intensified use of bank outlets as a complementary capillary distribution channel.[18]

Future growth should come from expansion into eight new provinces. All of these provinces represent attractive target markets because of their large population that is quickly gaining purchasing power. Unfortunately, the outbranching speed is restricted by the CIRC as it approves only two licences per year to foreign companies whereas domestic firms can receive up to 10–12 licences in one approval. To reach the goal of becoming the leading international life insurer in China, Allianz created a rather unique strategic position with a multi-channel distribution system that was strongly dependent on bancassurance.

This is not an easy undertaking considering the numerous changes and additions of regulations in the Chinese insurance market. For instance, starting in 2000, foreign firms were no longer allowed to have controlling stakes in JVs and only the legal form of a 50/50 joint venture was allowed. Business success in China often depends on political interests. Such regulations could further decrease the already low market share of foreign insurers of roughly 2 per cent in 2008. This stands in strong contrast to the Indian insurance market development where foreign insurers claim an overall market share of up to 30 per cent in the life segment. Foreign ownership in Indian insurance firms is limited to 26 per cent, but beyond this restriction, free competition can take place because domestic as well as foreign companies are liable to the same laws.

The acquisition of Dresdner Bank by Allianz in 2001 added banking branches in Shanghai and Beijing that offer investment banking services as well as transaction and credit products to corporate clients. Dresdner Bank has a small but profitable business in China, but potential synergies are not actively sought because costs are too high for the approval of necessary licences and implementation costs.

In February 2003, Allianz entered the property/casualty segment with the creation of the branch Allianz Insurance Company Guangzhou (AZCN). The branch is wholly owned by Allianz Deutschland, which on the one hand provides the advantage of having full control but on the other hand does not allow for AZCN to open new branches by itself. Under Chinese regulations, only full subsidiaries have permission to open other branches. To enter fund management markets Allianz initiated cooperation activities in 1994 with

Guotai Junan Securities Co., Ltd., and received authorization in April 2003 to establish the joint venture GTJA (Junan Allianz Fund Management Co.). In 2003, Mondial Assistance China was established to enter the market segments of roadside assistance and travel medical assistance services.

Competition Develops as Fast as the Business Grows

Since the opening of the Chinese insurance market, competition has been growing steadily as the market is highly attractive:[19]

- Number of potential customers is huge
- Chinese save approximately 25 per cent of their income
- One-child policy reduces obligations of family support
- Population is rapidly ageing (approximately 23 per cent will be over 64 by 2050)
- Salaries are rising and an affluent middle class is growing quickly
- Substantial migration from rural to urban areas ensures constant growth rates around big cities

In 2006, total market share of foreign joint ventures accounted for 5.9 per cent of the Chinese life insurance market. Measured by GWP, Allianz ranks fourth with a 5 per cent share of the rather small market served by foreign joint ventures[20] after AIG with 29 per cent, Generali with 22 per cent, and Prudential with 7 per cent.[21] When performance is measured in Annual Premium Equivalent (APE),[22] Allianz drops to fifth place. The strong market position among the foreign joint ventures of AIG derives from AIG's early and committed entry into the Chinese insurance market. The regulations were less strict at that time, and AIG has developed better government relationships compared to its peers, which translates into a 44.5 per cent market share of APE among the foreign financial services firms. One explanation could be that AIG fully owns its subsidiaries in China, possible due to its early entry.

High competition has been emerging since the opening of the Chinese insurance market as foreign insurance players establish their brands and develop a strong customer base. The pressure for Allianz to strengthen its unique strategic position is increasing. Rivalry among established and new firms is not as high as in developed markets since the overall market size is huge and growing. This is reflected by the fact that the Chinese hold around 40 per cent of their bank deposits as a reserve for health care and retirement.[23] Nevertheless, domestic- and foreign-funded companies search for differentiation potential and develop ways to block new entrants.[24] To reach a critical mass in the retail business, strong relationships with the government and top banks are essential key success factors. Chinese customers still have to be educated on financial services products and therefore mainly trust in brands or personal relationships when choosing their suppliers. The product innovation rate is nevertheless rather high. Prudential's track record in product innovation is unparalleled and it attempts to use cross-selling initiatives to guide customers towards more sophisticated products. In a nutshell, competitors refine their own strategic positions by establishing their brands, developing their distribution mix, and delivering more sophisticated products even though competitive rivalry still remains low.

Preparing for Stronger Competition: Marketing Activities of Allianz

Foreign financial services firms can choose rather disparate competitive strategies. However, in the fast growing areas of China, domestic and foreign financial services firms are not forced to strongly differentiate their offers. This might be different in more mature areas around the big cities. Differentiation begins with a long firm history and large size, which can impress Chinese customers and influence their decision-making process. With almost 100 years' history in China and its cooperation with ICBC as the world's most valuable bank and CITIC, AZCL is appealing for Chinese customers. AZCL invested in various marketing activities with a multi-million Euro budget in 2007, since Christian Molt, the CEO of AZCL, considers brand building as a key success factor.

To create a brand identity and brand awareness, AZCL organizes road shows and engages strongly as a sponsor of sport and other events worldwide. A downscaled model of the famous Munich Allianz Arena was built in Shanghai, and Allianz also sponsored the Formula 1 event in 2007 in Shanghai. Allianz engages in the German initiative 'Deutschland—Land der Ideen' (i.e. 'Germany—land of ideas') within which people tour for three years through China representing Germany with its culture and values. For many Chinese, Germany still stands for quality, solidity, and trust. Another high-impact marketing event was organized in January 2008, where the Chinese Olympic soccer team played against FC Bayern Munich in the Allianz Arena in Germany. This event was advertised locally and widely broadcasted on Chinese free TV, connecting technical innovation (i.e. the Allianz Arena) and German cultural values with the Allianz brand.

The Allianz sales academy is another building block of the marketing and sales strategy of AZCL. In most countries of presence, Allianz uses a multi-channel strategy where the weights of the single channels can vary considerably, especially as bancassurance becomes more important throughout Asia. Allianz has created an academy in cooperation with Shanghai University of Finance & Economics. The goal of this unit is to provide high-quality training for insurance agencies as well as for bank representatives and agents. As such, it efficiently transferred insurance product know-how to banking staff in the branches, for example, through e-learning modules.

AZCL monitors and improves the quality of its services by cooperating with the International Association of Registered Financial Consultants (IARFC), a firm with global presence and active in the field of training, support, and improvement of the professionalism of financial advisers. Within IARFC, 110 Allianz China Life agents graduated from internationally registered qualification courses in August 2006.

The Multi-Channel Distribution Approach

A key driver of AZCL's success in the Chinese insurance market is its multi-channel distribution system. The distribution system aims to establish new branches and thus a higher presence in and penetration of approved provinces, enabling a broader market reach. The system embraces professional agent teams, agency companies, and brokers as well as direct sales teams, especially for key account corporate customers and bank branches. The distribution mix is still country-specific, as seen in Figure 8.2.

To reach critical mass in China, AZCL is able to use the capital inflow from the bancassurance business, accounting for 73 per cent, to build up a stable agency structure. The quality of products and services launched by the insurer was secured by a new agency model which enhances training and performance management of local agents. In this context, the emergence of an e-agency platform as well as the foundation of ABA acts as energizing pillars. AZCL aggressively recruits agents and denoted triple-digit growth in number of agents in 2006, accounting nationwide for 4,000. At the beginning of 2008, AZCL recruited its 10,000th agent. Top bank outlets

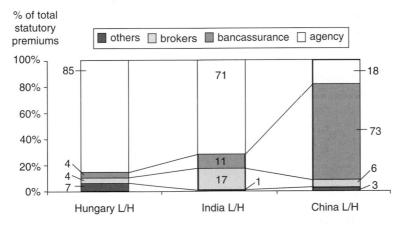

Figure 8.2. Multi-channel distribution of Allianz in selected countries 2006 (Allianz July 2007)

selling Allianz products more than quadrupled to more than 800 by the end of 2006.

It is not possible to scale a blueprint multi-distribution-channel system from one country to another without significant adaptations. In Japan, for instance, bancassurance was completely prohibited until April 2001 when the government loosened the restrictions step-by-step and finally opened up bancassurance entirely in December 2007. In Korea, regulation was even higher as the government restricted product sales of a financial institution in collaboration with an insurance company to 25 per cent of its total insurance sales, forcing a bank to cooperate with at least four insurance companies. Deregulation in the Korean market began in 2003 and is ongoing. In China, on the contrary, bancassurance business for Allianz with 800 bank outlets, of which 474 belong to ICBC, is the leading and most important distribution channel. This evolved from the strong demand of banks to sell insurance products as premiums are easily earned money, although at lower margins. Finally, in India Allianz sells around 80 per cent of its insurance products via agency and even though bancassurance consists of cooperations with up to 100 banks, this only makes up 10–12 per cent of the distribution mix.

Allianz had to adapt to many different conditions in new target markets, which formed their individual business-level strategy. Nevertheless, adaptation developed specific know-how and Allianz is now able to flexibly set up an efficient distribution system adapted to country-specific conditions and respective market demand.

Bancassurance grew into the strongest distribution channel and is expected to further dominate distribution channels in the future. The support of major banks (Agricultural Bank of China, China Construction Bank, Bank of China, Industrial and Commercial Bank of China, Bank of Communication) was critical for success in the Chinese market.[25] The CEO of Prudential insists on claiming that everyone who wants to build a stable insurance business in Asia must establish an agency network.[26] Overall sales in the Chinese insurance market are driven by agents (54 per cent)[27] even though these agents are typically untrained and not productive, and high turnover is prevalent.

Bancassurance distribution mainly sells single premium products of low margin due to a lack of product knowledge and poor training systems. Via the direct sales channel, large group policies of low margins are mainly sold, as seen in the case of Generali.[28] As shown in Figure 8.3, for Allianz, bancassurance is presently the most important sales channel (73 per cent Life/Health segment). In order to meet this demand, Allianz established a bancassurance academy (ABA). Allianz (18 per cent premiums generated by agency in 2006) continues to work on the development and training of its agency. AIG, Prudential (88 per cent premiums generated by agents in 2006, 91 per cent

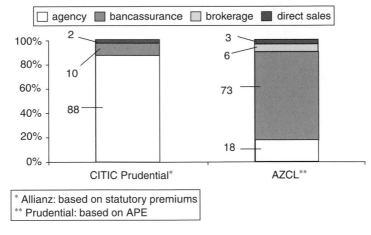

Figure 8.3. Towards unique strategic positions in China: multi-channel distribution of two foreign JVs in 2006 (Jones 2006)

of sales is regular premium mode) and Generali all count on the strength of a well-established agent network but also further growth through additional distribution channels like cooperation with banks, brokerage, and direct sales.

Allianz plans to have a network of 40,000 agents by 2010 and trains them using its in-house agency model but also including Professional Patterns of Management training (best practice education of a partner sales consulting firm). AIG built up actuarial centres approved by the US Society of Actuaries, makes use of LOMA training services and uses quality certificates by Société Générale de Surveillance (SGS) as an independent quality signal. Agency accounted for 88 per cent in Prudential's distribution mix in 2006. Prudential put so much weight on agency because this is the distribution channel selling high-profit products and able to practise cross-selling. Significantly more motivation by incentives can be generated in terms of external bank staff. Prudential makes use of classroom training and live experience as well as personal effectiveness training. Within this context, talented professionals from across the Chinese-speaking area are used as mentors and educators for Prudential's local resources.

Prudential recruited its 14,000th agent by the end of 2006 compared to Allianz's 10,000th agent in January 2008. Prudential developed the capability to set up country- and market-specific distribution systems like Allianz. Prudential and Manulife also set the pace in market penetration as measured by licensed provinces (Table 8.1).

To signal the importance and quality of the IPO of ICBC, Allianz became a strategic partner of ICBC with an investment of USD 1 billion. This was advance proof of trust and opened the doors for the strategic cooperation

Table 8.1. Licensed provinces in China in 2006 (Jones 2006)

	AIG	Manulife	Prudential	Generali	Allianz
Number of provinces	4	7	7	3	4
Number of cities	8	15	14	6	8

with ICBC in 2006. ICBC in turn supported Allianz with its branch system. This agreement was made in collaboration with Goldman Sachs and American Express, with a total value of USD 3.78 billion. The investment corresponded to 7.2406 percentage in total shares of ICBC in January 2008.[29] Goldman Sachs held 4.9327, Allianz 1.9258, and American Express 0.3821 percentage of total shares.[30]

In order to develop into a modern financial services group, ICBC bought a large amount of expertise in an area in which ICBC did not have many alternatives in the choice of its strategic partners. BofA (CCB, June 2005),[31] RBS (BoC, August 2005),[32] and HSBC were already engaged in partnerships and Citigroup and Deutsche Bank were not interested in a cooperation.[33] Goldman Sachs provides know-how in corporate governance, internal control, and risk management as well as for operational processes like treasury and closure of bad loans. American Express supports ICBC in the bank card business and Allianz enhances the bancassurance division of China's largest retail and wholesale bank with leading and innovative products and services. Together with Allianz, ICBC launched a new e-sales system on their website.

In the context of bancassurance education, ABA plays a decisive strategic role in Allianz's Asian expansion and strategic positioning. The increasing number of partnerships in Asia led to a higher contribution and consequently, a sharp appreciation of the bancassurance distribution channel. Its percentage rose by 22 per cent in five years from initially 3 per cent in 2001 to 25 per cent in the year 2006 in Asia.[34] The ABA therefore is not a one-off event but the first of the seven planned Allianz Bancassurance Academies in the insurer's seven Asian bancassurance markets. The Allianz Bancassurance Academies tackle the lack of qualified agents in several ways. First, Allianz addresses the lack of professional labour, which is partly due to the novelty of the distribution channel but also to the fact that many workers prefer to work for local companies due to perceived better career opportunities.[35] Second, Allianz tries to compensate its loss of control due to the restricted possibilities of entry modes in Asia, especially in the Chinese market. Wholly owned subsidiaries bear higher risks but also enable the parent company to more easily achieve, retain, and control business processes like building a brand identity in foreign markets. To insure quality of service and products, by means of ABA, Allianz is able to directly infuse its enormous experience in the global insurance industry and teach Allianz's best practices not only to new agency staff but also to employees of banking partners like ICBC. This will possibly create coherence with the insurer's other worldwide business operations and result in a globally cohesive brand identity and strengthen the partnership with key distribution channels. In addition, innovation is stimulated and will assist in the brand image building process. Finally, this is complemented by Allianz's chair at Tongji University, offering postgraduate programmes and a degree in insurance business management, and furthered by Dresdner Bank's chair for studies and research in the finance sector at Tongji University.[36]

Governing the Chinese Operations

The operational management concerning for instance IT, product development, monitoring and controlling is coordinated from the local head office in Singapore which is also the contact for reporting. The Chinese units are also directly coupled to Allianz SE in Munich in terms of capital needs and general strategic direction. The Chinese operations have an exceptional position because of their size, specific requirements, and growth potential. The connection to the head office in Munich is therefore very close.

The Singapore Regional Office directly monitors the profitability of the single initiatives in China and observes the development in a rather detailed way. A representative regularly visits China to discuss financial needs and opportunities for complementary resources provided by the head office. Another governing mechanism comes from the selection of key local decision-makers. Allianz's global governance model positions successful and reliable German managers from headquarters in key positions in the subsidiaries. Consequently, the CEO of AZCL, Christian Molt, is a German and local managers are used only in positions where more local comprehension and knowledge is necessary such as in marketing or distribution.

Outlook

In 2008, Allianz had roughly 1,400 employees in China in nearly all of its core businesses, namely, life and health insurance, property and casualty insurance, asset management, banking and assistance services as well as travel assistance. The total premium income in 2006 in China reached EUR 135 million, which indicates more than 250 per cent increase compared to 2005. The future outlook also looks good as the expected market growth in China for the property/casualty (P/C) and life/health (L/H) segments amounts to EUR 97 billion in 2010, which represents a CAGR of 15 per cent referring to the market volume of EUR 55 billion in 2006.

Allianz aggressively expands its businesses mainly via AZCL but also by means of other partnerships. Allianz tries to catch up to its main competitors like AIG and Generali by applying a differentiation strategy, which is mainly supported by its brand awareness programme and the strong relationships with key stakeholders such as ICBC and other well-known and locally recognized banks. Next to the multi-distribution channel system and Allianz's long experience in international risk management, the set-up of the ABA is a distinctive investment to create another unique selling proposition. The education of an excellent sales force with specific Allianz know-how can lead to a perceived differentiated service of higher quality for the customer once growth rates slow. Finally, Allianz sets a rapid pace by devoting itself to high company goals such as the achievement of EUR 1 billion GWP, to triple its revenues from bancassurance, enlarging the agency force to as many as 40,000 agents to further strengthen distribution, and gain economies of scale by 2011. Allianz aims to become the leading and most preferred international insurer in China in order to achieve high performance results.

HBOS: Transferring the Cost-Leadership Strategy Abroad

HBOS (Halifax Bank of Scotland) managed to rough up the British financial services landscape with a clear cost-leadership strategy, simple but customer-centred products and a focused internationalization strategy. The 'new force in the UK' was created by the merger of Halifax and Bank of Scotland in September 2001. Halifax was founded in 1853 and had run businesses in stock brokerage, personal banking, real estate, and insurance. Before the merger, Halifax was the UK's largest mortgage lender. The roots of Bank of Scotland date back to 1695, making it Scotland's oldest bank. In the 1970s, the Bank of Scotland entered a phase of product as well as geographical diversification. A dedicated Oil Division was created to offer field exploration services and, as a consequence, the first overseas office in Houston (Texas, United States) was founded. Branches in Moscow, Hong Kong, and Singapore followed. Through the acquisition of Countrywide in New Zealand in 1987 and Bank of Western Australia in 1995, the Bank of Scotland also entered into geographically very distant markets.

HBOS is headquartered in Edinburgh and experienced a fast growth phase. It advanced to become the fourth largest bank in the UK in 2007 behind HSBC, Royal Bank of Scotland, and Barclays Bank.[37] HBOS is the largest mortgage and savings provider in the UK, employing 73,500 people worldwide and serving around 23 million customers. The operational businesses are spread over five divisions:

- Retail banking
- Corporate banking
- Insurance and investment management
- Treasury and asset management
- International

Building Sources of Sustainable Competitive Advantage

The merger between Halifax and Bank of Scotland was announced in May 2001 and was approved in July of the same year. The operational units kept their original brand names, following a multi-brand strategy, and HBOS was created as a holding company. From the beginning of the merger, the management team announced that it would execute a growth strategy in which it would aggressively compete against the established banks by attacking their market share based on cost efficiency. At HBOS cost leadership is taken very seriously and penetrates the daily activities. As Phil Kershaw, Operations Director for HBOS International, states: 'Cost-leadership begins with the hearts and minds of a company; with its culture.'[38] The cost-leadership philosophy has to be endemic in employees' daily business and thus be embedded in the organization's DNA.

Besides its general attention to cultural aspects, another core pillar of the cost-leadership strategy of HBOS is its constant search for low-cost locations. HBOS has only two prestigious offices: one in Edinburgh and one in London. Mostly, the bank locates its operations in low-profile buildings and places that are geographically close but not expensive—such as Leeds or Halifax. In these cities employers do not have to pay a premium price for their workforce. But HBOS does not believe in aggressive offshoring activities because it might be possible to reduce costs once but it is difficult to constantly lower the expenses for even basic activities by 10 per cent every year if the processing centre is far away or even outsourced.

A third building block of HBOS's cost-leadership strategy is based on its capability to design lean business processes. The bank tries to implement processes that follow the 'one and done' principle. The goal is to avoid having too many papers flying around, the bank clerks in the retail branch will verify the customers' requests and then make the changes themselves if possible. This way not only are costs driven down but the service level increases as well. Customers can get an approval for a credit card application or a mortgage loan in real time. The essential leverage for cost efficiency is hence to design administrative processes in such a way that fewer employees and layers are involved. This results in high responsiveness and fast execution as seen when customer data need to be changed; an employee would directly arrange changes with the client in the system instead of triggering a long bureaucratic chain.

The fourth building block is that overheads are kept low. The international business of HBOS is run by a very small team of six members, and most of their time is spent working on concrete projects in the foreign locations.

A fifth aspect of HBOS's cost-leadership strategy is to reduce the overall purchasing costs. The IT system of the bank is fairly old but built for scale and low cost. New purchasing systems allowed the reduction of the number of suppliers and increasing transparency of costs.

The merger between Halifax and Bank of Scotland led to a substantial reduction of costs. Such cost reductions began with the very beginning of the merger as it provided total cost benefits of about GBP 620 million per year in three years following the merger.[39] Both parties contribute with complementary capabilities: Halifax has extensive know-how in personal finance products and Bank of Scotland in corporate banking and the credit card business. The merger resulted in 2,000 lay-offs, which is relatively small considering the size of the merger. This can be attributed to small redundancies and no expected branch closures. The two merging banks had almost no geographical or industry overlaps.[40]

The first big cost-cutting potential was identified during procurement, which at the time of the merger reached a spending volume of GBP 1.7 billion per year. The total of suppliers, around 100,000 just after the merger, was reduced to 28,000 and the number of procurement account codes was reduced from 17,000 to 27 commodities that were separated into 142 categories.[41] Through the HBOS supplier relationship management system (SRM) the bank planned to save GBP 300 million (EUR 469 million) by mid-2005[42] mainly by integrating the diverse operational systems and duplicated data of the merged financial services firms. The increased flexibility of the new HBOS SRM would make it easy to switch to the euro currency and to take full advantage of increased visibility of group expenditure. Cost savings were achieved by tight monitoring of costs and increased bargaining power with suppliers due to order grouping and conducting an actual-target comparison.[43]

Positioning HBOS as a cost leader in the UK financial services sector paid off, as Phil Hodkinson, the former Group Finance Director, emphasized: '... cost efficiency is a source of sustainable competitive advantage'.[44] By steadily improving the cost structure evident from a declining cost–income ratio that dropped from 45.2 per cent in 2002 to 40.9 per cent in 2006,[45] targeting the mid-30s by 2010, HBOS became the second largest bank in the UK measured by earnings. But a low-cost structure does not necessarily mean a low service quality. HBOS was capable of delivering lowest prices while at the same time delivering high service, which resulted in an annual increase of 6 per cent in productivity. HBOS achieved this by gaining market share and thus increasing revenues by 12 per cent per year while costs increased by only 6 per cent per year.[46]

HBOS Attacks Incumbent UK Banks

As part of its strategy, HBOS undertakes aggressive measures to grow its business in its UK home market and compete against the domestic 'big four': HSBC Holdings, Royal Bank of Scotland, Barclays, and Lloyds TSB, which controlled 83 per cent of the small business banking market in December 2001[47] compared to HBOS's 3 per cent market share.[48] The predominant banks have enjoyed generous margins thus far. There was little incentive for them to deliver innovative services or change their basic competitive approach. HBOS's strategy aims at shifting the operating model to a point where competitors simply cannot follow. The goal is to become the cost leader, which will provide HBOS still with big or even higher margins than its competitors and put it into a position to drive down costs continuously year by year and at the same time return created value to the customer. For instance, HBOS launched several products at considerably lower prices or higher interest rates. At the end of 2001, HBOS launched a business current account for small and medium enterprises (SMEs) that gave 2 per cent (raised to 3 per cent one year later) credit interest on savings while the big four paid 0 per cent to their customers. Bank of Scotland announced it would double its market share of the UK's SME banking sector to 6 per cent by the end of 2004. Despite this high ambition, HBOS reached 5 per cent by the end of 2007. In 2006, 15,800 and during 2007 about 14,600 SME businesses switched to HBOS which contributed substantially to the 16 per cent increase in total income of the business banking during 2007.[49] In the current account market HBOS increased its market share from initially 12 per cent by the end of 2002 to 15 per cent in 2005 and to an estimated market share of 22 per cent in 2007.[50] Since the launch of the new business current account in 2001, HBOS realized an outstanding track record, gaining 1.6 million new customers until September 2002 when it again raised the interest rate to 3 per cent. In 2003, HBOS gained another 900,000 new customers and acquired 879,000 new customers in 2006 and 1 million new accounts in 2007.[51]

Another smart competitive move was made in 2003, when HBOS launched a free 'packaged account' which had lower requirements to be opened, thus aiming at a broader range of customers and offering more transparent additional services that are regularly used by the customers and imply a direct value-added effect. Along with this service HBOS provided account-switching services to keep switching costs low (e.g. a two-minute application or extended free overdraft during the switching process),[52] a practice that was introduced four years later to the Italian market by UniCredit Group. At the beginning of 2008, HBOS offered a current account with a 6.17 per cent interest rate for up to GBP 2,500 and the requirement for a monthly fund of at least GBP 1,000.

Another element of the cost-leadership strategy of HBOS was to divest from unprofitable businesses. The bank also attempted to create a culture of cost discipline and frugality. HBOS also announced a savings plan in 2006 to improve the cost structure by GBP 300 million annually in savings until the end of 2009. Capital discipline is an essential cultural element to achieve cost leadership. This translates into treating capital as a scarce resource and growing by own financial strength, that is, organically, as a first priority. Each business grows by its own funding. HBOS plans to fund 13 per cent of its annual asset growth internally. This capital discipline is driven by the management team's interpretation of its mission primarily to deploy shareholder capital as efficiently and sustainably as possible at all levels of the organization.

Another strategic pillar at HBOS is 'colleague development', which aims to anchor the cost efficiency attitude in employees', especially managers' and top executives', daily operational behaviour. This general goal should be achieved by specific training programmes, the creation of a positive working environment, and an incentive system that involves ownership by colleagues.[53]

To summarize, HBOS executes its cost-leadership philosophy to deliver a more efficient cost structure than its main competitors. Gained profits can in turn be reinvested and used to offer customers low-priced products that provide more value added than those of competitors as quality and service remains at least at the same level if not even higher. Despite having a clear focus on developing cost leadership, HBOS did not lose contact with its customer needs and declared the ability to identify and meet customers' needs and intensify the quality of the relationship as key drivers for shareholder value.[54] The execution of a consequent cost-leadership strategy, which is at the very core of HBOS, means a sustainable lead in cost reduction over its rivals. HBOS was able to achieve the lowest cost–income ratio with 39.9 per cent among the top five UK banks by mid-2007. Lloyds TSB, RBS, and Barclays denote cost–income ratios of 48.3 per cent, 49.1 per cent, and 56.4 per cent, respectively, at the same time.

Focused International Expansion—Replicating Cost-Leadership Strategy

Before venturing into international markets, most firms prefer to consolidate the home market position. HBOS aims at 15–20 per cent market share for its main products, which it had already achieved for mortgages and savings partly due to Halifax's extensive market share before the merger (Figure 8.4).

HBOS built a solid financial foundation and home customer base and decided to intensify its international engagement in 2004. The bank intensified international activities in Ireland and Australia as well as North America

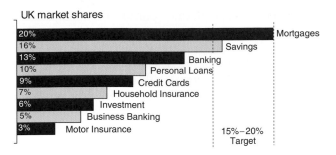

Figure 8.4. HBOS: Product market share in UK market in 2007 (HBOS Annual Report 2007: 8; www.hbosplc.com, March 2008: 8)

and Europe. Figure 8.5 shows the split-up of the International division and the overall product portfolio. In 2006, the company recorded slightly lower revenues, from GBP 23,617 million in 2005 to GBP 22,714 million in 2006 (3.8 per cent drop), which can be attributed to unrealized net investment revenue of the insurance and investment business.[55] Nevertheless, compared to 2002, revenues still increased 301 per cent. Alongside net profits, total assets and shareholder value were substantially increased and profit before tax increased on average 20 per cent per annum from 2001 until the end of 2004.

Considered to be at an early stage of internationalization in terms of the size of business conducted abroad in 2008, HBOS combines activities overseas in an international division responsible for Ireland, Australia, and Europe and North America (ENA). Foreign sales in 2007 accounted for roughly 13 per cent,[56] which is rather low compared to its national peers.

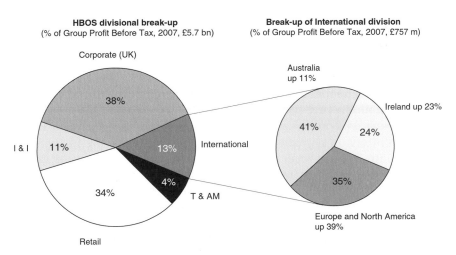

Figure 8.5. HBOS: Profit split in 2007 (www.hbosplc.com, March 2008)

Nevertheless, HBOS's offered product portfolio abroad is diversified as it includes retail, corporate, insurance, and investment products in Australia, full service retail and business banking products in Ireland and selected corporate, retail, and investment businesses in the area of ENA.

At first glance, the overall international strategy appears to be confined to attempts to grow businesses internationally by replicating the success formula that fits HBOS's growth model in its home markets. But more specifically HBOS replicates the DNA of the UK formula and attaches a country-specific style to it. For instance, it locally adapts marketing campaigns. HBOS's international strategy is based on four core elements:

- To grow nationally across Australia
- To create a full service bank in Ireland
- To develop niche markets in Europe and North America, offering a narrow range of services for selected industries
- To scale the cost-leadership capabilities internationally[57]

Due to cultural, tax, regulatory, and legal issues, it is not easy for HBOS to realize cross-border synergies. In fact, operational synergies have been very low across national markets. Despite these differences, HBOS wants to expand European activities in such a way that it can realize more cross-border synergies.

Putting Business Strategy into Practice

Until July 2007, the internationally sizeable business of HBOS could only be found in Ireland and Australia due to two major acquisitions. BOS acquired BankWest in 1995 and Equity Bank as well as ICC Bank in Ireland in 1999 and 2001. Further market penetration in Ireland and Australia was achieved partly due to similar market conditions compared to the UK banking industry. Ireland and Australia have a similar legal system[58] to the UK and already established brands like BOS Ireland and BankWest that serve as a solid foundation for market penetration. Both markets are dominated by big incumbent competitors claiming a large part of the market for themselves, happy with their current situation, and consequently, creating a low degree of rivalry. HBOS, on the contrary, is aggressive and eager to challenge the big incumbents' margins with low-cost retail products. HBOS systematically reinvests earned profits to introduce constantly new, innovative, and challenging products to expose customers to a real alternative to products offered by established big players or as BankWest Retail Chief Executive Ian Corfield coins it, providing 'a better deal'.[59]

HBOS's cost-leadership strategy has successfully transferred to international markets. As in the UK, the bank aims at delivering value for money products that are simple, innovative, and significantly break from standards set by incumbents. After acquiring 100 per cent of BankWest from the Australian government in 1995, BOS sold 49 per cent through an IPO on the ASX in 1996. Funded through internal capital and motivated by its international expansion strategy, HBOS bought back remaining outstanding shares (43 per cent) in 2003.[60] Full ownership of BankWest serves as a stepping stone towards the expansion of overseas activities in Australia. In 2008, BankWest, which is headquartered in Perth, provides a diversified financial services product portfolio to around 660,000 customers through its own branch network, agencies, and electronic banking services.

Competitive Strategy in Australia

Similar to the UK market, HBOS faces four main players in the fairly concentrated Australian banking sector: National Australia Bank (NAB), Commonwealth Bank of Australia (CBA), Australia and New Zealand Banking Group (ANZ), and Westpac Banking Corporation (Westpac). Seventy per cent of the Australian banking sector's market share as well as 80 per cent of banking assets were claimed by those four banks in 2007.[61] HBOS aims to take market share from those incumbent banks by again pursuing aggressive product offerings and high-profile service. Examples of those products were the launch of a high-interest deposit in 2004 that immediately attracted 20,000 new customers and one year later, the introduction of an innovative credit card. Both launches were accompanied by extensive marketing activities making use of television and print media. Rolling out the BankWest Hero Transaction account with no monthly fee, 5 per cent interest paid up to the first AUD 5,000 and no minimum balance put market share of the big four under pressure in October 2007.

Operations were concentrated on the west coast of Australia even though 80 per cent of the Australian population lives in the eastern portion of the country and 50 per cent of these accumulate in the three major cities: Sydney, Brisbane, and Melbourne. Consequently, HBOS announced in July 2007 that it would expand its eastern branching network over a time period of three to four years via 160 new branches from initially four, of which 125 would offer retail services and 35 would be specialized to business customers. Doubling its branch network gave HBOS access to no fewer than 11 million potential new customers, almost half of its current UK customer base. To emphasize its considerable differentiation from established banks, HBOS simultaneously extended opening hours and provided personal customer service seven days a week. Its branches were placed in high-traffic points of the cities like shopping malls and high streets.[62]

Competitive Strategy in Ireland

Roots in Ireland date back to 1933 when the ICC Bank was founded. After acquiring Equity Bank, which was established in 1965, BOS merged with ICC Bank in 2001 to form Bank of Scotland Ireland. BOS Ireland itself is a wholly owned subsidiary of HBOS Holding. The local bank remained faithful to the low-cost–radical innovation strategy inherited by its UK parent. In 1999, for example, BOS radically changed the Irish mortgage market by introducing several value for money home loans. The Irish banking sector is dominated by two major competitors, namely Bank of Ireland and Allied Irish Banks (AIB), which together make up 70 per cent of financial services market share and served 91 per cent of Irish customers in 2005.[63] Similar to Richard Branson with his Virgin franchise, HBOS was attracted by this high industry concentration and aspired to disturb the peace of the incumbent financial services firms. HBOS replicated the UK's retail strategy by offering simple and low-cost retail products accompanied by aggressive marketing campaigns.

For both incumbent banks, such an aggressive competitor was a new experience. To gain higher market reach and lure away customers, BOS Ireland announced its plans in 2004 to create a nationwide branch network from scratch within two years starting from January 2006. This branch network was built on the acquisition of 54 shops of Electricity Supply Board (ESB) in March 2005, accounting for GBP 83 million.[64] After being reopened as Halifax branches, the retail network provides HBOS with access to roughly 67 per cent of the Irish population. Along with the experienced workforce, HBOS also acquired the FinancElectric consumer loan book from the 95 per cent state-owned energy utility company and offers ESB's Billpay and cash payment services, opening access to 185,000 new potential customers.[65] Preceded by a marketing campaign advertising HBOS's new retail products including Ireland's at that time best savings account paying 3.75 per cent interest, 46 branches were rolled out—3 branches per month over a total period of 14 months. With the introduction of the best value current account in spring 2007 by Halifax, BOS Ireland's personal banking product portfolio was completed and turned into a full service bank. To further differentiate from competitors and create more customer convenience, opening hours were extended up to 50 per cent compared to Bank of Ireland or AIB.[66]

Expansion Plans for Europe and North America (ENA)

Businesses in the ENA area include retail banking, corporate banking, and investment products. Although the geographical span of the ENA area is huge, the business is rather small, leaving the main part of the 13 per cent of sales derived from foreign activities to business in Ireland and Australia.[67] The ENA area is a very peculiar geographical segment since it basically entails 'the rest of the world' for HBOS's presence. In the ENA area, retail business is restricted to the Spanish market, represented by the growing branch network (five new branch offices in 2006) of Banco Halifax Hispania and to an online and intermediary mortgage business undertaken by BOS Netherlands. Investment products are foremost sold in the German life assurance and pension market via the brands Clerical Medical Europe and Heidelberger Leben. Corporate banking is offered in North America in sectors of oil and gas, and gaming and real estate. To achieve a minimal critical mass in this market, HBOS acquired a life insurance portfolio from MLP, which allows HBOS to expand its regional banking partnership network to take advantage of commercial lending opportunities. In July 2006, for example, activities of corporate Europe were expanded to Sweden by setting up a corporate office in Stockholm.

Transferring the Home Market Competitive Recipe

HBOS developed its international businesses following a certain pattern. So far it had chosen markets with big complacent players where it could build on existing business and had good opportunities to grow organically. With Ireland and Australia, HBOS entered highly concentrated markets dominated by a few incumbent banks with a robust economic growth. HBOS faced low expansion barriers in terms of rivalry and retaliation of incumbents but had to find a way to achieve a minimal scale in a short period of time. HBOS developed its businesses very quickly, which can be attributed to its ability to execute and implement its strategy very fast. It organized in a lean way, resulting in high flexibility and short decision-making processes with few people involved. The headquarters decides the investment and leaves the rest to the local CEO and management team with sufficient input. HBOS was able to penetrate international markets because it followed a multi-brand niche strategy in most geographical areas and a low-cost/innovation strategy in a few selected markets (Table 8.2).

The predominant banks were able to make generous margins and were not eager to change their comfortable situation. Based on detailed customer and market research, HBOS managed to regularly launch simple and innovative products that enabled the bank to quickly attract new customers, for example, 44,000 new retail customers in Ireland in 2006. In addition to low-cost offers, HBOS differentiated itself from competitors through improved services like longer opening hours or comfortable home banking solutions. In terms of products and services HBOS always raised standards substantially above competitors' offers. To lure customers away from competitors, switching teams and an online switching tool are available, which reduces the hassle customers have when changing their supplier of financial services. Although it was involved in bidding processes in Ireland for buying the National Irish Bank in 2004 and rumoured to be interested in buying Australia's fifth biggest

Table 8.2. Overview of main market conditions and characteristics of HBOS's business-level strategy in 2007

	United Kingdom	Ireland	Australia
Competitors	4 big players • Barclays • HSBC • Royal BOS • Lloyds TSB	2 big players • Allied Irish Banks (190 branches) • Bank of Ireland (265 branches)	4 big players • NAB • Commonwealth Bank • ANZ • Westpac (1,000 branches apiece)
Market power of incumbents	• 83% of SME banking market controlled	• 70% of financial services market controlled • Relationship to 91% of banking customers	• 80% of banking assets possessed • Market share of 70%
Country economic conditions	• High interest rates • Slowing demand for mortgages as of January 2006 • Increased competition	• Continued strong economy • Robust savings culture • Young, growing population • Similar regulatory system to UK	• Prevalent higher margins • Similar banking and regulatory system to UK • Strong economy • Relatively fast economic growth
Outbranching measures by HBOS	• 3-year structured recruitment programme; 1,500 people for Business Banking Division • Use of existing 800 Halifax branches in UK	• 46 branches rolled out over 14 months • (Starting Jan 2006)	• 160 branches rolled out over 3–4 years • (Starting end of 2007)
Volume of expected potential access to new customers	• Cross-selling among 20 m existing customers • Switching customers from incumbents	• 2/3 of Ireland's adult population • 185,000 existing ESB customers	• Access to 11 m new potential customers
Main executing brands	• BOS/Halifax	• BOS Ireland/Halifax	• BankWest

Major investments for functional operations	• HBOS merger • providing a new account to existing SME customers cost £20m • BOS's Corporate Banking Division raises interest paid to customers cost £9m	• Acquisition of ESB retail business and rollout of branch network £109m (€160m)	• £160m for the first two years for set-up of retail network including IT, new branches
Additional services outperforming competitors	• 'Easy to join' switching team	• Longer opening hours, up to 50% more than competitors	• Extended opening hours: full telling services 7 days a week • New branches design reminds of a café
Expansion goal regarding competition	• Market share (current accounts) from 12% to 15% within 3 years (2003–2006) • Market share of the SME banking sector from 3% to 6% over 3 years (2002–2005)	• Focus on winning customers of the big 2	• Concentrate on winning customers of the big 4
Retail placement	• Major urban centres across the UK	• Convenient main streets • Shopping centre locations	• High streets • Major East Coast shopping centres • Retail precincts

bank in 2007,[68] HBOS's future international expansion is planned to be based primarily on organic growth initiatives.

Alternative Competitive Strategies

The Allianz case and the HBOS description show that there are many different ways to create a sustainably unique strategic position in foreign markets. Competitive strategies are the result of entrepreneurial calculation, changeable customer requirements, and competitors' and suppliers' strategies. The PEST (political, economic, social-cultural, and technological) environment plays a critical role too. In the financial services industry, the regulatory framework is obviously shaping competitive strategies of foreign financial services firms.

The Allianz case has specifically pointed at the pivotal role of the bancassurance alliance with ICBC. For a foreign financial services firm, it is extremely difficult to gain market share without a strong local ally. Another striking learning point of this section is that no global distribution recipe was used by Allianz. The German financial services firm drew on a broad mix of different channels in the various countries. The recruiting, training, and retaining of single brand agents therefore turned out to be a key competence in the Chinese market where foreign brands so far cannot guarantee access to a broader client base. Another principal discussion point that can be taken from the case description of Allianz in China refers to their governance system. Allianz, as opposed to Zurich FS for example, believes in a home-market-centric control and coordination model in which a German expatriate is country head even in such a difficult and culturally distant market as China.

The description of Allianz illustrated how a foreign-diversified financial services firm tries to enter an emerging country. The case of HBOS complemented the insights gained by exploring competitive strategies in mature countries. The HBOS case shows how a successful strategy can be exported to culturally, administratively, and economically similar markets. The case illustrated how a bank can create a cost-leadership strategy based on five main elements: its low-cost culture, the constant search for low-cost locations, the capability to design lean business processes, the drive to keep overheads low, and the programmes to reduce the overall purchasing costs. Based on these and other sources of competitive advantages, the case shows how large incumbent banks can be attacked first in the home market and then in two selected foreign markets, that is, Ireland and Australia. In other European and North American markets, HBOS decided to expand with a limited product range to prepare the market (and the company) for bigger future investments.

Both cases have hinted at the three generic drivers of success in foreign markets: the ability to differentiate the service offerings, the ability to deliver them at lower costs, and the capability to sub-segment lucrative markets and develop a specific service offering for them. As the HBOS case clearly illustrated, these three competitive strategies can be combined to achieve unique strategic positions. Lean and low-cost processes at the bank branch can at the same time increase customer value by enhancing the convenience for the customer of getting certain decisions and documents immediately. The following sections describe those differentiation, cost-leadership, and focus strategies in greater detail.

Drivers of Differentiation: Towards Customers' Care?

Why do customers prefer an Audi over a Skoda, despite the fact that the cars are largely identical? Why do people take a British Airways flight for GBP 400 when they could fly with easyJet or Ryanair for GBP 99? What attracts people to expensive restaurants when they can eat their fill at a lower cost in a fast-food joint? Differentiation means offering customers products or services that provide them with additional utility. Differentiation strategies aim at increasing the performance of services rather than reducing their costs. Customers opt to buy products or services not on the basis of prices, but because they provide additional value for which they are prepared to pay a premium price.

Yet, how different are financial services firms? Good differentiators usually have superior marketing capabilities and product engineering skills. They are able to obtain price premiums due to the creativity of designers and researchers, which are driven by a culture encouraging innovation, individuality, and risk-taking. In the financial services industry, increasingly informed clients are becoming more and more difficult to please. They expect high levels of service, and consider many services that once were thought to denote exceptional service as simple routine activities that banks must carry out. Safety, privacy, interest rates, speed, close contact, and the human touch are just some of the ingredients that constitute excellent customer service in the minds of banks' clients. As far as Internet banking is concerned, it is not surprising that in those countries where e-commerce has had a hard time taking off (e.g. Italy), this tool has yet to prove its full potential to the public. The country's culture and habits play a very important role in determining the success of this device, which should one day unleash its customer service upgrading resources. Clients feel the need to lead their relationship with their banks towards a more human and personal one, and this need changes not only in the type of services offered by local banks, but also in their physical layout. Most importantly, this implies the retraining of front-office employees and the reorganization of their priorities by putting customer satisfaction at the centre of their job objectives. However, pure Internet banks such as ING Direct in Italy or ING-DiBa in Germany and Austria have managed to gain substantial market share and attract international customers with their lucrative current accounts.

Financial services firms are often accused of not differing significantly. In some countries, customers may even perceive the financial services industry as organized by a cartel that offers rather homogeneous products. In many markets, it might be the case that limited competition has led to a stagnation of innovation and differentiation efforts. It is, however, also true that many final customers have difficulties in assessing product differences. Only the so-called 'self-directed investors' may be able to, or take the time to, really understand service differences. Many other customers just take whatever their consultant is offering because they trust a strong brand and the person representing that brand.

As shown by the example of HBOS, market share can be gained by developing simple products that customers can understand and invest substantially in marketing to explain the difference. In fact, HBOS claims to have the largest share of the switcher market with 22 per cent in 2003.[69] The recipe to make customers choose the offerings of HBOS are aggressive pricing, comparative advertising, and a sophisticated switcher service. But to keep customers, HBOS has to please them with more than just low costs. Differentiation drivers in financial services are many: security, convenience, information quality, tailor-made information, or processing speed, just to mention a few. As described in the case, HBOS executes its cost-leadership philosophy to deliver a more efficient cost structure than its main competitors but the UK bank reinvests the profits gained to offer customers low-priced products that provide more value added than those of competitors as quality and service remains at least at the same level if not even higher. Successful banks can effectively differentiate if they manage to communicate the distinctive features to the market. Referring to its retail business in 2003, HBOS indicates eight differentiation drivers:[70]

- *Broad customer base*: HBOS has a rather broad customer base of around 22 million customers, which means that two out of every five adults in the UK have a relationship with one or more of the companies linked to HBOS, indicating that some customers might prefer to be served by a bank that has a larger customer base.

- *Transparent products*: This is a key point in HBOS national as well as international strategy. Simple and transparent products are easier to explain to financial consultants and clients. The simpler the product, the easier it is to compare it to competitors' products. However, this does not mean that only commodity-like financial services products are sold.

- *Strong financial services brands*: In contrast to many large financial services firms, HBOS does not invest in developing an umbrella brand. Instead, it values the existing strong local brands. Branding decisions are based on large-scale empirical customer research. HBOS receives and analyses feedback from 45,000 customers every week. Different brands serve different segments and allow for varied pricing schemes.

- *Multi-channel distribution*: Relying on more than one distribution channel is crucial not only in emerging markets such as China, as seen in the Allianz case. In addition, in developed markets it is of central importance to develop agents, branches, telephone, mobile, and the Internet as sales channels.

- *A strong sales culture*: It is essential to train and provide incentives for the sales staff. HBOS has clear volume- and value-driven measures at branch, team, and individual level. Most of the measures are volume based in clearly indicated categories because they are easier to explain to sales people, but if unsecured loans are given or early cancellations happen, sales bonuses can be reduced. An average branch would have around 12 sales targets that would also include service quality aspects. Sales efforts are made proactively based on an analysis of the customer database and frequent review meetings at the branch level. Another key aspect of the HBOS sales culture is the transparency and visibility it creates in the sales performance of individuals, teams, and branches. Benchmarking motivates and allows for identification and dissemination of best practices.

- *Aggressive marketing*: HBOS believes in aggressive and comparative marketing. With several focused brands and based on a clear profitability analysis of customer segments, HBOS develops simple and understandable messages for end consumers.

- *Superior risk management*: HBOS claimed to have 92 per cent secured assets in 2003. This is indeed a differentiating factor, not only for clients but also for refinancing institutions or other stakeholders.

- *Consistent focus on improving productivity*: HBOS is committed to keeping costs down and allowing for a maximum increase in cost equal to the inflation rate. Central purchasing, resource pooling, divestments from costly businesses, or selected outsourcing are only some of the avenues to improved costs. On the other hand, HBOS constantly increases productivity on the revenue side. Every employee, for example, can consult the 'sales eye', the individual sales performance of the previous day, by 8 am the following day. Even the sales of other branches, the call centre, or other regions are available.

Every financial services firm has to go through the process of identifying differentiation drivers through the value creation processes, and then test them regarding their value for customers, their uniqueness, and the isolation mechanisms that can help to protect them.

Drivers of Cost Leadership: Towards Customers' 'Scare'?

A second generic competitive strategy is to position a company as the cost leader. A company that is a cost leader in a specific industry segment has succeeded in obtaining a competitive advantage by establishing a comprehensive lead in cost reduction over its rivals. In other words, it is the most cost-efficient producer in its segment. Its cost leadership relates to average total costs and creates potential for the company to cut prices. Its fundamental aim is to reduce costs below those of its competitors, but without falling below the minimum level of service and quality its customers expect. In financial services, it is difficult in many segments to follow a pure cost-leadership strategy because financial services products are generally complex and hard to evaluate ex ante by the consumer. What is the total cost of an investment certificate? Is the price fair compared to competitive offers? Few financial advisers are really able to answer those questions, let alone the final customer. Cost leaders are therefore keen on delivering simple and transparent products with prices that can be compared. HBOS, for example, follows a cost-leadership strategy but at the same time offers high-quality services. Cost leadership at HBOS means that many investment products have a 'no load' pricing strategy with no initial charges and no exit penalties but only a single annual management fee.

The ability to reduce costs depends on different capabilities and resources, such as access to capital and tight cost control systems combined with frequent reporting. Cost leaders in the manufacturing industry invest in scale-efficient plants and design their products for ease of manufacture and not necessarily to please the final consumer and the internal marketing department. They are able to control overheads and often avoid serving marginal customer accounts if this requires similar efforts compared to large customers. A cost leader is able to instil a penny-pinching culture of procedural discipline paired with the continuous search for new sources of cost reduction.

Experience shows that most markets require firms to reduce costs by 10–20 per cent annually. Innovative firms may perceive less pressure to do so but increase margins if they are able to control for costs as well as sell at premium prices. Cost pressure is usually stronger in the last two phases of a product life cycle (Figure 8.6). In a start-up phase, innovative products can achieve a price premium and can therefore afford higher cost positions. In a growth phase, selected innovative products are quickly introduced to a larger customer base. Competition is still not high and innovative traits of products and greater demand than supply keep cost pressure low. This changed substantially in the last two phases.

However, we need to clearly distinguish between cost and price leadership. Cost leadership does not just mean being cheaper than the competition. In essence, cost leadership means having a relative advantage in total costs

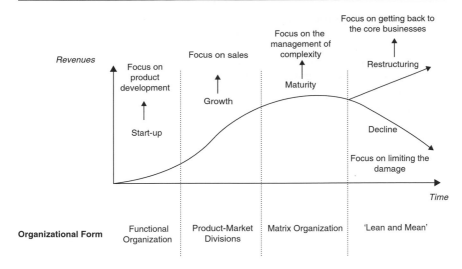

Figure 8.6. Business challenges through the evolution of the firm

that is also generally reflected in low prices. However, the level of quality and service expected in the particular market segment in question must also be maintained, but the price effect should not be given undue prominence. Cost advantages initially impact a company's profitability, which generates resources for additional investment, for example, in research, improved production processes, or expanding the company (increasing market share through acquisitions). Such investment can lead, in turn, to increases in overall productivity.

Focus Strategy

In contrast to the broadly based cost-leadership and differentiation strategies, a focus (or niche) strategy is geared towards a clearly delimited, tightly defined market segment. Many financial services firms have only recently invested substantial energy into understanding, segmenting, and targeting specific markets. This activity is especially important during international expansion. HBOS developed niche markets in Europe and North America, offering a narrow range of services for selected industries. Corporate banking in North America, for example, focuses on specific sectors such as oil and gas, gaming, and real estate. These spearhead operations are often used as a test of higher commitment entry modes in a later stage.

To serve a specific niche means to develop a differentiated offer for problems and needs posed by a clearly identifiable group of customers. Companies that have adopted a focus strategy develop special capabilities and resources to satisfy customer requirements in the particular niche. The value chain of such companies is generally narrow, because it is focused on a small number of products and markets. Niche strategies have several characteristics:

- Niche suppliers are 'masters' of their own special areas. By concentrating on a particular sphere of application, on specific technologies, or on clearly defined groups of customers, niche suppliers are able to achieve a high level of quality and process as well as market competence. Over time, niche suppliers become better and better at what they do.

- All the supplier's energies are focused on a single objective. On the one hand, this constitutes a high-risk strategy; on the other, it brings with it a compulsion to become the undisputed leader in the market segment in question.

- Customers' requirements are optimally satisfied, which in turn gives rise to a high degree of customer loyalty. Exit barriers for customers are extremely high. Close cooperation with customers produces a wide range of different feedback effects (information, suggestions for improvement, organizational interlocking, and many others), which further optimize the service provided for the target group.

- The barriers to entry for competitors are raised, because it is difficult to achieve the leading niche supplier's level of competence while persuading customers to abandon the (supposedly) leading supplier.

Orchestrating Functional Strategies

Generic business strategies have to be broken down to functional policies. Take Allianz as an example. The German financial services firm decided to

- Invest in China (market selection)

- Grow mainly by strategic alliances with local partners (entry mode)

- Position itself as a high-quality supplier of a relatively broad range of financial services such as life and health insurance, property and casualty insurance, asset management, banking and assistance services, as well as travel assistance (competitive business strategy)

As a next step, Allianz has to orchestrate the functional strategies as described in the case illustration: marketing, HR, sales, production, ICT, etc. The business unit strategy provides a general orientation as to how competitive advantages can be developed, but specific sets of measures for effective implementation of these business unit strategies are first formulated at the functional level. The management team thus describes, in terms of a step-by-step plan, the operational consequences resulting from the corporate strategy and the business unit strategy for the individual functions.

The functional strategy is therefore a bridge to implementation, because the level of planning detail is increased and specific action instructions are given. As such it represents the bridge between strategy creation and execution. Up to now, this book has discussed how financial services firms should hammer out an appropriate strategy for internationalization moves: 'Action without a strategy is a nightmare' was the message. The next part of this book will discuss how strategies can actually be implemented since: 'Strategy without action is a daydream'.

Part III

Strategy Execution

How much are good strategic ideas worth when initiatives are delayed or shelved and no sense of urgency for the key strategic issues is perceived? In dynamic financial services markets, where strategies of competitors can be easily identified and copied, it is fast and deterministic strategy execution that secures competitive advantage. But what do we know about the effective implementation of internationalization strategies in financial services? The extent of national differentiation in financial services in terms of regulatory differences, institutional divergence, customer demand, and cultural diversity has meant that the financial services sector is one of the most complex sectors within which to conduct cross-border activities, yet the recipes given by specialized consultants still read like a simple operation: choose growth coun-tries that suit the DNA of the company; assemble an adequate management team that fits the local culture; adapt the business model to local conditions; choose killer products to hook new clients to the company; develop efficient credit-risk assessment and management processes; and finally, start making money.

However, the way to implementing those and other strategies is rife with pitfalls and trade-offs. During the empirical data collection phase for this book, many executives interviewed stated that one key element of their success in mastering some of these issues was that they insisted on bold imple mentation: 'Implement today, perfect tomorrow'. By applying the Pareto principle to their actions, that is, 80 per cent of the effects come from 20 per cent of the causes, they managed to stay focused on the main issues and pushed for quick implementation with fine-tuning postponed until a later phase.

Execution hurdles in an international context are numerous. Changes are usually associated with strong emotions, and demand modifications to indi-vidual custom and practice. Organizational routines are important to ensure that the day's business is carried out efficiently, but they can hamper strategy execution if not adequate. The larger and older an organization is, the more difficult it is to alter these routines. Organizational history matters: many managers had to recognize that firms are path-dependent, that is, they are restricted in their evolutionary scope. Past decisions and actions to a large extent prescribe the future development of the company. It is very difficult for companies to develop fundamentally new resources and capabilities. Excellence in one dominant discipline (e.g. marketing) reinforces the development of this particular field, but at the same time inhibits the development of other expertise (e.g. technology).[1] Although the increased path dependency leads to a narrower set of options, on the other hand, it lends increased importance to strategic thinking. Because firms are path-dependent it is more important to blaze a trail in advance.

To create a great strategy that challenges the conventional industry logic and detects potential sources of competitive advantage is surely difficult, but to make employees abide by it requires more patience and 'volition',[2] for example, the willpower that enables managers to execute disciplined action even when they lack desire, expect not to enjoy the work, or feel tempted by alternative opportunities. Change processes need a certain psychological pressure from outside if they are actually to be put into effect. It is particularly difficult in successful companies to achieve broad consensus that a need for action exists.

Change is initiated if either the pressure exerted by the forces for change is raised or the barriers opposing change are reduced. Raising the pressure for change often leads to an increase in resistance and can become a zero-sum game. Organizations can be modified in a three-stage process: 'unfreeze–change–freeze'.[3] This is an easy principle to understand, but is difficult to implement. To unfreeze means to create a general awareness that change is needed. Leaders create a sense of urgency and seriously challenge existing ways of doing things. Only when a large part of the organization is ready for change can the adjustment be pursued in a purposeful manner. Changes in structures, systems, people, and culture are introduced. Although the maxim 'change is the only constant in today's world' enjoys general acceptance, fundamental changes to processes and procedures should be regarded as complete only after some time has elapsed. Perceived achievements are celebrated, and once again work can start on developing the routines necessary for dealing with day-to-day happenings.

The third part of this book deals with selected aspects of internationalization strategy execution. Chapter 9 describes how financial services firms attempt to create organizational architectures that allow for central control and standardization as well as local entrepreneurship. We will look at the ways corporate headquarters add value to their international business units. Organizational issues linked to the trade-off between local responsiveness and global efficiency will be discussed.

Chapter 10 discusses how cross-border synergies can be created in banks and insurance companies by enabling the transfer of knowledge within the network of international units. This chapter highlights the critical role of knowledge and knowledge sharing in making internationalization strategies work. We describe nine elements of an organizational culture that facilitates cross-border knowledge sharing and show how to design a system that supports the international flow of knowledge. The chapter concludes with a reflection on the limits of cross-border knowledge sharing.

Finally, Chapter 11 discusses how financial services firms attempt to energize international corporate entrepreneurship and thereby leverage the innovative and entrepreneurial potential of their geographically dispersed assets. This chapter identifies three types of entrepreneurial uncertainty that hamper the cross-border flow of entrepreneurial activities: communicative, behavioural, and value uncertainty. The chapter concludes by proposing organizational mechanisms that have the power to facilitate international corporate entrepreneurship.

9

How to organize? International organizational architectures

The choice of the organizational design of the international financial services firm directly affects the benefits and costs of international expansion as described in earlier chapters. Therefore, firms must consider effective organizational routines to coordinate and control the international network of subsidiaries. To what extent should a firm coordinate the linkages between geographical units and create global synergies? What is the optimal level of autonomy the foreign subsidiary should have? These strategy execution decisions mainly depend on the motives for internationalization. If the main trigger for internationalization was to reap economies of scale and scope across national borders, an organizational model with increased centralization is more adequate than a multi-domestic approach with strong delegation of decision rights. Execution entails that the strategic position along the continuum of local responsiveness versus global efficiency described in the second part of the book needs to be translated into organizational structures and processes.

A foreign multinational company facing local competition needs to overcome its liability of foreignness and gain competitive advantage by making use of the big company network. At the same time, the local subsidiary needs to react individually to the local competitive forces. The majority of research on multinational corporations has focused on economic reasons and effects of foreign market entry.[1] As a consequence, it seems that we still know more about the problems of becoming a multinational than about strategies for managing an established multinational. Collis and Montgomery[2] state that 'most multi-business companies are the sum of their parts and nothing more. Although executives have become more sophisticated in their understanding of what it takes to create competitive advantage at the level of individual business, when it comes to creating corporate advantage across multiple businesses, the news is far less encouraging.' However, substantial research efforts have been made in the last decade to close that gap. When financial services firms broaden their geographical scope, they frequently go through three different stages:

1. Prepare for cross-border activities through national consolidation
2. Set up (or buy) international operations that are run on arm's length principles after an initial phase of restructuring
3. Consolidate the international network of subsidiaries through increased central coordination and control

The order in which these stages occur depends on, among other factors, the nature of the business (i.e. how local it is) and the structure of the home market. The Swiss UBS, which operates in naturally regional or global businesses such as wealth management, tends to create strong interdependencies between geographically dispersed units immediately and therefore may skip stage 2. For many retail banks an initial phase of fairly decentralized foreign operations often precedes the creation of a more integrated network. On the other hand, even fairly integrated financial services firms that have entered the third stage of value creation can further pursue national integration if opportunities arise (as seen with the acquisition of the Capitalia Group).

This chapter is mainly concerned with what corporate headquarters do to add value to their family of international business units. The primary purpose is to gain an understanding of the potential to add value through a brief synopsis of a selected sample of the corporate strategy literature and exploring the complex and delicate relationship between MNC headquarters and subsidiaries. A description of the key pillars for corporate headquarters' roles and functions in the modern international financial services firm will be followed by case examples of the organizational structures of UniCredit Group and Erste Bank. This chapter concludes with reflections on how to balance the trade-off between local responsiveness and global efficiency.

How Headquarters Can Add Value

In the context of increased multinational presence, what is the role and function of corporate headquarters? The early literature on corporate strategy is concerned with top management activities such as fulfilling legal requirements (e.g. preparing annual reports, submitting tax returns, ensuring compliance with health and safety regulations, or environmental legislation) and basic governance functions (e.g. establishing a structure for the company, appointing senior management, raising capital and handling investor relations, implementing basic control processes, authorizing major decisions, guarding against risky or fraudulent decisions, and checking on delegated responsibilities).

The fashion for diversification and portfolio management that prevailed in the 1960s and 1970s brought mergers and acquisitions, and consequently, horizontal diversification and vertical integration, into the focus of corporate headquarters. These ideas were quickly replaced by a philosophy of 'sticking to the knitting', and refocusing portfolios on core business areas, a view that dominated the 1990s.[3] The main proposition was that corporate headquarters should identify and develop core competences (e.g. commonly shared technologies and knowledge across business units) and develop processes that augment and leverage the competences to develop related business. Initial fascination with the colourful concept of 'core competences' has left many corporate managers puzzled over how to realistically put this concept into practice.

Creating Parenting Advantage

The next big concept was 'parenting advantage'.[4] As business units' aim should be to create competitive advantage, it is the goal of the corporate headquarters to create parenting advantage by adding more value to their subsidiaries than any other parent could. Complementary to competitive advantage, parenting advantage emerges by influencing (i.e. 'parenting') the business units. 'The best parent companies create more value than any of their rivals would if they owned the same businesses. Those companies have what we call parenting advantage.'[5] Parenting advantage is achieved through a fit between the business unit and the corporate headquarters (Figure 9.1).

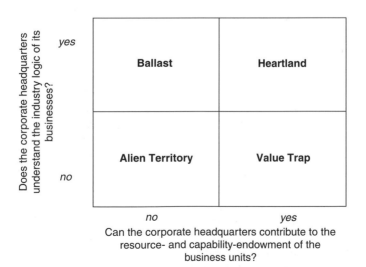

Figure 9.1. Creating parenting advantage (based on Campbell, Goold et al. 1995)

There are two prerequisites for the creation of parenting advantage: the corporate centre should be able to understand the business units' markets and should have something to offer in terms of complementary capabilities and resources. Looking at the relationship between the headquarters and the local subsidiary, four distinct approaches may be distinguished:

- *Alien territory*: Headquarters do not understand their subsidiary's business (e.g. nobody in the headquarters has spent significant time physically present in the subsidiary market) and has no complementary resources and capabilities to offer (i.e. there is already a strong local management team with all it needs to run a focused business). The generic strategic approach to managing such a subsidiary would be either to guide the subsidiary as a financial holding and not influence their business, sell the subsidiary to a better parent, or to increase the parent company's industry understanding as well as complementary resources and capabilities. There are several examples of relatively small retail banks that decided to enter specific investment banking segments without understanding the business logic and lacking the ability to significantly contribute to the resource and capability endowment of the new units. Such 'alien territory' investments have had devastating implications for many of those banks in the course of the subprime crisis.

- *Ballast*: Headquarters understand their subsidiary's industry but have little to offer to the autarkic local business. In this situation, the headquarters should be very slim and attempt to develop complementary resources and capabilities. ABN AMRO, for example, did not manage to extensively reduce redundant resources in their foreign retail markets and create benefits from cross-border arbitrage and aggregation. Many of their foreign subsidiaries could have been placed in the 'ballast' quadrant which resulted in higher cost–income ratios.

- *Value trap*: If the opposite happens, that is, headquarters has something to offer but does not understand the local industry, influencing the subsidiary could lead to negative results. Headquarters must increase their local market understanding before offering their support. Like the German Allianz, many multinational financial services firms name home-market executives as local CEOs which increases not only coordination and control but also the risk of interventions that are not adequate for the local market.

- *Heartland*: Only if headquarters understand the local market and also own complementary resources and capabilities, are they able to add value to the subsidiaries and thereby turn into 'heartquarters'. Headquarters contribute with cognitive impulse and make the most of strategic decisions. 'Heartquarters' recognize that strategic decision-making needs to be largely decentralized to be effective and see their tasks as providing the company with energy, passion for the business, and a sense of direction. Heartquarters create strategic experiences for their subsidiaries and divisions rather than a set of PowerPoint slides.

In summary, corporate headquarters should treat with caution subsidiaries whose business logic it does not understand, perhaps by developing the subsidiary as a financial holding or even selling the unit. Even if headquarters thoroughly understands the subsidiary environment, influencing its business might only create value if there are complementary resources or capabilities that can be offered. Not many headquarters seem to be able to place their subsidiaries into the heartland quadrant, and as a consequence, many corporate headquarters have come under attack. They are too big and costly. Only a small number of corporate headquarters manage to add value to their business units.[6] Even if corporate managers worked for free, the argument goes, they would often destroy value by choosing the wrong acquisition targets, hiring the wrong key executives, implementing the wrong control mechanisms, or influencing operational decisions on a business unit level without a sound knowledge of industry dynamics.

Why are most business unit managers not happy to receive a visit from the headquarters? Admittedly, the vanity of not being influenced by others in decision-making processes can play a role, but most often, corporate headquarters does not provide concrete help. Even worse, the pure fact that there is a corporate headquarters may have the negative psychological effect of 'financial safety' even if the market success is missing. However, this also shows that there might be little concrete support coming from the top, and instead business managers perceive the close collaboration with headquarters as control without headquarters knowing the market well. Intrapreneurs turn into managers just because they know that their existence may not be endangered if the business unit fails to deliver results. Other indicators for a negative impact of corporate headquarters on the performance of business units are the numerous successful de-mergers or management buyouts. By implication, to create value for their business units, corporate headquarters need to carefully define their roles.

Typical Headquarters Roles and Activities

Although the task profile of corporate headquarters varies substantially among the leading financial services firms, in general, headquarters may perform the following activities:[7]

1. *Portfolio strategy*: The centre decides upon the composition of businesses (e.g. vertical integration and diversification); the corporate headquarters acts as an investor in businesses and manages the fund allocation

231

process among subsidiaries. Headquarters evaluates profit prospects of each business unit, steers corporate resources into the most attractive strategic opportunities, and divests businesses that are not profitable or fit poorly with the overall firm.

2. *Negotiation and control of business unit performance:* The centre supports the formulation of subsidiary strategies, discusses past business performance with subsidiary managers, and defines new targets and incentive schemes together with the subsidiary management; the centre periodically controls the performance of the foreign units.

3. *Directly contribute to the resource and capability endowment of the business units*: Headquarters, for example, assigns key management positions and performs certain activities for which single subsidiaries do not have the scale or experience (such as ICT services or stakeholder management).

4. *Initiate coordination and collaboration within the network of subsidiaries*: When firms enter the third phase of value creation,[8] they aim at consolidating the international network of subsidiaries through increased central coordination and control; since all subsidiaries are in internal competition for financial resources and management attention, it is not very likely that they will attempt to create cross-border synergies spontaneously. Corporate headquarters has the responsibility to detect opportunities for collaboration and create systems that favour such initiatives.

Corporate strategy for diversified multi-business companies is intimately linked to competitive advantage at the business unit level. Competition occurs at the business unit level. Diversified companies do not compete— only their business units do. By implication, successful corporate strategy must grow out of and reinforce competitive strategy on a subsidiary level. If the corporate HQ is to enhance subsidiary performance, it must find ways to encourage subsidiaries to make decisions and contributions, which they would not make if they focused solely on the business of their own unit, that increase the firm's overall performance. For example, one business unit might acquire a system for inventory management that could be expanded to handle inventory in another business with little incremental cost. A product innovation in one unit might confer a first mover advantage on another unit that produces a complementary product in the MNC. Beneficial as such value creation opportunities might seem, unless corporate headquarters intervenes, subsidiaries will not engage in behaviour that contributes to other subsidiaries performance for two reasons.[9]

First, as subsidiaries are specialized and focused on their own business, they lack an overview of business needs of other units. Most managers within a business unit care most about their own business, but do not know how their actions and investments could affect the performance of other units. Thus, it is corporate managers responsible for overseeing a number of business units who can recognize that investments made in one unit might have a payoff in another unit.

Second, unless corporate headquarters intervenes, subsidiaries have little incentive to share their assets, even if they would understand and know who else could use them in the MNC. It is the responsibility of corporate management to establish the appropriate organizational context and design appropriate cross-unit linkages to unlock profit potentials available in the multi-business firm.

To illustrate the HQ's function in a multinational bank, UniCredit Group may serve as an example. Its CEE Division has seven key responsibilities:[10]

- Define and set the strategy and targets
- Choose and develop key people
- Facilitate integration within the Group
- Ensure key project implementation
- Support creation of synergies and sharing of best practices
- Support the local banks in reaching key objectives
- Monitor the achievement of targets

In summary, corporate-level interventions that add value to a family of business units in the modern corporation result from (a) the ability to identify, select, and leverage valuable knowledge[11] as well as (b) corporate systems of planning and control that seek to tailor headquarters' interventions according to their own characteristics in relation to the needs of subsidiaries.[12]

The Changing Role of Subsidiaries

Subsidiary roles have changed from mere sales outlets to active contributors to the resource endowment of the MNC. In early stages of international presence, ownership-specific advantages are mainly developed at the headquarters site and leveraged abroad.[13] It becomes increasingly evident that these subsidiaries develop distinctive resources and competences as they grow in size. Competitive advantage, therefore, does not come from the corporate headquarters alone but from a network of subsidiaries that interact with each other and their headquarters.[14] Although this phenomenon is more recent in financial services, we can observe that decentralized competence centres emerge that take up a strongly contributing role within the network of operating units.

As financial services firms become more international, subsidiaries have increasingly gained importance as sources of competitive advantage in the MNC, and as a consequence of their growth, we can observe the emergence of various subsidiary types. The multinational financial services firm does not rely solely on sources of competitive advantage created in the home country, but facilitates the peripheral development of knowledge, competences, or other sources of competitive advantage. Knowledge transfer among subsidiaries provides opportunities to improve an MNC's performance.[15] In the first half of the twentieth century, the dominant model for knowledge sharing in the MNCs was to govern the subsidiaries in a 'paternalistic' way to make sure that home-country innovations would be introduced across affiliated subsidiaries.[16] As MNCs grew, subsidiaries were not only used as mere sales units but also tasked to scan their environment for new ideas and technologies. 'Competence Centres' were created that signalled to other units that they had the mission (to the exclusion of other subsidiaries) to innovate in a certain area. While this second model of organizing the MNC worked well during the 1970s and 1980s, new governance models based on a more liberal management philosophy later emerged. The basic idea was that new knowledge could emerge from everywhere in the MNC and the headquarters needs to pursue a more democratic approach to the pursuit of new opportunities. In contrast to this centre-dominated view of the MNC, the liberal perspective purports that subsidiaries are capable, encouraged to develop strategies on their own, and do not exclusively rely on the role assigned by the headquarters.[17] This discussion hints at the eternal trade-off between centralizing decision power and the delegation of authority to decentralized units.

As a result, most financial services firms are not confronted with the choice between a paternalistic and a liberal model, but rather an issue of combining the two. In other words, knowledge exploration and knowledge exploitation have to be carefully balanced. Knowledge exploration is about developing options for the organization by activities such as search, variation, risk-taking, experimentation, play, flexibility, discovery, and innovation.[18] Exploitation, on the other hand, aims at ensuring survival by using existing resources for rent creation. Traditional managerial activities such as planning, organizing, controlling, or product-market positioning are in the foreground. Balancing the need for a democratic and liberal approach to facilitate innovation and exploration with the need for a more paternalistic approach to ensure operational efficiency, survival, and exploitation implies two fundamentally different ways in which power is distributed and used in the MNC. Autonomous strategic behaviour of subsidiaries creates new knowledge and hence new entrepreneurial options for the MNC. However, for the innovative idea to be successfully implemented in the organization, it has to be integrated into its concept of strategy.

Control Mechanisms in the Multinational Firm

To structure the relationship with headquarters and subsidiaries within an international financial services firm, various approaches beyond the mere design of line functions may be used. Such control systems allow senior management to determine whether a business unit is performing satisfactorily. They also provide sufficient motivation for local management to see that the business unit continues to do so.[19] As such, the activity of controlling involves negotiating objectives, measuring performance against those objectives, feedback on the results achieved with corresponding incentives or sanctions.

Control systems not only coordinate business unit activities in complex organizations and motivate managers to achieve performance targets but also give corporate headquarters management an idea of when to intervene. Control systems ensure that strategic decisions are made based on relevant data; they create the conditions for a consensus among key decision-makers by managing relative power among managers.[20] Corporate headquarters may use behavioural control mechanisms that monitor and reward inputs into strategic decision-making through supervision and approval as well as output control, which manages the performance outcomes of decisions. Controlling structures in the MNC increasingly refer to the ends of strategy making but not the means.[21] Corporate headquarters of successfully operating multinational firms increasingly delegate the responsibility of strategy making to the local subsidiaries while insisting on tight performance controls.

Control mechanisms in the MNC need to take differences in subsidiary evolution into account. As a consequence, while designing control mechanisms, one may need to take into account that in the same MNC a broader variety of control mechanisms may be used according to the subsidiary context (e.g. subsidiary charter, market size, geographical distance) as well as the headquarters' characteristics (e.g. their business understanding, availability of complementary resources and capabilities, historical relationships with key subsidiary managers).[22] While multiple control mechanisms and performance measurement procedures may vary, corporate headquarters nevertheless attempt to exercise procedural justice to avoid de-motivation of subsidiary management teams.[23]

However, the design of control structures does not only vary according to subsidiary characteristics. Most MNCs are complex organizations with different subsidiary types and various product divisions. Control systems have to reflect that complexity. It is therefore essential for corporate headquarters to design the control systems in a way that does not harm the mutual trust and motivation of subsidiary management teams. Differences in input,[24] process,[25] or output[26] control systems may be well accepted by subsidiary management teams if procedural justice[27]—the extent to which the dynamics of the decision process are judged to be fair—is guaranteed by headquarters. Procedural justice contributes to obtaining voluntary cooperation of individuals during strategy formation and implementation processes.

235

Aligning Interests between Headquarters and Subsidiaries

To address problems of incentive alignment and achieve better coordination, headquarters can engage in several interventions. For example, corporate headquarters may devise a way for the investing or contributing unit to get 'credit' for the value their investment creates in other units (e.g. providing incentives). The headquarters can also intervene through providing public acknowledgement and support for subsidiary concerns, and by influencing corporate career paths in the MNC for subsidiary managers (e.g. non-monetary incentives). Vertical linkages are established by headquarters through personal supervision of the subsidiary manager by HQs (e.g. sending expatriate managers as monitors) and establishing bureaucratic mechanisms including rules, programmes, and planning procedures to achieve coordination and to monitor subsidiaries.

HQs can also influence mutual understanding by establishing cross-linkages in vertical HQs-subsidiary as well as inter-subsidiary relations. For example, HQs may offer subsidiary managers headquarters-based training programmes, executive development programmes that include participants from headquarters, and headquarters mentors for managers of foreign subsidiaries (e.g. vertical linkages). In addition, corporate management may sponsor and encourage inter-subsidiary linkages, for example, through joint decision-making using inter-unit committees and supervisory boards consisting of subsidiary managers to evaluate threats to corporate technology. Alternatively, centralizing investments in a valuable asset such as a brand name or shared R&D facilities by creating a unit that manages the assets for several business units (e.g. designing an organizational context) might create opportunities to realize economies of scale and scope in addition to making appropriate investments that individual subsidiaries would not be willing to bear. More avenues for HQ influence on subsidiaries are possible as indicated with examples in Table 9.1.

Headquarters need to critically evaluate when such interventions add value. For example, to monitor a subsidiary, top management needs to understand the business of the subsidiary and its current situation. To apply financial incentives, there should be a strong positive correlation between the behaviour of subsidiary managers and subsidiary results. If this relation is weak, financial incentives might be reducing subsidiary performance. If financial performance-based incentives work well, they may undermine appeals to common goals as attempted by vertical integration mechanisms. Financial incentives force subsidiary managers to focus on their businesses, but this focus might lead to the neglect of common goals. Therefore, HQs should select appropriate interventions and apply them with care to add value, taking interactions between interventions into account.

Table 9.1. Corporate interventions*a*

Corporate Interventions	
Intervention	Example
Monitoring: Activities or mechanisms used by headquarters to obtain information about the behaviours and decisions of subsidiary management.	• Personal supervision of subsidiary manager
Contribution to value added: HQ seeks to close knowledge gaps with subsidiaries.	• Expatriate managers as monitors • Bureaucratic mechanisms, including rules, programmes, and planning procedures
Financial incentives: A portion of subsidiary management's compensation is outcome-based.	• Pay might be linked to MNC performance
Contribution to value added: Bargaining costs between subsidiaries reduced; aligned interests.	• Pay might be linked to other subsidiary performance • Pay might be linked to own subsidiary performance
Non-monetary incentive: Align interest between subsidiary managers and HQ through non-financial means.	• Provide public support for subsidiary concerns
Contribution to value added: Aligned interest results, even if financial incentives do not work.	• Corporate career path in the MNC for subsidiary managers • Assignment of highly skilled and experienced human resources from throughout the corporation to the subsidiary
Vertical integration mechanisms: Make individuals identify with the MNC organization and goals; make subsidiary managers identify with values and norms of good citizenship behaviour.	• Regular meetings or visits from MNC top management
Contribution to value added: Results in shared understanding between headquarters and subsidiaries; coordinating activities will be more effective based on common understanding and goals.	• Exposure and contribution to MNC vision and strategy process • Include assignments at corporate headquarters, headquarters-based training programmes, executive development programmes that include participants from headquarters, and headquarters mentors for managers of foreign subsidiaries
Lateral integrating mechanisms: Refers to activities that facilitate contact among managers of different foreign subsidiaries.	• HQ encourages joint decision-making using inter-unit committees
Contribution to value added: Results in shared understanding between subsidiaries; coordinating activities will be more effective based on common understanding and goals.	• HQ encourages inter-subsidiary liaison personnel, meetings, and training programmes

a Based on O'Donnell (2000); Björkman, Barner-Rasmussen et al. (2004).

Knowledge Flows within the Multinational Firm

The role of the corporate parent in the MNC as argued in the last section is more complex as compared to locally operating firms, and corporate interventions have to vary according to subsidiary characteristics. Corporate interventions also need to vary according to the degree of their respective knowledge inflow and outflow, which shows the degree of interdependence between a subsidiary and other MNC units.[28] Different subsidiaries call for differences in the application of, for example, vertical and horizontal integration mechanisms, as well as incentives.

'Local innovators' are characterized by few knowledge transactions between other units of the MNC. Consequently, local innovators will most likely have a low need for vertical integrative mechanisms and a low level of horizontal linkages with other units. Because local innovators are most likely not responsible for other units' businesses, the performance bonus of local innovators will most likely not depend on a larger cluster of subsidiaries. Within the general trend towards outcome measures,[29] it is more likely that local innovators will be measured on performance outcomes than on behaviour controls. MNC headquarters are simply not likely to fully understand all of the subsidiary's businesses and required behaviour well enough. In contrast, 'integrated player' subsidiaries need more support from headquarters in terms of a horizontal integration mechanism. 'Implementors' just apply knowledge received from other units. In a multinational financial services firm, it is not necessary that all units contribute as competence centres with specific knowledge. If units are small, operating in a specific context, or with no relevant competences for the group, it may make sense to limit the units' knowledge outflow. 'Global innovators' are typically self-sufficient in their own knowledge creation, but have a great responsibility to share their knowledge with other units. Citigroup's software development subsidiary in Bangalore is such a case. For these units, the creation of horizontal integration mechanisms like socialization opportunities is the most important corporate intervention. To the extent that headquarters understands little of what the subsidiary does, the value-adding influence of headquarters is to enable the subsidiary to share its knowledge.

To summarize, the likelihood of corporate interventions to be successful depends on both subsidiary and headquarters characteristics. In particular, the smaller the gap between what a subsidiary needs and what headquarters can provide, the greater the likelihood of successful direct interventions. In some situations, however, it will be beneficial for headquarters not to intervene directly, but rather act as a parent, providing a value-adding infrastructure to otherwise relatively autonomous subsidiaries (e.g. local innovators, subsidiaries outside the heartland). The next section is concerned with intervention styles (direct vs. indirect) and degrees of intervention (hands-off, hands-on, or selectively).

UniCredit Group: Creating the First Truly European Bank

Most financial services firms exploit growth potential in their home markets before they expand abroad. Obviously, in smaller home markets like

Switzerland (UBS, Credit Suisse, etc.), the Netherlands (ING, ABN AMRO, etc.), or Belgium (Fortis), this point of saturation is reached much earlier. The development of the UniCredit Group illustrates the three stages of value creation clearly.

National consolidation and integration before attempting cross-border activities was essential to UniCredit's success in international markets. In 1999, UniCredit started to invest in Eastern European banks while carefully integrating the affiliated national banks, first through a federal model and then in 2003 through the creation of three separate banks dedicated to distinct customer segments:

- UniCredit Banca serving household clients and small businesses
- UniCredit Banca d'Impresa targeting larger corporations
- UniCredit Private Banking

In the same year, the 'New Europe Division' was created with the charter to coordinate and control the newly acquired businesses in the Eastern European countries. One year later, with the creation of the Global Banking Services Division, responsible for the optimization of cost structures and the Group's internal processes by bringing about further synergy and cost savings, another step was taken towards the creation of cross-border synergies.

Following the corporate transactions that led to the implementation of Project S3, the UniCredit Group allocated the remaining subsidiaries of the company, such as UBM and its product and financial services companies, to the appropriate division and transferred all other strategic and core equity investments previously held by the Federated Banks to the company. The three new divisions joined the already existing New Europe division created in 2001 to supervise and coordinate the UniCredit Group's business in Central and Eastern Europe.

Organizational Structure

The organizational structure of the UniCredit Group in 2008 reflects the strategic approach underlying the Project S3 reorganization (Figure 9.2). The UniCredit Group conducts its operations through four business divisions: Retail, Corporate and Investment Banking, Private Banking and Asset Management, and New Europe. Each of these divisions is established within the company and organized around one or more lead banks which, through its distribution network, commercialize products and services engineered and packaged by the other banks and financial services companies comprising the division. In addition, the company established the Global Banking Services division to operate as the UniCredit Group's execution unit and provide group-wide services to all business lines in the areas of human resources, IT,

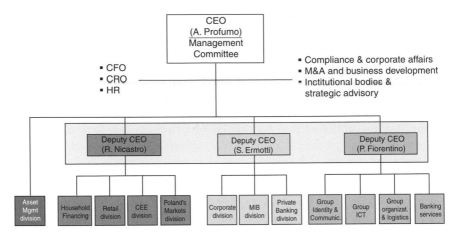

Figure 9.2. Organizational structure of UniCredit Group in 2008 (www.unicreditgroup. eu)

organization, operations, procurement, security, and building/facility management.

The main driver for internationalization into CEE countries was 'market seeking' and not 'efficiency seeking'. As a consequence, the distribution of financial services products needs to be managed locally. With increasing maturity and size of the decentralized operations, however, economies of scale in the production of banking services have become more important. To realize cost-saving potential and boost process and product innovation, UniCredit changed its organizational architecture from a multi-brand and multinational blueprint with high national subsidiary autonomy to an integrated structure with five product divisions (Retail, Corporate, Private & Asset Management, Investment Banking, and Commercial Real Estate Financing), two area divisions (CEE and Poland), and one functional division (Global Banking Services).

Creating Cross-Border Synergies

By 2008, UniCredit aims to realize EUR 900 million in cost synergies. EUR 492 million will be made from restructuring the newly acquired firms by using the global IT platform, restructuring the branch network, personnel cuts, and the optimization of the product portfolio. An additional EUR 241 million is expected from the rationalization of the corporate centre and the redesign of central processes such as the credit process and several back-office activities. Finally, EUR 67 million of cost savings will be achieved through the centralization of procurement for selected product and service categories and other cost management initiatives. The total cost of integration until 2008 is estimated at EUR 1.25 billion and should be covered by extraordinary gains.

Effective cost management as well as revenue-generating initiatives led to a reduction of the overall cost/income ratio from 69 per cent in 1999 to 55 per cent in 2004, where it has stabilized. Tight risk control measures have improved asset quality substantially. Employees per branch were reduced from 37 in 1999 to 22 in 2004 while revenues per branch increased from EUR 1.1 million to EUR 1.4 million in the same time period. The improved product mix and shift towards service fees increased the weight of the net commission on total revenues from 19.1 per cent in 1999 to 24.2 per cent in 2004.

UniCredit creates value by acquiring foreign banks and transforming them into more efficient businesses. Two types of acquisitions can be distinguished. In some cases, the main objective during the post-merger integration phase is to realize these cost synergies and 'squeeze the lemon' as much as possible. This approach is chosen if the target bank is relatively large in size and the UniCredit position in this country is already close to the desired level. In other cases, it is more important to grow quickly and achieve a respectable size. UniCredit aims at a minimum market share of 10 per cent in each country it enters. Among the cardinal mistakes that the UniCredit management team admits are some minor acquisitions that absorbed substantial management attention during the integration phase. If it was not possible to acquire a major player in a country, a key lesson for the management team was to buy a small bank, make quick and minor 'stand-alone' improvements, and then focus on further growth, either through complementary organic growth or through additional acquisitions. Only when the operation had become large enough would full-scale integration into the group's organizational architecture be considered.

The low cost-to-income ratio of UniCredit's Italian operations reflects the deep knowledge of its business model in the core areas of retail and corporate banking. These superior banking capabilities together with 'exportable' IT platforms allowed UniCredit to acquire foreign banks and transform those banks using a fairly standardized process. The highly profitable international-ization expansion was mainly the result of finding the right targets, negotiat-ing the right price, the creation and usage of a global service centre, aggressive commercial capabilities, and the transfer of business excellence across newly acquired units.

Creating Coordination Mechanisms: The New Europe Division

UniCredit's New Europe division had the charter to steer the development of the group's newly acquired banks in the Eastern European countries by supporting their planning and control as well as their loan processing. The New Europe division intends to develop into a leading cross-border network of retail banks and the best risk manager in New Europe by creating a structure guided by strong central directives still capable of adapting to local differences. In this context, the more established New Europe banks will focus on continuing to improve their financial results and fulfil their institutional role within local markets, and the emerging New Europe banks will focus on growth in selected customer segments and/or products.

The local companies find competent staff as well as slack resources necessary to carry out many initiatives, such as:

- Large strategic projects (such as redesigning information systems and the loan process, creating product factories, developing multi-channel distribution systems, or creating client-focused divisions)
- Provision of immediate operational support with the development and launch of new products
- Optimization of production processes
- Implementation of planning systems
- Internal monitoring
- Creation of modern incentive systems
- Upgrading of the information systems

The new information systems used by the UniCredit Group's New Europe banks, together with the redesign of the New Europe banks' loan approval, monitoring and recovery processes, led to a reduction of operational risks, which had a positive impact on costs.

Creation of Competence Centres

Although most multinational banks are still organized around geographical divisions, UniCredit unifies its product excellence in global product factories or competence centres. In early 2006, the investment banking activities were unified and headquartered in Munich with strategic operations in London, Milan, Vienna, the United States, Asia, and CEE. This unit develops new products and coordinates investment banking activities globally. The multi-national composition of the Executive Management Committee facilitates the alignment of product and geographical interests. This role has been assigned for seven years.

Another strong impact on sales as well as costs was the creation of a pan-European platform in the credit card sector as a result of a partnership with Servizi Interbancari, which UniCredit expects will allow its New Europe banks to benefit from significant economies of scale and competitive advantages. In addition, the UniCredit Group has further developed its 'New Europe desks', which provide integrated services and closer coordination between its Italian operations and its New Europe banks. These desks help the UniCredit Group's Italian corporate banking customers seek investment opportunities in New Europe and carry out their foreign transactions and business ventures through specific support in the banking area in addition to providing commercial, legal, and tax services.

The principal strategic objective of the Global Banking Services division is to maximize cross-division synergies and UniCredit Group efficiency through the redesign of key processes. Its main objectives include 'right sizing' the UniCredit Group's staff, optimizing the UniCredit Group's non-core assets, rationalizing the UniCredit Group's real estate portfolio, and further rationalizing the UniCredit Group's corporate structure through the streamlining of its legal entities.

Cultural Changes

Although quick improvements of the cost–income ratio can be made through a substantial reduction of the workforce and other cost-reducing measures, the division also initiated a series of projects aimed at increasing the revenue-generating capacity of the local banks. Customers in the CEE countries show a strong demand for traditional interest-based banking products such as bank deposits, credit loans, mortgage loans, or leasing contracts. Service fees are becoming increasingly important as asset management products are sold. The creation of a 'sales performance culture' was facilitated by making the Uni-Credit Group's sales support tools, training, and planning procedures available throughout the network. The development and retention of the customer base was bolstered and further supported by the restructuring of the distribution networks to client-focused divisions to better tailor the UniCredit Group's product offerings.

Erste Bank: Creating Decentralized Power through Independence and Distinctiveness

Erste Bank cleared its way towards international markets by restoring profitability through a restructuring of the domestic business without any major acquisitions. A key pillar of the success strategy of Erste Bank was to uncompromisingly tackle low-return domestic businesses. A key element was to give the 64 independent savings banks, for which Erste acted as central banker, branches owned by Erste Bank in return for an increased equity stake in the focal savings bank. This approach led to a reduction of Erste Bank's own branches from 270 in 1998 to 144 in 2004 and gave rise to a better exploitation of the synergy potential.

In fact, the Austrian savings bank sector seemed to be more willing to consider moves towards cooperation than is seen in other markets. Erste Bank increasingly served as the backbone for the affiliated savings banks that signed a cross-guarantee agreement in 2001. Now, Erste Bank additionally provides IT support, pools marketing budgets to promote a single brand for all savings banks, and develops new financial products for the entire network. This increased collaboration helped to minimize the structural causes of low profitability in the Austrian operations; however, there were still some firm-specific issues to tackle.

Organizational Complexity

In 1996, Erste Bank was not a terribly complicated bank, with only 3,600 employees, 230 branches in one country with one language, and five board members. In 2007, after 11 years of international expansion, the Erste Group was composed of nine banks, around 50,100 employees, 2,700 branches in nine countries with nine different languages, and 45 board members. However, the organizational structure was still basically the same as it was in 1996 and hence a new organizational form had to be found. One of the central issues was solving the trade-off between fostering decentralized entrepreneurship deeply rooted in local expertise and the need to develop and use profound knowledge and capabilities to create parenting advantages on a global scale. Up to this point, subsidiaries were managed in a rather decentralized way to avoid negative influence from the centre. Most strategic decisions such as product development, marketing, or branch development were made at the country level. To coordinate the network of decentralized units and reap profits from the international presence, Erste Bank created several steering committees composed of functional heads of the country organizations meeting to make decisions about common standards and applications. Decisions were made through voting, and Austria had only one vote, as did the other countries. This way, Erste Bank had an implicit matrix organization combining geographical business units with functional lines of responsibility. There were several goals for this organizational model. It should create economies of scale, making use of the common client base wherever possible. Some products or services, such as cash management, need a supra-regional basis and know-how transfer from developed markets in the treasury or real estate business to create additional value for the affiliated banks. Internal benchmarking processes further increase the efficiency and effectiveness of the operations.

Towards a New Organizational Model

The goal was to create a 'common consolidation', which meant performing some activities centrally but as a community rather than exclusively driven by corporate headquarters. Before the reorganization, three types of governance existed in the organization. A fairly centralized model was applied in treasury; retail banking was purely local; a federative model using steering committees and cross-border boards was applied for IT issues. In fact, numerous group boards existed, such as the retail board, the large corporate board, the IT council, the procurement board, and several project boards (such as the Basel II steering committee). A group steering committee composed of top managers in the centre as well as in country organizations hovered above the entire global organization with a vague definition of their relationship to the group boards. In mid-2005, three alternative governance models were discussed:

- The group steering committee would formally empower the group boards to make decisions, and only take notice of these decisions. If necessary, this committee would act as an 'escalation board'.
- The group steering committee asks the group boards to submit proposals to be evaluated and ratified by the group steering committee.
- Group boards are dissolved and the group steering committee decides on issues where (a) group responsibility is defined, (b) local responsibility is defined, and (c) responsibility of the group steering committee is defined.

The three alternative models may appear to increase the complexity of decision-making, '... but this is the price we have to pay for not having a traditional holding company. [...] There are no role models we can follow, which means that we have to find our own way.'[30] As structure follows strategy, the new group architecture should help Erste Group live up to its declared strategic aspirations:

- To further promote 'entrepreneurial space and culture'
- To exploit further external growth perspectives
- To leverage cross-country business opportunities
- To utilize Erste Group's unique customer potential with over 15 million customers
- To increase cultural cohesion in the Group
- To create excess leadership capacity
- To significantly increase focus on clients

The old organizational structure (see Figure 9.3) had several shortcomings: unbalanced top management composed largely of executives from the Austrian operations led to a strong historic focus on Austrian interests at the cost of a Group/CEE perspective. Decentralized units were given high levels of autonomy to serve the local clients best and create an entrepreneurial spirit in the foreign bank subsidiaries. The downside of this decentralized structure, however, was that Erste Group did not make use of the cross-border synergy

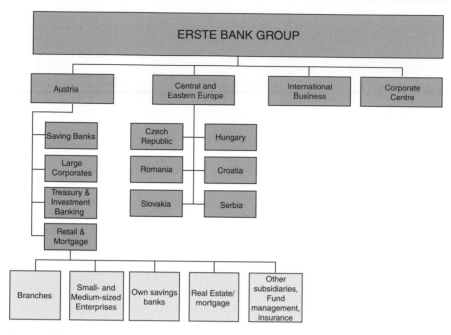

Figure 9.3. Organizational structure of Erste Bank before the reorganization in 2007

potential by acting as a 'true' group rather than pursuing local interests. Collaboration in the Group was still perceived as 'painful' and 'tiring'. Decisions at the Group level were difficult to finalize and local execution often did not work. Local banks often did not fully understand the Group alignment.

Erste Bank in 2008

The main objective of the reorganization was to create transparency through the separation of the Group from local Austrian interests. A clear overall Group governance blueprint was developed and transparency was increased through the definition of unambiguous roles and responsibilities of the holding vis-à-vis local banks and vice versa. The conscious combination of centralized (i.e. Group Divisions) and decentralized elements (e.g. Retail, Corporate/SME) created a simultaneous focus on Group synergies as well as local entrepreneurship and liberated management capacity for business and client activities. The new structure also allowed for increased activity in human resources development, Group-wide performance management with uniform standards, and a more intense collaboration and interaction in Group-wide leadership networks.

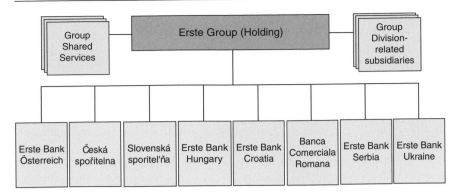

Figure 9.4. Organizational structure of Erste Bank in 2008

The new Erste Group structure consists of four building blocks:

- Regional business lines (retail, corporate, and SME businesses)
- Product divisions Group Capital Markets (GCM) and Group Corporate and Investment Banking (GCIB)
- Centre functions such as HR or Strategy
- Group shared services (including Group IT operations)

These elements are supported by a new committee and board structure. The Group board is supported by an executive committee. The regional business lines have two boards: one for the retail business and one for the corporate and SME business. Both product divisions have a board (i.e. GCM and GCIB). In addition, a functional board ensures coordination between Group and local functions and coordinates IT initiatives (Figure 9.4).

Relying on this new organizational architecture, the Holding identified several areas where it can add value. The Group performance management function develops standard performance matrices and provides external benchmarking. This is an essential step to identifying best practices across borders and matching them with areas where knowledge and capabilities are not at group-standard level. The Group HR function gets the opportunity to engage in systematic top executive development and the creation of an expert talent pool programme. Furthermore, HR has the charter to develop interactive leadership networks and communities as well as other initiatives that contribute to increased cultural cohesion. The Group strategy function overlooks the portfolio of strategic initiatives and monitors the functioning of the Group architecture. In addition, it is responsible for mergers and acquisitions initiatives (country and target analysis) as well as the further development of strategic alliances. To reflect the diversity of the Group, it is the goal of Erste Group to staff the Group Centre functions with approximately 30 per cent CEE personnel in the long run (Figure 9.5). Steering functions at the headquarters level consists of Holding Steering functions with no respective local responsibility and Group Centre functions with the charter to align the local approaches according to predefined responsibilities/competences. The Holding functions entail group development initiatives, strategic group development, investor relations, group secretariat, strategic group products, and group procurement. Group Centre functions include group marketing, group communications, group HR, group audit, group performance management, group accounting, group risk management, international risk management, group legal services, and group compliance.

IT and Operations provide the Group with infrastructure and focus on synergies. Over the past few years, Erste Group has successfully implemented several initiatives to align its IT and operations infrastructure, including a core SAP system, a core banking system, and anti-money laundering systems. To reach a higher level of synergies, the Group COO function receives increased competences vis-à-vis local banks. In particular, the COO is responsible for providing the Group-wide common IT platforms based on local/divisional business needs but with a much stronger focus on group alignment and the realization of synergies. The integration between local IT functions and central operations is ensured by strong alignment in the Group, implementing a direct reporting line from the local banks to the central IT Shared Services. By contrast, Group Organization is designed as a competence centre for processes and already aligned systems in the Group (e.g. SAP) and has a matrix responsibility, that is, a dotted reporting line towards local banks. Group Operations is a fairly autonomous nucleus for Group shared services in the operations area (e.g. group payments).

The new divisional structure of GCIB lays the foundation for continued growth. The GCIB Division is governed by the GCIB Board as a true decision-making body with full profit and loss responsibility across the Group. The Group Competence Centres with group-wide management aim to increase operational efficiency and develop stronger product expertise through the transfer of best practices and the utilization of resources as well as the elimination of intra-group competition in the areas of real estate/leasing, infrastructure finance, investment banking, and international business/syndication. The mission of the newly created International Customers unit is to acquire customers that are based outside the extended home market (i.e. Austria plus CEE).

GCM aims to become the leading CEE specialist in capital markets. The sales and trading units are led by Group heads with full profit and loss responsibility across countries. A direct reporting line exists from local operations to the relevant department head in the Holding, which is also primarily responsible for HR decisions. Those sales and trading units are located in the Holding or any of the local banks/investment banks. Local heads have the full responsibility for local sales and interface management with trading units.

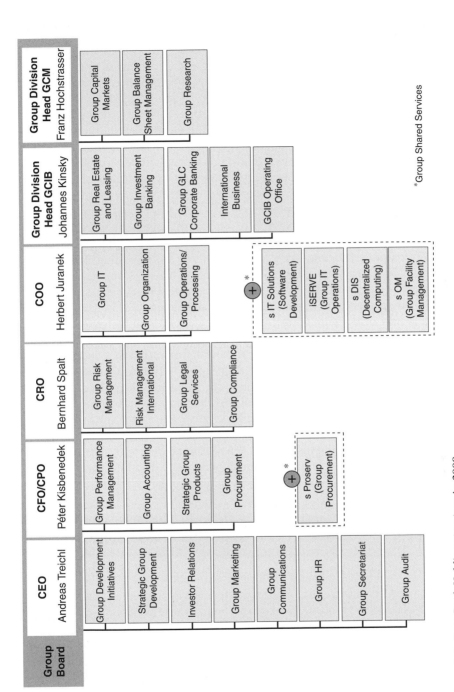

Figure 9.5. Erste Bank Holding structure in 2008

Group Board	CEO Andreas Treichl	CFO/CPO Péter Kisbenedek	CRO Bernhard Spalt	COO Herbert Juranek	Group Division Head GCIB Johannes Kinsky	Group Division Head GCM Franz Hochstrasser

CEO Andreas Treichl:
- Group Development Initiatives
- Strategic Group Development
- Investor Relations
- Group Marketing
- Group Communications
- Group HR
- Group Secretariat
- Group Audit

CFO/CPO Péter Kisbenedek:
- Group Performance Management
- Group Accounting
- Strategic Group Products
- Group Procurement
- (+)* s Proserv (Group Procurement)

CRO Bernhard Spalt:
- Group Risk Management
- Risk Management International
- Group Legal Services
- Group Compliance

COO Herbert Juranek:
- Group IT
- Group Organization
- Group Operations/Processing
- (+)* s IT Solutions (Software Development)
- iSERVE (Group IT Operations)
- s DIS (Decentralized Computing)
- s OM (Group Facility Management)

Group Division Head GCIB Johannes Kinsky:
- Group Real Estate and Leasing
- Group Investment Banking
- Group GLC Corporate Banking
- International Business
- GCIB Operating Office

Group Division Head GCM Franz Hochstrasser:
- Group Capital Markets
- Group Balance Sheet Management
- Group Research

*Group Shared Services

Interface Management: Subsidiaries versus Headquarters

This new organizational architecture creates major implications for all local entities. The Holding sets strategic guidelines and directions as well as group standards, acting as a performance coach to support local entrepreneurship and unlock group synergies. Each local bank is served by one of the Group board members as well as an overall country contact. This way, the viewpoints of the local banks are adequately represented in Group board discussions. In addition, the Group board member serves as a contact for the local CEO and board, especially in cases where mediation of escalations between local banks and Group Centre functions is required. Serving as chairmen of the local banks' supervisory board, the Group board members ensure that centrally taken Group decisions are implemented. On the other hand, core decision-makers in local banks are involved in Group management via the Group Executive Committee, the Group Division Boards, and Functional Councils. The Group Centre functions have a clearly defined matrix responsibility vis-à-vis local banks. In addition, the Holding established new Group management processes together with the local banks, particularly in the areas of performance management and human resources management.

In this new organizational architecture, the extent of involvement of the Holding differs in the case of the regional business lines as opposed to the two divisional businesses. The former is basically managed in a decentralized manner with the exception of selected group-wide business initiatives (e.g. cards business). The central boards have the mere function of an information exchange platform in the areas of distribution and sales, product management, and customer interaction and service. The latter shows a clearly centralized structure with the division board chairman given the ultimate decision right concerning his business line. Although key staff may be located at the headquarters or a local bank, the boards of the divisions decide on the nomination, compensation, and bonus payments of key staff members.

The Eternal Trade-Off: Local Responsiveness versus Global Efficiency

The cases of Erste Bank and UniCredit show how retail banks organize across borders and solve the local responsiveness–global efficiency trade-offs in fairly distinct ways. Erste Bank grants much more autonomy to its local subsidiaries and strongly believes in the local nature of retail business that requires decentralized entrepreneurship. UniCredit, on the other hand, seeks to centralize and standardize operations to create efficiency gains but also a higher reliability and quality of services provided. Which approach will be more successful?

Towards Increased Standardization?

A relevant managerial issue is to understand where and how standardization of services increases leads to competitive advantage. While it is tempting to assume that Wal-Mart offers a standardized set of products in all of its outlets this is simply not the case. Each store manager has the responsibility for selecting and stocking the items most in demand in his or her region. On reflection, this is not that surprising given the vast diversity that we know exists on the American continent. For instance, winter clothing and snow equipment will be in much greater demand in the chilly northern states than the milder western and southern regions of the country. Wal-Mart's success, therefore, does not arise from providing a standardized and consistent menu of products like McDonald's. Rather, a large degree of Wal-Mart's success can be attributed to back-office or logistical integration. Wal-Mart derives great efficiencies through the integration of warehousing, transport, ordering, and information systems. Information from thousands of stores flows immediately back to central warehouses enabling shelves to be replenished within hours and extra inventory automatically ordered from suppliers. Thus, the use of common systems and centralized warehousing enables significant economies of scale to be realized. Well-developed relationships also exist with suppliers and elaborate IT systems enable 'cross-docking' to occur—the ability to unload supplier deliveries directly onto trucks bound for individual stores, thus saving on warehouse storage and unloading/reloading expenses.

Similarly, Amazon.com provides a highly customized service to millions of Americans, literally being able to deliver a personal selection from the world's largest catalogue of books directly to a customer's door within a few days. Once again, the key to the system is not so much standardization as logistical integration. Amazon operates its own servers and warehouses which enable over 95 per cent of orders to be dispatched the same business day. The use of a common carrier, UPS, enables a high degree of efficiency in delivery (not to mention an impressive diversity of delivery options) as well as the ability for customers to track their orders. While Amazon and Wal-Mart represent a high level of logistical integration, we also see relatively simple levels of continental integration in North America that are currently unachievable in Europe. For instance, it is relatively simple (even trivial) for an American business to set up a toll-free (800/888) number that will operate across the United States and Canada. Tariffs exist not only for continental-range numbers but also for toll-free numbers operating in one or a few states.

Thus, a company like British Airways is able to offer a single contact number for all its customers flying throughout North America (with separate numbers for its business class and frequent flyers). British Airways cannot offer this level of integration in Europe, relying instead on a separate set of numbers for each country in Europe. It is clear that there are substantial economies of scale involved in achieving logistical (or back-office) integration in the service industry. We have managed to illustrate a couple of the better known examples. However, it should be noted that American companies have made great strides in integrating a wide range of service businesses, including banking services, information technology, retailing, and health services at the continental level.

A similar trend can be observed in financial services. There is an increase in the number of firms that create regional product factories and operational back-office centres that develop and process the financial services products from various countries.

Recognizing Market Differences

The way companies are organized should reflect the magnitude and type of differences of the countries they operate in. To participate in multiple national markets complicates corporate strategy. The key challenge is to understand the degrees of similarity and difference across markets, and to exploit these similarities and differences through an adequate organizational design. It is, for example, a corporate strategy task to decide whether subsidiary units should cater for variations in preferences for products or services sold in different markets, which would in turn compromise benefits of standardizing products across various national operations. However, it is not only customers that have different tastes and habits; employees cannot be treated equally all over the world. Another central issue is consequently whether a multinational financial services firm should apply a set of common processes across all its geographically dispersed units or alternatively grant autonomy to regional units to accommodate local customs and norms. Organization design is the top management task that must accommodate the specific challenges in operating across national boundaries. These challenges can be grouped into two opposing forces: local responsiveness, global efficiency.[31]

Organizational design geared to achieve global efficiency is appropriate if country markets exhibit similarities. The potential to use similarities of market has increased due to three driving forces:[32]

- Improvements in both international and national transportation infrastructures have reduced the costs of transporting goods and people.

- Diffusion of telecommunication technologies and Internet-based systems has enhanced the ability of firms to coordinate a dispersed network of businesses.

- Efforts to harmonize intellectual property law, contract law, and other forms of the legal infrastructure have also facilitated convergence in the economic organization of industries and markets.

As discussed earlier in this book, markets sometimes resisted complete harmonization and firms started to adapt their approaches accordingly. The music channel MTV started its international operations with a global approach, airing its content developed in the United States in Europe without significant adaptations, until local competitors emerged and disputed MTV's supremacy. In Germany, the local television station Viva started in 1993 to broadcast German songs and shows moderated by Germans for Germans. Two years later, Viva Zwei ('Viva Two') was launched. MTV reacted to this threat by adding regional content to its global programme and finally decided to forge alliances with local TV channels to better customize its content. This battle for local customers ended by Viacom—MTV's parent company—buying 98 per cent of Viva and thereby virtually creating a monopoly for music television in Germany.

The organizational challenge is to become globally efficient by reaping economies of scale and scope in processes, transferring best practices from one place to another, tapping into location advantages, and leveraging firm-specific advantages across countries through similar processes. Organizational processes need to be designed to take advantage of cross-country similarities to the greatest extent.

On the other hand, many characteristics of doing business internationally remain localized. Country variations reflect, for example, differing needs of consumers in different regions of the world. Such differences in consumer tastes are one issue among others that require local responsiveness in the MNC's processes in addition to providing the chance to engage in arbitrage. If different countries served have special social, institutional, and economic features, MNCs must accommodate country-specific practices that deviate from other processes in the MNC. A key complication of corporate strategy is then to grant subsidiaries autonomy without losing control or acquire the necessary knowledge that makes a particular subsidiary locally successful.

An MNC entering a new market may confront unfamiliar laws, regulations, and institutional procedures. Foreign firms partnering with a domestic partner seek to use their local knowledge. Firms also must adapt to how buyers or governments will respond to establishing local production facilities or using local suppliers. In addition, informal requirements that local culture, customs, and beliefs impose are often less obvious to the foreign MNC. Even if the firm's existing strategy remains useful in the new country, the processes and capabilities that supported it in the home country may not work in the new environment.

The extent to which local differences will matter for a particular MNC also depends on the type of business pursued by the MNC. Cross-border flows of cement are more sensitive to the effects of geographical distance than cross-border flows of satellite TV programming, but less subject to cultural (as in linguistic) differences or administrative restraints due to political sensitivity.

Table 9.2. Local responsiveness versus global efficiency[a]

Responsiveness	Global efficiency
HQ seeks value added through segmentation and arbitrage	HQ seeks value added through leveraging firm-specific knowledge
Key questions:	*Key questions:*
How do countries differ? What does this imply for MNC strategy and organization?	*How are countries alike? What does this imply for MNC strategy and organization?*
• Adapt to culture	• Reap economies of scale
• Adapt to institutions and law	• Reap economies of scope
• Adapt to norms and values	• Transfer best practices
• Adapt to consumer tastes	• Exploit firm-specific knowledge

[a] Bartlett and Ghoshal (1990); Ghemawat (2003).

The cement industry has seen a surge in global concentration in the last 15 years driven by economies of scale and scope. In contrast, the satellite television industry has seen attempts by companies to (re)broadcast the same content in additional countries, but this idea has run up against both cultural preferences for local language programming and administrative restraints. Country differences may be exploited by the MNC as indicated in Table 9.2 through market segmentation, which compromises economies of scale. However, such differences can be exploited through arbitrage (e.g. French cuisine, wines, and perfumes are sold as premium brands around the world, as is American fast food and pop culture, and Italian fashion).[33]

Balancing Local Responsiveness versus Global Efficiency

Addressing the challenges of local responsiveness and global efficiency is demanding because it requires coordination and aligning of headquarters' interests with the interests of subsidiaries. A multinational financial institution must distinguish between knowledge that can add value in other locations and knowledge that is idiosyncratic to one particular location only. The more subsidiary knowledge creation is specific to the local context, the greater the difficulties, and hence costs, in inter-subsidiary knowledge sharing. The same variety that produces innovation locally makes it difficult for headquarters to recognize which innovations could have value for the firm as a whole. There are three issues that MNC headquarters need to address with respect to learning processes in the tension field between global efficiency and local responsiveness.

A multinational firm needs to be able to create mechanisms for variety creation including identifying novel ideas and knowledge, selecting them according to local, regional, or global usefulness, and diffusing the innovation throughout the company.[34]

Table 9.3. Aligning corporate interventions to the local context[a]

	Corporate interventions
Intervention type	Country differences
Monitoring: Activities or mechanisms used by headquarters to obtain information about the behaviours and decisions of subsidiary management.	The greater the differences between locations, the more difficult monitoring becomes as headquarters lack location-specific knowledge; lack of headquarters' knowledge leads to more decentralization (e.g. country units are monitored by regional units).
Financial incentives: A portion of subsidiary management's compensation is outcome-based.	The greater the differences between locations, the more difficult the application of financial incentives; the less headquarters understands regional differences, the harder it is to make financial incentives fair across locations.
Non-monetary incentive: Align interest between subsidiary managers and HQ through non-financial means.	The greater the differences between locations, the more important non-monetary incentives become; non-monetary incentives need to be earned by local business through convincing headquarters by signalling their knowledge.
Vertical integration mechanisms: Make individuals identify with the MNC organization and goals; make subsidiary managers identify with values and norms of good citizenship behaviour.	The greater the differences between locations, the more important vertical integration mechanisms become; if financial measurement and other incentives are hard to apply, the greater the importance of commonly shared goals.
Lateral integrating mechanisms: Refers to activities that facilitate contact among managers of different foreign subsidiaries.	The greater the differences between locations, the more important horizontal integration mechanisms become; if financial measurement and other incentives are hard to apply, the greater the importance of headquarters enabling subsidiaries to share their knowledge through providing infrastructure.

[a] Inspired by Ouchi (1977); Ouchi (1979); O'Dell and Grayson (1998); Muralidharan and III (1999).

- *Variety*: The greater the country differences, the greater the exposure to a variety of new innovative knowledge, but the greater the costs of sharing such knowledge across other units.

- *Selection*: The more centralized the process of selecting valuable knowledge, appropriate for the MNC (e.g. located at the HQ), the more difficult it is for decision-makers to know what local innovations have occurred and their usefulness beyond the region of discovery.

- *Exploitation*: The more similar country markets are, the greater the likelihood that knowledge valuable in one location will be useful in another location.

If local differences between countries are large, the MNC faces a great deal of variety of external learning opportunities. Because exposure to new knowledge is great, learning processes need to focus on selecting knowledge that can be locally, regionally, or globally exploited. The greater local differences are, the less likely it is that corporate headquarters will be able to distinguish purely locally specific knowledge from more generally applicable knowledge. Accordingly, the selection process in the MNC cannot be completely centralized, but requires the active involvement of regional managers and decision-making units. If differences between country units are small, the MNC faces a low variety of external learning opportunities, and accordingly, new knowledge development stems largely from knowledge combination between internal units. Due to greater levels of similarity, the selection process can be much more centralized, and achieving economies of scale and scope through knowledge sharing becomes possible. With this argument in mind, one can revisit corporate intervention mechanisms and map the impact of country differences on their applicability (as outlined in Table 9.3).

To conclude, creating an effective organizational design in a multinational firm is more challenging compared to a purely domestic operation. This is largely due to similarities and differences in the country contexts in which the MNC operates. Similarities between country operations provide the chance for MNC headquarters to achieve global efficiency that cannot be matched by locally competing firms; differences in market contexts provide opportunities for market segmentation and arbitrage. However, profiting from international presence should not be taken for granted, but has to be achieved through an adequate organizational design. Multinational firms need to identify the trade-off between local responsiveness and global efficiency for their operations and align their corporate intervention mechanism accordingly. The likelihood of successful deployment of corporate interventions depends not only on the diversity of contexts in which the MNC operates, but more importantly, on the relationship between corporate headquarters and their subsidiaries.

10

How to accelerate learning? Facilitating cross-border knowledge transfer

A key element of executing a cross-border integration strategy is to enable decentralized units to share knowledge. To organize and incentivize knowledge sharing is one important avenue for headquarters to add value. Andrea Moneta, former head of the organizational unit that steers the CEE countries at UniCredit, views knowledge management as central to the success of international business, and adds: 'To facilitate cross-border knowledge flows is one of the most important tasks at the corporate headquarters.'[1] Like Moneta, many managers in the financial services industry have come to the conclusion that knowledge is strategically important. Most of them have also realized how difficult it is to facilitate lateral knowledge flows. In fact, after more than two decades of articles and projects around the management of knowledge (KM), we see a high degree of dissatisfaction with KM as a managerial tool in the MNC.[2] It is increasingly evident that KM systems that are designed on an ad hoc basis often do not survive beyond initial fascination.

UniCredit's knowledge management system includes the most frequent elements—both hard (ICT) and soft (human relations) building blocks can be found. The bank soon recognized that to facilitate knowledge flows across national borders, they had to streamline communication via a unified Intranet infrastructure. This allowed all employees worldwide to have one sole workplace desktop. In addition, UniCredit substantially invests in various types of training, the development of an international meeting culture or creates organizational structures that serve as competence relays for specific knowledge areas. But to fundamentally change the way a company that grew to a large extent through acquisitions manages its knowledge is a long and painful process.

'Knowledge is power', says the philosopher Francis Bacon. 'So why should I share it?' is a frequent managerial reply. If executives want to become the next 'oracle manager' in their companies, they had better hide what they know. 'We have difficulty in developing incentive systems that facilitate knowledge sharing', according to many managers in charge of knowledge management. 'We cannot link promotions or bonuses to knowledge-sharing activities since we cannot measure knowledge.' Because formal systems so far only provide limited support to knowledge exchange, companies, as their first priority, need to change their culture. Arie de Geus from Shell knows: the learning culture is the only source of sustainable competitive advantage. Everything else is quite easy to copy. As positive as this might sound for Shell, it is hard for a company that is not used to sharing knowledge.

Investment banks like Goldman Sachs or Deutsche Bank face a trade-off when allowing single experts to grow their knowledge to the point where these experts become celebrities. On the one hand, the experts are providing a competitive advantage the investment bank needs, but on the other hand, it is extremely hard to keep them inside the firm. Those experts earn several times that of the CEO's compensation package. This changes the role of the CEO. Soccer teams have a similar problem: they need excellent players to win but if they become stars, it is hard to control and motivate them. Firms cannot afford to follow Bayern Munich's coach in the idea to have a rotation plan for all players besides the goalkeeper, can they? As a response to individual experts leaving the company with critical knowledge, firms have started to create teams that share similar knowledge. This knowledge protection strategy resulted—above all in knowledge-intensive financial services segments such as investment banking—in entire teams jumping to competing firms or starting their own venture. These short episodes illustrate how central and difficult at the same time knowledge management is for multinational firms in general and for knowledge-intensive sectors like the financial services industry in particular.

This chapter aims at contributing to an increased understanding of knowledge management issues in multinational financial services firms in three ways. First, we attempt to show that there are several good reasons to assume that it is absolutely critical to manage company knowledge in a multinational financial services firm. Second, we describe nine elements of an organizational culture that supports cross-border knowledge sharing. Third, we show how to design a system that supports the international flow of knowledge. The chapter concludes with a reflection on the limits of cross-border knowledge sharing.

The Impact of Knowledge on Business Performance

After its first appearances in the late 1980s and early 1990s, knowledge management developed into a major subject of crucial concern for the management of modern multinational firms.[3] Decisive in the proliferation of KM were the writings of Alvin Toffler[4] on the 'knowledge society' and

Nonaka and Takeuchi[5] on knowledge creation in companies, as well as Grant and Baden Fuller[6] and Grant[7] on knowledge integration. The main message was: Knowledge has taken precedence over traditional organizational resources such as labour, capital, and land. Consequently, business writers and several progressive MNCs began to think about how crucial knowledge can be captured, shared, and exploited to achieve competitive advantage. International competition has not only intensified, it has also become more knowledge-based.[8] Where the sources of competitive advantage have shifted from physical assets to intellectual resources, knowledge-based competition raises some particularly significant organizational challenges for firms competing internationally. For example, integrating knowledge development efforts across countries may become more important as this eliminates duplication of efforts and saves costs, identifying and learning from the best in class, assigning knowledge development tasks to specific entities, and offering it to other units.

For financial services firms, this is quite a challenge, given divergent regulatory frameworks and local business characteristics, but they nevertheless search for 'best practices' in their network of largely independent local operations. Common performance standards are a first step to achieving comparability of practices and the identification of advanced knowledge. Many financial services firms have realized that the multinational production and distribution of knowledge yields advantages over competitors who rely on knowledge development either as a purely domestic process or as a portfolio of independent activities in different countries. Regional and global headquarters are sometimes used as relay stations for knowledge exchange. However, when firms leverage ideas generated in one geographic market into other geographic markets, it is increasingly hazardous to communicate knowledge first from a subsidiary to the headquarters and then back to another subsidiary. Instead, local subsidiaries need to have direct access to all other local units in need of, or in possession of, critical knowledge.

Many authors[9] view the modern multinational financial services firm as a 'differentiated network'. The importance of knowledge flows between subsidiaries and their headquarters for the MNC performance is widely acknowledged. To make use of the valuable knowledge developed decentrally, local managers aim to increase the absorptive capacity[10] of the single units and at the same time fuel the network with their unique knowledge. Unfortunately, success is not often achieved: many managers who attempt to implement knowledge management systems seem to be disappointed with the effectiveness of KM as a managerial instrument to achieve competitive advantage. A survey[11] involving 214 executives from different North American and European companies evaluated the effectiveness of 25 top management tools. On a scale from 1 (highly dissatisfied) to 5 (highly satisfied), knowledge management ranks 25th. Clearly, knowledge management today is less favourably regarded compared to its past euphoria. Has KM fallen from grace in the eyes of top management?

Some companies have invested heavily in information and communication technology (ICT) to support knowledge management initiatives, but employees involved in business operations have made little use of this technology. Other companies were betting on grassroots initiatives in the belief that knowledge management only works when people involved in business operations engage in communities of practice that work largely untouched by managerial intervention, only to be later disappointed that the initiative had little to do with the strategic concerns of the company. Some companies provide incentives to store knowledge on electronic knowledge-sharing systems, only to see employees upload irrelevant knowledge and others waste precious time searching unstructured databases. Some companies have made knowledge creation and sharing a special responsibility of centres of excellence, but then central experts left the centres to pursue innovative ideas on their own. Unfortunately, many knowledge management systems suffer from lack of leadership and flawed design.

The list of system elements (e.g. communities of practice, corporate university, centres of excellence, knowledge portals) in knowledge management practices has reached a substantial dimension and there is nothing inherently wrong with such lists of recommended tools and general advice. The problem is, however, that these lists are not particularly helpful when system elements are not aligned with the organization and a company's strategy through sound knowledge system design. The challenge for companies is to understand how to select and align knowledge system elements in a complementary way by considering a set of system design choices.

The Opportunity of Decentralizing Learning

Central office dictates could not turn Intel into a marketing company, nor would they turn IBM into a software company. Nor will the flipchart-sized 'The Learning Organization Chart', developed by management, turn Chevron into a learning organization. Nor will any CEO's talk of removing not-invented-here syndromes, giving credit for ideas, empowerment, and promoting the 'right' people have any effect unless knowledge can be developed freely wherever and whenever it is needed. Often that will mean that knowledge is developed locally and independently of central management's knowledge or control! Each individual, each business unit, and the company as a whole will have to learn what 'marketing', 'strategy', and 'core competence' mean for each individual. And they might each need to learn very different things. There are few prescriptions in modern management theories on how to 'manage' such a situation. What we know since Shell experimented with scenarios in the 1970s is that you need to identify the key decision-makers with the power to implement new ideas and help trigger their learning process. This dimension examines which individuals in a company possess decision rights with regard to both creating and sharing knowledge.

Decentralized knowledge management systems emerged from the initiative of the firm's employees, with management involved only in loose coordination of the process. Solutions and problems tend to be unique to the context of its creation and as a result are difficult to codify in standard formats that can be used elsewhere in the company. Consequently, lessons from the firm's experience are hard to categorize, thus possibilities for management intervention seem to be limited, for example, management cannot prescribe to employees what topics they should concentrate upon. Instead individuals decide on their own initiative to invest their time in codifying knowledge and making it available through their personal networks and internal markets. The clear advantage of this type of knowledge management system is that it is rooted in individuals' initiative and requires little administrative overhead expenditures. As knowledge is created by users themselves individually or in communities of practice,[12] few agency costs are incurred on behalf of the organization to align interest through incentives and monitoring. On the other hand, knowledge production costs may be high due to increased redundancies.

More centralized knowledge management systems are built and managed from the top. They typically organize knowledge creation through a large central department, for example, what has been labelled centres of excellence, whose task consists of creating, synthesizing, and distributing the firm's knowledge.[13] The main advantage of central system design is that it provides the opportunity for visionary breakthroughs, management can focus employees to certain strategically important areas or topics, and due to higher control and monitoring, the knowledge management system is more likely to be well organized. However, the disadvantages are that central systems require higher overhead expenditures because they are closely monitored and managed. In addition, knowledge transfer costs are high due to the geographical separation of knowledge creation and use.

Central organization of knowledge creation has been applied in many corporations including firms like AT&T, IBM, and Microsoft.[14] The key advantage of this approach is that long-term, explorative and risky attempts at knowledge creation are protected from the pressures of daily operations and budget constraints. However, the remoteness to current business may make knowledge creation unresponsive to market demands, leading to slower knowledge commercialization, and also poses the threat of inbreeding in self-contained think tanks that follow their intellectual curiosity rather than furthering the company's aspirations. On the other hand, dispersed knowledge creation may lead to double invention, locally contained solutions, and thinking in functional silos.

Because both approaches to knowledge system design have advantages and disadvantages, choosing between them forces the question of what the system should achieve. March[15] differentiates between two learning processes within organizations that knowledge system design may achieve—namely, exploitation and exploration. The essence of exploitation is the refinement and extension of existing knowledge. It is an incremental learning process[16] and its returns are highly predictable. On the other hand, exploration centres on the experimentation with new alternatives, and its returns are uncertain, distant, and at times negative.[17] The focus here is on developing innovation and creative breakthrough that deviates substantially from what organizations already know and do. Due to the degree of uncertainty involved, there is a tendency to overemphasize exploitation of known alternatives and downplay the exploration of unknown territories, but to adapt successfully over time, exploitation and exploration need to be balanced. Therefore, the question of decentralized versus centralized knowledge system design depends on the question of what the system is supposed to achieve. When cost-intensive exploration with global exploitation of standardized knowledge is attempted, the firm may tend to design knowledge management systems centrally.

In one company, a central supervisory board or steering committee (i.e. knowledge management board) was created to make sure that knowledge was developed in a directed and efficient way. The board allocates decision rights to expert groups that had the task to identify, develop, and use new knowledge. However, it has been argued in academic articles that knowledge-based competition requires employee autonomy to unlock high involvement in self-managed teams.[18] But those expert groups are distinct from 'communities of practice' defined as groups of people who are informally bound together by shared expertise and a common interest for a knowledge area.[19]

The probability that communities of practice were autonomously emerging and taking care of diligently defined knowledge management issues was very low. This seemed to be more likely to happen in smaller organizations where everybody knows everybody. 'How long do you want to wait until an expert from Brunei calls up his German colleague?' Another risk the company feared was that those communities of practice would end up as 'discussion clubs' without any pressure to produce results. Consequently, the knowledge management board nominated an expert group with an expert leader for each strategic knowledge area. The communities of practice would autonomously form themselves around the expert groups and support them with ideas and feedback. Different decision rights were given to each group by the knowledge management board.

The Power of Networks

Knowledge sharing largely depends on the strengths of the networks. Companies wire their R&D people to ensure knowledge sharing and push down time-to-market. Ericsson, for instance, has 17,000 engineers in 40 research centres in 20 countries worldwide tied into a single network. Likewise, the number one R&D spender in the pharmaceutical industry, Hoffman La Roche, is attempting to turn itself into a real-time research operation by connecting its R&D teams in the United States, Japan, and Europe via various kinds of information technology. The idea is to have their research work bridge time zones. An internal approach to networking was taken by the fifth largest aluminium company in the world, Hydro Aluminium. Supported by advanced information technology, Hydro has linked five small smelters located in remote parts of Norway into what it describes as a single 'virtual plant'. Rather than placing centralized functions at corporate headquarters, one or more of the plants volunteered to 'specialize' in that function and become a resource for the rest of the company. Functions that did not require or benefit from centralized control were delegated to the plants individually.

One of the plants has a corporate-wide responsibility for ecological issues, like understanding and working with the life span of aluminium. A second plant is responsible for personnel and process safety issues. A third plant takes care of the health issues. Yet another plant is responsible for the external environmental issues throughout the corporation. This responsibility does not mean to merely carry out directives sent out from top management. Rather, it means a responsibility to implement current routines as smoothly as possible as well as develop new knowledge regarding what can be the routines of tomorrow. Thus, rather than having a corporate 'head' separated from an operational 'body', knowledge now resides (and is constantly created) in a complex web of interaction among the plants. The first step was to take on health and environmental issues; the next step will be personnel issues.

These 'network' organizations are the oracle manager's worst nightmare. Communication can take place—and knowledge can be created—between any two or more people in the organization, and in some instances, at any point in time. Communication does not need to be filtered through a top manager. In fact, keeping track of communications flow in this sort of networked company is virtually impossible and the manager's status as the 'overseer' and ultimate source of company knowledge is dramatically altered, if not completely shattered.

Dee Hock, the founding CEO of Visa International, took an uncommon pride in his 'inability' to force any of his member banks to follow his dictates, since he technically worked for them rather than the other way around. Yet he credits this openness with the ultimate success of the credit card system. He once glorified in his own limited knowledge saying, 'No part knows the whole, the whole does not know all the parts and none has any need to. The centre only does what cannot reasonably be done by a more localised part, which turns out to be remarkably little.' To the oracle manager, this apparent loss of control over knowledge is unthinkable, but few bankers would choose to return the incredible profits made possible by the Visa network.

Similarly, the Swedish finance and insurance company Skandia AFS draws its organizational chart in the form of an onion. The skin represents the customer base, which makes up part of the organization. Peeling the skin, you discover the brokers, followed by the employees—the first on the payroll. Corporate headquarters is located at the centre of the onion. The heart is where the energy derives; the head only gives a cognitive impetus. If managers want to be part of the knowledge-building process in increasingly networked companies, they must dive fully into the dynamic conversations taking place among the people in the plants. They cannot retreat to the rarefied air of their corporate Delphis.

Developing a Culture for Cross-Border Knowledge Sharing

To achieve knowledge sharing and combination across boundaries requires a 'transnational organization'[20] in which specialized units are linked into an integrated network that enables them to achieve their strategic objectives of foreign market entry such as efficiency, responsiveness, and learning. In an ideal world, a multinational financial services firm manages to combine the advantages of decentralized learning and knowledge sharing with the efficiency of centralized decision-making—and thereby optimally solve the trade-off between local adaptations versus global standardization. Although challenging, in order to surf on the third wave of value creation, it is necessary to address the issues involved in the creation of a decentralized knowledge-sharing network.

Multinational financial services firms need to discuss and choose among a variety of knowledge-sharing goals, knowing that not all of them can be pursued with the same intensity. Managing company knowledge is context-sensitive: different market situations as well as firm characteristics require different knowledge management systems. Part of the frustration with knowledge management systems comes from the unreflected use of available tools. It is a common mistake to think that the more knowledge management tools are applied, the better the system. How can you manage what you know? The answers to that question by authors or appointed 'Chief Knowledge Officers' read like a list of best practices: create a 'yellow pages' directory for your firm knowledge, develop knowledge maps, introduce knowledge brokers, create competence centres, feed information into knowledge databases, develop a knowledge vision, work on your conversation culture, create a virtual university, develop guidelines for documentation, reward knowledge transfer, turn new knowledge into product innovations, or create an invisible asset monitor.

The list of best practices in knowledge management has reached a substantial dimension. How can managers choose the appropriate tools and approaches? Should they intuitively pick some of the tools and start to implement them (mostly managers would start with storing and measuring their knowledge)? Or is there already a coherent system or logic behind the set of best practices integrated into the current management system? Yes, there is one. Managers need to understand their knowledge culture and choose the tools that best fit into their 'way of knowing'. In most books on knowledge management, the valuable comment that the knowledge management system has to fit the proper knowledge culture comes in one of the last chapters and is dealt with in a couple of pages.

The challenge is to understand the way a company develops knowledge before starting to introduce knowledge management tools, just as a Western manager would familiarize himself with basic behavioural rules of the Japanese culture before entering into contract negotiations in Tokyo. Knowledge potential can be realized if knowledge is thoroughly identified, measured, developed, linked to the organizational task system, and converted into innovations. Companies need to concentrate on the design of practical models which support both the maintenance of resource knowledge and the incorporation of knowledge into value-adding processes.

The following sections describe cultural elements that possibly lead to an increased capability of creating and sharing knowledge across national boundaries. These potential knowledge-sharing avenues are summarized in Table 10.1.

Increase the Speed of Knowledge Representation

The first goal of a powerful knowledge management system is to increase the speed of knowledge representation to better grasp upcoming business opportunities and meet challenges. The faster a firm achieves knowledge representation, the better it performs in comparison with a relatively slower competitor. Knowledge representation refers to the process of coding, storing, and retrieval of knowledge. There are at least three ways to achieve rapid knowledge representation.

First, encourage parallel processing of information, which often involves simultaneous execution of several related activities. For example, when Norwegian oil operator Statoil built the technically demanding Statfjord A, B, and C platforms for North Sea oil production, they introduced a substantial

Table 10.1. Developing a culture for cross-border knowledge sharing

Increase the speed of knowledge representation	• Encourage parallel processing of information • Distinguish between learning by and learning before doing • Redesign horizontal process in the company
Increase the power of knowledge representation	• Ensure effective encoding and storage of information • Boost the storage capacity of knowledge • Ensure effective and efficient retrieval of information
Increase the reliability of knowledge representation	• Increase the validity of representation through a regular updating of information • Enhance validity by using multiple sources of data for a representation • Increase validity of a representation through a common understanding of the representation
Connect people with people	• Facilitate exchange and processing of information through connecting employees via their PC • Balance the use of electronic communication with the rich, multi-sensuous experiences of face-to-face meeting • Facilitate connection between the company and the outside world
Connect people with information	• Develop a climate and practices of open storage and retrieval of information in databases • Systematically identify the people who have certain knowledge • Ensure that the network extends to where the most interesting information is created, and/or is available
Stimulate heedful, collective action	• Institutionalize social rules of behaviour and action that stimulate heedful interrelating • Care for newcomers into the network • Involve increasingly advanced levels in the company
Recognize the individuality of knowledge development	• Care for distinctions made throughout the organization • Stimulate people to challenge assumptions already made by others, and often taken for granted in the company • Work on people's scaling capabilities
Balance authority and self-reference	• Use authority only when knowledge is exploited, not in situations when knowledge is supposed to be developed • Review the work procedures of project teams • Internalize the distinction between authority and self-reference
Create a climate for learning conversations	• Distinguish between the conversations that are primarily focused on executing existing routines within a business and those trying to create a space for something new to take shape • Establish rules for strategic conversations • Inculcate the idea of knowledge development as a responsibility, or even a 'right' as part of the identity of the company

concurrent engineering practice. A platform typically consists of three major parts: the deck (production facilities), the gravity base structure (concrete), and the hotel (living quarters). Normally, knowledge of production system design is needed before designing the hotel and gravity base structure. In the case of Statfjord, a substantial overlap was achieved between the designs of the three components, reducing the total time to completion. This involved an impressive management of information between a large number of sub-contractors, engineering firms, construction companies, and technical consultants. A list of drafts, design documents, and technical specifications representing at each stage the current state of knowledge were prepared and the flow of these documents was planned.

A strategy development project is another type of project where knowledge development is involved. In most firms, a typical strategy development project involves at least the following steps: determine a business mission, analyse the opportunities and threats of the business environment, identify strengths and weaknesses of the firm, identify long-term goals, develop alternative strategies, choose a strategy that allows the company to reach its goals, implemented through developing operational policies and directives, and finally, monitor the results of the strategy implementation. If executives want to follow this first rule of thumb, these tasks should not be completed sequentially. They should start with analysis during goal formulation, strategy development during analysis, choice during development, and implementation during choice. Finally, constant monitoring of how the organization receives the strategy process should be allowed, not only how the organization receives the strategy itself.

In achieving parallel processing, strategic knowledge is of crucial importance. In a strategy process, if one does not have any information about the development of the industry, it is quite difficult to make a clear, realistic, and adapted business strategy on how to compete. In an offshore petroleum engineering project, it is quite difficult to design the pipes if you do not know how much petroleum will be produced. Strategic knowledge sets out to define information gaps: What information is available? How does this compare to information needed to execute a task?

A second way to increase the speed of knowledge representation is to distinguish between learning by and learning before doing. If you know a lot, encourage learning before doing; if you know little, encourage learning while doing. Some companies that have substantial knowledge of the same or a related production process can reduce time to market for drug development through encouraging learning before doing through the scaling up of production. These companies simulate the full-scale production process, and thereby define its characteristics. For a drug where the company has little knowledge of the production process, the process of learning while doing is more likely to deliver desired results by starting production and adjusting the characteristics of the process gradually. In other words, full-scale efficient production is reached through trial and error.

What is the lesson here? Parallel processing of information is not the only crucial role for successful knowledge management. Knowledge about tasks where the company's knowledge can be applied is highly critical in deciding whether to engage in learning before doing or learning by doing. It is quite paradoxical that most implementation of strategies developed by top management teams, even if they are path-breaking, based on radical innovation, quite complex in their formulation, and involving major change, follows the learning-before-doing principle. If there is a lack of this kind of 'extensional' knowledge, one would expect the reverse to be the case—more learning by doing. In fact, if a strategy is an extension of previous strategies, one would very much expect extensional knowledge to allow learning before doing (e.g. discussion and simulation of what could go wrong in strategy implementation, for example, using scenario techniques).

When IBM launched its USD 5 billion project in 1963, the organization was taking on a major corporate transformation project, making IBM an integrated computer manufacturer, covering everything from software to chips. The project set out to create an integrated, compatible, multi-usage computer—the 360 series. Rather than finalizing a strategy before launching the project, IBM management mapped the strategic direction of the company as the project played out. They gradually became more knowledgeable about technology, markets, and the technical design of the product. They were learning while doing. If strategies are radical, like the 360 series, one would tend to expect more learning by doing, more experimentation in action.

A third way to increase the speed of knowledge representation, and perhaps the most well known, is to redesign horizontal processes in the company to allow for effective information flow. During their international expansion, many financial services firms have redesigned their governance mechanisms and created structures and processes that facilitate the lateral flow of knowledge. Relatively global (or at least regional) businesses such as investment banking, wealth management, or large corporate banking have recently been organized as cross-national business divisions in many banks. Knowledge representation speeds up by assigning central responsibility for service categories and standardizing report structures.

Increase the Power of Knowledge Representation

Management efforts should aim to increase the power, or in other words, the capacity for knowledge representation or information processing. Like a computer, the more memory the computer has, the more powerful it is. Companies, however, are slightly more complex, and one needs to add the dimension of accessibility. While computers have input/output sockets preparing them for access, organizations tend to lose overview of their real resources. It is not enough to have the brightest people on the payroll if these people do not use their full potential, solving the most difficult tasks. Firms need some way of accessing them easily.

First, the company needs to be effective at encoding information, making it possible to store it correctly in the organizational memory. The brain works in a similar way. It takes in signals from the environment and codes them into categories. For example, most human beings when perceiving a green, round, sweet smelling object would encode it as an apple. One can assume that the company should work in a similar way. An incoming letter from an angry customer needs to be coded as a 'matter for the complaints department'. Information about a competitor entering a foreign market needs to be encoded as 'strategic marketing information'. Upon encoding, the organization ensures that the information ends up in the right place. One might think that the most important encoders are in the mail office or in your secretarial office, and that might very well be so. However, most employees are engaged in coding activities all day long; for example, when receiving an incoming telephone call from an interesting job seeker looking for a job in product development. One could encode the matter as 'product development'. Perhaps one even runs one's fingers through the company phone book, and gives the applicant a name in product development. Perhaps one may code it as a matter for 'personnel', and ask the candidate to send his application to the personnel office. Another alternative might be to say, 'Send me your application, and I'll review it myself.' After having looked at it one decides how to encode it—where to send it. Encoding happens every day, but how do we get it to function more effectively? The idea is to continuously develop both the company knowledge road—who, what, when, where, and why—and the procedural knowledge road map—what to do.

A second way to increase the power of knowledge representation is to boost the storage capacity of knowledge. Information is stored in the heads of organizational employees. Information, in the form of memos, letters, personal notes, reports, procedures, etc., is also stored in computer files, archives, and private files. With prices dropping for computer hardware, storage space is becoming less of a critical factor in increasing the power of information processing of the organization. Employees are able to store all e-mails, which makes it easier for them to keep track of their own communication both within and outside the company.

A third way to increase the power of knowledge representation is to ensure effective and efficient retrieval of information. In other words, companies need to get the correct information as fast as possible. This means working on many fronts. Computer databases need to be made easily accessible for employees, easy to read, and easy to operate. Archives need to be kept in a known location; they need to be tidy, clean, and easy to operate. There needs to be a filing system that can be operated on a need-to-know basis. Perhaps the ideal model is one of a library; here every layman can retrieve information easily and painlessly.

Before moving on to discuss the importance of enhancing accuracy of knowledge and information, there are three things to keep in mind when increasing the power of knowledge development in a company. First, guarantee that there is effective coding of information. Second, make sure there are sufficient, effective storage capacities. Third, ensure effective systems for retrieval of information.

Increase the Reliability of Knowledge Representation

Perhaps the toughest challenges of knowledge management concern the quest for accuracy and reliability. How does one know that your company really knows the 'truth' about its industry? How does one ensure that the assumptions about new product development at competitors are correct? How does one make sure that understanding changes in the industry corresponds to reality? These questions are particularly relevant for companies that find themselves in emergent industries where roles are evolving. A competitor today might become a supplier tomorrow. A new entrant may become a customer. In addition, power relations are not fixed. The bargaining power of a customer is unclear as the degree of integration of the industry rapidly changes.

Although for many decades it was rather static, the financial services industry has become an emergent industry where roles and power bases change constantly. Industrial firms, online banks, direct insurers, or the French retailer Carrefour are turning the industry more dynamic. In such industries, it is difficult to create accurate representations of the industry landscape—and many firms fall into the 'paralysis by analysis' trap. Companies constantly have to change their representations and make strategic decisions based on limited and incomplete information. Knowledge developed today might be wrong tomorrow. Any industry analysis, identifying players, is rapidly outdated. Against this background, it becomes very important to develop what one can call representational validity (i.e. that the company's representation of the environment is valid). There are four ways to increase the validity of knowledge representations.

First, the validity of these representations can be increased through a regular updating of information. A company represents its environment in many forms: sales charts, industry models, trends, shareholder value analysis, market studies, customer interviews, strategic analyses, purchasing procedures, supplier appraisals, etc. Frequent gathering and updating of company, business, and generic knowledge is necessary, and especially important is knowledge of recent events that could change a representation.

Second, validity can be enhanced greatly by using multiple sources of data for a representation. For example, if a public company wants to assess its ability to create shareholder value, it might draw a comparison with the most important, publicly listed firm. Validity of the representation would be greatly enhanced if comparisons were also made with other stock market indexes, like

Nikkei 500, Netherlands Index, or Standard & Poor 500. The secret of validity lies in comparisons. What does one source of data say in comparison with another source? Why? What do discrepancies tell us?

Third, validity of a representation is also enhanced through a common understanding of a representation. For example, when management teams are asked to estimate the impact of investments in marketing on market share and profitability of a firm, normally one gets as many answers as there are managers. A challenge for management teams is to achieve a common understanding of what the information at hand might mean, and what the information does not tell them. Discussions then typically revolve around questions such as: How do you define market share? Is that product share? Share of a customer's mind? Share of time and attention of the customer? How much can you read out of a market share? Assuming that you invest in developing a market, how can you evaluate the return on that investment?

Discussions about the fundamentals behind data seem much more fruitful in achieving common understanding than a pure disagreement or agreement on the implications of information. In building validity, managers should ask themselves about the extent of their knowledge. Where is our knowledge valid? How much do we really know about this phenomenon? This is what established bankers might ask themselves when confronted with new electronic media. What can we really do with this development? This is also what insurance firms ask about financial services; what does it take to successfully integrate financial services and insurance into packages that benefit the customer?

Finally, to increase the validity of knowledge representations, managers should ask actors outside the company, whether customers, suppliers, or government officials, if their knowledge of the environment is accurate. How many firms invite customers to share their views on the company? As a part of a major quality and productivity transformation programme, Siemens invited selected customers to visit and speak openly about their quality and service level. The television manufacturing branch of Sony Europe buys tubes and other components from Siemens. Their reactions gave the Siemens managers a major shock—their customer service was below an acceptable level, and their delivery times were far too high. Siemens had to rethink the validity of its business knowledge of a satisfied, smiling, happy customer, and use this new insight to boost the transformation programme.

Connect People with People

Yet, knowledge is not only stored in brains and machines, but also in the patterns of a certain practice, values, and attitudes. It is stored in the way a task is performed. Take a Xerox copier, a highly complex product with a very high

271

number of possible failure modes. The copier repairmen that frequently visit your office have gone through a number of training sessions. They also have instruction manuals on how to diagnose a technical problem, and how to correct it. The transfer of knowledge from one repairman to another, however, does not go via the manual, but rather through a kind of master–apprentice relationship in which the young apprentice learns the tricks of the trade on site. He learns by watching the patterns of practising repairs by his master. The information is stored in the way repairs are practised. This occurs in many areas; just think of banking, the medical field, sales, carpentry, plumbing, law, etc.

To boost cross-border knowledge flows, financial services firms have to connect the people within their organizations, and connect employees with the outside world. This includes linking PCs into local and wide area networks and into Intranets and the Internet. There are many more ways to connect people in companies, ranging from memo, fax, e-mail, voice mail, over the telephone, and video, to larger meetings and face-to-face meetings. The aim is to stimulate employees to share existing company information with one another and to access and store new information more effectively. There are at least three ways to connect people with each other from a knowledge management perspective.

The first way is to 'wire' the company that is connecting employees via their PC. The aim is, of course, to facilitate exchange and processing of information. The rationale is that the beliefs that direct communication and exchange of objective information are facilitated among employees because it is easier to send information across time and space. In turn, this improves the flexibility of the company, which is a key characteristic of a networked organization. Although many companies are getting wired to speed up internal processes and learning, much remains to be done the problem is not with the technology, but with corporate processes. Companies must fundamentally change the way they do business, and that is a difficult task.

To wire a company, however, requires that employees are computer-literate beyond word processing. In the spirit of moving the computer/employee ratio towards 1 or above, management needs to stimulate the introduction and use of e-mail, give access to databases, sometimes even to the Internet. Some retail banks even in developed countries spend hundreds of millions of euros on fancy PR programmes or bonuses for their top performers but are cheese-paring when it comes to ICT infrastructure of their branches.

The Swedish insurance company Skandia has integrated a PC-use ratio in its visualization of how much its 'structural capital' has grown over time. Computer literacy among employees, seen as a premise for connectivity, has become an important variable in this 140-year-old insurance company. Likewise, at Hewlett Packard, 100,000 employees used 120,000 computers in

1996. Despite the huge costs involved (PCs turnaround in three years!), the benefit is substantial.

A second way to increase connectivity among employees is to balance the use of electronic communication with the rich, multi-sensuous experiences of face-to-face meetings. Face-to-face interaction and electronically mediated information exchanges differ in several fundamental ways. In face-to-face meetings, the participants are always sharing time and space, which is not the case for electronic interaction. From a knowledge management perspective, this makes an enormous difference.

First, face-to-face meetings involve more sensuous experience than an electronic information exchange; face-to-face meetings provide for a much richer information exchange. In fact, from a pure biological perspective, e-mail and even video-based exchange seems somewhat bizarre. The PC/TV monitors screen out all the smells, sounds, and textures of the environment that we normally pick up in face-to-face meetings. It emphasizes the natural power of the eye to look at things from afar, while de-emphasizing the other senses engaged in human communication. Although it is consistent with the visual and textual biases of Western views of knowledge production, electronically mediated communication clearly reduces the participants' potential of knowing during the interaction/communication. Furthermore, the learning context of face-to-face meetings is better because each party—in real time—has the possibility to partly access the other's learning process by asking questions like 'How did you reach that conclusion?' Despite the tremendous advances in technology, it would be very hard to reintroduce the social context in electronically, inter-organizational or intra-organizational communications.

Acknowledging some of the implications of these fundamental differences, several managers we have met use some heuristics to achieve the balance between face-to-face and electronic communication. Although equipped with the latest video-conferencing technology, for instance, top management of Skandia AFS apply the rule that one in every three group communications should be face-to-face.

A third way to increase the connectivity among employees is to facilitate connection between the company and the outside world. The aim is to break with the industrial view of setting up as many barriers as possible between a company and the rest of the world. Interestingly, new communication technology is consistent with Western ideals of democracy; in theory, everybody can contribute ideas, facts, and opinions to, and access, 'free' information across time and space. In practice, this is not the case in many companies and countries.

Riding on the wave of business process thinking, many companies are improving their connections with suppliers in addition to their customers; they are coordinating the whole supply chain (on a global scale). These connections are about information, not just the flow of physical products, including joint planning, coordination of organizational processes, etc. Such connections encompass a huge potential for knowledge development if they are seen in a knowledge management perspective. It is the number and quality of the connections that counts.

There are many practical problems to address when trying to connect people with people. Typical challenges that need to be addressed include when people can send messages on what vehicle, what is the required response time, what is the priority of processing messages, and what is the security of interaction in the network. In addition to more fundamental questions of robustness of the networks, issues of confidentiality, identity, anonymity, and integrity of messages are raised daily in most companies with advanced, electronically based communication networks. These are very mundane challenges, seemingly requiring traditional control approaches. In most companies, each employee has the right to access all information needed but firms sometimes monitor the traffic in terms of large variance of end-user addresses usage and addresses for non-business information.

Connect People with Information

A second task of knowledge management is to connect people with information. Although partly overlapping with the first task—connecting people with people—there are some distinct conceptual and practical features of this task that are worth highlighting. Knowledge resides in the network, and knowledge is only considered organizational knowledge if it has been stored and is accessible to others. There are at least three ways to connect people with information.

The first way is to develop a climate, and practices of open storage and retrieval of information in databases, analogous to the brain. These databases constitute an important part of the 'memory' of the company. This is what will make the people develop a shared understanding of the world. Because of electronic communication technology, people have the potential to access considerably more people with one of the most frequently asked questions in companies: 'Does anybody know . . . ?' With a small effort it is possible to leverage, in principle, all brains in the network! This information, however, needs to be stored in some kind of 'public' database, or archived to be considered organizational knowledge. For instance, electronic 'storage files' accessible to all can make this happen. These files contain not only answers to the question posed by network members, but also what people in the network wanted to know, that is, the questions asked.

In some companies the main knowledge management task concerns the continuous conversion of what is in the heads of employees into databases. At Skandia, the key task is to convert 'human capital' into 'structural capital'. Structural capital is everything that is left in the company when employees go home, and as one of their managers told us, 'It is structural capital that is the most valuable part of the company, not the human capital.' It encompasses organizational routines and processes of all kinds. It is the infrastructure of the organization, including its memory.

Of course, in many instances it is impossible to give all people in the network free access to all information for reasons of confidentiality. Categories of employees are typically denied access to parts of databases. So-called 'firewall' software and other filtering mechanisms make it increasingly easy to distinguish layers, or classes of accessibility to information in the network.

The challenge of knowledge management goes beyond keeping tidy databases of information, however. The challenge for most companies is how to retrieve business, company, and generic knowledge of its people. There are two central questions to be asked in this respect. How do companies retrieve historical knowledge, and how do they link that knowledge to current tasks? Perhaps one can develop a genealogy of a task, like some families keep detailed records of their ancestors (the task here, of course, is breeding). One can look at a task and then trace the people who have worked on that task in the company. Some of the knowledge carries over from generation to generation. A 'master' in accounting hands over knowledge to the 'apprentice'. The apprentice gradually becomes a master by improving the accounting practices of the company. In some instances, people move from one job to another. If firms want event knowledge of how the company tackled a crisis in its accounting, they might want to find people that were around at the time.

Therefore, a second way to connect people with information is to systematically identify the people who have certain knowledge. Many firms have encouraged their managers to become 'brokers' of knowledge. A manager is supposed to connect people with different knowledge, connect ideas, and disseminate and pass on information. These firms have also developed what they call the 'yellow pages', a directory of knowledge. This is a solution to the problem of finding out who has knowledge about a particular problem. The approach is to list relevant expertise/knowledge and who has it. Furthermore, the key point is to do yellow pages by acclamation, not by organizational chats, and distribute them to everybody in the company. This approach is claimed to lead to reduced time for identifying expertise, and has also helped in encouraging the role of knowledge brokers. Other organizations list 'competence areas', the people who know something about these areas, and/or list competence area by person. Such cross-referencing makes the retrieval of information quite easy. Of course, any attempt to develop yellow pages must ensure continuous updating to capture new employers, new knowledge, and other changes in the workforce.

A third way to connect people with information is to ensure that the network extends to where the most interesting information is created, and/or is available. Phillips has extended its organizational network in the multimedia realm this way. They house employees from other parts of the organization to work in the San Francisco Bay area. That is where the new multimedia ideas, capabilities, and products are developed, but this is also where the new initiatives on educational reforms are taking place, that is, the users of multimedia products. Phillips feels that it simply has to tap into it by extending its network.

Stimulate Collective Action

Based on an information infrastructure around employees, a third knowledge management task is to stimulate 'collective action' throughout the organization. The idea is to make the whole company work together as one huge network that through coordinated behaviour and action will do 'the right thing' in all situations. A simple example of collective action is when one employee asks the others for advice, and gets quick answers on how to solve a particular problem. The company is seen as analogous to a neural network, a kind of 'collective mind' residing in the connections among employees. Collective action is based on the principle of parallel processing among 'interrelated processing units', that is, employees. It requires effective connections between people and between people and information. It is the joint situation that is the focus, not the local.

Weick and Roberts[21] called such collective actions the outcome of 'heedful interrelating'. To be heedful simply means that one combines behaviour in an intelligent, rather than haphazard way. People act heedfully when they are careful, critical, conscious, purposeful, etc., that is, heeding is a set of qualities of mind with respect to an action. Collective action is a complex process. While envisaging the collective action of the whole network, group members subordinate their action to that of the envisioned, collective action of the group. The outcome of collective action, however, depends very much on which activities are tied together. Collective action in handling a customer complaint by the sales group is different from that taken by the top management team in developing a new vision. Several ways to stimulate collective action exist.

A first way is to infix social rules of behaviour and action that stimulate heedful interrelating. One method of doing this is to develop a social contract of 'pre-emptive generosity' among employees in the network; that is, a generosity in information, not monetary terms. The rule is simple: I contribute the information I have and judge relevant to the task at hand, and I expect everybody else in the network to do the same. I simply assume that my fellow employees will contribute their best over time, and therefore I behave accordingly. In practice it is difficult to motivate employees to contribute their very best whenever it is needed, and it is especially difficult in a network primarily resting on electronic communications. Few people want to 'sign up' for pre-emptive generosity via a 'socially castrated' communication tool like e-mail.

A second way to stimulate collective action is to care for newcomers in the network. Because newcomers cannot envision collective actions by the network they have joined, they are in constant danger of making errors. They act heedlessly simply because they have not yet learned about the heedful interrelations in the network. While being great learning events, of course, these mistakes can also have devastating effects on the company.

This is more than a top management responsibility; it is a shared responsibility among the network members. There are several ways to help newcomers act heedfully, rather than heedlessly in their new organizations. Employees can, for instance, relate 'war stories' to the new people. These stories typically integrate different themes of previous heedful actions that might help the newcomer better envision what future actions the group might possibly take. Needless to say, social interaction, rather than electronic communication, is crucial.

A third way to stimulate collective action is to involve more and more advanced levels in the company. Clearly, heedful interrelating and collective action can occur between two or more people. The unit of analysis in the previous section was a group in the company, like a project team. Obtaining truly heedful collective action is a major challenge in a group of, say, three people. A firm can probably, over time and with the right skills and context, push forward the scale of heedful collective action. What about the sales group? The R&D team? The new cross-functional group of 11 people? The whole SBU? The company? The third way to stimulate collective action is to strive in this direction. Few companies have yet achieved this, however.

This dimension of knowledge management goes way beyond connecting people with one another, and people with information. The requirements for heedful collective action are not trivial. It will require continuous and deep interaction among group members. For the many reasons outlined above, this interaction is not primarily done via electronic communication.

Recognize the Individuality of Knowledge Development

The primary task is to recognize the individuality of knowledge development—everything known is known by somebody—and align the organization accordingly. This means that all organizational members feel that they have the potential to develop new knowledge all the time, and this also means that management must figure out a way for all members (the SBU manager, the support staff person, and the call centre operator) to allocate some of their time, energy as well as company money to develop new knowledge.

To successfully stimulate people to venture into the unknown, management needs to understand norms, beliefs, values, and world views of employees, groups, units, and the whole company. What people see when they venture into the unknown depends on who they are. Should all employees run around and randomly develop knowledge? Should the office clerk develop knowledge about the next possible acquisition? No, that is not the idea, as will be discussed later but the idea is that each employee has a potential to develop knowledge, that is, to both think and do, that can be stimulated to be unleashed.

It is really about viewing employees as humans rather than man-as-a-machine, and thus allowing them to fulfil their potential as knowing organizational members. This may sound obvious to some readers, but considering how companies operate today, it does not seem to be common practice in most companies. We suggest the following three rules of thumb for managers wanting to facilitate employee stimulation.

First, care for distinctions made throughout the organization. All employees have a unique set of experiences that help them to make their own personal distinctions in life. Knowledge enables distinction making and distinctions, in turn, enable the development of new knowledge. So, the more knowledgeable one is, the more distinctions one can make. The more knowledgeable a manager is about the wealth management industry, the finer the distinctions he or she can make regarding the development, production, and distribution of certificates. The company's knowledge is therefore all the different distinctions made by the organizational members, as well as the potential new distinctions they can make in the future.

Sometimes employees distinguish something that could evolve into an immense strategic problem for the company, like the 'little warning signs' in Barings Bank before it went down, or in Société Générale before the French President asked the CEO to step down because of illegal trading operations by a broker in the lower hierarchies. Before management knows it, the company has an unexpected crisis, just because of a tiny little event that seemed so uninteresting when somebody did it, or observed it. We are certain that in all the companies that have been forced into a situation of crisis change, some employee, on some organizational level, saw it coming. In our language any crisis situation typically means that top management did not make the distinctions they should have made. This is not surprising since it is extremely difficult for any top manager in the knowledge economy to be the all-knowing oracle of the industrial economy.

A second way to facilitate individual knowledge development is to stimulate people to challenge assumptions already made by others, often taken for granted in the company. Tradition derives from the act of handing down something from generation to generation, and/or the principles held and generally followed by any branch of knowledge, acquired from and handed down by experience and practice. In the language of distinction making, tradition means making increasingly finer distinctions resting on the same basic assumptions.

Many of our social rules tell us that traditions are important in our private lives as well as in organized life in companies. We recruit new employees by selecting and promoting the people that we feel will 'fit' into our organization. The natural lack of diversity in basic views that will result will make any organization vulnerable to quick changes inside and outside its boundaries. This is why it is sometimes necessary to reconsider basic assumptions. However, in practice, it is extremely difficult to break with tradition. It is a painstaking approach that requires identification and examination of assumptions previously made by oneself or others, and seeking out possible new branches of knowledge, that is, making a new distinction that may give rise to a new tradition. For instance, most of what we call 'conceptual breakthroughs' are examples of the rethinking form of distinction making because these insights break with the traditional view, for instance, the Earth is round versus flat.

A third way to facilitate individual knowledge development is to work on people's scaling capabilities. Scaling is like taking off or landing in an aircraft. One is able to see both the small and the big picture. Patterns will occur at different altitudes that one has not seen before. Scaling means moving back and forth between fine and more rudimentary distinctions. There is an inherent positive feedback potential in knowledge development; the more I know, the more I have the potential to know. Likewise, the better the organizational members are at scaling, the greater the opportunity to develop more knowledge simply because they can connect with more people on more issues.

Emergent patterns from scaling always arise in the eye of the observer. If the top management team of a particular bank may see the growing business potential in 'assurance and financial services', or see them as a threat, and change the bank's corporate behaviour accordingly, top management teams of other banks may not see any patterns at all. As argued above, 'what you see depends on who you are'. This simply means that although presented with the same facts, or inputs, people will interpret these facts/inputs differently. Thus, it is not advisable to expect top managers to see all the patterns that might be relevant to others.

Balance Authority and Self-Reference

While the exercise of command authority, where one individual tells another individual what to do, is sometimes necessary, excessive reliance on authority is an enormous barrier to the availability and creation of knowledge within a firm. It prohibits individuals from successfully self-referencing and, therefore, from realizing their potential as knowing humans.

Self-referencing refers to the common sense, everyday observation that all humans have a unique set of experiences that makes us see and react to things differently. This is why it matters who did the industry analysis, who made the claim about emerging technology, or who did the market segmentation. Although the differences between people's views eventually converge and become trivial on routine matters, they are the essential building blocks for the creation of new knowledge. This is also why every company develops an ever-changing knowledge base. There are several ways to balance authority and self-reference.

A first way is to ensure that authority is used only when knowledge is exploited, not in situations when knowledge is supposed to be developed. When a firm is in survival mode, that is, implementing what is already known to it during standard operations, authority is the appropriate modus operandi. Based on the assumption that they know more, managers should tell the next layer what to do. It is in the advancement, or knowledge development, mode that this kind of command authority is most inappropriate. Consequently, managers must figure out other ways 'to get things done'. This is also where most managers fail, simply because their experience restricts their span of possible actions.

Closely related to the previous rule, the second rule of thumb in balancing authority with self-reference is to make even more use of project work. The reason might seem obvious by now; project work is a vehicle for advancement activities and, thus, provides a natural boundary for when to stop using command authority. This may not seem to be a new idea, not least because most readers are probably involved in several projects right now. Many factors influence the possibility to balance authority with self-reference via project teams, including who is participating, the mandate for the work, time constraints, measurement of progress, etc. The problem is that the nature of project work in many companies is more of another survival activity, rather than an advancement activity geared towards knowing more.

A third way to balancing authority with self-reference is to one way or another help employees internalize the distinction between authority-based management and self-reference. It is not until this distinction is part of the deep structure or the basic assumptions of organizational members that the benefits will pay off. It is not sufficient only to realign the organizational routines accordingly, or write another instruction that it must happen. In addition to such artefacts, the underlying values, that is, what is considered good and bad, or right and wrong, of organizational members must reflect the distinction between authority-based management and self-reference. Ultimately this means that the distinction should not be an issue in the organization; it should be so natural that people do not need to talk about it any more—it is embodied. The transparent assumptions on which employees base their values are that command authority simply is not used when people are in a knowledge development mode.

Create a Climate for Learning Conversations

The development and diffusion of knowledge in a company depends to a great extent on the development and diffusion of language. The development and diffusion of language, in turn, is about the art of conversation. Conversations are the backbone of business because few decisions are taken without at least two people talking about it, and if they do not understand each other, things can go terribly wrong. A word or phrase may embody a marvellous idea, but it cannot really be called 'language' until it is successfully used in conversations. This is why the creation of a climate for learning conversations needs to be a central concern of every manager who wishes to succeed in a knowledge-intensive age.

Language here refers to different concepts and the meanings they carry. To create a common language is much more than just the decision to use English as the company language. Every company has its own unique set of concepts and phrases—its own language—that cannot be easily translated or adopted by anyone else. Unless you are part of the conversations that made the language, and continually remake it, important meanings can be totally missed. Stimulate language, and over time an internal company lexicon emerges. This means spending time and resources on discussing and giving meaning to new and old words, concepts and phrases, as well as innovating own concepts and phrases. This is what is played out in many industries today, including such diverse businesses as pharmaceuticals, educational software, consumer electronics, and financial services.

Given the centrality of conversations to both the routine operation and the future success of business, it is ironic how few managers pay the slightest attention to it or to the conversations that give rise to it. There are few strategic planning documents with 'manage the business conversations better' as a major issue, but with the increasing cultural diversity of internationalizing financial services firms, the time has come to put it near the top of the list. There are several ways to create a climate for learning conversations.

A first method is to make and use the distinction between the conversations that are primarily focused on executing existing routines within a business and those trying to create a space for something new to take shape. The former covers issues that have been talked about previously. Perhaps these issues were new to everyone at some time in the past, and once required more extensive conversation, but not any longer. The latter calls for people to move into new and unfamiliar territory by talking about things that have never been discussed before. Operational conversations are about exploiting the knowledge gained in the past and present. Strategic conversations are about creating the knowledge, and the language to diffuse it, that will be necessary for a successful future.

Many managers seem to instinctively do a better job at operational conversations than the strategic ones. People who are proficient at talking about the day-to-day challenges of their businesses have trouble translating that success into their strategic conversations. 'Strategy sessions' often focus on day-to-day operational details, or become over-structured, boring and political; in short, a waste of time. The exceptions to this pattern are fondly remembered, but remain exceptions nonetheless. In the days when a business strategy took years to unfold and was tied to a fairly stable set of products and services, this limitation did not carry a great cost. Now, even previously slow-moving financial services firms are under pressure to change direction in a matter of weeks or months. Like the obsolescence of computer equipment, a strategy may have a very short shelf life. If managers are not proficient at talking about the future, their company will not have a future.

A second way to create a climate of learning conversations is to establish rules for strategic conversations. A common reason why managers have less success with strategic conversations is that they try to utilize the same rules and tools that they do in operational conversations. At first glance, one might think that the skills are transferable. A conversation is just a conversation, after all. Unfortunately, it does not work that way. In most companies, many common elements of operational conversations are in fact active barriers to successful conversations about the future.

An example of a rule for a strategic conversation is to focus only on building shared meaning, rather than on 'who's right'. Strategic conversations must be a dialogue for understanding rather than advocacy for agreement. If an adversarial tone is allowed into strategic discussions, then the creation of new knowledge and language will stop. The full language surrounding the future of the company does not yet exist; it must be created. All of the conversations that will eventually give rise to operational routines have not yet taken place. There are no right or wrong answers.

Another example of such a rule is to abolish the use of authority in strategic conversations. Although one's current organizational authority may be relevant to operational conversations, it is meaningless to strategic ones. As soon as authority is used in a discussion, it ceases to be a strategic conversation and becomes operational. More extreme uses of power, such as threats and intimidation, are even less compatible with learning conversations.

A final method to create a climate of learning conversations is to inculcate the idea of knowledge development as a responsibility, or even a 'right' as part of the identity of the company. This means that all the routine systems are aligned to this. In particular, incentive schemes need to encourage active participation in learning conversations. It also means that value judgements in the company are positive towards learning conversations. It must be considered 'good', 'fine', 'valuable', etc. to spend time developing options for the future through conversations in addition to implementing what is already known today.

Designing Cross-Border Knowledge-Sharing Systems

Knowledge management systems are effective if their elements complement each other. Activities are complements if doing more of one thing increases the returns to doing more of the others.[22] The challenge is to develop the knowledge strategy that best fits the current competitive challenges and the company's culture.

Designing a new knowledge management system can follow these steps:

- Outline the impact of knowledge on corporate success
- Conduct a knowledge audit
- Implement 'quick wins'
- Change knowledge management culture

Outline the Impact of Knowledge on Corporate Success

Before investing in costly knowledge management systems and activities, one needs to get a sound understanding of the general business logic and profit drivers of the single segments. How does knowledge influence the creation of positional advantages within a given industry? How does knowledge influence the creation of cost and differentiation advantages?

Key knowledge areas need to be identified that have a substantial impact on the performance of the firm. Not all business segments gravitate around the same relevant knowledge categories. In retail and corporate banking, customer knowledge is essential to assess the risk level of lending activities. In investment banking, knowledge about the technical product construction and the trends of reference asset markets is crucial. Not all knowledge areas deserve the same level of attention. The next step, the knowledge audit, should centre on the identified core areas and make sure that knowledge creation and exchange is happening there. If the knowledge management system works in those areas, it will inevitably involve other, less relevant, knowledge categories.

Conduct a Knowledge Audit

For the knowledge areas that have been identified, the next step of the process schedules a detailed analysis of how knowledge is identified, developed, exploited, and measured. Figure 10.1 lists the major questions that have to

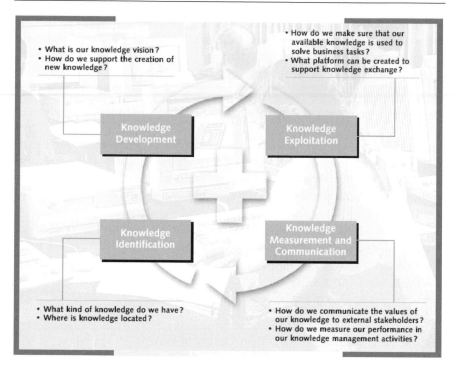

Figure 10.1. Knowledge audit

be addressed in each phase of a knowledge audit. The first phase, knowledge identification, aims at (*a*) locating existing knowledge (related to the key knowledge areas) and (*b*) understanding the shape of that knowledge (i.e. is it codified or embodied in people's brains?). Aids such as knowledge maps, yellow pages systems, best practice libraries, or knowledge brokers may help in understanding location and shaping existing key knowledge.

The second step consists of understanding how the financial services firm develops new knowledge. The Swedish financial services group Skandia AFS may illustrate this step. The company was growing at a fast pace in the early 1990s and the top management feared that it would not be able to grow its intellectual capital at the rate of its revenues. One of the central concerns was how the necessary knowledge could be transferred to all the branches that were newly opened. In addition, Skandia feared that knowledge was too fluid: 'How much of the intellectual capital remains in our company when the employees go home?' was a key question during those times.

At Skandia, intellectual capital (or knowledge) was composed of human capital (or tacit knowledge) and structural capital (or codified knowledge). As Figure 10.2 shows, there are six fundamental processes that have the power

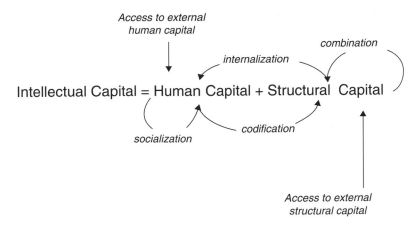

Figure 10.2. Knowledge development processes (for a detailed discussion of knowledge processes, see Nonaka and Takeuchi 1995)

to enhance intellectual capital. The following paragraphs describe the four central processes in more detail.

1. *Socialization*: Human capital is knowledge that resides in the body and brain of the employees and can therefore only be transferred and developed through the interaction between employees. It is hard to learn how to negotiate a merger deal from manuals. It is rare that people read a book about designing a new investment certificate and are able to perform this task in an investment bank. Socialization helps an apprentice observe and experience the actions of a master and learn how to perform certain tasks. In the past, investment banks tried to protect themselves from powerful individuals by facilitating the creation of teams—with the result that entire teams now move from one bank to another.

2. *Codification*: A second knowledge development process is the creation of structural capital: corporate insurance consultants that codify their client site visits in a brief report, creating structural capital. An M&A team that describes its post-merger-integration experience and makes it available in a best practice database likewise creates structural capital.

3. *Internalization*: Creating databases without ensuring that they are used is of little value. Internalization describes the process of finding codified knowledge in a database or a library and connecting it to one's existing knowledge base while reading it. Experience shows that many senior managers in consulting companies prefer to use best practice databases just to identify the most adequate project leader and then engage in socialization. In other firms, managers prefer to invent a proper solution to an existing and recurring problem instead of reading about previous

285

project results. Facilitating internalization processes is often at least as difficult as pushing for codification efforts.

4. *Combination*: Some firms are able to present a client presentation with over 300 PowerPoint slides with the client's name and tailored content on each page only 24 hours after the first project briefing. Those firms combine existing pieces of codified knowledge and assemble them in a new way.

The third step of the knowledge audit is to understand how knowledge is exploited. This is especially tricky in multinational firms where tasks in one part of the world need to be connected with knowledge in another part of the world. One solution to this challenge is that upcoming tasks are classified and coordinated by a global practice leader or competence centres. A best practice database or yellow pages system might help managers in search of existing solutions. Incentive systems and managerial mechanisms that facilitate the transfer of knowledge from one country to another must be put in place. Even if subsidiary managers are good corporate citizens, they do not always send out their best people to solve problems elsewhere.

The knowledge audit concludes with an analysis of how the value of intellectual capital is communicated to the stakeholders and the performance of the knowledge management system is evaluated and corrective actions are taken. The sometimes huge difference between book and market value of firms is partly because knowledge is not properly represented in the balance sheets of financial services firms. Skandia developed a supplement to the annual report to illustrate the value of its intellectual capital to shareholders. To do this, Skandia used a balanced scorecard approach and left the decision to develop measures for knowledge to the decentralized units. Other firms limit their knowledge communication and measurement activities to simple items like the annual goal setting of employees by including 'professionally manages knowledge' as an evaluation criterion.

Implement 'Quick Wins'

After a sound understanding of where knowledge is located, how it is developed, exploited, measured, and how the efficiency of the knowledge management processes are appraised, small changes in the knowledge management system with a strong impact can be tackled. These 'quick wins' can be found at several places:

- *Meetings*: It is sometimes appalling to see that people who should meet never do. Sometimes the creation of new types of meetings or the re-composition of the meeting members adds substantial value to cross-border knowledge flows of a firm. The use of video conferencing or

Internet-based meeting tools may not be immediate for some firms but is potentially a quick win for many organizations.

- *Intranet*: Fast and direct access to relevant databases accelerates cross-border knowledge transfer. In one company, the European subsidiaries had a link to the online knowledge management system on their home page, whereas their American colleagues needed to click through three pages before accessing the same system. To create similar Intranet systems with fast and direct access to relevant pages does not cost much time and can have a huge impact on knowledge exchange.

- *International job rotation*: Systematic and professional knowledge transfer across borders can be effectively organized through an international job rotation programme. Such initiatives can be organized relatively quickly and do not require massive financial investments.

- *Project management*: Knowledge transfer can be improved by marginally changing the project guidelines. To make sure that existing solutions are sought before starting a project, project leaders of, for example, ICT initiatives could be forced to sign a milestone document stating to what extent existing solutions within the company can be used to achieve the desired goals. In the final report, milestones could be to summarize project experiences and inserted in the best practice library.

- *Reporting system*: To change the distribution list of key documents could also create substantial benefits for the company without much effort.

- *Yellow pages system*: To allow the search for expertise instead of names, this system facilitates the creation of links between tasks and knowledge. The challenge lies in motivating experts to signal their areas of expertise on, for example, personal CV Intranet pages. Some firms facilitate the feeding and updating of the personal CV online by assigning international career opportunities based on this database or by granting bonuses for specific achievements (such as patents filed or articles published) that have been indicated on the site.

These are just some examples of quick wins that financial services firms might implement after their knowledge audit. This phase is essential because it keeps the enthusiasm for knowledge management high and opens up for deeper change programmes linked to the culture of the company.

Change the Knowledge Management Culture

To achieve deeper and fundamental change in the way a multinational company generates and distributes knowledge, cultural aspects have to be addressed. National, industry, and firm-specific cultural elements all influence

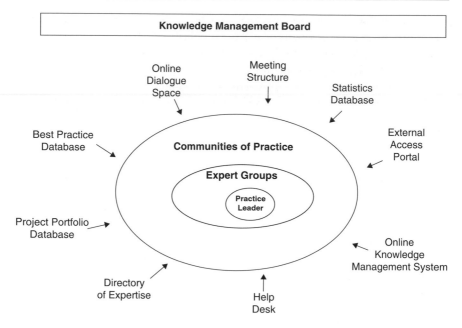

Figure 10.3. Changing the knowledge management culture

how knowledge is managed. To achieve fundamental change, a multi-layer system, as depicted in Figure 10.3, might help.

At the heart of the model are the practice leaders that have been nominated to spend most of their time facilitating the management of their respective key knowledge area. An expert group is composed of members nominated by a board that filters applications of overconfident managers and finds experts that are excessively modest. The reason for installing a 'filter' function for membership of expert groups is mainly due to different self-perceptions of what it means to be an expert; in some cultures, employees might expose themselves too early as experts and in other cultures, the true experts are hiding themselves because they fear being inundated with additional work. The filter also ensures the strategy fit of the expert groups, that is, they concentrate on strategically important knowledge areas.

The expert groups develop project reports, collect existing best practices, screen and disseminate external literature, and embark on selected knowledge development projects. They also act as a switching board, connecting tasks to knowledge on an international basis. Whereas internally in a community of practice no significant hierarchy can be identified, it is a major career step for an expert to be nominated as leader of an expert group. However, the tasks of the practice leader are more linked to coordination than to control. It is then up to the expert group to translate the task into a work programme. Resources can be requested by the expert groups, which are then assigned by the Knowledge Management Board, which also has the right to withdraw the resources and thereby close an expert group.

Since the Knowledge Management Board assigns tasks and resources, it also monitors the performance. Whereas the line management rewards the group members, the Knowledge Management Board is responsible for feedback to the line managers regarding performance of individuals. The Knowledge Management Board is composed of experts that are able to assess the technical quality of the project work. In addition, the success—measured for example by downloads and Intranet-site traffic as well as an online survey—of the publications of the expert groups is an indicator for the performance of the expert group. The members of expert groups are highly self-motivated because they are given the possibility to follow their interests and work on the edge of the research front in their knowledge area. However, the Knowledge Management Board can influence career decisions of members of expert groups and provide additional incentives.

In support of the expert group is the community of practice, which is defined as a group of experts who are informally bound to one another by exposure to and interest for a common class of tasks. They exist for an undefined period of time, and come together virtually (Intranet) or face-to-face to exchange knowledge. Members of a community of practice can come from different units, functions, and hierarchical positions within the organization. The participation in a community is not mandatory; hence, employees are not assigned to a specific community of practice. The main goal is to generate new knowledge for personal use in operational activities. Therefore, it is the community itself, or more precisely the individual members, that defines the tasks of the community. The scope of the tasks and activities has to be within the limits of the personal time and resources those individuals obtain from their operational units.

A community of practice can be converted into an expert group with more resources and responsibilities (subject to approval by the Knowledge Management Board). The monitoring and rewards of the results are therefore not standardized or intense. It is up to the line managers of each participant to decide whether the time spent by an employee is beneficial for the personal development of the single member of the community.

To change the knowledge management culture is obviously not an easy task and does not follow cookbook-like approaches. The creation of a knowledge management board that nominates practice leaders for core knowledge areas, expert teams in their support and encourages employees to actively participate in communities of practice is nevertheless a concrete start for a long journey towards a cross-border knowledge-sharing culture.

When Too Much Knowledge Sharing Hurts Company Performance

To conclude this chapter on lateral knowledge flows in multinational financial services firms, a warning note for excessive knowledge sharing needs to be placed. Decentralized units such as subsidiaries or foreign office managers tend to make implicit cost–benefit calculations before engaging in knowledge-sharing activities with other company units. From a subsidiary perspective, there is an optimal level of knowledge sharing. With a too high level of knowledge sharing, the costs of knowledge outflow generated by the time intensity of communication as well as knowledge codification and adaptation exceed the benefits of knowledge sharing in the form of formal recognition and rewarding. At the subsidiary level, cost–benefit reflections of knowledge outflows may diverge from those made at the headquarters since the interests are often not completely overlapping. To align interests in the MNC and achieve the optimal level of knowledge sharing, organizational mechanisms need to be developed to calibrate the various components of costs and benefits of knowledge sharing.

At its extremes, there are two very different knowledge management strategies available to firms depending on their overall competitive strategy.[23] Applying a people-to-document approach, a company attempts to extract knowledge from the person who developed it, make it independent from that person, and store it in databases, where it can be accessed and used by others in the company. This approach is called the codification strategy. Following this type of strategy opens up the possibility of achieving scale and scope in knowledge re-use. Examples of firms using this strategy are, among others, Ernst & Young and Deloitte Touche—companies that provide services with standardized service components and processes that can be re-used on a number of occasions.

In other companies, where services and products depend more on individual expertise that cannot be easily standardized, direct person-to-person contacts seem more appropriate to develop and share knowledge. Firms applying this strategy are, among others, Boston Consulting Group and McKinsey—companies that provide solutions to unique customer problems. The knowledge management strategy chosen depends among other things on a company's competitive strategy and product market positioning. If a company provides standardized solutions with high degrees of reliability, a codification strategy is the obvious choice, but if it offers client solutions that are rich in tacit knowledge and offerings are highly customized and innovative, a personalization strategy seems more appropriate. While companies need to make choices on their primary strategy to the design of knowledge management systems, companies offering unique solutions will also have processes and routines that are stable and occur frequently. If this is the case, companies need to distinguish between codification and personalization strategies to the design of knowledge management systems based on a thorough analysis of knowledge types involved in a particular activity.

Lest knowledge involved in a particular activity become completely tacit, companies have the choice to invest in externalization, detaching knowledge from knowers involved in activities, and codification to quickly share and leverage available knowledge across time and place as well as use and users. When knowledge is codified it can not only be more easily shared and replicated to support geographic or product line expansion, but additionally, it may help establish understanding needed for process improvement. Alternatively, companies may leave possibilities of codification unused to operate with higher degrees of tacit knowledge. Knowledge sharing is still possible in this case, but it is limited in that it relies on costly and slow methods of sharing such as personal transfer or apprenticeship. Additionally, when high levels of tacit knowledge are coupled with causal ambiguity, process improvements may be confined to unsystematic trial and error learning. While personalization strategies incur fewer fixed costs of codification, they also exhibit higher variable costs each time knowledge is shared. Codification of knowledge should thus be seen as an investment, the costs of which are determined by the prevalent knowledge type (e.g. tacit vs. explicit). Codification investments also need justification by future savings realized through economies of scale and scope of knowledge re-use as well as reduced variable costs of knowledge sharing.

11

How to boost innovation across borders? International corporate entrepreneurship

Another avenue to create value out of a network of decentralized organizational units is to tap into innovative ideas locally and turn them into inventions that can be commercialized across geographical boundaries. The relevance of innovation as an engine of economic growth in advanced economies is widely acknowledged. In recent years, the revolution in information and communication technologies and the emergence of a knowledge-based economy have altered firms' traditional competitive strategies, leading to a radical change of their perspectives. In this evolving context, the service sector has assumed a central position and service innovation has become a topic of increasing interest among economists and scholars in the technology and innovation field.[1]

Two main research streams on innovation can be distinguished. The economics-oriented research tradition[2] explores macro issues such as diffusion patterns of innovations and inter-sector differences in innovation propensity. The organization-oriented tradition[3] looks at micro issues in product innovation such as the influence of structures, processes, and people on innovation processes. Within the last decade there has been a considerable flourishing of service innovation literature, although without a systematic approach.[4] We still have a poor understanding of how service inventions are created and commercialized, how value is generated and distributed among the actors involved in the innovation process, and of the economic role that innovation plays in the contemporary service industries.

The financial services sector provides a striking illustration of how the multinational firm can address challenges of reaping returns to innovation. In some protected markets, the need to speed up innovation might be low, but many countries now liberalize financial markets and competition increases the pressure to innovate in product and process areas.

Compared to other industries, innovation in financial services can be hampered by higher degrees of government regulations, lower technological dynamism, difficulty in appropriation of value from service innovations, and customers' low propensity for experimentation. However, the situation has changed during the last decade and the financial sector in most European countries has become fairly dynamic.[5] There are many examples of financial services innovation that have been triggered by local changes in regulations, such as mandatory pension contributions or tax relief on savings vehicles, but most financial services firms are still not proficient at facilitating the identification and diffusion of subsidiary innovations—an activity that bears too many entrepreneurial uncertainties for the actors involved.

This chapter explores how financial services firms facilitate international corporate entrepreneurship within their multinational networks of affiliated firms. If financial services firms want to generate value out of their network of subsidiaries, they need to be able to leverage the innovative and entrepreneurial potential of their geographically dispersed assets. Subsidiaries contribute to the innovative strength of a multinational firm with strategic initiatives, defined as a discrete, proactive undertaking that advances a new way for the corporation to use or expand its resources. Initiative taking is an entrepreneurial process, beginning with the identification of an opportunity, culminating in a commitment of resources to that opportunity and the distribution of the value generated. In this process, headquarters and subsidiaries have often divergent interests that have to be aligned. This chapter identifies three types of entrepreneurial uncertainty that hamper the cross-border flow of entrepreneurial activities: communicative, behavioural, and value uncertainty. We conclude by proposing organizational mechanisms that have the power to facilitate international corporate entrepreneurship.

Service Innovation

Despite the undisputed importance of services for the world economy, and the importance of innovation for the service sector, only a few empirical studies have explored the specifics of innovation processes in service firms.[6] One explanation for infrequent studies of service innovation could be that we assume that insights from existing studies on physical goods can be transferred to services. However, as discussed earlier, services have a number of characteristics that distinguish them from other product types (such as physical goods or digital goods): intangibility, inseparability, perishability, and heterogeneity. Services are intangible because they have to be experienced and can most often not be touched, seen, transported, or lifted.[7]

The intangibility of services makes it more difficult to protect service innovations through patents. Nevertheless, when searching the US patent database with the keyword 'banking' we get over 10,000 hits. Most of those inventions are related to technological hardware components. But many of them are business methods. Yahoo!, for example, filed a patent to protect its financial information portal in 2001 with the following abstract:[8]

A system for a financial institution or other information maintainer has a list of its account holders that also have accounts with a portal and have agreed to link their portal account and user account with the financial institution or other information maintainer. When a user logs onto the user's portal account, the portal server can request information from the user account over a trusted link to the financial institution or other information maintainer. The portal can request data for a particular user over the trusted link or can request bulk data for all users, using portal authentication data, as opposed to user authentication data. In the preferred embodiment, the actions allowed on a user account by the portal authentication data are more restrictive than the actions allowed by the user authentication data. As an example, a brokerage house might allow the portal to read recent transaction data for the user but not to make trades on the user's account, while the brokerage house would allow the user to perform many more actions if the user logged on directly to the brokerage house's system using the user's authentication data.

Although Yahoo! attached 16 claims to the specific patent application, there are many financial portals that have very similar business methods which may lead to the conclusion that it is still difficult to effectively protect business methods or financial services products that are not linked to some hardware components. The fact that the production and consumption of many services cannot be separated also makes it difficult to observe potential patent infringements.

Due to the close contact with the single consumer, it is quite hard to standardize and control the quality of the service offer, at least at the customer interface. The customer involvement in the production process also makes it necessary to have a local presence and adapt to cultural and language differences. Furthermore, services perish after their consumption and cannot be stored. Consequently, service firms need to plan their capacity carefully and are more likely to provide excess capacity. On the other hand, the ownership of services remains with the seller. These differences call for fundamentally distinct approaches towards service innovation as opposed to the innovation of physical goods.

Many studies on service innovation recognize that there are differences, but most of them are not explicit in pinpointing those differences in a detailed manner. Vermeulen,[9] for example, reports that many banks and insurance companies do not systematically facilitate innovation processes and rarely involve customers, front-office personnel, or intermediaries in the development of new services. Vermeulen's study was based on a multi-method approach involving 120 interviews and panel discussions with representatives from the Netherlands' 10 largest financial services firms. The product innovation process largely followed a four-phase process: idea generation, concept development, building, and implementation. Vermeulen concluded his study by suggesting that financial services firms need to explicitly designate a 'place' for product development, create a culture for innovation, and remove IT as an innovation barrier.

The relatively simple innovation process suggested by Vermeulen's empirical study resembles the one used by Bank of America[10] and many other service firms. What exactly are the differences between service and physical goods innovation? Lyons, Chatman, and Joyce[11] support the proposition that service innovation has specific traits and dynamics, and point out several differences. They suggest avoiding several pitfalls when attempting to develop and sustain an innovation culture:[12]

Trap No. 1. Avoid the creation of a central innovation team
Trap No. 2. Avoid the search for radical and short-term innovation
Trap No. 3. Avoid the creation of a separate start-up unit
Trap No. 4. Avoid the search for innovation without clear leadership from the top

The authors' list of pitfalls has been previously pointed out as success recipes by renowned experts in innovation management and to a large extent contradicts much of received wisdom. The suggestions by Lyons, Chatman, and Joyce are based on the study of an investment bank and cannot be easily generalized to other services categories. Are those pitfalls equally important for retail banks? Why did Citigroup nominate Amy Radin as Chief Innovation Officer and fall into traps 1, 2, and 3? She created a central innovation team that acted as an internal venture capital firm in search of radical innovation, for example, in payment systems. Why did the World Bank organize innovation markets without clear leadership and fall into traps 3 and 4? The winners from the innovation markets were sponsored to create separate start-up units without clear indications and leadership from the top. Why did Bank of America create an Innovation and Development Center in Atlanta and fall into traps 1, 2, and 4? The innovation centre was a dedicated innovation team that worked with a clearly identified set of bank branches to radically and incrementally improve the services provided to retail customers.

The truth is that there are probably many answers to the question of how innovation processes can be organized in financial services firms. Hard services, such as retail banking, most likely require different approaches as opposed to soft services, such as investment banking. No uniform innovation recipe can be defined. The following examples illustrate how financial services firms aim to facilitate corporate entrepreneurship.

Innovation Markets at the World Bank

At the World Bank, a small team of the corporate strategy unit created the idea of a 'Development Marketplace'.[13] The idea behind the new space for innovation was that someone should organize a market for ideas; headquarters should be in charge of bringing together people that have good ideas with colleagues who are willing and able to fund and sponsor the ideas, with the goal to increase speed by responding faster to client needs, quality by delivering to clients the experience of many countries, adapted to local conditions, and innovation by not just doing better than in the past, but by bringing new services, finding and testing what had never been done before. To achieve these goals, the World Bank facilitates cross-border knowledge sharing by

- building communities of practice
- establishing help desks/advisory services
- building a directory of expertise
- establishing direct access to development statistics
- developing a best practices library of past projects
- building an online dialogue space
- providing external access for clients, partners, and stakeholders
- developing an online knowledge base in which the bank's know-how is stored and made widely accessible

However, innovation management at the World Bank is not just reduced to facilitating cross-border knowledge sharing. Selected innovation initiatives are identified and sponsored. The World Bank's first Development Marketplace consisted of 44 teams from around the world that received innovation grants. The entire innovation process lasted three years and was designed by a small team from the World Bank's corporate strategy unit. Through the Innovation Marketplace, the international funding agency discovered new ways to tackle the issue of economic prosperity. The applied methodology allowed small-scale experiments and informed decision-making before investing large amounts of money in substantial projects. With this programme, the World Bank managed to reach out for innovative ideas across geographical areas and organizational hierarchies. Innovative ideas blossom through experimentation without committing huge sums controlled by accounting executives.

The World Bank programme for innovation is a good example of focused corporate entrepreneurship,[14] but to make a sustainable impact on the problem of poverty, the World Bank 'must make the marketplace for innovation more than a biannual extravaganza, it needs to be open 365 days a year'.[15] To complement the well-organized series of high-profile events, the World Bank needs to develop a more comprehensive capability for innovation. Most firms are able to establish some sort of innovation processes at random, which may produce occasional success stories but fall short in creating systematic learning opportunities that strengthen the consistency and productivity of service development.[16]

The Innovation and Development Centre of Bank of America

Another example of 'focused' corporate entrepreneurship comes from the Bank of America.[17] Similar to the previous example from the World Bank, a team from corporate headquarters was set up to facilitate the exchange of new ideas. The Innovation & Development (I&D) Team is located at the headquarters level and has the responsibility to facilitate product and service development at the bank, especially for their customers of retail branches.

The customer is at the centre of the innovation process at the Bank of America. To make small-scale experiments in a big environment that enables robust feedback, the bank created an Innovation and Development Center in Atlanta. Initially, 20 of the 200 branches in Atlanta participated in the innovation market. They had to commit to partly funding the initiatives from their own budgets but hoped to compensate these investments with some early mover advantages from innovative services.

The innovation process was not terribly different from approaches in other industries and followed five steps:

- *Evaluate ideas*: Conceiving, assessing, and prioritizing ideas with the goal of accessing internal and external sources and creating awareness and commitment by bank staff.
- *Plan and design*: Ensures that a service prototype matches the initial expectations and is developed in a short period of time.
- *Implement*: The test branches are now introduced to the new service concepts, which are made ready for use.
- *Test*: The performance of the service prototype is monitored and the service concept is eventually modified.
- *Recommend*: Based on the test run with the 20 branches in Atlanta, the innovation team makes recommendations for a nationwide rollout and testing.

Although just an example of an innovation process that is confined to one nation, we can imagine how this process can be leveraged internationally; test branches would need to come from a larger geographical variety and the organization of the idea collection process would also increase in its complexity.

Innovation at Citigroup

Innovation at Citigroup has a figurehead: Amy Radin.[18] She created that position in 2005 to facilitate service innovation within the giant financial services firm. The model she has chosen resembles that of a venture capitalist,[19] supporting innovative ideas in areas such as contactless payments, mobile payments, or P2P money transfers. For example, together with the transaction processor Elan Financial Services, Citi announced it would prepare tests of mobile payment systems that would allow users to send and receive payments linked to an Obopay account card through cellular phone software supported by text messages. The users would be able to fund their Obopay accounts with Citi debit and credit cards.[20]

Similar to the previous case illustration, Radin believes in small-scale experiments—even in areas where investments in technology need to be made.[21] Given the bigger international retail network, Citigroup has started to roll out some of its inventions in foreign countries first. The introduction in 2006 of automatic biometric cash machines in India is just one example. Citibank decided to develop and install fingerprint-reading ATMs for their Indian customers first and not for the significantly richer home-market clients. The system allows clients to substitute banking cards with their fingerprints complemented by a PIN code to access the services offered by ATMs.[22]

These fingerprint ATMs target the large group of so far 'unbanked' poor Indian customers with micro-finance products. This business will be lucrative if Citibank can efficiently serve this population with lending products at an interest rate comparable to that of the developed countries. Since bad loan levels in micro-finance markets are estimated as being as low as 2 per cent, this is not a far-fetched possibility.

Citigroup is not the first bank to introduce modern technology in emerging countries. Automatic biometric cash machines were introduced in Bolivia in 2001 by the Private Financial Fund 'Prodem FFP', operating 90 branches and serving around 250,000 customers in Bolivia.[23] The goal of this non-profit organization is to serve bottom-of-the-pyramid customers by developing solutions based on proprietary technology that lowers processing costs while solving the specific needs of largely illiterate customers.

These short case illustrations show that financial services firms have started to invest in creating innovation. The roots of their innovation capabilities are found in their home market operations but some of them are setting out to scale new technology, service concepts, or organizational processes on an international level.

A Process Framework for International Corporate Entrepreneurship

Entrepreneurship can be defined as a process by which individuals—either on their own or inside the organization—pursue opportunities (i.e. future situations that appear to be desirable and feasible) without regard to the resources they currently control[24] through innovations that eventually lead to new positioning in target markets.[25] The field of entrepreneurship can be divided into three main areas: results, motives, and processes of entrepreneurial action.

The desired result of entrepreneurial action is primarily innovation and ultimately, increased profit through the creation of new business activities within the scope of the existing organization, organizational renewal that alters existing resource patterns, and Schumpeterian innovation or 'frame breaking change'.[26] Innovations disrupt the market equilibrium and create 'new combinations' in at least five areas:[27]

- new good or a new quality of a good
- new method of production
- opening of a new market
- conquest of a new source of supply
- changing of the industry structure

The second area within the field of entrepreneurship is concerned with the motives for entrepreneurial action. Psychological characteristics of individuals, such as creativity, readiness to take risks, or flexibility, can be distinguished from environmental factors like sociological traits. Cultural differences within the multinational firm substantially influence the triggers for entrepreneurial action. The extent to which it is accepted to fail as an entrepreneur may serve as an example; whereas it is absolutely normal—or even a distinction—to file for bankruptcy with new ventures before making the first million in the US business society, the German culture blames entrepreneurs for failing experiments.

The third area looks at how entrepreneurs act—what is between the triggers for and the results of entrepreneurship. We can distinguish between focused and dispersed corporate entrepreneurship.[28] The former is sometimes also called corporate venturing and assumes that entrepreneurship and management are two fundamentally different activities and, as a consequence, are difficult to be effectively performed by the same organizational structures. The most typical form of focused corporate entrepreneurship is the development of a dedicated New Venture Division whose mission is to identify and nurture new business opportunities.

Dispersed corporate entrepreneurship (or intrapreneurship), on the other hand, is based on the assumption that managers have the capacity for

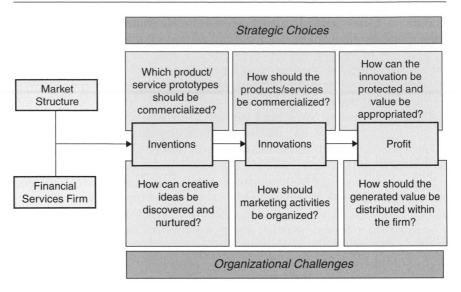

Figure 11.1. An integrative process framework for corporate entrepreneurship

managerial and entrepreneurial behaviour at the same time. As a substitute of the dedicated New Venture Division, dispersed corporate entrepreneurship is facilitated by an entrepreneurial corporate culture. However, it is most likely the combination of both corporate entrepreneurship types that would yield the best results.[29]

Corporate Entrepreneurship

The entrepreneurial process is induced by external and internal triggers that eventually lead to an invention which may then turn into an innovation through its commercialization, finally leading to increased profit through value appropriation (Figure 11.1).

Even though innovation processes are relatively non-discrete and non-sequential streams of activities,[30] Figure 11.1 attempts to bundle the tasks and activities involved in an innovation process for purposes of description and diagnosis.[31] In this process model, invention stands for the creation of new products, services, and processes. An innovation, on the other hand, describes the initial commercialization of the invention by producing, marketing, and selling the product or service or by applying the new method of production. The three main process steps are

- triggering inventions
- commercialization
- value appropriation

Triggering Inventions

An entrepreneurial organization is one that pursues opportunities, regardless of the resources it currently controls. The level of entrepreneurship within the firm is critically dependent on the attitude of individuals below the ranks of top management.[32] Hence, the traits of the individuals within the organization are fundamental for the study of corporate entrepreneurship. Organizations will be able to accelerate corporate entrepreneurship by putting individuals in a position to detect opportunities, by training them to do so and by rewarding them. The incentives to question the status quo need to be strong enough to engage in potential power games, and the negative effects of potential failures have to be limited.

Entrepreneurs within large multinational financial services firms may well be 'recruiting mistakes'. Most large firms look for well-educated MBA graduates that have focused on getting good grades instead of pursuing different types of experiences. Entrepreneurs typically have attributes such as the following:

- proactive (which does not necessarily mean willingness to take risks)
- aspirations beyond current capabilities
- capability to resolve dilemmas
- learning capabilities[33]

The capability to recognize patterns in internal and external trends and to develop new knowledge based on trends is essential for innovation processes. Sources of innovation can come from within and outside the organization. Entrepreneurs look for new knowledge from unexpected events, process needs, and changes in industry perception, the demographic composition of potential customers, or the like.[34] Many innovative ideas have accidentally popped up but a systematic approach to the creation of entrepreneurial concepts should complement innovation systems.

After an innovative idea has been detected, the prototype has to be developed and tested. Depending on the service type, this can be done in a couple of hours (e.g. a new product type in investment banking) or several months (e.g. a new security feature for credit cards). The degree of involvement of the customer and market research also depends on the nature of the service type and the investments required. Where small-scale experiments are possible (e.g. a new investment certificate or a new savings account), learning by doing innovation approaches can work. A new feature of ING Direct's Internet site can be quickly launched and customer feedback is immediately available. Costs to adapt the new concept are relatively low. Where inventions require new technologies, significant changes in ICT or other large-scale investments that are hard to reverse (e.g. introduction of automatic biometric cash machines or the introduction of a new brand), learning before doing modes are more appropriate. Before Bank of America decides to change the outfit of all branches worldwide, the new branch concept undergoes several tests.

Commercialization: Turning Inventions into Innovations

When should an invention be turned into an innovation or—put in other words—when should a new product or service be commercialized? When should a new method of production be applied? Once the time is ripe for commercialization, how should that process be carried out? Financial services firms are often accused of being too conservative and less innovative than other industries, but compared to other sectors, such as the white goods industry which saw its major innovation in the invention and commercialization of the first microwave in 1947, many financial services firms have managed to revolutionize or create segments by pioneering new products or distribution systems.

Innovation in the financial services industry is less visible and obvious than in other industries. In 1950, for example, Diner's Club was born, enabling customers to dine now and pay later. The consumer credit card business was launched and subsequently triggered numerous innovations in transaction processing, targeting, additional service types, security features, or physical card types. Contrasting the conservative image of the financial services industry, the list of innovations is surprisingly long. Even in apparently less dynamic contexts such as retail branch, reintroduction to work after one year of paternity leave is not easy. A substantial amount of new products, technologies, and procedures have to be learned. Three main innovation types in financial services can be distinguished:

- service or product innovations (e.g. new derivatives, account types, mortgage products)
- process innovations (e.g. loan tracking systems, telephone banking, customer profitability analysis)
- process and service innovations (e.g. Internet banking, ATMs, home banking)

An invention turns into an innovation through its commercialization or application to the value-generating system of the firm. With this, the financial services firm has to prove that it is not only good at exploration but also can keep the balance with its exploitation capabilities. The commercialization speed is essential in the financial services industry where it is hard—but not impossible—to protect new product ideas through patents.

"If you can't convince them – confuse them"

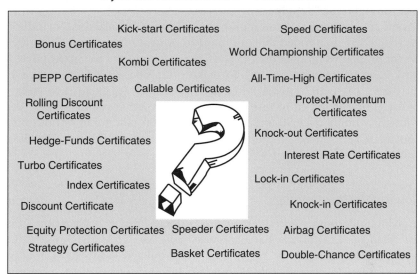

Figure 11.2. Product innovation in the certificates market

Value Appropriation: Turning Innovation into Increased Profits

Innovations do not always provide value to the final consumer. Innovation in the financial sector has often meant achieving higher margins for the bank by means of creating and selling more sophisticated investment products. Looking at the Italian investment certificates market, for example, it is legitimate to ask why Italian final consumers need 4,859 different investment certificates. Figure 11.2 lists a selection of labels that have been invented for the various certificates products; 'if you can't convince them, confuse them' seems to be the marketing strategy. The proliferation of certificate types is even higher in other European countries.

A recent online survey conducted in Italy showed that it is rather difficult for self-directed investors and financial services advisers to understand how the certificates are constructed and assess the potential risk/profit relation.[35] Many innovative financial products for the average investor are therefore not experience but 'credence goods', that is, even after consumption it is hard to assess the quality of the service for customers. It is equally difficult to assess who participates in what degree from the value that has been created with a specific certificates product. What is a 'fair' price that allows investment banks, their distribution channels, and customers to profit from the certificate in an adequate way? This question has a less obvious answer compared to other sectors where it is possible to assess the value added of each participating actor through reverse engineering.

Another brief note on value appropriation in the financial services industry: it is frequently mentioned that it is hard to protect innovation. This may be true for numerous product innovations, but it is certainly not appropriate for many basic banking operations. To make online banking more secure and worry-free, payment systems faster and more reliable, or to save costs by applying Internet-based technologies to the company's phone system, Bank of America holds over 50 and has filed over 100 patents in various areas. Innovation can indeed be protected in many areas—and innovation speed is not the only means to achieve protection.

Subsidiary Entrepreneurship

To facilitate corporate entrepreneurship in local firms is a demanding task. Few financial institutions have seriously addressed the challenge to link innovation capabilities of the major decentralized units in a multinational setting. In general, subsidiaries can take up four distinct innovation tasks:[36]

- *Innovation task 1*: New products, services, or processes are created and used locally.
- *Innovation task 2*: The subsidiary can be required to adopt innovations developed by other units of the MNC.
- *Innovation task 3*: The subsidiary can be asked to contribute to the diffusion of local innovation to other units.
- *Innovation task 4*: New products, services, or processes are created, used locally, and diffused to other units.

As the multinational financial services firm grows, the decentralized units become more responsible for business processes. It is therefore more likely that entrepreneurial thrusts can come also from subsidiary managers and not just from headquarters. Such initiatives often lead to an increase in international responsibilities for the subsidiary. The factors that have the power to influence the level of strategic initiatives at the subsidiary level are numerous:[37]

- Local resource endowment
- Intensity of parent–subsidiary communication
- Degree of subsidiary autonomy
- Subsidiary charter
- Subsidiary credibility
- Distinctive subsidiary capabilities
- Dynamism of the local market context
- Entrepreneurial traits of the local management team

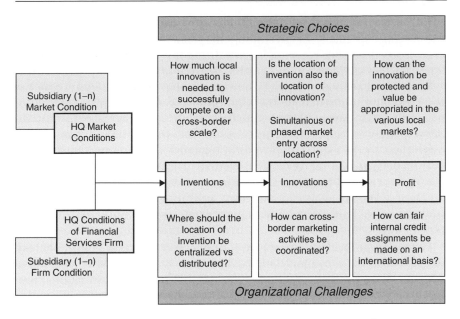

Figure 11.3. Extended innovation process framework in multinational firms

This list is not exhaustive but shows that subsidiary entrepreneurship can be influenced by a large number of factors. This does not mean that every subsidiary should, or will, be highly innovative. Depending on the context, it might make sense to limit the innovation task of some subsidiaries to innovation task no. 1 (i.e. locally used innovation). Moving from local innovation to global innovation (i.e. innovation types 2 to 4) enlarges the set of strategic choices and complicates the resulting organizational challenges, which MNC managers then have to address (Figure 11.3).

There are at least three important areas where innovating in locally operating service firms differs from the innovating MNC. First, antecedents to invention move from a single market context to a multi-market context because the MNC simultaneously operates in several markets. It is not only the firm context of the HQs that matters, but also the firm contexts of all MNC subsidiaries. The variety of knowledge sources and knowledge combination possibilities increases substantially in the MNC to induce innovation. Accordingly, managers of a multinational financial services firm need to decide whether subsidiaries should be used for creating variety and assuming responsibility for local, regional, or global inventions. In general, the more decentralized this responsibility is across subsidiaries, the greater the variety of invention that can be expected. Unfortunately, however, if knowledge and invention emanate from a local context, their use without substantial adaptation might be confined to the regional context from which they originated. Although the

MNC has the advantage of learning from its diverse local contexts, the greater the location specificity of invention, the greater the difficulties of sharing knowledge. A possible response is centralizing inventions in centres of excellence, but this sacrifices variety benefits in favour of global knowledge sharing.

Second, unlike local innovators, a multinational financial services firm has the possibility to disentangle the location of invention from the context of innovation (i.e. invent service ideas in Atlanta and use them in Canada; develop software applications in India for use in the United States). This might lead to the exploitation of local expertise in different subsidiaries to eventually speed up the commercialization of invention. However, because inventions could be further developed into innovation in a different location, a crucial problem emerges in the MNC: how to reward and assign credit to inventing subsidiaries so that they remain motivated to continue sharing their innovations.

Finally, while local innovators are confined to a particular market context, where returns to innovation could be difficult to realize, the MNC operates in several market contexts simultaneously. Accordingly, the multinational firm has to choose its strategic position depending on competitors' strategic moves as well as external conditions. For example, while eBay was a market leader in Germany, it took a late mover position in Japan, where AOL was a first mover in the commercialization of consumer auctions. To assume different strategic postures in alternative locations enables an MNC to hedge innovator risks across locations, increase the speed of innovation and the life cycle of products, or eventually cross-subsidize product launches in different markets.

Synchronizing or phasing market entry across locations is a formidable source of added value for headquarters. However, reaping benefits to innovation in the MNC poses challenges of resolving power struggles, knowledge sharing to enable cross-market learning, and avoiding the pitfalls of selective interventions where headquarters has little market knowledge and no complementary resources to offer.

The Role of Entrepreneurial Uncertainty

Agency problems arise whenever the complexity of a task makes it necessary to divide labour and one party (the principal) delegates decision-making authority or/and control over resources to another party (the agent). The nature of the internationalization business implies division of labour since headquarters cannot centrally execute all tasks in foreign countries. To exploit entrepreneurial opportunities in foreign countries, financial services firms need to organize the assembly and the coordination of resource allocation as well as the appropriation and internal distribution of the value created.

To efficiently perform these tasks, firms often decide to create a new entity in the foreign country. An MNC decides to internalize problematic future transactions in a foreign country because it might be easier to monitor and control all parties involved in those transactions within the boundaries of the same firm. However, given that the MNC seeks to overcome its liability of foreignness, it often shares ownership of subsidiaries with local entrepreneurs. To facilitate international corporate entrepreneurship, interests between the principal and the agent have to be aligned, particularly when the entrepreneur is the agent.[38] Table 11.1 lists frequently found conflicts of interest in multinational firms along with entrepreneurial phases of opportunity recognition, resource mobilization, and value appropriation. This list is obviously not complete, but gives an idea of the potential extent of divergent interests. Successful multinational firms are able to map those interests and address them individually with adequate organizational mechanisms.

Entrepreneurial activities, by definition, are tainted with economic uncertainties.[39] Uncertainty is different from risk:[40] risk refers to a situation in which all possible future outcomes with their probability of occurrence are known at the time the decision is made. For uncertain investments, on the other hand, neither the possible outcomes nor their probability of occurrence is known when committing resources. If divergent interests add too many additional uncertainties to the organization of opportunity recognition, resource mobilization, and value appropriation, the result will be low entrepreneurial intensity. To facilitate the process of international corporate entrepreneurship, several types of uncertainties have to be reduced and overcome. Three broad categories of entrepreneurial uncertainties can be distinguished: communicative, behavioural, and value uncertainty.[41]

Communicative Uncertainty

Observing large complex MNCs, it soon becomes clear that decentralized entrepreneurship includes several communicative uncertainties. At first, a local entrepreneur who has an innovative idea and is seeking support from headquarters or other MNC units needs to find a 'principal' that is in possession of required resources and has the power to assign them to interesting proposals. 'Who should I talk to in order to get funding for my project?' In some MNCs, formal positions or units foster focused entrepreneurship. In others, the search for a sponsor for the idea is more hazardous. Often, subsidiary managers have to convince not only one person but also several members of the dominant coalition. Sometimes it is difficult to find an appropriate stage and audience for presenting innovative ideas, maybe because through the knowledge-sharing process with the proposing manager, HQ managers become partly co-entrepreneurs with certain responsibilities associated with that role.

Table 11.1. Alignment of interests in entrepreneurial processes—an example

Entrepreneurial phases	Headquarters interests	Subsidiary interests
Opportunity recognition What triggers innovative thinking on the subsidiary level? How can subsidiaries be directed to the 'right' type of subsidiary initiative?	• To increase market penetration first and then search for other opportunities • To keep product development as HQ's responsibility and market development as subsidiary responsibility • To systematically organize market research activities • To identify opportunities that may be leveraged within the MNC and transferred to other subsidiaries	• To search for businesses with a high degree of novelty for the firm • To influence product development in such a way that local needs are respected • To get slack resources for investment in systematic opportunity recognition • To search for opportunities that involve M&A
Resource mobilization How are the resource allocation mechanisms for entrepreneurial activities organized? What increases the ability of organizing wealth-generating relationships between factors of production in the MNC?	• To get investment proposals that are presented in a fully standardized report with cash flow predictions • To decide on bigger investments and to be informed by the subsidiaries about all initiatives • To make major resource allocation decisions in line with the annual budgeting process • To delegate decision power without losing control	• To have the possibility to present an idea in a concise and informal way during early stages • To get feedback on proposals in a quick and informal manner • To take on also bigger investment projects in a fairly autonomous way • To get resources for projects at any time of the year
Value appropriation How should the allocation of entrepreneurial rents be organized?	• To coordinate value appropriation on a worldwide basis (i.e. tax optimization, portfolio reasoning) • To steer resources into attractive new businesses • To see 'good citizenship' behaviour of subsidiaries	• To get rewarded for successful innovation at the subsidiary as well as a personal level • To increase subsidiary charters related to successful entrepreneurial activities • To be able to apply favourable transfer pricing schemes on activities related to a subsidiary initiative

A second communicative uncertainty may come from an information gap regarding the presentation format. What is the look and feel of my business idea proposal? Some firms are known for their one-page memos; others require a rigid financial analysis with cash flow projections and several hundred PowerPoint slides and market intelligence reports. In other firms, it might be enough to pitch the idea to the CEO during a coffee break. Similar to submitting a paper to a scientific journal, subsidiary managers need to know how to structure the proposal in terms of length, language style, level of detail, etc.

A third source of communicative uncertainty concerns the timing of the submission. Sometimes innovative ideas are not followed up because the annual formal planning process is already at an advanced stage and the proposal cannot be included. When is the right time to pitch an idea? The creation of presentation opportunities during ideas fairs, innovation workshops, or business plan contests not only facilitates the codification, socialization, and internalization of ideas, but also makes sure that distant subsidiaries get the opportunities to communicate their entrepreneurial ideas. Optimal commercialization timing and speed of entrepreneurial activities often require high flexibility in proposal submission timing.

In summary, finding out when to present what type of proposal in what format to which HQ manager on what occasion creates information search costs and therefore represents a barrier to decentralized entrepreneurship. Of course, similar communication uncertainties exist in later phases of the entrepreneurial process, whether it is the resource coordination phase or the communication of the project progress and final value added.

Behavioural Uncertainty

Behavioural uncertainty may be most important in the opportunity exploitation phase. However, MNCs face the challenge of reducing behavioural uncertainty as early as when identifying and legitimizing opportunities. Subsidiary entrepreneurs might fear losing ownership of the idea when proposing and therefore hesitate to test their ideas. Ideas might be presented in an overconfident manner to get the attention of HQ managers and win the race against competing internal proposals from other subsidiaries.

It is therefore a challenge for the HQs to assess the quality of the data presented. Information gathering and interpretation in entrepreneurial processes is complex and reflects the inherent risk of innovative ideas, but the purposeful distortion of data to increase the attractiveness of the proposal represents a major source of behavioural uncertainty and needs to be addressed when designing organizational mechanisms that foster subsidiary entrepreneurship.

Value Uncertainty

Value uncertainty in entrepreneurial processes plays an essential role in the last phase, that is, when the economic and non-financial benefits of the entrepreneurial initiatives are evaluated and entrepreneurial gains are distributed to the parties involved in proportion to their contribution. However, knowing how the value assessment and appropriation for individual managers or the subsidiary as a whole is done is essential for stimulating the submission of entrepreneurial proposals. Why should subsidiary managers invest time and money in opportunity identification to submit risky proposals that put them under even greater performance pressure? If the response to that question is not straightforward, entrepreneurs are facing value uncertainty that could reduce their drive to propose new ideas.

Freedom within Boundaries: Getting Organized for International Corporate Entrepreneurship

There are several organizational mechanisms that have the power to reduce entrepreneurial uncertainties and thereby facilitate international corporate entrepreneurship. The goal of most financial services firms is not to get as many subsidiary initiatives as possible but as many as are necessary. To a large extent, subsidiaries are tasked to just use the innovative concepts developed elsewhere; not all firms can become centres of excellence and take the lead in innovation. Headquarters has to strike the balance between incentivizing subsidiaries to use their freedom to innovate and setting the boundaries for the scope of innovation.

Generally, three types of organizational forms can be identified that can structure entrepreneurial investment decisions under uncertainty:[42]

- clan-based entrepreneurial firms[43]
- expert-based entrepreneurial firms
- charisma-based entrepreneurial firms

Clan-based governance is not easy to scale. Although in small family-owned companies the possibility that there are enough (capable) relatives for key positions in a company may be high, this governance model is not sustainable if the company wants to grow. However, clans can also be constructed in a different way. As seen in the Allianz case, many financial services firms prefer to create strong relationships with managers in headquarters (often with the home market nationality) and send them out to foreign markets. Multinational financial services firms face the trade-off between naming a member of the HQ's clan as head of the subsidiary and naming a local manager who might not belong to the 'inner circle'. How likely is it that a local subsidiary head in China becomes part of the global firm's clan?

The expert-based model of governance is also difficult to implement on an international level. Developing expertise in a certain area is costly and time-consuming. How difficult is it for the local controller to hide important facts from the central internal auditor? How long does it take for a HQ manager to understand a local market initiative in detail? Recent scandals have shown that it even seems to be difficult to know what key managers and traders are doing when they sit right next door.

Charisma-based organizational models depend on a personal trait of HQs managers as well as the capability to develop a vision and communicate that vision effectively to the subsidiaries.

From an agency theory perspective on the roles of the board of directors,[44] there are several ways to align HQ's interests with those of the subsidiaries. Drawing on an application of agency theory to board roles, the corporate headquarters can take up several roles to steer and facilitate international corporate entrepreneurship.

HQ Task 1: Strategic Agenda Setting

The corporate headquarters is legitimized to set the strategic agenda of the MNC and has the responsibility of early identification and fast response to relevant events and trends in the markets the MNC is operating. Strategic issue management[45] is one of the key roles that headquarters takes in relation to its subsidiaries. A strategic issue is a '... forthcoming development, either inside or outside of the organization, which is likely to have an important impact on the ability of the enterprise to meet its objectives'.[46] To ensure an early identification and fast response to strategic issues, strategic issue management systems steer the selection of strategic issues as they get the decision-makers' attention and are addressed by the organization.

The legitimization of strategic issues and administrative routines such as meetings and conferences to process the issues are of focal interest. National cultures influence the perceptions of environmental uncertainty and organizational control and therefore alter the interpretation and response to strategic issues.[47] The corporate headquarters needs to be sensitive to local interpretations of strategic issues since they trigger different decision processes and behaviour.

HQ Task 2: Top Management Selection

Corporate headquarters has the right to select the top management team members and therefore influence the dominant coalition within the subsidiary. Complex decisions and entrepreneurship are influenced by behavioural factors rather than on the basis of economic optimization.[48] As a consequence, the top management team composition has a decisive influence on organizational outcomes through a set of complex decisions made by powerful members of the subsidiary that reflect their values and cognitive bases. The decision whether to appoint local managers or use expatriate managers from the corporate centre illustrates the impact top management selection has not only on subsidiary performance but also on the subsidiary–headquarters relationship.

HQ Task 3: Definition of Subsidiary Charters

The evolution of a subsidiary depends on both the enhancement of the capabilities in a subsidiary and the explicit change in the subsidiary's charter. The subsidiary role can be measured in terms of specific businesses, or elements of the business, the subsidiary undertakes and for which it has responsibility.[49] Three factors determine the subsidiary role, and thereby its evolution:

- head office assignments perceived as decisions regarding the allocation of activities to the subsidiary
- subsidiary choices regarding those activities
- local environment determinism conceived as environmental influences on both subsidiary and head office decisions

HQ Task 4: Resource Allocation

A major characteristic of strategic decisions is that they involve resource commitment under conditions of uncertainty. The resource allocation process in a multinational firm can start from the top (allocating surplus cash) or from the subsidiaries (applying for additional resources to follow up on strategic initiatives). The internal competition for scarce resources and management attention plays a central role in the life of the MNC.[50] Several methods can be applied to make resource allocation decisions: portfolio matrices, past performance tracks, net present values of expected future cash flows, or real options models. Subsidiaries can attempt to influence resource allocation decisions by leveraging a central position in the MNC network, for example, arising from the dependence of headquarters and other subsidiaries on their unique resources. The higher the knowledge intensity (i.e. knowledge output of subsidiary to other MNC units) of a subsidiary, the higher is its bargaining power.[51]

HQ Task 5: Monitoring and Rewarding

Corporate headquarters can use behavioural control mechanisms that monitor and reward inputs into strategic decision-making through supervision and approval as well as output control which manages the performance outcomes of decisions. Strategic control systems shifted in the late 1990s from being focused on the content of strategy (i.e. behavioural control) to one based upon outcomes in terms of performance items (i.e. output control).[52] Negotiating, monitoring, and rewarding the achievement of financial performance goals became the dominant theme in strategy meetings between headquarters and geographical divisions. As a consequence, strategy plans became less detailed on the qualitative side but more focused on numbers. By doing so, corporate headquarters negatively influence the entrepreneurial drive of divisional top management teams.[53] The more corporate staff were involved in influencing divisional strategies, the greater the erosion of divisional responsibility and accountability.[54] Negotiating goals, monitoring, and rewarding should therefore be labelled 'long-term resources plans' and not mistakenly called 'strategy plans'.[55]

Epilogue: Sustainable International Development after the Subprime Crisis

The subprime crisis shook the financial services market and will substantially change its nature. Early warning signals indicating that not all was well could be detected as early as in 2006. But most industry players realized just in July 2007 how big the problem was—and one year later it is still not clear how long the crisis will last. Affected is not just the 'hall of shame', as The Economist[1] called the 10 financial institutions with the biggest write-downs.[2] The global credit crunch affects the financial services firms that have been active on international investment banking markets as well as the local banks that face difficulties in borrowing on the dry interbank market. As a result, it is increasingly expensive and in some cases impossible to borrow money for corporate and retail clients. This, of course, has a negative effect on the growth prospects of the global economy.

After the Internet bubble burst and the 9/11 crisis slowed the economy down, the low interest rate policy by Alan Greenspan made it easier to borrow money and paved the way for the credit crunch. But the subprime crisis has developed because too many managers were guided by erroneous ethical principles, incentive systems, or just plain ignorance. Many financial institutions and their customers were chasing after easy profits and deliberately ignored the risks associated with them. Mortgage agencies brokered home loans to customers that could not afford the loans. The agencies passed on the risks associated with those loans to the borrowing retail banks and cashed in their service fees. The retail banks took the loans because of the commercial pressure from their bosses, assuming that real estate prices would always increase, and the loan surplus they granted to their clients would help them pay the rates for the first couple of years. To get this risk off their balance sheets, financial engineers from investment banks helped the retail banks create sophisticated debt instruments. The yield-hungry financial markets happily bought these complex and innovative financial products, sometimes without a clear understanding of the associated risks. Rating agencies had a hard time assessing the risks associated with these products but they did not even question the lending procedures: home loans in the United States were given without any official certification of total income of the customer or even their social security number.

If we compare the managerial processes that led to the subprime crisis to other industries, it becomes clear that financial services firms need to fundamentally review their leadership and governance models. At Toyota, for example, Katsuaki Watanabe (CEO) is known for his habit of test-driving all Toyota prototypes and many of the competing cars. He challenges his engineers with ideas and carefully monitors the results. When launching a new car, Toyota has a clear business model and orchestrates over 300,000 employees worldwide. Financial services firms need to develop new systems that allow them to govern and align the interests of powerful investment bankers with ethical standards, the overall objectives of their bosses and, ultimately, the stakeholders.

Clearly, the global subprime crisis and the resulting credit crunch have influenced the international strategies of financial services firms in multiple ways. Many mostly passive investors from emerging economies get the opportunity to acquire a share in some of the most prestigious financial services firms. New clearing platforms for investment vehicles will appear to create transparency and restore trust. The government and the central banks are facing a 'moral hazard' problem: not supporting the financial institutions could seriously harm the global economy. Injecting liquidity to restore financial stability and not at all punishing aggressive bank practices would on the other hand increase the incentives for improper behaviour by banks. Regulations will therefore have to change to put more pressure on the financial institutions and their business partners to create more transparency in business processes and financial services products.

Some of the big financial institutions will have to sell parts of their businesses to make up for their huge write-downs. New governance models need to be found to establish process standards and managerial practices that stabilize the financial services systems. But maybe more importantly, financial services firms need to find new ways to attract and keep talents without losing control over their activities. To align the interests of the shareholders and the brightest investment bankers, new incentive systems need to be created that make sure the composition and timing of bonuses reflect the real long-term value they created for the company.

To sustainably build an international financial services firm, executives therefore cannot just place bets on highly risky products but need to carefully understand the value drivers of cross-border businesses. There is no general correlation between the size of the firm and its economic performance, nor is there a universal causal relationship between the degree of international expansion and the profitability of the firm. As pointed out throughout this book, it is the quality of strategic decision-making and strategy execution that creates value for shareholders in foreign markets. The subprime crisis has just accelerated the decisions of some financial services firms to reduce their international exposure and to concentrate on fewer geographical markets. To build an international financial services firm does not necessarily mean to grow as fast and as large as possible but rather to design and execute credible corporate- and business-level strategies based on a sound analysis of core competences and market structures. Not all financial services firms will be able to—and have to—initiate an internationalization process. There currently is, and will continue to be in the future, space for local champions.

Notes

Preface

1. Buzzell, Gale et al. (1975).
2. Kogut (1984).
3. Phil Hodkinson (14 May 2007), Speech of Group Finance Director of HBOS at the UBS Conference.
4. Berger, DeYoung et al. (2000: 35); Llewellyn (1999).

Introduction

1. Grosse (2004).
2. Casson (1990).
3. Berger and Smith (2003).
4. Rugman (2000).
5. Ghemawat and del Sol (1998).
6. Hitt, Bierman et al. (2006).
7. Capar and Kotabe (2003).
8. Contractor, Kundu et al. (2003).
9. Li, Goerzen et al. (2005); Ruigrok and Wagner (2005).
10. Hennart (2007).
11. Aliber (1984); Berger, Hanweck et al. (1987); Dermine (2002); Grubel (1977); Llewellyn (1999); Slager (2006).
12. Venzin, Kumar et al. (2008).
13. Berger, DeYoung et al. (2000).

Part I

1. Hornby (Mar 2007).

Chapter 1

1. www.historyworld.net.
2. Rothbard (1983).
3. www.en.wikipedia.org.
4. de Roover (1948).
5. Sedillot (1998).
6. Channon (1988).
7. Baron and Besanko (2001).
8. Rudy (1975).

Notes

9. www.citigroup.com.
10. Geoghegan (2007).
11. Saunders and Millon Cornett (2004).
12. Figures relate to 2005.
13. www.prosper.com.
14. Grosse (2004).
15. Boddewyn, Halbrich et al. (1986).
16. Vandermerwe and Chadwick (1989).
17. Patterson and Cicic (1995).
18. Slager (2006).
19. Capar and Kotabe (2003).
20. Anderson and Gatignon (1986).
21. Buckley (1988); Delios and Beamish (1999).
22. Kogut (1985).
23. Berthon, Pitt et al. (1999).
24. Anderson and Narus (1995); Lovelock (1992).
25. Lovelock and Yip (1996).
26. Feketekuty (1988).
27. Reardon, Erramilli et al. (1996).
28. See Mahnke and Venzin (2003).
29. See Mahnke and Venzin (2003).
30. Nelson, R. R. (May 1970). 'Information and Consumer Behavior'. *Journal of Political Economy*, 311–29.
31. www.ingdirect.ca/en/; Ryans, Deutscher et al. (2007); Ryans (1999); Verweire and Van den Berghe (2007).
32. Verweire and Van den Berghe (2007: 6).
33. Ryans, Deutscher et al. (2007: 3).
34. Verweire and Van den Berghe (2007).
35. Robertson and Francis (2003); Verweire and Van den Berghe (2007).

Chapter 2

1. Sullivan (1994).
2. Geringer, Tallman et al. (2000); Ruigrok and Wagner (2003).
3. See Claudio Dematté (2004: 266 ff), on Pan-European strategies.
4. Bartlett and Ghoshal (1991); Ghoshal (1987); Kobrin (1991); Prahalad and Doz (1987).
5. Ghemawat and Spence (1986: 63).
6. www.atkearney.com.
7. Birkinshaw, Morrison et al. (1995); Kobrin (1991).
8. Rugman (1979).
9. Geringer, Tallman et al. (2000).
10. Lu and Beamish (2004).
11. Hannan and Freeman (1984).
12. Nelson and Winter (1982); Stinchcombe (1965).
13. Henderson (1999).
14. Grosse (2004).

15. See Venzin, Kumar et al. (2008).
16. Slager (2005).
17. Slager (2005).
18. Nocera, Iannotta et al. (2007).
19. Ayadi and Pujals (2005).

Part II

1. Root (1994).
2. Mintzberg (1994: 190).

Chapter 3

1. The Merriam-Webster's online dictionary.
2. Mankins (2004).
3. D'Aveni (1994).
4. Grant (2003).
5. Glaister and Falshaw (1999).
6. Glaister and Falshaw (1999: 115).
7. Eisenhardt (1999).
8. Campbell, Goold et al. (1995).
9. Inkpen and Choudhury (1995).
10. Grant (1998: 17).
11. Amram and Kulatilaka (1999: 104).
12. Gabriele Werzer (2005).
13. Grant (2003).
14. Weick (1995).
15. Martin Wohlmuth (2005).

Chapter 4

1. See Dermine (2002); Forestieri (1993).
2. CEE here defined as Bosnia and Herzegovina, Bulgaria, Croatia, Czech Republic, Estonia, Hungary, Latvia, Lithuania, Poland, Romania, Russia, Serbia, Slovakia, Slovenia, Turkey, and Ukraine.
3. See also Mottura (2007: 168ff).
4. Smith (1776).
5. Ricardo (1821).
6. Ohlin (1933).
7. Posner (1961).
8. Linder (1961).
9. Hymer (1976).
10. Knickerbocker (1973).
11. Vernon (1966).
12. Casson (1983).
13. Hymer (1960).
14. Dunning (1981).

15. Ghoshal (1987); Gupta and Govindarajan (2001); Hout, Porter et al. (1982); Kogut (1985).
16. Bartlett and Ghoshal (1991); Prahalad (1976); Prahalad and Doz (1987); Stopford and Wells (1972).
17. Stopford and Wells (1972).
18. Chandler (1966).
19. Hout, Porter et al. (1982); Prahalad and Doz (1987).
20. Bartlett and Ghoshal (1988, 1991).
21. Chi and Nystrom (1998); Hennart (1982, 1991); Rugman and Verbeke (1992).
22. Birkinshaw and Hood (1998).
23. DeYoung and Nolle (1996).
24. Ghemawat, Ballarin et al. (2006).
25. Berger and DeYoung (2001); Siddharthan and Lall (1982).
26. Hedlund and Ridderstrale (1997).
27. Ghoshal and Bartlett (1990); Kogut and Zander (1993).
28. Saunders and Walter (1993).
29. Slager (2006).
30. Grubel (1977).
31. Engwall and Wallenstal (1988).
32. Kogut (1985).
33. Berger and Hannan (1998).
34. Ghemawat (2007).
35. Ghemawat (2007); Rugman (2000).
36. Hymer (1976); Kindleberger (1969).
37. Hannan and Freeman (1984).
38. Nelson and Winter (1982); Stinchcombe (1965).
39. Henderson (1999).
40. Demsetz (1988).
41. Ansoff (1957); Canals (1997: 84 ff).
42. Jamie Damon (16 July 2007), Interview with Spiegel Online.
43. Ghemawat (2007).
44. Ghemawat (2007: 28 ff).
45. Berger and Smith (2003: 384).
46. Berger and Smith (2003: 384).
47. Berger and Smith (2003: 384).
48. See Ghemawat (2007: 30).
49. For an overview on strategy and organization in corporate banking, see Laurentis (2004).
50. Llewellyn (2002).
51. Llewellyn (2002: 27–8).

Chapter 5

1. Bond and Green (2003).
2. Kumar, Stam et al. (1994).
3. Sakarya, Eckman et al. (2007).
4. www.state.gov.

5. Excluding Taiwan since the United States has acknowledged the Chinese position that Taiwan is part of China.
6. www.atkearney.com.
7. Barth, Caprio et al. (2004).
8. Claessens and Janssen (2000); Claessens, Demirgüç-Kunt et al. (2001).
9. Satta (2004).
10. Demirgüç-Kunt, Laeven et al. (2003).
11. Bettis and Hall (1981); Haspeslagh (1982).
12. Morrison and Wensley (1991).
13. Armstrong and Brodie (1994); Hambrick, MacMillan et al. (1982); MacMillan, Hambrick et al. (1982).
14. 1994.
15. Haspeslagh (1982).
16. Buzzell, Gale et al. (1975).
17. Hedley (1977); Wensley (1981).
18. Day (1977).
19. Armstrong and Brodie (1994).
20. 1977.
21. 1982.
22. Morrison and Wensley (1991).
23. Wensley (1981).
24. Christensen, Cooper et al. (1982).
25. 1982, p. 13.
26. Day (1977).
27. 1991, p. 110.
28. Guillén and Tschoegl (2000).
29. Crawford (01 Feb 2002).
30. Erramilli (1991).
31. www.scip.org.
32. Amit, Domowitz et al. (1988: 431).

Chapter 6

1. Slaughter (1990).
2. Courtney, Kirkland et al. (1997).
3. Schoemaker (1995); Schwartz (1996); Van der Heijden (1996).
4. Dixit and Nalebuff (1991).
5. Senge (1990).
6. Casti (1997).
7. Dixit and Pindyck (1995).
8. Beinhocker (1999).
9. Kaufmann (1995).
10. Beinhocker (1999: 53).
11. Glaister and Falshaw (1999).
12. Amram and Kulatilaka (1999: 104).
13. March (1994: 174).
14. Weick (1995).

15. Eisenhardt (1999).
16. Shaw, Brown et al. (1998).
17. Sanders (1998).
18. Weick (1995: 25).
19. Polanyi (1966).
20. Nonaka and Takeuchi (1995: 11).
21. Shapiro and Spence (1997: 63).
22. Khatri and Ng (2000: 59–60).
23. Khatri and Ng (2000).
24. Shapiro and Spence (1997).
25. A free download of the book 'The Delphi Method: Techniques and Applications', edited by Harold A. Linstone and Murray Turoff, can be found at the following website: http://www.is.njit.edu/pubs/delphibook/.
26. Lieberman and Montgomery (1988, 1998).
27. Suarez and Lanzolla (2007).
28. Berger and Dick (2007).
29. Rumelt (1987).
30. Lieberman and Montgomery (1998).
31. Johanson and Vahlne (1990).
32. Lieberman and Montgomery (1998).
33. Carpenter and Nakamoto (1989, 1994).
34. Kardes and Kalyanaram (1992).
35. Beggs and Klemperer (1992); Farrell and Shapiro (1988, 1989).
36. Katz and Shapiro (1985).
37. Arthur (1990).
38. Liebowitz and Margolis (1995).
39. Farrell and Saloner (1985, 1986).
40. Shapiro and Varian (1998).
41. Berger and Dick (2007).
42. Markides and Geroski (2004).
43. Tellis and Golder (2002).
44. Lieberman and Montgomery (1988).
45. 18 April 2006.
46. Karsch (2007).
47. Kardes and Kalyanaram (1992).
48. Kardes, Kalyanaram et al. (1993).
49. McDougall and Oviatt (1994).
50. Knight and Cavusgil (1989).
51. Sharma and Johanson (1987).
52. Buckley and Casson (1976).
53. Macquarie Bank, Annual Review (2006: 3).
54. Penrose (1959).
55. Cohen and Levinthal (1990).

Chapter 7

1. Grubel (1989); Huertas (1990).

2. Alavarez-Gil, Cardone-Riportella et al. (2003); Blomstermo, Sharma et al. (2006); Erramilli (1990, 1992); Erramilli and Rao (1990, 1993); Sanchez-Peinado, Pla-Barber et al. (2007).
3. Sarkar, Cavusgil et al. (1999).
4. Bell (1995).
5. Coviello and Munro (1995).
6. Johanson and Vahlne (1977, 1990).
7. Coase (1937).
8. Dunning (1988).
9. www.atkearney.com.
10. Generali Corporate Communication (Feb 2005: 1).
11. www.bloomberg.com.
12. Generali China Life News Center (01 Nov 2006).
13. Generali China Life News Center (29 Apr 2007).
14. Generali Group (Oct 2007: 26).
15. www.geb.generali.com.
16. www.geb.generali.com.
17. Quoted in Euromoney, Sep 2005, p. 285.
18. Bain (1956).
19. Lubatkin (1983); Singh and Montgomery (1987).
20. Fowler and Schmidt (1989); Kitching (1967); Kusewitt Jr. (1985).
21. The Banker (2007).
22. A. T. Kearney's Global PMI Study, 1998–9.
23. Haspeslagh and Jamison (1991: 15).
24. Birkinshaw (1999); Birkinshaw, Bresman et al. (2000); Empson (2000).
25. Chaudhuri and Tabrizi (1999).
26. Capron, Mitchell et al. (2001); Karim and Mitchell (2000).
27. Birkinshaw (1999); Birkinshaw, Bresman et al. (2000); Haspeslagh and Jamison (1991).
28. Glaister and Buckley (1996).
29. Das and Teng (1999).
30. Park and Russo (1996).
31. Bleeke and Ernst (1992).
32. Goerzen (2005).
33. Ernst and Halevy (2000); Gulati and Singh (1998); Peng and Shenkar (2002).
34. Arino, de la Torre et al. (2001).
35. For the first three approaches, see Root (1994).
36. Grubel (1977).
37. Miller and Parkhe (1998).
38. Ball and Tschoegl (1982).
39. Johanson and Vahlne (1977).
40. Anderson and Gatignon (1986).
41. Kogut and Singh (1988).
42. Barkema and Vermeulen (1998); Kogut and Singh (1988).
43. Hultman and McGee (1989); Yamori (1998).
44. Eisenhardt (1999).

Chapter 8

1. Markides (1999).
2. Based on Reuters portfolio top 500 financial services firms (retrieved on 29 Feb 2008).
3. Based on The Banker (2007) and Annual Reports.
4. Grant (2008: 205–9).
5. *Financial Times*, Friday, 15 Feb 2008, p. 16.
6. Hamel (1996).
7. Markides (1999).
8. Strebel (1995: 11).
9. Kim and Mauborgne (1997).
10. Prahalad and Bettis (1986).
11. Prahalad and Bettis (1986: 491).
12. Hedberg (1981).
13. Whittington (1999).
14. D'Aveni (1994).
15. Grant (2008: 211–14).
16. The case was developed based on interviews with Tobias Meckert (Allianz SE, Asia, Middle East, North Africa) and secondary data.
17. The case was developed based on an interview with Phil Kershaw (Operations Director for HBOS International) and secondary data.
18. Molt (2007: 45).
19. Jones (2006).
20. The market share refers to the foreign JVs. The overall market share of Allianz is just 0.295 per cent.
21. Molt (2007: 39).
22. www.moneyterms.co.uk defines annual premium equivalent as 'the total amount of regular premiums from new business + 10% of the total amount of single premiums on business written during the year'. This measure is used to compare the actual sales performance of insurers within a given time period.
23. Jones (2006).
24. www.businessweek.com (16 Oct 2007).
25. Shek (2006: 244).
26. Stowe (Dec 2006).
27. Jones (2006).
28. Jones (2006).
29. www.allianz.com.cn.
30. www.icbc.-ltd.com.
31. http://news.bbc.co.uk.
32. http://en.epochtimes.com.
33. Guerrera (26 Jan 2006).
34. www.allianz.com (07 May 2007).
35. Anderlini (15 Aug 2007).
36. Dresdner Bank stopped funding for its chair at Tongji in 2008.
37. The Banker (2007).

38. Phil Kershaw, 17 Mar 2008, Interview with Operations Director for HBOS International.
39. Bank of Scotland press release (17 Jul 2001).
40. http://news.bbc.co.uk (04 May 2001).
41. www.computingbusiness.co.uk (15 Oct 2003).
42. Ezingeard (2003).
43. www.computingbusiness.co.uk (15 Oct 2003).
44. Hodkinson (Jun 2007).
45. HBOS Annual Report (2006).
46. Hodkinson (Jun 2007).
47. HBOS press release (05 Dec 2001).
48. http://news.bbc.co.uk (05 Dec 2001).
49. HBOS press release (23 Aug 2007); HBOS Annual Report (2007).
50. HBOS press release (25 Sep 2002).
51. HBOS Annual Report (2007).
52. HBOS press release (29 Jul 2003).
53. HBOS Annual Report (2006).
54. www.hbosplc.com.
55. www.datamonitor.com (Nov 2007).
56. www.hbosplc.com (Mar 2008).
57. HBOS Annual Report (2006).
58. Croft (13 Jul 2007).
59. HBOS press release (04 Oct 2007).
60. Fifield (19 Aug 2003).
61. Croft (13 Jul 2007); http://uk.reuters.com (12 Jul 2007).
62. HBOS press release (12 Jul 2007).
63. Croft and Murray Brown (11 Jan 2006); Thomas and Murray Brown (10 Jan 2006).
64. Croft (20 Jun 2005).
65. Bank of Scotland Ireland press release (16 Mar 2005).
66. Thomas and Murray Brown (10 Jan 2006).
67. Croft and Murray Brown (11 Jan 2006).
68. http://uk.reuters.com (12 Jul 2007).
69. HBOS (Dec 2003: 19).
70. HBOS (Dec 2003: 5–6).
71. Based on www.forbes.com.
72. Allianz (Jul 2007).
73. Jones (2006).
74. HBOS Annual Report (2007: 8); www.hbosplc.com (Mar 2008: 8).
75. www.hbosplc.com (Mar 2008).
76. Jones (2006).

Part III

1. Leonard-Barton (1992).
2. Ghoshal and Bruch (2003).
3. Lewin (1947); Zand and Sorensen (1975).

Chapter 9

1. Dunning (1988).
2. Collis and Montgomery (1998: 71).
3. Prahalad and Hamel (1990).
4. Campbell, Goold et al. (1995).
5. Campbell, Goold et al. (1995: 121).
6. Goold, Campbell et al. (1994); Koch (2000).
7. Grant (1998).
8. See Chapter 4.
9. Buckley and Carter (2003).
10. Zadrazil, 19 September (2007).
11. Buckley and Carter (2004).
12. Björkman, Barner-Rasmussen et al. (2004); Goold and Campbell (1987).
13. Dunning (1981); Vernon (1966).
14. Bartlett and Ghoshal (1989).
15. Gupta and Govindarajan (2000); Kogut and Zander (1992); Mudambi and Navarra (2004); Tsai and Ghoshal (1998).
16. Birkinshaw and Hood (2001).
17. Delany (2000).
18. March (1991: 71).
19. Goold and Quinn (1990).
20. Doz and Prahalad (1984).
21. Grant (2003).
22. Gupta and Govindarajan (1991).
23. Kim and Mauborgne (1991, 1995, 1998).
24. Controlling for amount of resources used such as time and money.
25. Controlling for the nature of a process such as the single steps in credit assignment decisions.
26. Controlling for results produced such as revenues, margins, or product quality.
27. Kim and Mauborgne (1998).
28. Gupta and Govindarajan (1991).
29. Grant (2003).
30. Andreas Treichl, CEO of Erste Bank quoted by Martin Wohlmuth, Head of Strategic Management Erste Bank, 2005.
31. Bartlett and Ghoshal (1990).
32. Hill (2004).
33. Ghemawat (2003).
34. Forsgren (1997); March (1991); Saloner, Shepard et al. (2001).

Chapter 10

1. Andrea Moneta, November 2005, Interview with Head of Poland Markets Division UniCredit Group.
2. Rigby (2001).
3. Bartlett and Ghoshal (1989).
4. Toffler (1990).

5. Nonaka and Takeuchi (1995).
6. Grant and Baden-Fuller (1995).
7. Grant (1996).
8. Child and McGrath (2001); Prahalad and Hamel (1990); Stewart (1997).
9. Bartlett and Ghoshal (1989); Gupta and Govindarajan (1991, 2000).
10. Cohen and Levinthal (1990).
11. Rigby (2001).
12. Wenger, McDermott et al. (2002).
13. Sarvary (1999).
14. Leonard-Barton (1995).
15. March (1991).
16. Sanchez and Mahoney (1996).
17. March (1991).
18. Cohen, Ledford et al. (1996).
19. Wenger and Snyder (2000: 139–40).
20. Bartlett and Ghoshal (1989).
21. Weick and Roberts (1993).
22. Milgrom and Roberts (1995).
23. Hansen, Nohria et al. (1999).

Chapter 11

1. Barras (1986); Gallouj and Weinstein (1997); Metcalf and Miles (2000); Thomke (2003).
2. Dosi (1988); Nelson and Winter (1977).
3. Cooper and Kleinschmidt (1987); Damanpour (1991).
4. Evangelista (2000); Gallouj (2002).
5. Flier, van den Bosch et al. (2001).
6. Lyons, Chatman et al. (2007); Thomke (2003); Vermeulen (2004).
7. Dahringer (1991).
8. Retrieved from USPTO patent full-text and image database (www.uspto.gov/patft) 15 May 2008.
9. Vermeulen (2004).
10. Thomke (2003).
11. Lyons, Chatman et al. (2007).
12. Lyons, Chatman et al. (2007).
13. Wood and Hamel (2002); www.worldbank.org.
14. Birkinshaw (1997).
15. Wood and Hamel (2002: 7).
16. Thomke (2003).
17. Case illustration based on Thomke (2003); Annual Reports; www.bankofamerica.com.
18. www.citigroup.com.
19. Business Week, 19 Jun 2006 (accessed electronically at http://www.businessweek.com).
20. Wolfe (Mar 2007).
21. www.businessinnovationinsider.com.

22. Hammond, Kramer et al. (2007).
23. Hernandez and Mugica (2003); www.prodemffp.com.
24. Stevenson, Roberts et al. (1989).
25. Stopford and Baden-Fuller (1994).
26. Stopford and Baden-Fuller (1994: 522).
27. Schumpeter (1934).
28. Stevenson and Jarillo (1990).
29. Birkinshaw (1997).
30. Kanter (1988).
31. Daft (1982); King (1992).
32. Stevenson and Jarillo (1990: 23–4).
33. Stevenson and Jarillo (1990: 25).
34. Drucker (1991).
35. Venzin, Reitzig et al. (2005).
36. Birkinshaw (1997); Ghoshal and Bartlett (1988).
37. Birkinshaw (1997, 1999).
38. Jones and Butler (1992: 73).
39. Jones and Butler (1992).
40. Alvarez and Barney (2005).
41. Mahnke, Venzin et al. (2007).
42. Alvarez and Barney (2005).
43. Ouchi (1980).
44. Zahra and Pearce (1989).
45. Ansoff (1980); Dutton and Duncan (1987).
46. Ansoff (1980: 133).
47. Schneider and Meyer (1991).
48. Cyert and March (1963).
49. Birkinshaw and Hood (1998: 775).
50. Birkinshaw, Bouquet et al. (2007).
51. Mudambi and Navarra (2004).
52. Grant (2003).
53. Koch (2000).
54. Grant (2003).
55. Rumelt, Aug 2007.

Epilogue

1. The Economist (2008).
2. Write-downs from January 2007 to the end of April 2008: Citigroup with over USD 40bn is heading the list followed by UBS, Merrill Lynch (both over USD 30bn), Bank of America, RBS, Morgan Stanley, HSBC, JP Morgan Chase, Credit Suisse, and IKB.

Bibliography

Alavarez-Gil, M. J., C. Cardone-Riportella, et al. (2003). ' "Financial Service Firms" Entry-Mode Choice and Cultural Diversity: Spanish Companies in Latin America'. *International Journal of Bank Marketing*, 21(3): 109–21.

Aliber, R. Z. (1984). 'International Banking'. *Journal of Money, Credit and Banking*, 16(4): 661–78.

Allianz, S. E. (Jul 2007). 'Allianz in Growth Markets'. Allianz Capital Markets Day 2007.

Alvarez, S. A. and J. B. Barney (2005). 'How Do Entrepreneurs Organize Firms under Conditions of Uncertainty?' *Journal of Management*, 31(5): 776–93.

Amit, R., I. Domowitz, et al. (1988). 'Thinking One Step Ahead: The Use of Conjectures in Competitor Analysis'. *Strategic Management Journal*, 9(5): 431–42.

Amram, M. and N. Kulatilaka (1999). 'Disciplined Decisions: Aligning Strategy with the Financial Markets'. *Harvard Business Review*, 77(1): 95–104.

Anderlini, J. (15 Aug 2007). 'Investing in China: Insurance Invasion That Never Was'. *Financial Times*.

Anderson, E. and H. Gatignon (1986). 'Modes of Foreign Entry: A Transaction Cost Analysis and Propositions'. *Journal of International Business Studies*, 17(3): 1–26.

Anderson, J. C. and J. A. Narus (1995). 'Capturing the Value of Supplementary Services'. *Harvard Business Review*, 73(1): 75–83.

Ansoff, I. H. (1957). 'Strategies for Diversification'. *Harvard Business Review*, 35(5): 113–24.

Ansoff, I. (1980). 'Strategic Issue Management'. *Strategic Management Journal*, 1(2): 131–48.

Arino, A., J. de la Torre, et al. (2001). 'Relational Quality: Managing Trust in Corporate Alliances'. *California Management Review*, 44(1): 109–31.

Armstrong, J. S. and R. J. Brodie (1994). 'Effects of Portfolio Planning Methods on Decision Making: Experimental Results'. *International Journal of Research in Marketing*, 11: 73–84.

Arthur, B. (1990). 'Positive Feedbacks in the Economy'. *Scientific American*, 262 (February): 92–9.

Ayadi, R. and G. Pujals (2005). *Banking Mergers and Acquisitions in the EU: Overview, Assessment and Prospects*. Vienna, SUERF—Société Universitaire Européenne de Recherches Financières.

Bain, J. S. (1956). 'Advantages of the Large Firm: Production, Distribution, and Sales Promotion'. *Journal of Marketing*, 20(4): 336–46.

Ball, C. and A. E. Tschoegl (1982). 'The Decision to Establish a Foreign Bank Branch or Subsidiary: An Application of Binary Classification Procedures'. *Journal of Financial and Quantitative Analysis*, 17(3): 411–24.

Bank of Scotland Ireland press release (16 Mar 2005). Bank of Scotland (Ireland) to Open Nationwide Branch Network.

Bank of Scotland press release (17 Jul 2001). Halifax and Bank of Scotland Welcome Office of Fair Trading Approval of HBOS Merger Proposals.

Barkema, H. G. and F. Vermeulen (1998). 'International Expansion through Start up or Acquisition: A Learning Perspective'. *Academy of Management Journal*, 41(1): 7–26.

Baron, D. P. and D. Besanko (2001). 'Strategy, Organization and Incentives: Global Corporate Banking at Citibank'. *Industrial and Corporate Change*, 10(1): 1–36.

Barras, R. (1986). 'Towards a Theory of Innovation in Services'. *Research Policy*, 15: 161–73.

Barth, J. R., G. Caprio, Jr., et al. (2004). 'Bank Regulation and Supervision: What Works Best?' *Journal of Financial Intermediation*, 13(2): 205–48.

Bartlett, C. A. and S. Ghoshal (1988). 'Organizing for Worldwide Effectiveness: The Transnational Solution'. *California Management Review*, 31(1): 54–73.

——— (1989). *Managing across Borders: The Transnational Solution*. Cambridge, MA: Harvard Business School Press.

——— (1990). 'Matrix Management: Not a Structure, a Frame of Mind'. *Harvard Business Review*, 90(4): 138–45.

——— (1991). *Managing across Borders: The Transnational Solution*. Boston, Mass.: Harvard Business School Press.

Beggs, A. and P. Klemperer (1992). 'Multi-Period Competition with Switching Costs'. *Econometrica*, 60(3): 651–66.

Beinhocker, E. (1999). 'On the Origin of Strategies'. *The McKinsey Quarterly*, 4: 38–45.

Bell, J. (1995). 'The Internationalization of Small Computer Software Firms—A Further Challenge to "Stage" Theories'. *European Journal of Marketing*, 29(8): 60–75.

Berger, A. N. and A. A. Dick (2007). 'Entry into Banking Markets and the Early-Mover Advantage'. *Journal of Money, Credit and Banking*, 39(4): 775–807.

—— and D. C. Smith (2003). 'Global Integration in the Banking Industry'. *Federal Reserve Bulletin*, 89(11): 451–60.

—— and R. DeYoung (2001). 'The Effects of Geographic Expansion on Bank Efficiency'. *Journal of Financial Services Research*, 19(2/3): 163–84.

—— and T. H. Hannan (1998). 'The Efficiency Cost of Market Power in the Banking Industry: A Test of the "Quiet Life" and Related Hypotheses'. *Review of Economics and Statistics*, 8(3): 454–65.

—— G. A. Hanweck, et al. (1987). 'Competitive Viability in Banking: Scale, Scope and Product Mix Economies'. *Journal of Monetary Economics*, 20(3): 501–20.

—— R. DeYoung, et al. (2000). 'Globalization of Financial Institutions: Evidence from Cross-Border Banking Performance'. *Brookings-Wharton Papers on Financial Services*, 23–158.

Berthon, P., L. Pitt, et al. (1999). 'Executive Insights: Virtual Services Go International: International Services in the Marketspace'. *Journal of International Marketing*, 7(3): 84–105.

Bettis, R. A. and W. K. Hall (1981). 'Strategic Portfolio Management in the Multibusiness Firm'. *California Management Review*, 24(1): 23–38.

Birkinshaw, J. (1999). 'The Determinants and Consequences of Subsidiary Initiative in Multinational Corporations'. *Entrepreneurship: Theory & Practice*, 24(1): 9–36.

——and N. Hood (1998). 'Multinational Subsidiary Evolution: Capability and Charter Change in Foreign-Owned Subsidiary Companies'. *Academy of Management Review*, 23(4): 773–95.

——— (2001). 'Unleash Innovation in Foreign Subsidiaries'. *Harvard Business Review*, 79(3): 131–8.

——A. Morrison, et al. (1995). 'Structural and Competitive Determinants of a Global Integration Strategy'. *Strategic Management Journal*, 16(8): 637–55.

——H. Bresman, et al. (2000). 'Managing the Post-Acquisition Integration Process: How the Human Integration and Task Integration Processes Interact to Foster Value Creation'. *Journal of Management Studies*, 37(3): 395–425.

——C. Bouquet, et al. (2007). 'Managing Executive Attention in the Global Company'. *MIT Sloan Management Review*, 48(4): 39–45.

Birkinshaw, J. M. (1997). 'Entrepreneurship in Multinational Corporations: The Characteristics of Subsidiary Initiatives'. *Strategic Management Journal*, 18(3): 207–29.

Björkman, I., W. Barner-Rasmussen, et al. (2004). 'Managing Knowledge Transfer in MNCs: The Impact of Headquarters Control Mechanisms'. *Journal of International Business Studies*, 35(5): 443–55.

Bleeke, J. and D. Ernst (1992). 'The Way to Win in Cross-Border Alliances'. *The McKinsey Quarterly*, 1: 113–33.

Blomstermo, A., D. D. Sharma, et al. (2006). 'Choice of Foreign Market Entry Mode in Service Firms'. *International Marketing Review*, 23(2): 211–29.

Boddewyn, J. J., M. B. Halbrich, et al. (1986). 'Service Multinationals: Conceptualisation, Measurement and Theory'. *Journal of International Business Studies*, 17(3): 41–57.

Bond, S. J. and S. Green (2003). 'The World's Local Bank: Strategic Overview'. HSBC Investor Day, 27 November 2003.

Buckley, P. and M. J. Carter (2003). 'Governing Knowledge Sharing in Multinational Enterprises'. *Management International Review* (Special Issue 3): 7–25.

Buckley, P. J. (1988). 'The Limits of Explanation: Testing the Internalization Theory of the Multinational Enterprise'. *Journal of International Business Studies*, 19(2): 181–93.

——and M. Casson (1976). *The Future of the Multinational Enterprise*. New York: Holmes & Meier.

——and M. J. Carter (2004). 'A Formal Analysis of Knowledge Combination in Multinational Enterprises'. *Journal of International Business Studies*, 35(5): 371–84.

Buzzell, R. D., B. T. Gale, et al. (1975). 'Market Share—A Key to Profitability'. *Harvard Business Review*, 53 (Jan/Feb): 97–106.

Campbell, A., M. Goold, et al. (1995). 'Corporate Strategy: The Quest for Parenting Advantage'. *Harvard Business Review*, March–April 120–32.

Canals, J. (1997). *Universal Banking: International Comparisons and Theoretical Perspectives*. Oxford: Oxford University Press.

Capar, N. and M. Kotabe (2003). 'The Relationship between International Diversification and Performance in Service Firms'. *Journal of International Business Studies*, 34(4): 345–55.

Capron, L., W. Mitchell, et al. (2001). 'Asset Divestiture Following Horizontal Acquisitions: A Dynamic View'. *Strategic Management Journal*, 22(9): 817–44.

Carpenter, G. S. and K. Nakamoto (1989). 'Consumer Preference Formation and Pioneering Advantage'. *Journal of Marketing Research*, 26: 285–98.

—— —— (1994). 'Reflections on Consumer Preference Formation and Pioneering Advantage'. *Journal of Marketing Research*, 31: 570–3.

Casson, J. (1990). 'Evolution of Multinational Banks: A Theoretical Perspective', in G. Jones (ed.), *Banks as Multinationals*. London: Routledge.

Casson, M. (1983). *The Growth of International Business*. London: Allen and Unwin.

Casti, J. (1997). *Would-Be Worlds: How Simulation is Changing the Frontiers of Science*. New York: John Wiley & Sons.

Chandler, A. D. (1966). *Strategy and Structure*. Cambridge, MA: MIT Press.

Channon, D. F. (1988). *Global Banking Strategy*. New York: John Wiley and Sons.

Chaudhuri, S. and B. Tabrizi (1999). 'Capturing the Real Value in High-Tech Acquisitions'. *Harvard Business Review*, 77(5): 123–30.

Chi, T. and P. Nystrom (1998). 'An Economic Analysis of Matrix Structure, Using Multinational Corporations as an Illustration'. *Managerial and Decision Economics*, 19: 141–56.

Child, J. and R. McGrath (2001). 'Organization Unfettered: Organizational Forms in an Information Intensive Economy'. *Academy of Management Journal*, 44(6): 1135–48.

Christensen, H. K., A. C. Cooper, et al. (1982). 'The Dog Business: A Re-Examination'. *Business Horizons*, 25(6): 12–18.

Claessens, S. and M. Janssen (eds.). (2000). *The Internationalization of Financial Services—Issues and Lessons for Developing Countries*. The Hague, Boston, London: Kluwer Law.

—— A. Demirgüç-Kunt, et al. (2001). 'How Does Foreign Entry Affect Domestic Banking Markets?' *Journal of Banking and Finance*, 25(5): 891–911.

Coase, R. H. (1937). 'The Nature of the Firm'. *Economica*, 4: 386–405.

Cohen, S. G., G. E. J. Ledford, et al. (1996). 'A Predictive Model of Self-Managing Work Team Effectiveness'. *Human Relations*, 49: 643–76.

Cohen, W. and D. Levinthal (1990). 'Absorptive Capacity: A New Perspective on Learning and Innovation'. *Administrative Science Quarterly*, 35: 128–52.

Collis, D. and C. A. Montgomery (1998). 'Creating Corporate Advantage'. *Harvard Business Review*, 76(3): 70–83.

Contractor, F. J., S. K. Kundu, et al. (2003). 'A Three-Stage Theory of International Expansion: The Link between Multinationality and Performance in the Service Sector'. *Journal of International Business Studies*, 34(1): 5–18.

Cooper, R. G. and E. J. Kleinschmidt (1987). 'New Product: What Separates Winners from Losers?' *Journal of Product Innovation Management*, 4(3): 169–84.

Courtney, H., J. Kirkland, et al. (1997). 'Strategy under Uncertainty'. *Harvard Business Review*, November–December 67–79.

Coviello, N. and H. Munro (1995). 'Growing the Entrepreneurial Firm'. *European Journal of Marketing*, 29(7): 49–62.

Crawford, L. (01 Feb 2002). 'Spain still Banking on a Latin America Bonanza'. *Financial Times*.

Croft, J. (13 Jul 2007). 'HBOS Moves to Expand in Australia'. *Financial Times*. London.

332

——(20 Jun 2005). 'HBOS to Dispose of Branches as it Outlines Irish Plan'. *Financial Times*.

——and J. Murray Brown (11 Jan 2006). 'HBOS to Take on Ireland's Big Two through Launch of 46 Branches'. *Financial Times*.

Cyert, R. M. and J. G. March (1963). *A Behavioral Theory of the Firm*. Englewood Cliffs, NJ: Prentice-Hall.

D'Aveni, R. A. (1994). *Hypercompetition—Managing the Dynamics of Strategic Maneuvering*. New York: Free Press.

Daft, R. (1982). 'Bureaucratic Versus Non Bureaucratic Structure and the Process of Innovation and Change', in S. Bacharach (ed.), *Research in the Sociology of Organizations*. Greenwich, CT: JAI Press, 1: pp. 129–66.

Dahringer, L. D. (1991). 'Marketing Services Internationally: Barriers and Management Strategies'. *Journal of Services Marketing*, 5(3): 5–18.

Damanpour, F. (1991). 'Organizational Innovation: A Meta-Analysis of Effects of Determinants and Moderators'. *Academy of Management Journal*, 34(3): 555–90.

Das, T. K. and B.-S. Teng (1999). 'Managing Risks in Strategic Alliances'. *Academy of Management Executive*, 13(4): 50–62.

Day, G. S. (1977). 'Diagnosing the Product Portfolio'. *Journal of Marketing*, 41(2): 29–38.

de Roover, R. A. (1948). *The Medici Bank: Its Organization, Management, and Decline*. London: Oxford University Press.

Delany, E. (2000). 'Strategic Development of the Multinational Subsidiary through Subsidiary Initiative-Taking'. *Long Range Planning*, 33: 220–44.

Delios, A. and P. W. Beamish (1999). 'Geographic Scope, Product Diversification and the Corporate Performance of Japanese Firms'. *Strategic Management Journal*, 20(8): 711–27.

Demattè, C. (2004). *Il mestiere di dirigere*. Milan: Etas.

Demirgüç-Kunt, A., L. Laeven, et al. (2003). 'Regulations, Market Structure, Institutions, and the Cost of Financial Intermediation'. *NBER Working Papers 9890*, National Bureau of Economic Research, Inc.

Demsetz, H. (1988). 'The Theory of the Firm Revisited'. *Journal of Law, Economics and Organization*, 4(1): 141–61.

Dermine, J. (2002). 'Banking in Europe: Past, Present and Future'. *Second ECB Central Banking Conference: The transformation of the European financial system*. Frankfurt, Germany.

DeYoung, R. and D. E. Nolle (1996). 'Foreign-Owned Banks in the United States: Earning Market Share or Buying it?' *Journal of Money, Credit and Banking*, 28(4): 622–36.

Dixit, A. and B. Nalebuff (1991). *Thinking Strategically: The Competitive Edge in Business, Politics and Everyday Life*. New York: W.W. Norton.

——and R. Pindyck (1995). 'The Options Approach to Capital Investment'. *Harvard Business Review*, May–June 105–15.

Dosi, G. (1988). 'Sources, Procedures, and Microeconomic Effects of Innovation'. *Journal of Economic Literature*, 26(3): 1120–71.

Doz, Y. L. and C. K. Prahalad (1984). 'Patterns of Strategic Control within Multinational Corporations'. *Journal of International Business Studies*, 15(2): 55–72.

Drucker, P. (1991). 'The Discipline of Innovation', in J. Henry and D. Walkner (eds.), *Managing Innovation*. London: Sage, pp. 9–17.

Dunning, J. H. (1981). *International Production and the Multinational Enterprise*. London: Allen & Unwin.

Dunning, J. (1988). 'The Eclectic Paradigm of International Production: A Restatement and Some Possible Extensions'. *Journal of International Business Studies*, 19(1): 1–31.

Dutton, J. and R. Duncan (1987). 'The Creation of Momentum for Change through the Process of Strategic Issue Diagnosis'. *Strategic Management Journal*, 8(3): 279–96.

Eisenhardt, K. M. (1999). 'Strategy as Strategic Decision Making'. *Sloan Management Review*, 40(3): 65–72.

Empson, L. (2000). 'Merging Professional Service Firms'. *Business Strategy Review*, 11(2): 39–46.

Engwall, L. and M. Wallenstal (1988). 'Tit for Tat in Small Steps. The Internationalization of Swedish Banks'. *Scandinavian Journal of Management*, 4(3/4): 147–55.

Ernst, D. and T. Halevy (2000). 'When to Think Alliance'. *The McKinsey Quarterly*, 4: 47–55.

Erramilli, M. K. (1990). 'Entry Mode Choice in Services Industries'. *International Marketing Review*, 7(5): 50–62.

—— (1991). 'The Experience Factor in Foreign Market Entry Behavior of Service Firms'. *Journal of International Business Studies*, 22(3): 479–501.

—— (1992). 'Influence of Some External and Internal Environmental Factors on Foreign Market Entry Mode Choice in Service Firms'. *Journal of Business Research*, 25(4): 263–76.

—— and C. P. Rao (1990). 'Choice of Foreign Market Entry Modes by Service Firms: Role of Market Knowledge'. *Management International Review*, 30(2): 135–50.

—— —— (1993). ' "Service Firms" International Entry-mode Choice: A Modified Transaction-Cost Analysis Approach'. *Journal of Marketing*, 57(3): 19–38.

Evangelista, R. (2000). 'Sectoral Patterns of Technological Change in Services'. *Economics of Innovation and New Technology*, 9(3): 183–221.

Ezingeard, J.-N. (2003). 'Managing Supply Chain Information at HBOS: The SRM (Supplier Relationship Management) Initiative'. *ECCH—The European Case Clearing House*.

Farrell, J. and C. Shapiro (1988). 'Dynamic Competition with Switching Costs'. *Journal of Economics*, 19(1): 123–37.

—— —— (1989). 'Optimal Contracts with Lock-In'. *American Economic Review*, 79(1): 51–68.

—— and G. Saloner (1985). 'Standardization, Compatibility, and Innovation'. *Rand Journal of Economics*, 16(1): 70–83.

—— —— (1986). 'Installed Base and Compatibility: Innovation, Product Preannouncements, and Predation'. *American Economic Review, Papers and Proceedings*, 76(5): 940–55.

Feketekuty, G. (1988). *International Trade in Services: An Overview and Blueprint for Negotiations*. Cambridge, MA: Ballinger Publishing Company.

Fifield, A. (19 Aug 2003). 'HBOS Wins Australian Takeover Vote'. *Financial Times*.

Flier, B., F. A. J. van den Bosch, et al. (2001). 'The Changing Landscape of the European Financial Services Sector'. *Long Range Planning*, 24: 179–207.

Forestieri, G. (1993). 'Economies of Scale and Scope in the Financial Services Industry: A Review of the Recent Literature'. *OECD—Financial Conglomerates*, 63–124.

Forsgren, M. (1997). 'The Advantage Paradox of the Multinational Corporation', in I. Björkman and M. Forsgren (eds.), *The Nature of the International Firm*. Copenhagen: Copenhagen Business School Press.

Fowler, K. L. and D. R. Schmidt (1989). 'Determinants of Tender Offer Post-Acquisition Financial Performance'. *Strategic Management Journal*, 10(4): 339–50.

Gallouj, F. (2002). 'Innovation in Services and the Attendance Old and New Myths'. *Journal of Socio-Economics*, 31(2): 137–54.

—— and O. Weinstein (1997). 'Innovation in Services'. *Research Policy*, 26: 537–56.

Generali China Life News Center (01 Nov 2006). Generali China Head Office is to be Relocated to Beijing—GC Guangdong Branch as the future Coordination Center in South China, Generali China Life.

—— (29 Apr 2007). Generali China Life Insurance Co., Ltd. has been growing steadily; both of the shareholders have increased their capital investment once again, Generali China Life.

Generali Corporate Communication (Feb 2005). Generali China Life enters the group policies sector in China. *Generali News*, Assicurazioni Generali.

Generali Group (Oct 2007). Strategic Plan Update—Accelerating the Pace of Change. Merrill Lynch—Banking & Insurance CEO Conference.

Geoghegan, M. (2007). 'Think Joined up'. Presentation at Morgan Stanley Investors Conference.

Geringer, J. M., S. Tallman, et al. (2000). 'Product and International Diversification among Japanese Multinational Firms'. *Strategic Management Journal*, 21(1): 51–80.

Ghemawat, P. (2003). 'Semiglobalization and International Business Strategy'. *Journal of International Business Studies*, 34(2): 138–52.

—— (2007). *Redefining Global Strategy: Crossing Borders in a World Where Differences Still Matter*. Boston: Harvard Business School Publishing.

—— and A. M. Spence (1986). 'Modelling Global Competition', in M. E. Porter (ed.), *Competition in Global Industries*. Boston, MA.: Harvard Business School Press, pp. 61–79.

—— and P. del Sol (1998). 'Commitment vs. Flexibility'. *California Management Review*, 40(4): 26–42.

—— E. Ballarin, et al. (2006). 'Santander's Acquisition of Abbey: Banking across Borders'. *ECCH—European Case Clearing House*, 18.

Ghoshal, S. (1987). 'Global Strategy: An Organizing Framework'. *Strategic Management Journal*, 8(5): 425–40.

—— and C. A. Bartlett (1988). 'Creation, Adoption and Diffusion of Innovations by Subsidiaries of Multinational Corporations'. *Journal of International Business Studies*, 19(3): 365–88.

—— —— (1990). 'The Multinational Corporation as an International Network'. *Academy of Management Review*, 15(4): 603–25.

—— and H. Bruch (2003). 'Going Beyond Motivation to the Power of Volition'. *MIT Sloan Management Review*, 44(3): 51–7.

Bibliography

Glaister, K. W. and J. R. Falshaw (1999). 'Strategic Planning: Still Going Strong?' *Long Range Planning*, 32(1): 107–16.

—— and P. J. Buckley (1996). 'Strategic Motives for International Alliance Formation'. *Journal of Management Studies*, 33(3): 301–32.

Goerzen, A. (2005). 'Managing Alliance Networks: Emerging Practices of Multinational Corporations'. *Academy of Management Executive*, 19(2): 94–107.

Goold, M. and A. Campbell (1987). *Strategies and Styles: The Role of the Centre in Managing Diversified Corporations*. London: Basil Blackwell Ltd.

—— and J. J. Quinn (1990). 'The Paradox of Strategic Controls'. *Strategic Management Journal*, 11(1): 40–50.

—— A. Campbell, et al. (1994). *Corporate-Level Strategy: Creating Value in the Multibusiness Company*. New York: John Wiley & Sons Inc.

Grant, R. (2008). *Contemporary Strategy Analysis*. Oxford: Blackwell Publishing.

—— and C. Baden-Fuller (1995). 'A Knowledge-Based Theory of Inter-Firm Collaboration'. *Academy of Management Best Paper Proceedings*, 17–21.

Grant, R. M. (1996). 'Toward a Knowledge-Based Theory of the Firm'. *Strategic Management Journal* 17 (Winter Special Issue): 109–22.

—— (1998). *Contemporary Strategy Analysis. Concepts, Techniques, Applications*. New York: Blackwell.

—— (2003). 'Strategic Planning in a Turbulent Environment: Evidence from the Oil Majors'. *Strategic Management Journal*, 24: 491–517.

Grosse, R. (2004). 'Are the Largest Financial Institutions Really "Global"?' *Management International Review*, 44(4): 127–42.

Grosse, R. E. (2004). *The Future of Global Financial Services*. Padstow, Australia: Blackwell Publishing.

Grubel, H. (1989). 'Multinational Banking', in P. Enderwick (ed.), *Multinational Service Firms*. London: Routledge, pp. 61–78.

Grubel, H. G. (1977). 'A Theory of Multinational Banking'. *Banca Nazionale del Lavoro Quarterly*, 30 (123): 345–63.

Guerrera, F. (26 Jan 2006). 'ICBC Draws on Foreign Expertise Before Listing'. *Financial Times*.

Guillén, M. F. and A. E. Tschoegl (2000). 'The Internationalization of Retail Banking: The Case of the Spanish Banks in Latin America'. *Transnational Corporations*, 9(3): 63–98.

Gulati, R. and H. Singh (1998). 'The Architecture of Cooperation: Managing Coordination Costs and Appropriation Concerns in Strategic Alliances'. *Administrative Science Quarterly*, 43(4): 781–814.

Gupta, A. K. and V. Govindarajan (1991). 'Knowledge Flows and the Structure of Control within Multinational Corporations'. *Academy of Management Review*, 16(4): 768–92.

—— —— (2000). 'Knowledge Flows within Multinational Corporations'. *Strategic Management Journal*, 21(4): 473–96.

—— —— (2001). 'Converting Global Presence into Global Competitive Advantage'. *Academy of Management Executive*, 15(2): 45–56.

Hambrick, D. C., I. C. MacMillan, et al. (1982). 'Strategic Attributes and Performance in the BCG Matrix—A PIMS-Based Analysis of Industrial Product Businesses'. *Academy of Management Journal*, 25(3): 510–31.

Hamel, G. (1996). 'Strategy as Revolution'. *Harvard Business Review*, 74(4): 69–82.

Hammond, A. L., W. J. Kramer, et al. (2007). *The Next Four Billion: Market Size and Business Strategy at the Base of the Pyramid*. Washington, DC: World Resource Institute and IFC.

Hannan, M. T. and J. Freeman (1984). 'Structural Inertia and Organizational Change'. *American Sociological Review*, 49: 149–64.

Hansen, M., N. Nohria, et al. (1999). 'What's Your Strategy for Managing Knowledge?' *Harvard Business Review*, 77(2): 106–19.

Haspeslagh, P. (1982). 'Portfolio Planning: Uses and Limits'. *Harvard Business Review*, 60(1): 58–73.

Haspeslagh, P. C. and D. B. Jamison (1991). *Managing Acquisitions: Creating Value through Corporate Renewal*. New York: Free Press.

HBOS, Annual Report 2006.

HBOS, Annual Report 2007.

HBOS (Dec 2003). Retail Investors Seminar.

HBOS press release (05 Dec 2001). A fair deal.

—— (25 Sep 2002). HBOS increases its Current Account market share target.

—— (29 Jul 2003). A better deal for Big Four customers.

—— (12 Jul 2007). HBOS launches biggest ever Australian banking expansion programme.

—— (23 Aug 2007). HBOS response: Competition Commission report on SME banking services.

—— (04 Oct 2007). HBOS launches market-beating 5% current account in Australia.

Hedberg, B. (1981). 'How Organizations Learn and Unlearn', in P. Nystrom and W. Starbuck (eds.), *Handbook of Organizational Design*. Oxford: Oxford University Press.

Hedley, B. (1977). 'Strategy and the Business Portfolio'. *Long Range Planning*, 10: 9–15.

Hedlund, G. and J. Ridderstrale (1997). *Toward a Theory of the Self-Renewing MNC*. Columbia, SC: University of South Carolina Press.

Henderson, A. D. (1999). 'Firm Strategy and Age Dependence: A Contingent View of the Liabilities of Newness, Adolescence, and Obsolescence'. *Administrative Science Quarterly*, 44: 281–314.

Hennart, J. F. (1982). *A Theory of Multinational Enterprise*. Ann Arbor: University of Michigan Press.

—— (2007). 'The Theoretical Rationale for a Multinatinationality – Performance Relationship'. *Management International Review*, 47(3): 423–52.

Hennart, J.-F. (1991). 'The Transactions Cost Theory of Joint Ventures: An Empirical Study of Japanese Subsidiaries in the USA'. *Management Science*, 37: 483–97.

Hernandez, R. and Y. Mugica (2003). What Works: PRODEM FFP's Multilingual Smart ATMs for Microfinance: Innovative Solutions for Delivering Financial Services to Rural Bolivia. World Resource Institute.

Hill, C. W. L. (2004). *International Business: Competing in the Global Marketplace*. New York: Irwin/McGraw-Hill.

Hitt, M. A., L. Bierman, et al. (2006). 'The Importance of Resources in the Internationalization of Professional Service Firms: The Good, the Bad, and the Ugly'. *Academy of Management Journal*, 49(6): 1137–57.

Hodkinson, P. (Jun 2007). 'Speech Transcript'. Goldman Sachs Conference, Group Finance Director HBOS: 1.

Hornby, A. (Mar 2007). 'Sustainable Growth'. Speech at Morgan Stanley European Banks & Financials Conference, CEO HBOS.

Hout, T., M. Porter, et al. (1982). 'How Global Companies Win Out'. *Harvard Business Review*, 60(5): 98–108.

http://en.epochtimes.com. (26 Aug 2005). 'Royal Bank of Scotland Buys into Bank of China'. Retrieved 27/03/2008, from http://en.epochtimes.com/news/5-8-26/31628.html.

http://news.bbc.co.uk. (04 May 2001). 'HBOS: The Merger Benefits'. Retrieved 16/02/2008, from http://news.bbc.co.uk/1/hi/business/1312791.stm.

——(05 Dec 2001). 'HBOS Takes on Big Four "Cartel"'. Retrieved 18/02/2008, from http://news.bbc.co.uk/2/low/business/1693226.stm.

——(17 Jun 2005). 'Bank of America Invests in China'. Retrieved 27/03/2008, from http://news.bbc.co.uk/2/hi/business/4102670.stm.

http://uk.reuters.com. (12 Jul 2007). 'HBOS's BankWest Expands with 160 Australia Branches'. Retrieved 27/03/2008, from http://uk.reuters.com/article/businessNews/idUKL1261169820070712?pageNumber = 1&virtualBrandChannel = 0.

Huertas, T. F. (1990). 'US Multinational Banking: History and Prospects', in G. Jones (ed.), *Banks as Multinationals*, London, UK and New York, USA: Routledge, pp. 248–67.

Hultman, C. W. and L. R. McGee (1989). 'Factors Affecting the Foreign Banking Presence in the U.S.'. *Journal of Banking and Finance*, 13(3): 383–96.

Hymer, S. H. (1960). The International Operations of National Firms: A Study of Direct Foreign Investment. PhD Dissertation, MIT. Published by MIT Press in 1976.

Inkpen, A. C. and N. Choudhury (1995). 'The Seeking of Strategy Where it Is Not: Towards a Theory of Strategy Absence'. *Strategic Management Journal*, 16: 313–23.

Johanson, J. and J. E. Vahlne (1977). 'The Internationalization Process of the Firm—A Model of Knowledge Development and Increasing Foreign Market Commitments'. *Journal of International Business Studies*, 8(1): 23–32.

————(1990). 'The Mechanism of Internationalization'. *International Marketing Review*, 7(4): 11–24.

Jones, G. (2006). *Prudential: Leading in Asia Presentation*. China: Prudential plc, pp. 142–62.

——and J. E. Butler (1992). 'Managing Internal Corporate Entrepreneurship: An Agency Theory Perspective'. *Journal of Management*, 18(4): 733–49.

Kanter, R. M. (1988). 'When a Thousand Flowers Bloom. Structural, Collective, and Social Conditions for Innovation in Organizations', in L. L. Cummings and B. Staw (eds.), *Research in Organizational Behavior*. Greenwich, CT: JAI Press, 10: pp. 169–211.

Kardes, F. R. and G. Kalyanaram (1992). 'Order-of-Entry Effects on Consumer Memory and Judgment: An Information Integration Perspective'. *Journal of Marketing Research*, 29: 343–57.

————et al. (1993). 'Brand Retrieval, Consideration Set Composition, Consumer Choice, and the Pioneering Advantage'. *Journal of Consumer Research*, 20(1): 62–75.

Karim, S. and W. Mitchell (2000). 'Path-Dependent and Path-Breaking Change: Reconfiguring Business Resources Following Acquisitions in the U.S. Medical Sector, 1978–1995'. *Strategic Management Journal*, 21(10/11): 1061–81.

Karsch, W. (2007). 'Direct Banking in Deutschland: Wettlauf im Web'. *Die Bank* (12).

Katz, M. and C. Shapiro (1985). 'Network Externalities, Competition, and Compatibility'. *American Economic Review*, 75: 424–40.

Kaufmann, S. (1995). *At Home in the Universe: The Search for the Laws of Self-Organization and Complexity*. New York: Oxford University Press.

Khatri, N. and H. A. Ng (2000). 'The Role of Intuition in Strategic Decision Making'. *Human Relations*, 53(1): 57–86.

Kim, W. C. and R. Mauborgne (1991). 'Implementing Global Strategies: The Role of Procedural Justice'. *Strategic Management Journal*, 12(4): 125–43.

——— (1995). 'A Procedural Justice Model of Strategic Decision-Making: Strategy Content Implications in the Multinational'. *Organization Science*, 6(1): 44–61.

——— (1997). 'Value Innovation: The Strategic Logic of High Growth'. *Harvard Business Review*, 75(1): 103–12.

——— (1998). 'Procedural Justice, Strategic Decision Making, and the Knowledge Economy'. *Strategic Management Journal*, 19(4, Special Issue: Editor's Choice): 323–38.

Kindleberger, C. P. (1969). *American Business Abroad: Six Lectures on Direct Investment*. New Haven/London: Yale University Press.

King, N. (1992). 'Modeling the Innovation Process: An Empirical Comparison of Approaches'. *Journal of Occupational and Organizational Psychology*, 65: 89–100.

Kitching, J. (1967). 'Why Do Mergers Miscarry?' *Harvard Business Review*, 45(6): 84–101.

Knickerbocker, F. T. (1973). *Oligopolistic Reaction and Multinational Enterprise*. Boston: Harvard University Press.

Knight, G. A. and S. T. Cavusgil (1989). 'Innovation, Organizational Capabilities, and the Born-Global Firm'. *Journal of International Business Studies*, 35(2): 124–41.

Kobrin, S. J. (1991). 'An Empirical Analysis of the Determinants of Global Integration'. *Strategic Management Journal*, 12 (Special Issue: Global Strategy): 17–31.

Koch, R. (2000). *The Financial Times Guide to Strategy*. London: Prentice-Hall.

Kogut, B. (1984). 'Normative Observations on the International Value-Added Chain and Strategic Groups'. *Journal of International Business Studies*, 15(2): 151–67.

—— (1985). 'Designing Global Strategies: Comparative and Competitive Value-Added Chains'. *Sloan Management Review*, 26(4): 15–28.

—— and H. Singh (1988). 'The Effect of National Culture on the Choice of Entry Mode'. *Journal of International Business Studies*, 19(3): 411–32.

—— and U. Zander (1992). 'Knowledge of the Firm, Combinative Capabilities, and the Replication of Technology'. *Organization Science*, 3(3): 383–97.

——— (1993). 'Knowledge of the Firm and the Evolutionary Theory of the Multinational Corporation'. *Journal of International Business Studies*, 34(6): 516–29.

Krabichler, T. and I. Krauss (2003). 'Konsolidierung im europäischen Bankenmarkt—die Laender der EU im Vergleich, Institut fuer Bankeninformatik und Bankstrategie an der Universität Regensburg (ibi)'. Institut für Bankinformatik und Bankstrategie an der Universität Regensburg, 02/2003.

Kumar, V., A. Stam, et al. (1994). 'An Interactive Multicriteria Approach to Identifying Potential Foreign Markets'. *Journal of International Marketing*, 2(1): 29–52.

Kusewitt, J. B., Jr. (1985). 'An Exploratory Study of Strategic Acquisition Factors Relating to Performance'. *Strategic Management Journal*, 6(2): 151–69.

Laurentis, G. D. (ed.). (2004). *Strategy and Structure in Corporate Banking*. Frankfurt a.M.: Springer Verlag.

Lavallo, D. and L. Mendonca (2007). 'Strategy's Strategist: An Interview with Richard Rumelt'. *The McKinsey Quarterly*, 4: 56–67.

Leonard-Barton, D. (1992). 'Core Capabilities and Core Rigidities: A Paradox in Managing New Product Development'. *Strategic Management Journal*, 13 (Special Issue Summer): 111–25.

——(1995). *Wellsprings of Knowledge: Building and Sustaining the Sources of Innovation*. Boston, MA: Harvard Business School Press.

Lewin, K. (1947). 'Frontiers in Group Dynamics'. *Human Relations*, 1: 2–38.

Li, L., A. Goerzen, et al. (2005). 'Multinationality and Performance: Theoretical Development and Future Research'. *Academy of International Business Annual Meeting*. Quebec City, Canada.

Lieberman, M. B. and D. B. Montgomery (1988). 'First-Mover Advantages'. *Strategic Management Journal*, 9: 41–58.

—— ——(1998). 'First-Mover (Dis)advantages: Retrospective and Link with the Resource-Based View'. *Strategic Management Journal*, 19 (12): 1111–25.

Liebowitz, S. J. and S. E. Margolis (1995). 'Are Network Externalities a New Source of Market Failure?' *Research in Law and Economics*, 17: 1–22.

Linder, S. (1961). *An Essay on Trade and Transformation*. New York: John Wiley.

Llewellyn, D. T. (1999). *The New Economics of Banking*. Amsterdam: Société Universitaire Européenne de Recherches Financières.

—— (2002). *The Future for Small & Regional Banks in Europe*. Vienna: Société Universitaire Européenne de Recherches Financières.

Lovelock, C. H. (1992). 'A Basic Toolkit for Service Managers', in C. H. Lovelock (ed.), *Managing Services: Marketing, Operations, and Human Resources*. Englewood Cliffs, NJ: Prentice-Hall, pp. 17–30.

——and G. S. Yip (1996). 'Developing Global Strategies for Service Businesses'. *California Management Review*, 38(2): 64–86.

Lu, J. W. and P. W. Beamish (2004). 'International Diversification and Firm Performance: The S-Curve Hypothesis'. *Academy of Management Journal*, 47(4): 598–609.

Lubatkin, M. (1983). 'Mergers and the Performance of the Acquiring Firm'. *Academy of Management Review*, 8(2): 218–25.

Lyons, R. K., J. A. Chatman, et al. (2007). 'Innovation in Service: Corporate Culture and Investment Banking'. *California Management Review*, 50(1): 174–91.

MacMillan, I. C., D. C. Hambrick, et al. (1982). 'The Product Portfolio and Profitability— A PIMS-Based Analysis of Industrial-Product Businesses'. *Academy of Management Journal*, 25(4): 733–55.

Mahnke, V. and M. Venzin (2003). 'The Internationalization Process of Digital Good Providers'. *Management International Review*, 1: 115–42.

—— ——et al. (2007). 'Governing Entrepreneurial Opportunity Recognition in MNEs: Aligning Interests and Cognition under Uncertainty'. *Journal of Management Studies*, 44(7): 1278–98.

Mankins, M. C. (2004). 'Stop Wasting Valuable Time'. *Harvard Business Review*, 82(9): 58–65.

March, J. G. (1991). 'Exploration and Exploitation in Organizational Learning'. *Organization Science*, 2(1): 71–87.

——(1994). *A Primer on Decision Making*. New York: Free Press.

Markides, C. (1999). *All the Right Moves: A Guide to Crafting Breakthrough Strategy*. Boston, MA: Harvard Business School Press.

Markides, C. C. and P. A. Geroski (2004). *Fast Second: How Smart Companies Bypass Radical Innovation to Enter and Dominate New Markets*. San Francisco: Jossey-Bass.

McDougall, P. P. and B. M. Oviatt (1994). *New Venture Internationalization, Strategic Change, and Performance: A Follow-up Study*. 1994 Academy of Management Conference, Dallas, TX.

Metcalf, S. and I. Miles (eds.). (2000). *Innovation Systems in the Service Economy: Measurement and Case Study Analysis*. London: Kluwer Academic.

Milgrom, P. and J. Roberts (1995). 'Complementarities and Fit: Strategy, Structure, and Organizational Change in Manufacturing'. *Journal of Accounting and Economics*, 19(2–3): 179–208.

Miller, S. R. and A. Parkhe (1998). 'Patterns in the Expansion of U.S. Banks' Foreign Operations'. *Journal of International Business Studies*, 29(2): 359–89.

Mintzberg, H. (1994). *The Rise and Fall of Strategic Planning*. Hertfordshire: Prentice-Hall, Inc.

Molt, C. (2007). 'Allianz in China'. *Allianz in Growth Markets*. Presentation at the Capital Markets Day 2007, Allianz SE, pp. 38–51. Retrieved from company web page, www.allianz.com.

Morrison, A. and R. Wensley (1991). 'Boxing Up or Boxed In?: A Short History of the Boston Consulting Group Share/Growth Matrix'. *Journal of Marketing Management*, 7(2): 105–29.

Mottura, P. (2007). *Banche: Strategia, Organizzazione e Concentrazioni*. Milan: Egea.

Mudambi, R. and P. Navarra (2004). 'Is Knowledge Power? Knowledge Flows, Subsidiary Power and Rent-Seeking within MNCs'. *Journal of International Business Studies*, 35(5): 385–406.

Muralidharan, R. and R. D. Hamilton, III (1999). 'Aligning Multinational Control Systems'. *Long Range Planning*, 32(3): 352–61.

Nelson, R. R. and S. G. Winter (1977). 'Simulation of Schumpeterian Competition'. *American Economic Review*, 67(1): 271–6.

————— (1982). *An Evolutionary Theory of Economic Change*. Cambridge, MA.: Harvard University Press.

Nocera, G., G. Iannotta, et al. (2007). 'Ownership Structure, Risk and Performance in the European Banking Industry'. *Journal of Banking and Finance*, 31: 2127–49.

Nonaka, I. and H. Takeuchi (1995). *The Knowledge Creating Company—How Japanese Companies Create the Dynamics of Innovation*. New York: Oxford University Press.

O'Dell, C. and C. Grayson (1998). 'If only we knew, what we know: identification and transfer of internal best practices'. *California Management Review*, 40(3): 154–74.

O'Donnell, S. W. (2000). 'Managing Foreign Subsidiaries: Agents of Headquarters, or an Interdependent Network?' *Strategic Management Journal*, 21(5): 525–48.

Ohlin, B. (1933). *Interregional and International Trade*. Cambridge, MA: Harvard University Press.

Ouchi, W. (1977). 'The relationship between organizational structure and organizational control'. *Administrative Science Quarterly*, 22: 95–113.

——— (1979). 'A conceptual framework for the design of organizational control mechanisms'. *Management Science*, 25(9): 833–48.

341

Ouchi, W. (1980). 'Markets, Bureaucracies and Clans'. *Administrative Science Quarterly*, 25: 129–41.

Park, S. H. and M. V. Russo (1996). 'When Competition Eclipses Cooperation: An Event History Analysis of Joint Venture Failure'. *Management Science*, 42(6): 875–90.

Patterson, P. G. and M. Cicic (1995). 'A Typology of Service Firms in International Markets: An Empirical Investigation'. *Journal of International Marketing*, 3(4): 57–83.

Pauly, C. and Balzli, B. (2007). 'Keeping the Hedge Funds in Check: Interview with JP Morgan Chase CEO Jamie Dimon.' Spiegel Online, 16 July 2007.

Peng, M. W. and O. Shenkar (2002). 'Joint Venture Dissolution as Corporate Divorce'. *Academy of Management Executive*, 16(2): 92–105.

Penrose, E. T. (1959). *The Theory of the Growth of the Firm*. New York: Wiley.

Polanyi, M. (1966). *The Tacit Dimension*. London: Routledge & Kegan Paul.

Posner, M. V. (1961). 'International Trade and Technical Change'. *Oxford Economic Papers*, 13(3): 323–41.

Prahalad, C. K. (1976). 'Strategic Choices in Diversified MNCs'. *Harvard Business Review*, 54(4): 67–78.

—— and G. Hamel (1990). 'The Core Competence of the Corporation'. *Harvard Business Review*, 68(3): 79–91.

—— and R. A. Bettis (1986). 'The Dominant Logic: A New Linkage between Diversity and Performance'. *Strategic Management Journal*, 7(6): 485–501.

—— and Y. L. Doz (1987). *The Multinational Mission: Balancing Local Demands and Global Vision*. New York: Free Press.

Reardon, J., M. K. Erramilli, et al. (1996). 'International Expansion of Service Firms: Problems and Strategies'. *Journal of Professional Services Marketing*, 15(1): 31–46.

Ricardo, D. (1821). *On the Principles of Political Economy and Taxation*. London: John Murray.

Rigby, D. (2001). 'Management Tools and Techniques: A Survey'. *California Management Review*, 43(2): 37–49.

Robertson, D. and I. Francis (2003). 'ING Direct: Your Other Bank'. *IMD—International Institute for Management Development*. Case Study from IMD; retrieved from ECCH.

Root, F. R. (1994). *Entry Strategies for International Markets*. San Francisco, CA: Lexington Books.

Rothbard, M. N. (1983). *The Mystery of Banking*. London: Richardson and Snyder.

Rudy, J. P. (1975). 'Global Planning in Multinational Banking'. *Columbia Journal of World Business*, 10(4): 16–23.

Rugman, A. (1979). *International Diversification and the Multinational Enterprise*. Lexington: Heath.

—— (2000). *The End of Globalization*. New York: Random House.

Rugman, A. M. and A. Verbeke (1992). 'A Note on the Transnational Solution and the Transaction Cost Theory of Multinational Strategic Management'. *Journal of International Business Studies*, 23: 761–71.

Ruigrok, W. and H. Wagner (2003). 'Internationalization and Performance: An Organizational Learning Perspective'. *Management International Review*, 43(1): 63–83.

———— (2005). Internationalization and Firm Performance: Meta-Analytic Review and Future Research Directions. *Academy of International Business* Conference.

Rumelt, R. (1987). 'Theory, Strategy, and Entrepreneurship', in D. J. Teece (ed.), *The Competitive Challenge*. Cambridge, MA: Ballinger Publishing, pp. 137–58.

Ryans, A. (1999). 'ING Bank of Canada (A): Launch of a Direct Bank'. *Richard Ivey School of Business—The University of Western Ontario*. Case Study, ECCH.

——T. Deutscher, et al. (2007). 'ING Direct USA—Rebel with a Cause'. *IMD—International Institute for Management Development*. Case Study, ECCH.

Sakarya, S., M. Eckman, et al. (2007). 'Market Selection for International Expansion. Assessing Opportunities in Emerging Markets'. *International Marketing Review*, 24(2): 208–38.

Saloner, G., A. Shepard, et al. (2001). *Strategic Management*. New York: John Wiley & Sons.

Sanchez-Peinado, E., J. Pla-Barber, et al. (2007). 'Strategic Variables That Influence Entry Mode Choice in Service Firms'. *Journal of International Marketing*, 15(1): 67–91.

Sanchez, R. and J. T. Mahoney (1996). 'Modularity, Flexibility, and Knowledge Management in Product and Organization Design'. *Strategic Management Journal*, 17: 63–76.

Sanders, I. (1998). *Strategic Thinking and the New Science*. New York: Free Press.

Sarkar, M. B., S. T. Cavusgil, et al. (1999). 'International Expansion of Telecommunication Carriers'. *Journal of International Business*, 30(2): 361–82.

Sarvary, M. (1999). 'Knowledge Management and Competition in the Consulting Industry'. *California Management Review*, 41(2): 95–107.

Satta, T. A. (2004). 'The Influence of Foreign Bank Entry on Lending to Small Firms in Tanzania'. *Journal of Policy Reform*, 7(3) (September): 165–73.

Saunders, A. and I. Walter (1993). *Universal Banking in the United States: What Could We Gain? What Could We Lose?* Oxford: Oxford University Press.

——and M. Millon Cornett (2004). *Financial Markets and Institutions—A Modern Perspective*. New York: McGraw-Hill/Irwin.

Schneider, S. C. and A. D. Meyer (1991). 'Interpreting and Responding to Strategic Issues: The Impact of National Culture'. *Strategic Management Journal*, 12: 307–20.

Schoemaker, P. (1995). 'Scenario Planning: A New Tool for Strategic Thinking'. *Sloan Management Review*, 36(2): 25–40.

Schumpeter, J. A. (1934). *The Theory of Economic Development*. Cambridge, MA: Harvard University Press.

Schwartz, P. (1996). *The Art of the Long View: Planning for the Future in an Uncertain World*. New York: Doubleday.

Sedillot, R. (1998). *Muscheln, Münzen und Papier. Geschichte des Geldes*. Frankfurt: Campus.

Senge, P. (1990). 'The Leader's New Work: Building Learning Organizations'. *Sloan Management Review*, 32(1): 7–23.

Shapiro, C. and H. R. Varian (1998). *Information Rules: A Strategic Guide to the Network Economy*. Boston, MA: Harvard Business School Press.

Shapiro, S. and M. T. Spence (1997). 'Managerial Intuition: A Conceptual and Operational Framework'. *Business Horizons*, 40(1): 63–8.

Sharma, D. D. and J. Johanson (1987). 'Technical Consultancy in Internationalization'. *International Marketing Review*, 4(4): 20–9.

Shaw, G., R. Brown, et al. (1998). 'Strategic Stories: How 3M is Rewriting Business Planning'. *Harvard Business Review*, 76(3): 41–50.

Shek, C. (2006). 'China: CITIC-PRU Building Scale in a Large and Fast Growing Market'. *Prudential: Leading in Asia Presentation*, Prudential plc pp. 239–54.

343

Siddharthan, N. S. and S. Lall (1982). 'The Recent Growth of the Largest US Multinationals'. *Oxford Bulletin of Economics and Statistics*, 44(1): 1–13.

Singh, H. and C. A. Montgomery (1987). 'Corporate Acquisition Strategies and Economic Performance'. *Strategic Management Journal*, 8(4): 377–86.

Slager, A. (2005). *Internationalization of Banks: Strategic Patterns and Performance*. Vienna: SUERF—The European Money and Finance Forum.

—— (2006). *Internationalization of Banks: Patterns, Strategies and Performance*. New York: Palgrave Macmillan Ltd.

Slaughter, R. A. (1990). 'The Foresight Principle'. *Futures* (October): 801–19.

Smith, A. (1776). *The Wealth of Nations*. Harmondsworth: Penguin Books.

Stevenson, H. H. and J. C. Jarillo (1990). 'A Paradigm of Entrepreneurship: Entrepreneurial Management'. *Strategic Management Journal*, 11: 17–27.

—— M. J. Roberts, et al. (1989). *New Business Ventures and the Entrepreneur*. Homewood, Illinois: Irwin.

Stewart, T. A. (1997). *Intellectual Capital: The New Wealth of Organizations*. New York: Currency Doubleday.

Stinchcombe, A. L. (1965). 'Social Structure and Organizations', in J. G. March (ed.), *Handbook of Organizations*. Chicago: Rand McNally.

Stopford, J. and L. Wells (1972). *Managing the Multinational Enterprise*. New York: Basic Books.

Stopford, J. M. and C. Baden-Fuller (1994). 'Creating Corporate Entrepreneurship'. *Strategic Management Journal*, 15(10): 521–36.

Stowe, B. (Dec 2006). CITIC Prudential Illustrated interview, CEO of Prudential Corporation Asia.

Strebel, P. (1995). 'Creating Industry Breakpoints: Changing the Rules of the Game'. *Long Range Planning*, 28: 11–20.

Suarez, F. F. and G. Lanzolla (2007). 'The Role of Environmental Dynamics in Building a First Mover Advantage Theory'. *Academy of Management Review*, 32(2): 377–92.

Sullivan, D. (1994). 'Measuring the Degree of Internationalization of a Firm'. *International Business Studies*, 25(2): 325–42.

Tellis, G. J. and P. N. Golder (2002). *Will & Vision: How Latecomers Grow to Dominate Markets*. New York: McGraw-Hill.

The Banker (2007). *Top 1000 World Banks 2007*. London: The Financial Times Ltd. Retrieved from www.thebanker.com.

The Economist (15 May 2008). 'Professionally Gloomy'. 11–14.

Thomas, H. and J. Murray Brown (10 Jan 2006). 'HBOS Launches Into Irish Retail Banking'. *Financial Times*.

Thomke, S. (2003). 'R&D Comes to Service'. *Harvard Business Review* April: 3–11.

Toffler, A. (1990). *The Third Wave*. New York: Bantam Books.

Tsai, W. and S. Ghoshal (1998). 'Social Capital and Value Creation: The Role of Intrafirm Networks'. *Academy of Management Journal*, 41(4): 464–77.

Van der Heijden, K. (1996). *The Art of Strategic Conversation*. New York: John Wiley & Sons.

Vandermerwe, S. and M. Chadwick (1989). 'The Internationalization of Services'. *The Service Industries Journal*, 9(1): 79–93.

Venzin, M., C. Rasner, et al. (2005*a*). *The Strategy Process—A Practical Handbook for Implementation in Business.* London: Cyan/Campus Books.

——M. Reitzig, et al. (2005*b*). *Innovazione Finanziaria: Caratteristiche e potenzialità di sviluppo dei Certificati in Italia.* Bocconi University.

Venzin, M., Kumar, V. and J. Kleine (2008). 'Internationalization of Retail Banks: A Micro-Level Study of the Multinationality–Performance Relationship'. *Management International Review,* 48: 463–85.

Vermeulen, P. (2004). 'Managing Product Innovation in Financial Service Firms'. *European Management Journal,* 22(1): 43–50.

Vernon, R. (1966). 'International Trade and International Investment in the Product Life Cycle'. *Quarterly Journal of Economics,* 80: 190–207.

Verweire, K. and L. A. Van den Berghe (2007). 'ING Direct—Rebel in the Banking Industry'. *Vlerick Leuven Gent Management Case Study,* ECCH.

Weick, K. and K. Roberts (1993). 'Collective Minds in Organizations: Heedful Interrelating on Flight Decks'. *Administrative Science Quarterly,* 38: 357–81.

Weick, K. E. (1995). *Sensemaking in Organizations.* London: Sage.

Wenger, E., R. McDermott, et al. (2002). *Cultivating Communities of Practice: A Guide to Managing Knowledge.* Boston, MA: Harvard Business School Publishing.

Wenger, E. C. and W. M. Snyder (2000). 'Communities of Practice: The Organizational Frontier'. *Harvard Business Review,* 78(1): 139–45.

Wensley, R. (1981). 'Strategic Marketing: Betas, Boxes, or Basics'. *Journal of Marketing,* 45: 173–82.

Werzer, G. (2005). Head of Investor Relations Erste Bank, Interview, Vienna.

Whittington, R. (25 Oct 1999). 'The "How" is More Important than the "Where"'. *Financial Times,* 4.

Wohlmuth, M. (2005). Head of Strategic Management, Interview, Vienna.

Wolfe, D. (Mar 2007). 'Testing, Testing: Citi and Obobay, Elan and Sapphire'. *American Banker.* Retrieved online from www.amaricanbanker.com.

Wood, R. C. and G. Hamel (2002). 'The World's Innovation Market'. *Harvard Business Review* November: 2–8.

www.allianz.com. (07 May 2007). 'Shanghai Sees Launch of First Allianz Bancassurance Academy'. Retrieved 27/03/2008, from http://www.allianz.com/en/ allianz_group/press_center/news/company_news/human_resources/news_2007-05-07.html?hits = Allianz + bancassurance + Academy.

www.allianz.com.cn. 'Allianz in China'. Retrieved 27/03/2008, from http://www. allianz.com.cn/allianzinChina_en.htm.

www.atkearney.com. 'Banks Shift Gears in Drive for Top-Line Growth: Focus Turns to Customers in the Financial Services Industry'. Retrieved 16/02/2008, from http://www.atkearney.com/shared_res/pdf/Banks_Shift_topLineGrowth_S.pdf.

——'Globalization Index 2007'. Retrieved 26/03/2008, from http://www.atkearney. com/main.taf?p = 5,4,1,127.

www.bankofamerica.com. 'The I&D Team'. Retrieved 28/03/2008, from https://www. bankofamerica.com.

www.bloomberg.com. (22 Mar 2005). 'AIG, Manulife Increase Life Insurance Market Share in China'. Retrieved 27/03/2008, from http://www.bloomberg.com/ apps/news?pid = 10000082&sid = atduDWqSW2hk&refer = canad.

www.businessinnovationinsider.com. (01 Dec 2006). 'Chief Innovation Officer'. Retrieved 28/03/2008, from http://www.businessinnovationinsider.com/2006/11/26-week/.

www.businessweek.com. (16 Oct 2007). 'Big Plans for China's Life Insurance Market'. Retrieved 31/01/2008, from http://www.businessweek.com/globalbiz/content/oct2007/gb20071016_422307.htm?chan = search.

www.citigroup.com. 'How Citi is Organized'. Retrieved 23/08/2007, from http://www.citigroup.com/citigroup/business/index.htm.

www.citigroup.com. 'Innovation Figurehead'. Retrieved 28/03/2008, from http://www.citigroup.com/citigroup/profiles/radin.

www.computingbusiness.co.uk. (15 Oct 2003). 'HBOS Merger made Easy'. Retrieved 27/03/2008, from http://www.computingbusiness.co.uk/computing/features/2072322/hbos-merger-made-easy.

www.datamonitor.com. (Nov 2007). 'HBOS plc—Company Profile'. *Datamonitor.*

www.en.wikipedia.org. 'History of Banking'. Retrieved 12/02/2008, from http://en.wikipedia.org/wiki/History_of_banking.

www.forbes.com. 'Forbes List: The World's 2,000 Largest Public Companies'. Retrieved 08/02/2008, from http://www.forbes.com/2007/03/29/forbes-global-2000-biz-07forbes2000-cz_sd_0329global_land.html.

www.geb.generali.com. 'Generali Employee Benefits Network'. Retrieved 27/03/2008, from http://www.geb.generali.com/gebcom/home.do.

——'Multinational Pooling'. Retrieved 27/03/2008, from http://www.geb.generali.com/gebcom/sezione.do?idItem = 1191&idSezione = 1190.

www.hbosplc.com. 'Our Strategy'. Retrieved 19/02/2008, from http://www.hbosplc.com/investors/inv_strategy1.asp.

——(Mar 2008). 'Latest Investor Pack'. Retrieved 27/03/2008, from http://www.hbosplc.com/investors/includes/2008.03.03%20Investor%20Presentation%20Pack.pdf.

www.historyworld.net. 'History of Banking'. Retrieved 06/01/2008, from http://www.historyworld.net/.

www.icbc-ltd.com. 'Shareholding Structure of ICBC'. Retrieved 27/03/2008, from http://www.icbc-ltd.com/jsp/en/template/docTemp.jsp?path = ROOT%3EInvestor+Relations%3EShare+Information%3EShareholding+Structure.

www.ingdirect.ca/en/. 'About ING Direct Bank Canada'. Retrieved 25/03/2008, from http://www.ingdirect.ca/en/.

www.moneyterms.co.uk. 'Annual Premium Equivalent'. Retrieved 27/03/2008, from http://moneyterms.co.uk/.

www.prodemffp.com. Retrieved 28/03/2008, from http://www.prodemffp.com.

www.prosper.com. 'About Prosper'. Retrieved 24/08/2007, from http://www.prosper.com/about/.

www.scip.org. 'The Society of Competitive Intelligence Professionals'. Retrieved 26/03/2008, from http://www.scip.org.

www.state.gov. 'Independent States in the World'. Retrieved 25/03/2008, from http://www.state.gov/s/inr/rls/4250.htm.

www.unicreditgroup.eu. 'Organigram'. Retrieved 18/02/2008, from http://www.unicreditgroup.eu/en/investor_relations/presentazioni/allegati/ppt/UBS_2008_02_01_WEB.pdf.

www.worldbank.org. 'Development Marketplace'. Retrieved 28/03/2008, from www.worldbank.org/developmentmarketplace.

Yamori, N. (1998). 'A Note on the Location Choice of Multinational Banks: The Case of Japanese Financial Institutions'. *Journal of Banking and Finance*, 22(1): 109–20.

Zadrazil, R. (19 Sep 2007). CEMS presentation of Bank Austria Creditanstalt. COO Bank Austria Creditanstalt.

Zahra, S. A. and J. A. Pearce (1989). 'Boards of Directors and Corporate Financial Performance'. *Journal of Management*, 15: 291–334.

Zand, D. E. and R. E. Sorensen (1975). 'Theory of Change and the Effective Use of Management Science'. *Administrative Science Quarterly*, 20(4): 532–45.

Zedelius, W. (2007). 'Allianz in Growth Markets—When Growth Meets Profitability'. *Allianz in Growth Markets*. Presentation at the Capital Markets Day 2007, Allianz SE, pp. 3–37.

Index

AAA (Adaptation—Aggregation—Arbitrage)
   triangle 113–15
ABA (Allianz Bancassurance Academy) 197,
   198, 200, 202
Abbey National 1, 4, 44, 104
ABN AMRO x, 4, *11*, *30*, 63, 135, 230
   takeover of 169–71, *172–4*
accelerated internationalization
      processes 154–7
   international governance mechanisms
      157
   international new ventures 154–5
   international niche markets 156–7
   role of networks 155–6
   scaling capabilities 157
ABN Bank (Algemene Bank Nederland) 169
Aetna Financial 36
AG Group 111
AGF Afrique 124
aggregation xiv
AIB (Allied Irish Banks) 160, 210
AIG 9, 155, 166, 195, 198–9
Algemene Bank Nederland (ABN Bank) 169
Allgemeine Hypothekenbank Rheinboden
   186
Allianz 3, 22, 97
   bancassurance academies (ABAs) 197, 198,
      200, 202
   business-level strategies 191–202
   and China 150, 155, 191–202, 214
   and Dazhong 192–3
   and Dresdner Bank 12, 35, 194
   and emerging countries 124–5
   functional strategy orchestration 220
   and Guotai Junan Securities C., Ltd.
      194–5
   and ICBC 155, 193, 199–200, 214
   marketing activities 196–7
   multi-channel distribution approach *197*,
      197–201
   and new foreign markets 150
   and offshoring 9
   Professional Patterns of Management
      training 199

and regional/global brands 105
strategic alliances 192–5
Allianz China Life Insurance Co. (AZCL) 193–4,
   196–7, *199*
Allianz Dazhong Life Insurance 192–3
Allianz Deutschland 194
Allianz EFU 124
Allianz Insurance Company Guangzhou
   (AZCN) 194
Allianz Insurance Limited 124–5
Allianz SE *11*, *30*, *122*, 134
Allianz Stuttgarter Verein 191
Allied Irish Banks (AIB) 160, 210
alternative competitive strategies
   cost leadership drivers 218–19
   differentiation strategies 215–17
   focus (niche) strategies 219–20
Amazon.com 54, 251
American Express 200
American International Group, Inc. *3*, *11*, *30*
Amsterdam-Rotterdam Bank (AMRO Bank)
   169
ANZ (Australia and New Zealand Banking
   Group) 209
AOL 306
arbitrage xiv, 114: *see also* CAGE
Argentina 135
Armstrong, J. S. 129–30
Arnold, L. x–xi
Arthur D. Little 131
Ashby, W. R. 80
ATM networks 6
AT&T *3*
Australia and New Zealand Banking Group
   (ANZ) 209
Austrian banks: profitability 89
authority 279–81
AVIVA 9, 160
AVS (DIE ERSTE österreichische
      Spar-Casse-Bank
      Anteilswervaltungssparkasse) 91
AXA *3*, 9, *11*, 12, *30*, 35–6
AXA Asia Pacific Holdings 125, 177, 160
AXA Gulf 125

AXA Philippines 177–8
AZCL (Allianz China Life Insurance Co.) 193–4, 196–7, *199*
AZCN (Allianz Insurance Company Guangzhou) 194

Bacon, F. 257
Baden-Fuller, C. 258–9
Balmer, S. 145
Banca Antonveneta 4, 171, *174*
Banca Commerciale Italiana 68
Banca Intesa 61, 63, *67*, 68, 134–6, 142
Banca Mediolanum 189
Banca Monte dei Paschi di Siena SPA (MPS) x, 25, *174*
Banca Popolare Intra 186
bancassurance academies (ABA) 197, 198, 200, 202
Banco Ambrosiano Veneto 68
Banco Bilbao Vizcaya Arqentaria SA, *see* BBV/BBVA
Banco Bradesco SA *30*
Banco Desio 186
Banco Halifax Hispania 211
Banco Santander *3*, *11*, *30*, 189
  and Abbey National 1, 104
  and ABN AMRO x, 170, 171, *172*, *174*
Banco Santander Central Hispano (BSCH) 4, 188
Banco Sudameris Brasil 135
Bank Austria 4, 67–8, *67*
Bank für Sparanlagen und Vermögensbildung AG in Frankfurt am Main 153
Bank Générale, Belgium 104
Bank Handlowy, Poland 158
Bank Mandiri, Indonesia 125, 177
Bank of America (BofA) 2, *3*, *11*, 13, *30*, *173*
  and innovation 295, 297–8
Bank of China 13, *30*
Bank of Communications, China 13, *30*, 38
Bank of Ireland 210
Bank of Scotland 202, 203, 204
BPH (Bank Przemyslowo Handlowy) 122–3
banks: and diversification 38
BankWest (Bank of Western Australia) 208–9
Barclays Bank *3*, *11*, 26, *30*, 205
  and ABN AMRO 170, *172*, *173*, *174*
Barclays International 28
Barings Bank 36
Bartlett, C. A. 103, 113–14, *114*
Basel Accord (1992) 43
BAT Industries PLC 4
BBV/BBVA (Banco Bilbao Vizcaya Arqentaria SA) 4, *30*, 61, *67*, 68, 134–5
BCG (Boston Consulting Group) viii, 129–33
Beamish, P. W. 64
Beinhocker, E. 144

Benelux countries 185: *see also* Belgium; Luxembourg; Netherlands
Berger, A. N. 20, 116–17, 152
Berkshire Hathaway *3*, *30*, 97
BHF-Bank 36
BNL (Banca Nazionale del Lavoro) 4
BNP Paribas *3*, *11*, *30*, 186
BofA, *see* Bank of America
Bolivia 298
Borsa Italiana 37
BOS Ireland 208, 210
BOS Netherlands 211
Boston Consulting Group (BCG) viii, 129–33
BP *3*
branding 32, 46
  Erste Bank 93, *93*, 105, 127
  experience goods and 105, 162
Branson, R. 132
Brazil 135
British Airways 251
Brodie, R. J. 129–30
Brussels Lambert 36
BSCH (Banco Santander Central Hispano) 4, 188
Buffet, W. 97
business-level strategies 184–221
  Allianz in China 191–202
  alternative competitive strategies 214–21
  competitive advantage 184–91
  HBOS 202–14, *212–13*

CAGE (cultural, administrative, geographical, and economic) differences xiii, xiv, 1, 5, 127, *133*, 136, 182
car manufacturers: and banking/insurance 36
Cariplo 68
CBA (Commonwealth Bank of Australia) 209
CC-Bank AG 188
CEE countries 43, 125, 141–2
  Bank Austria and 67–8
  Erste Bank and 44, 46, 67, 82–3, 91, 93–7, 103, 127–8, 141
CEMEX 54
central banks 27
Česká spořitelna 95–6
Chaebol, South Korea 156
Chandler, A. D. 102
Chase Manhattan 28
Chatman, J. A. 295
Chebron *3*
Children's Investment Fund (TCI), The 169–70
China Construction Bank 13
China Development Bank *173*
China Insurance Regulatory Commission, *see* CIRC
China Investment Corporation (CIC) 126
China Life *30*, 192

China Merchants Bank *30*
China National Petroleum Corporation
        (CNPC) 155, 165–6
China Pacific Insurance Co Ltd. (CPIC) 192
Christensen, H. K. 132
CIC (China Investment Corporation) 126
CIRC (China Insurance Regulatory
        Commission) 165, 166, 194
Citibank 2, 28, 29
CITIC Prudential 193, *199*
CITIC Trust (CITIC Trust and Investment
        Company Ltd) 193
Citigroup 1–2, *3*, 4, 12, *30*, 97, 180
    and innovation 295, 298
    international strategy 22, 124, 186
    market entry modes 158
    market segmentation 31
    organizational structure 32–3
    total assets (2007) *11*
Citizens Financial Group, Inc. 4
CNPC (China National Petroleum
        Corporation) 155, 165–6
Coca-Cola Company 115
collective action 276–7
Collis, D. 227
Comdirect Bank 153
command structures 180
Commerzbank AG *11*, 153, 187
Commonwealth Bank of Australia (CBA) 209
competition 232
competitive advantage (CA) 184–91, 224,
        233–4
    performance differences 186–9
    unique strategic position 189–91
competitive intelligence 134–40
    analysis 138–9
    application to strategic decisions 139–40
    distribution 139
    gathering 137–8
    planning 137
conflict resolution 180
ConocoPhillips *3*
Corfield, I. 208
corporate interventions *237, 255*
cost–income ratios: total assets and *118*
CPIC (China Pacific Insurance Co Ltd.) 192
Credem, Italy 186
credence goods 42
Credit Agricole SA *11*, 135
Credit Suisse 2, 12, 75–6, 112
Credit Suisse First Boston 179, 180
CRM (customer relationship management) 36
Croatia 142
cross-border knowledge sharing
        culture 264–83, *266*
    authority and self-reference 279–81
    collective action 276–7

connecting people with information 274–6
connecting people with people 271–4
individuality of knowledge development
        277–9
learning conversations climate 281–3
power of knowledge representation 268–70
reliability of knowledge representation
        270–1
speed of knowledge representation 265–8
cross-border knowledge sharing systems
        283–90
    impact of knowledge on corporate
            success 283
    knowledge audits 283–6, *284, 285*
    knowledge management 287–9, *288*
    knowledge transfer implementation 286–7
cross-border knowledge transfer 257–91
    cross-border knowledge sharing culture
            264–83
    cross-border knowledge sharing system
            design 283–9
    impact of knowledge on business
            performance 258–64
    knowledge sharing and company
            performance 290–1
cultural, administrative, geographical, and
        economic (CAGE) differences xiii, xiv, 1,
        5, 127, *133*, 136, 182
customer relationship management (CRM) 36
Czech Republic 46, 67, 82–3, 93–4, 95–7

DAB Bank 153
Daft, Douglas 115
Danske Bank 187, *187*
Day, G. S. 132
Dazhong 192–3
de Geus, A. 258
decision-making strategies 77–9
Delphi technique 147
Deutsche Bank *3, 11*, 44–5, 80, 97, 104, 153
Deutschland AG 155–6
Dexia SA *11*
DiBa AG 58–9
Dick, A. A. 152
digital information goods 48–59, *49*
    customer/product adaptations 56–7
    and first mover advantages 51
    new markets 54–6
    product adaptation costs 52–3, *53*
    (re-)production costs 51–2, *52*
    transportation costs 49–50, *50*
digital information goods providers
    market entry strategies 54–5
    and market penetration 58–9
digitalization
    entry modes and 160
    and internationalization 42

Dimons, J. 112–13
Diner's Club 302
dispersed corporate entrepreneurship 299–300
DNB (Dutch Central Bank) *172*
dog businesses 132–3
DOI (degree of internationalization) 61, 62
Dresdner Bank 12, 35, 104, 153, 194, 201
DSK Bank 125
Dunning, J. H. 102
Dutch Central Bank (DNB) *172*
Dutch East India Company 27
Dutch Investor's Association (VEB) *172,
173*

early mover advantages 149–52
East India Company 27
eBay 41, 55, 151, 306
economies of scale viii–x, 104–5
economies of scope viii, 105–6
Egg 42
Electricité de France *3*
Electricity Supply Board (ESB) 210
electronic banking 28
entrepreneurial uncertainty 306–10, *308*
  behavioural 309
  communicative 307–9
  value 310
entry modes: and digitalization 160
eQ Online, Finland 153
Equitable of Iowa 36
Equity Bank, Ireland 208, 210
Ericsson 263
Erste Bank 45, 64
  branding 93, *93*, 105, 127
  and CEE countries 44, 46, 67, 82–3, 91, 93–7,
    103, 127–8, 141
  and Czech Republic 46, 67, 82–3, 93–4, 95–7
  ESOP (Employee Stock Ownership
    Program) 94
  foreign market profitability 103
  and Girocredit 91
  growth options evaluation *110*, 110–11
  and Hungary 91, 95
  M-P relationships 67, *67*
  and Mezöbank 91
  MSOP (Management Stock Option Plan) 94
  organizational architecture 243–50
  pre-2008 organization 244–6, *246*
  in Slovakia 44
  strategy-making process 87–97
  2008 reorganization 246–50, *247, 249*
Erste Bank der oesterreichischen Sparkassen
    AG 91
ERSTE österreichische Spar-Casse—Bank,
    DIE 91
ERSTE österreichische Spar-Casse—Bank
    Aktiengesellschaft, DIE 91

ERSTE österreichische Spar-Casse—Bank
    Anteilswervaltungssparkasse (AVS),
    DIE 91
Estonia 142
exhanges 37
experience goods 31–2, 42
  and branding 105, 162
  character of 48–9
  see also digital information goods
ExxonMobil *3*

face-to-face meetings 273
Falshaw, J. R. 76
FDI (foreign direct investment) 101, 102, 158,
    182
Financ Electric 210
financial services
  competition 36–8
  definition of 6–7
  evolution/history of 23–9
  heterogeneity of 45
  inseparability of 43–5
  intangibility of 46
  most valuable (2008) *30*
  performance patterns 65–9
  perishability of 46–7
  product properties 38–47
financial services growth paradox vii–xiv
Financial Services Modernization Act (1999),
    USA 37
firm evolution *219*
first mover advantages 14, 46, 51
Fisher, M. *174*
flexibility–commitment trade-off 12–13
Forbes.com 2–4, *3*
forecasting methods 147–9
foreign direct investment (FDI) 101, 102, 158,
    182
Fortis N.V. 2, *11*, 12, 104, 111–12, 185
  and ABN AMRO x, 170, *172, 174*
France 186
Frankfurter Volksbank 186–7
Freame, J. 26
free rider effects 152
Friedman, T. 8
Fugger Bank 25–6
Furman Selz 36

GE-McKinsey matrix 129
GEB (Generali Benefits Network) 165, 166,
    167
General Electric *3*, 37
General Insurance Company Ltd., Pakistan
    124
Generali (Assicurazioni Generali S.p.A.) 155,
    165–7, 195, 199
Generali Benefits Network (GEB) 165, 166, 167

Generali China Life Insurance Company
    Limited 155, 165
Germany 121
  bank profitability 89, 186–7, 188
Ghemawat, P. 113, 115
Ghoshal, S. 103, 113
Girocredit 91
Glaister, K. W. 76
global efficiency: local responsiveness
    and 250–6, *254*, *255*
Global Payments Asia-Pacific Limited 160
Globalization Index 62
Goizueta, R. 115
Goldman Sachs Group *3*, *11*, *30*, 200
Gould, T. 26
Grant, R. 76, 258–9
Great Depression 27
Groenink, R. *174*
Grosse, R. 37
Groupe Caisse d'Epargne 186
Guotai Junan Securities C., Ltd. 194–5

Halifax 202, 203, 204: *see also* HBOS
Hang Seng Bank 22
HBOS *3*, 97
  business-level strategies 202–14, *212–13*
  Clerical Medical Europe 211
  competitive strategy in Australia 209
  competitive strategy in Ireland 210
  cost leadership 206–8, 218
  Europe and North America (ENA) expansion
    plans 210–11
  Heidelberger Leben 211
  international strategy 21–2
  and local brands 105
  product market share *207*
  profit split *207*
  total assets (2007) *11*
  and sustainable competitive advantage
    203–5
  and UK banks 205–6
headquarters
  control mechanisms 234–5, 312–13
  and entrepreneurship *308*, 310, 311–13
  and knowledge flows 237–8
  organizational architecture 228–38
  parenting advantage *229*, 229–31
  roles and activities 231–3
  and subsidiaries 233–4, 236, *237*
Hecksher-Ohlin theory 101
HeidelbergCement 54
Heidelberger Leben 211
Hewlett Packard 272–3
Hochstrasser, F. *249*
Hock, D. 263–4
Hodkinson, P. 204
Hoffman La Roche 263

Holcim 54
Hornby, A. 21–2
HSBC (Hongkong and Shanghai Banking
    Corporation Limited) 2, *3*, 6, 13, *30*,
    160, 186, 205
  M–P relationship *67*, 68
  organizational structure 34
  total assets (2007) *11*
HSBC France 186
Huijin Investment Co. 126
Hungary 91, 95
HVB (Hypovereinsbank) 1, 4, 13
Hydro Aluminium 263
Hymer, S. H. 101
hypercompetition 75
Hypovereinsbank (HVB) 1, 4, 13

i-Faber digital marketplace 38
IARFC (International Association of Registered
    Financial Consultants) 197
IBM 268
ICBC (Industrial and Commercial Bank of
    China) 1–2, *11*, *30*, 65, 126
  and Allianz 155, 193, 199–200, 214
ICC Bank, Ireland 208, 210
IKEA 41
India 9
India Allianz 198
Industrial and Commercial Bank of China, *see*
    ICBC
industrial corporations: and
    banking/insurance 36
industry breakpoints 190
ING (Internationale Nederlanden Groep) Groep
    N V. *3*, *11*, 12, *30*, 36
ING Bank online 43
ING-DiBa, Germany 153, 154
ING Direct 32, 36, 56, 57, 150
  and DiBa AG 58–9
  and digitalization 48, 54
  market entry strategies 55, 160
innovation 292–3
  invention and 302
  and profits *303*, 303–4
  service innovation 293–8
  subsidiaries and 304–6
insurance industry 35–6
  competition 36–8
  and offshoring 9
International Association of Registered
    Financial Consultants (IARFC) 197
international corporate
    entrepreneurship 292–313
  entrepreneurial uncertainty 306–10
  organizational mechanisms 310–13
  process framework 299–306, *300*, *305*
  service innovation 293–8

international corporate entrepreneurship
    framework 299–306, *300, 305*
  corporate entrepreneurship 300–2, *300*
  innovations 300, 301, 302–4
  inventions 300–2
  subsidiary entrepreneurship 304–6
international expansion benefits 103–8
  access to key factors 106
  agency motives 107–8
  economies of scale 104–5
  economies of scope 105–6
  gravitational pull effect 106–7
  market power, accumulation of 107
  satisfaction of shareholders' growth
    expectations 107
  X-efficiencies 106
international expansion costs 108–10
  coordination costs 109–10
  liabilities of foreignness 108–9
  liabilities of newness 64–5, 109
international strategies 22
  and service properties 39–43
internationalization
  cultural issues 1, 5
  drivers of 63
  impact of product features on 47–59
  and investment/retail banking 39
  profit impact of 60–9
  trade-offs 39–41
Internet 37
Internet banking 215–16
Intesa Sanpaola S.p.A. *30*, 134–5
intrapreneurship 299–300
intuition 146–7
investment banking 39, 160
I–R (integration–responsiveness)
    framework 103
Irevna, India 9
Isdell, N. 115
Italy: bank profitability 89, 186

Japan 156, 198
joint ventures 158, 160, 164, 177–8, 179–80,
    193–5: see also *individual joint ventures*
Joyce, C. 295
JP Morgan 28, 82–3
JP Morgan Chase *3, 11, 30*, 112–13
Junan Allianz Fund Management Co. 195
Juranek, H. *249*

Kaczynski, L. 123
Kearney, A. T. 62, 163, 171
keiretsu networks 155, 156
Kershaw, P. 203
Khatri, N. 147
Kinsky, J. *249*
Kisbenedek, P. *249*

KM, *see* knowledge management
knowledge and business performance 258–64
  decentralized learning 260–2
  networks 263–4
knowledge audits 283–6, *284, 285*
knowledge exploitation 234
knowledge exploration 234
knowledge management (KM) 257–60
  centralized/decentralized systems 260–2
  communities of practice 262
  cross-border knowledge sharing 264–83
  networks 263–4
  system design 283–9
knowledge representation 265–70
  power of 268–70
  reliability of 270–1
  speed of 265–8
knowledge transfer 234
Korea 198
Krungthei Bank, Thailand 178
Kuhlmann, A. 57

LaSalle 170, *172, 173*
late mover advantages 152–4
Latin America 134–6
Linder, S. 101
Llewellyn, D. 118–19
Lloyd, E. 26
Lloyds TSB 205
local responsiveness: and global
    efficiency 250–6, *254, 255*
LSE (London Stock Exchange) 37
Lu, J. W. 64
Lyons, R. K. 295

M–P (multinationality-performance)
    relationships 15, 61, 64, 66–7, *67*
M&A (mergers and acquisitions) 168–76
Macquarie Bank, Australia 39, 97, 156–7, 177
Macquarie Shinsei Advisory Co. Ltd
    (MSAC) 39, 177
Mankins, M. C. 74
Manulife 199
March, J. G. 261–2
market attractiveness 121–7, *122*
  emerging v. economically developed
    markets 124–6
  frameworks and governments 122–3
  inverse internationalization 126–7
market differences 252–4
market entry mode decision variables 159–63
  context sensitivity of 159–61
  market commitment/control 161–3
market entry modes 158–83
  ABN AMRO 169–71, *172–4*
  choice of mode 181–3
  decision variables 159–63

mergers and acquisitions 168–76
organic growth 163–7
strategic alliances 164, 177–81
market entry motives 134–5
market entry strategies 54–5
market entry timing/speed 141–57
accelerated internationalization
  processes 154–7
early mover advantages 149–52
late mover advantages 152–4
market foresight 143–9
market foresight 143–9
forecasting methods 147–9
intuition and 146–7
uncertainty 143–5
market penetrability 127–8
market segmentation 31–2
and organizational structure 32–5
market selection 120–40
competitive intelligence 134–40
market attractiveness 121–7, *122*
market penetrability 127–8
portfolio strategies 129–34, *133*
Mastercard 6
McKinsey 131
Medici Bank 25
mergers and acquisitions (M&A) 168–76
ABN AMRO 169–76, *172–4*
integration 171–6, *176*
process model for management of 171–6,
  175
Merrill Lynch & Co., Inc. *11*
Metro Bank 177–8
Mezöbank 91
Middle East and Indian Mercantile 68
Midland Bank 68
Minmetals, China 178
Mitsubishi UFJ Financial Group Inc. *11, 30*
Mittal, India 126
Mizuho Financia Group Inc. *11*
Molt, C. 196, 201
Mondial Assistance China 195
Moneta, A. 257
Monte dei Paschi di Siena (MPS) x, 25,
  174
Montgomery, C. A. 227
Morgan Stanley *3, 11*, 126–7
Morrison, A. 133
mortgages/mortgage loans 42
MPS (Monte dei Paschi di Siena) x, 25, *174*
MSAC (Macquarie Shinsei Advisory Co.
  Ltd) 39, 177
MTV music channel 253
multinational banks 28
multinational firms
evaluation of alternative growth
  options 110–13

exploiting cross-border differences 113–16
international expansion benefits 103–8
international expansion costs 108–10
international expansion limits/viability of
  local firms 116–19
value creation in 99–103, *100*
multinationality
measurement of 61–2
S-curve hypothesis 60, 63–5
multinationality–performance (M–P)
  relationships 15, 61, 64, 66–7, *67*

NAB (National Australia Bank) 209
Nan Tung Bank 126
NASDAQ 37
National Australia Bank (NAB) 209
national banks 27
National Westminster Bank 104
Nationale-Nederlanden 36
New York Stock Exchange 37
Ng, H. A. 147
NMB Postbank Groep 36
Nonaka, I. 146, 258–9
Nordea 97, 178
N.V. AMEV 111

offshoring xiv, 5, 9
Office Tiger, India 9
Ohlin, B. 101
operational conversations 281–2
oracle managers 77, 78, 79
organic growth 163–7
Generali in China 165–7
organic entry modes 163–5
organizational architectures 227–56
Erste Bank 243–50
headquarters 228–38
local responsiveness/global efficiency
  trade-offs 250–6
market segmentation and 32–5
UniCredit Group 238–43
OTP, Hungary 125

PAIC (Ping An Insurance Company) *30*, 192
parenting advantage *229*, 229–31
PayPal 6, 48
PBC (People's Bank of China) 192
peer-to-peer finance 36–7
People's Bank of China (PBC) 192
People's Insurance Company of China
  (PICC) 192
performance differences 186–9
Philips 275–6
PICC (People's Insurance Company of
  China) 192
Ping An Insurance Company (PAIC) *30*, 192
Poland 122–3

portfolio strategies 129–34
  BCG matrix viii, 129–33
  matrix construction 133–4
Posner, M. V. 101
Postbank 153
principal–agent conflicts xii
Private Financial Fund 'Prodem FFP,'
  Bolivia 298
Procter & Gamble 21
profitability 186–8, 187
Profumo, A. 79, 97, 99
Prosper 36–7
Prudential 193, 195, 196, 198–9

Radin, A. 295, 298
Raiffeisen Bank (RZB), Austria 158, 162
RBS (Royal Bank of Scotland) 4, 13, 104, 105,
  188, 205
  and ABN AMRO 170–1, 172, 174
RealiaStar 36
relational quality 181
resource allocation 312
retailers: and banking/insurance 36, 178
Ricardo, D. 101
risk exposure 159
  strategic alliances and 178–9
Roberts, K. 276
Royal Bank of Canada 30
Royal Bank of Scotland (RBS) vii, x, 3, 10, 11,
  30
Royal Dutch Shell 3
RR Donnelley 9
Rugman, A. 10
Russia 142
RZB (Raiffeisen Bank), Austria 158, 162

Santander Consumer CC-Bank 186, 188
SCIP (Society of Competitive Intelligence
  Professionals) 136
Scott-Barrett, Hugh 173
search goods 42
Second Banking Directive (1993), USA 43
self-referencing 280–1
service innovation 293–8
  Bank of America 297–8
  Citigroup 298
  World Bank innovation markets 296–7
Servizi Interbancari 242
SGS (Société Générale de Surveillance) 199
Shapiro, S. 147
shareholder returns x–xii, xi
shareholders: and top management xii–xiii
Shinsei Bank Ltd, Japan 39, 177
SIC codes 19
Siemens 180, 271
Skandia AFS 264, 272, 273, 274
  knowledge audit 284–6

Slager, A. 65–6
Slovakia 44, 142
SMEs 161, 205
Smith, A. 101
Société Générale de Surveillance (SGS) 199
Société Générale SA 3, 11, 124
Society of Competitive Intelligence
  Professionals (SCIP) 136
South Korea 156
South Sea Company 27
Spalt, B. 249
Spence, M. T. 147
Stack, J. 95, 96
Standard Bank, South Africa 126
Standard Chartered Bank 2
standard operating procedures 180–1
standardization 251–2
Statoil 265–7
Stopford, J. 102–3
strategic alliances 164, 176–81
  cross-border alliances 179–80
  governance of 180–1
  and risks 178–9
strategic conversations 282
strategic decision-making 74–9
strategic issue management 311
strategic knowledge 267
strategy execution 223–5
strategy-making process design 85–96
  business unit strategies development 92
  company analysis 89–90
  corporate strategies development 91–2
  functional strategies development 93
  market analysis 88–9
  performance management 87–8
  strategic agenda 88
  strategy implementation 93–6
  strategy process framework 86, 87
  strategy workshops 85–7
  vision/long-term objectives development
    90
strategy-making processes 74–9
  corporate planning 80
  formal strategic planning 85
  intuition 73, 76, 80, 83
  oracle managers 77, 78, 79
  organizational flexibility 80
  real option approach 80–1
  self-organized networks 77, 78–9
  strategy production process 81, 81–4
  see also strategy-making process design
subprime crisis 314–16
subsidiaries 164
subsidiary charters 312
Sudameris group 136
Sumitomo Mitsui Financial Group, Inc. 11
Systracom, Germany 153

Takeuchi, H. 146, 258–9
Tata Group, India 126
TC (transaction cost) theory 160
TCI (The Children's Investment Fund) 169–70
telecommunications industry: and
    internationalization 160–1
Temasek *173*
Toffler, A. 258
top management selection 311–12
Total *3*
total assets: and cost–income ratios *118*
Toyota Motor *3*, 315
transaction cost (TC) theory 160
transfer pricing 181
Travelers Group 35–6
Treichel, A. 88, 94, 95, 167, *249*
Turkey 142

UBS AG, Switzerland x–xi, 2, *3, 11, 30*, 105,
    180, 228
Unibail-Rodamco 187, *187*
UniCredit Banca 239
UniCredit Banca d'Impresa 239
UniCredit Banca Private Banking 239
UniCredit Group *11, 30*, 97, 167, 189, 238–43
    and Bank Austria Creditanstalt 4
    and CEE countries 103, 125
    competence centres 242–3
    coordination mechanisms 241–2
    cross-border synergies 240–1
    cultural changes 243
    and diversification 38
    Global Banking Services division 239,
        242
    and HVB (Hypovereinsbank) 1, 4, 13
    and i-Faber digital marketplace 38
    IT 75
    New Europe division 241–2
    organizational structure 33–4, *33*,
        238–43
    Poland Markets Division 75, 103–4, 123
    product divisions 239–40, *240*, 241–2
    and regional/global brands 105
    in 2008: 239–40, *240*

value creation in 99
vision statement 90
Unilever 21
United Kingdom: branch network structure
    121
United States of America: branch network
    structure 121
universal banks 12
US banks 28

Varle, J. *174*
VEB (Dutch Investor's Association) *172, 173*
Venezuela 135
Vermeulen, P. 294–5
Viacom 253
Virgin Group 132
Visa 6
Visa International 263–4
Viva (local German television station) 253
Volkswagen Bank 187
Vontobel, Switzerland 153
VSB (Dutch bank) 111

Wachovia Corporation *30*
Wal-Mart Stores *3*, 251
Walter, H. 153
Watanabe, K. 315
wealth management 160
Weick, K. 276
Weill, S. 17, 97
Wells Fargo & Company *30*
Wells, L. 102
Wensley, R. 133
Westpac Banking Corporation (Westpac) 209
Winterthur 12, 112
Woodruff, R. 115
World Bank 295, 296–7

Yahoo! 55, 56–8, 294

Zedelius, W. 122
Zopa 36–7, 48, 52–3
Zurich Financial Services 188
Zurich Group 4